EIGHTH EDITION

# CALIFORNIA
## REAL ESTATE FINANCE

Minnie Lush, BA, GRI, ABR

David Sirota, PhD

This publication is designed to provide accurate and authoritative information in regard to the subject matter covered. It is sold with the understanding that the publisher is not engaged in rendering legal, accounting, or other professional advice. If legal advice or other expert assistance is required, the services of a competent professional should be sought.

President: Dr. Andrew Temte
Chief Learning Officer: Dr. Tim Smaby
Executive Director, Real Estate Education: Melissa Kleeman-Moy
Development Editor: Adam Bissen

CALIFORNIA REAL ESTATE FINANCE EIGHTH EDITION
©2013 Kaplan, Inc.
Published by DF Institute, Inc., d/b/a Dearborn Real Estate Education
332 Front St. S., Suite 501
La Crosse, WI 54601

Printed in the United States of America
Second revision, August 2015
ISBN: 978-1-4277-4435-7 / 1-4277-4435-1
PPN: 1523-1308

# CONTENTS

## Part 3: What Kinds of Loans Are Available?

Part 4: How Do I Get a Loan?

# Part 5: What Happens After the Loan Is Made?

# Part 6: What Are the Financial Strategies and Math Calculations?

# PREFACE

Welcome to the intriguing and exciting world of real estate finance. Prior to 2008, California real estate markets had been experiencing a huge surge in property values in an atmosphere of stability and growth. Based on relatively low interest rates, controlled inflation, and stable employment, predictions were that this prosperity would continue at a steady pace. However, in 2009, national unemployment rates were near 10 percent, and the national foreclosure rate was 10 percent. The nation was fearful and the real estate market plummeted in many areas of the country. California was one of several states severely affected.

In October 2008, Congress passed a rescue bill to ease the credit crunch that resulted when the real estate bubble of the early part of this century burst. The bill included $700 billion to help lenders dispose of worthless defaulted loans and restart their lending activities. The federal government has taken a leading role in shoring up the credit industry to allow the economy to adjust to a new era of stricter oversight and more responsible underwriting.

It was shocking to observe how powerful the real estate financial markets were in bringing the world's economy to the brink of disaster with the proliferation of loans on properties evaluated beyond reason to borrowers without adequate credit. The recovery, now in process, is again based on long-term, fixed-interest-rate loans made to qualified borrowers financing reasonably evaluated real estate properties. Costs for securing these loans have risen substantially.

Although loans can still be secured through the Internet, underwriters will be screening these loans carefully to make sure the borrowers have verifiable credit histories and that the collateral properties are evaluated accurately. Nothing-down, interest-only, subprime loans are no longer acceptable.

Lenders must now adhere carefully to the underwriters' requirements in order to sell their real estate loans in the secondary markets.

In 2013, we see mortgage conditions improving because the sturdy fabric of capitalism is woven from the strong and resilient threads of partnership between the federal government and private enterprise. To a great extent, private enterprise depends on the ability of many individuals to comprehend and use real estate finance. Each participant need not know everything about all phases of financing real estate, but those who do understand the process are more likely to achieve success.

During the Great Depression of the late 1920s and 1930s, the capitalistic U.S. system was battered, torn, and generally worn threadbare. Safeguards from the government were woven carefully into the cloth, and the number and scope of these safeguards have increased over the years.

The safety measures that secured the government also protected people and their investments. People have depended, in ever-increasing numbers, on banks, thrift institutions, and life insurance companies to lend them the dollars they need to buy a piece of America. Some people bought large pieces, and some grouped together to buy even larger ones; but most people bought just the little piece they call home. The Federal Deposit Insurance Corporation (FDIC) stands behind everyone's deposits to a maximum of $250,000 per account.

This eighth edition has been designed to address the ever-increasing technological development. We need to know the hard and fast rules and techniques of the industry, and we need them explained concisely and plainly with plenty of examples. This book is written to meet our readers' needs.

This text is divided into two components: the principles of real estate finance are covered in the first half, while the practices and applications of California real estate finance are in the second half.

The book's sequence is designed to answer the following questions:

- What is finance and money?

- Where do we get the money?

- What kinds of loans are available?

- How do I get a loan?

- What happens after the loan is made?

- What are the financial strategies and math calculations?

Chapter 1 introduces the nature and cycle of California real estate finance. It includes a discussion of the state's credit system economy and nature of financing relationships, an examination of the local and national mortgage markets, the cyclical nature of the real estate market, and a view of the changing demographics affecting the future of the housing market in California.

Chapter 2 discusses money and the monetary system as directed by the major governmental influences in the financial markets: the Federal Reserve System, which regulates and controls the nation's money supply; the U.S. Treasury, which acts as the fiscal manager; and the Federal Home Loan Bank system, which directs the actions of this nation's thrifts.

Chapter 3 presents the institutional sources for providing funds for real estate finance, including banks, savings associations, and life insurance companies.

Chapter 4 describes other financial sources, such as mortgage brokers and bankers, trusts, bonds, endowment funds, private loan companies, and individuals.

Chapter 5 describes conventional, insured, and guaranteed loans in the context of the Federal Housing Administration and the Department of Veterans Affairs. It also includes a discussion of the California Veterans Loan Program.

Chapter 6 investigates the special category of agricultural lending and includes a review of the federal and state regulations affecting California real estate loans.

Chapter 7 examines the use of junior finance when structuring a real estate sale, an important tool in the California real estate market.

Chapter 8 describes contemporary real estate financial techniques in terms of variations of payments and types of loans.

Chapter 9 defines the various instruments used to finance California real estate, including the note and deed of trust, the note and mortgage, and the real property sales contract (land contract). It also provides descriptions of the many special provisions that can be included in these instruments in order to adjust them to more readily serve individual requirements.

Chapter 10 describes the process for underwriting a real estate loan by examining the creditworthiness of the borrowers and the value of the collateral.

Chapter 11 presents the techniques for closing a loan, including prorations and a closing statement.

Chapter 12 delineates the national secondary markets available for buying and selling real estate loans, including the Federal National Mortgage Association, the Federal Home Loan Mortgage Corporation, and the Government National Mortgage Association, now known as Fannie Mae, Freddie Mac, and Ginnie Mae.

Chapter 13 discusses the ramifications involved in loan defaults and foreclosures in California.

Chapter 14 addresses some alternative investment financing strategies, including seller carrybacks, equity participation, and tax-deferred refinancing.

Finally, Chapter 15 presents a comprehensive examination of the mathematics of California real estate finance.

At the end of each chapter, the reader will find a series of review questions and exercises. They have been designed to check comprehension of the chapter's information. Answers may be found in the answer key at the back of the book.

## ■ ACKNOWLEDGMENTS

Thanks go to the following, whose comments contributed greatly to this and prior editions of *California Real Estate Finance*: George W. Lawrence, California Association of REALTORS® Master Instructor Faculty; Leonel "Leo" Bello, MBA, City College of San Francisco; Rick Chehab, De Anza College; Ignacio Gonzales, Mendocino Community College; Kartik Subramaniam, ADHI Schools, LLC; Alan D. Tochterman, attorney-at-law; David Stuczynski, American Title Company; Abraham Farkas, Esq., West Los Angeles College; Steve Herndon, Santa Rosa Junior College; Leigh H. Conway; Bob Wynne, San Joaquin Delta College; Dr. Robert Gaber, College of San Mateo; Dr. Robert F. Bohn, Golden Gate University; Jeff Young, Los Angeles City College; Ronald Dean Schultz, Diablo Valley College; Thurza B. Andrew, GRI, Butte Community College; Dr. Donna Grogan, El Camino College; Fred Martinez, City College of San Francisco; and Roy Agall of Anthony Schools.

## ■ ABOUT THE AUTHORS

Minnie Lush, BA, GRI, ABR, REALTOR®, real estate broker, author, and lecturer, is acclaimed as one of the finest real estate speakers and trainers in California. Lush has taught all eight broker-qualifying courses, including courses of investment analysis, commercial property, and property management. For many years, she owned and operated her own real estate licensing examination preparation and training schools and was a consistent top producer while selling real estate. She periodically appears as a guest on talk shows and is an invited speaker for many organizations at the local, state, and national levels. In the past, Lush has served on a California State Department of Real Estate education committee. She is a master faculty member of the California Association of REALTORS®, lecturing throughout California in the Graduate REALTOR® Institute program. She has served as president of the Burbank Association of REALTORS® and has chaired many of its committees. Further, she was named REALTOR® of the Year and is a recipient of the distinguished Mary L. Vaughan award for excellence in leadership and training. Lush has taught at Los Angeles Community College and Azusa Pacific University. She is also the author of textbooks used by many private schools and California colleges and universities (e.g., *California Real Estate Exam Guide* and *California Real Estate Finance* [co-author], both published by Dearborn Real Estate Education). In 2011, Lush was the recipient of the prestigious Educator of the Year award from the California Real Estate Educators' Association (CREEA). Further, she serves as a volunteer member of the board of directors of the Burbank Housing Corporation, a city corporation that provides newly renovated housing for very low-, low-, and moderate-income families.

Dr. David Sirota of Green Valley, Arizona, has called upon 40 years of field experience and 10 years of academic training in the writing of *California Real Estate Finance*. After securing his doctorate in real estate from the University of Arizona in 1971, Sirota headed the Department of Real Estate at the University of Nebraska, Omaha, for four years. He then taught at Eastern Michigan University in Ypsilanti, National University in San Diego, and California State University in Fullerton. Sirota is the author of *Essentials of Real Estate Investment* and *Essentials of Real Estate Finance*.

## CHAPTER ONE

# NATURE AND CYCLE OF CALIFORNIA REAL ESTATE FINANCE

## ■ KEY TERMS

allodial system
bill of sale
bundle of rights
chattel
collateral
community property
concurrent ownership
condemnation
condominium
Consumer Financial
  Protection Bureau
  (CFPB)
cycle
deed
deed of trust
deregulation
disintermediation
Dodd-Frank Wall
  Street Reform
  and Consumer
  Protection Act

English common law
eminent domain
equitable title
Fannie Mae
fee simple absolute
Freddie Mac
freehold estate
Ginnie Mae
hereditaments
hypothecation
joint tenancy
land contract
leasehold estate
legal title
leverage
lien
mortgage
partnerships
personal property
police power
primary market

property
ranchos
real property
Roman Civil Law
SAFE Act
savings associations
secondary mortgage
  market
security agreement
Tax Reform Act of
  1986 (TRA '86)
Tax Relief Act of 1997
  (TRA '97)
tenants in common
thrifts
time-shares
trade fixture
zoning

# ■ HISTORICAL PERSPECTIVE

Fundamentally, the political, social, and religious structure of a society, no matter how primitive, determines the laws under which it will operate. Those laws that pertain to the acquisition, ownership, and disposition of land are as ancient as humanity. In the earliest times, uncodified laws of might and power determined the owner's "rights" to territory. More formal land laws were adopted by the Egyptians long before the first century AD. Our laws of property are derived from the English feudal system, which originated with the Norman conquest in 1066.

As the conqueror and lord, King William was the owner and source of all rights in land. He delegated these rights as rewards for service and loyalty and installed his knights in the castles previously owned by the defeated English king. In turn, these ruling knights could delegate interests in lesser parcels of land under their control to whomever they wished. In effect, this government transformed a military organization into an economic system for control and continuity of land possession. Those people in possession of land played dual roles, as tenants to their overlords and as lords to tenants, with the exception of the monarch, who retained the power of assignment at all times. Thus, the feudal system was one huge life estate, with the heirs of deceased landholders continuing their tenure only at the whim of the monarch.

Some individual rights in land ownership were recognized by the Magna Carta, granted by the King of England to the barons at Runnymede in 1215. This historically important document contains provisions for securing the personal liberty of all the people and their rights in property. These private property rights were delineated further in 1290 by a statute that recognized the feudal *tenant's* right to convey *that* interest in land. This statute, *Quia Emptores*, formed the basis for the development of land ownership in fee simple absolute—the form of ownership that we now enjoy under our private real property **allodial system**.

The individual property owner in this country holds rights in property that are subject only to taxation, eminent domain, escheat, and the police powers of government. Among the rights of property ownership is the right to finance real estate by pledging the property and/or rights in it as collateral for a loan.

# ■ NATURE OF REAL ESTATE FINANCE

No one can question the unmistakable importance of real estate in our lives.

Complementing its physical importance is the economic impact of real estate on our lifestyles. The industrial and commercial activities of our nation are completely dependent on the land and its natural resources for their very existence. Society cannot function without the food, lumber, minerals, water, and other parts and products of our land.

Many of us are involved, either directly or indirectly, in some activity concerning real estate. Farmers and miners, sanitary engineers, surveyors, land planners, homebuilders, furniture manufacturers, and paint purveyors—all of these people and more depend on real estate and its use for their livelihood. Millions of people are engaged directly in contract construction activities in the United States, with millions more providing them with the materials and peripheral services essential for their work.

The construction industry is vital to our country's economic well-being. Any changes in its activities soon affect everyone. A building slowdown results in layoffs and cutbacks; increased activity stimulates production and services in the myriad areas of endeavor associated with the industry. Not much construction is attempted without funding by loans secured from the various sources of money for real estate finance. In fact, most real estate activities rely on the availability of borrowed funds.

**Ownership of Property**   The private ownership of property in California mirrored its changes in governmental dominion. The Spanish Empire used the Roman Civil Law as the basis for ownership. Its elaborate and detailed codes were imposed through royal grants of land given to political or military agencies of the crown. Absolute title did not change hands, and these grants, ranchos, were made primarily for grazing and other agricultural purposes.

When Mexico achieved independence from Spain in 1821, formal land grants, known as *expedientes*, were filed and recorded in the new government archives.

Subsequently, and as a result of the Mexican-American War, California was ceded by treaty to the United States in 1848. During California's time as a U.S. possession, the expedientes were carefully reviewed and the owners' rights recognized officially by the new laws.

When California was admitted as the 31st state in the Union in 1850, the principles of ownership followed **English common law,** which was adhered to by the rest of the country.

**Property.**    **Property** is anything that can be controlled and owned. Is water property? Water falling from the sky in the form of rain is not property, nor is the water in the middle of the ocean. These waters are not "owned" by anybody. However, the water from a well is the property of its owner, as is distilled water in a container. The water in the navigable lakes and rivers of this country, as well as the land and water located up to 200 miles off our coasts, is the property of our government.

Is air property? The air all around us, clean or dirty, is not property. The air above the land is not property until it is encompassed within a structure; air in an oxygen tank is property.

Is an idea property? Not until an idea is converted into a patented invention or a copyrighted manuscript is it considered property.

The underlying thread of logic in this discussion is that property is not so much something that can be *owned* as it is something that can be *controlled*. Thus, a lease gives the tenant control. The landlord continues to benefit from the ownership. Our system of government has laws that protect both rights.

**Real Property.**    *Real estate* is described as the earth, the land, and all natural and man-made hereditaments found permanently attached thereto. **Hereditaments** are things capable of being inherited. Land, streams, trees, minerals, buildings, fences, and other features fixed permanently in place on the land are interpreted as real estate. Thus, real estate is an inheritable estate. **Real property** is all that is immovable.

Real property marries the legal concepts of ownership and control with the physical description of real estate. Now real property can be further defined as that **bundle of rights** in property, including possession, control, enjoyment, exclusion, disposition, and others, that enhance the inheritable ownership of the land and everything permanently affixed to it. Real property ownership is transferred by **deed** and encumbered by the use of a **mortgage,** a **deed of trust,** or a **land contract** when it is pledged as collateral for a loan. (*Real estate, real property,* and *realty* will be considered synonyms in this book.)

**Personal Property.**   Also called **chattel, personal property** is generally considered to be anything that is not real property, which presumes that it is mobile, *not* permanently attached to the earth. Thus, automobiles, furniture, clothing, and other portable objects are obviously personal property. A classic example of the various attributes of property is the tree that is *real* while growing on the land, *personal* when in the form of lumber, and *real* again when in the form of a home. Personal property ownership is transferred by a **bill of sale** and is encumbered with a **security agreement** when it is used as collateral for a loan.

Clear-cut classifications of real versus personal property are sometimes difficult to identify. For instance, mobile homes are often included in both categories. In some jurisdictions, mobile homes are considered real property when they are permanently affixed to a foundation on a lot. However, if the personal property taxes in the area are lower than the taxes on real property, mobile homes, even the largest double-wides, may be sitting precariously upon concrete blocks, with their wheels and tires still attached. Thus, some mobile homes are interpreted as real property, while others, though of similar size and construction, are personal property. Permanent attachment to the land then becomes the final arbiter between real and personal property. The term *manufactured home* is currently used in place of *mobile home.*

**Commercial Fixtures.**   The exception to the permanent affixation rule is the category of property classified as a commercial or **trade fixture.**

Personal property utilized by commercial tenants in pursuit of their occupations retains its personal property quality no matter how permanently it is affixed to the real estate. Heating units, coolers, walk-in refrigerators, floor coverings, interior partitions, shelves, counters, cabinets, dental chairs, and all other items that are installed by business and professional tenants remain their personal property and must be removed from leased premises before the expiration of the lease. In the event of a dispute in defining a fixture, the following tests are applied:

- Method or manner of annexation

- Adaptability or nature of use

- Relationship between the parties

- Intention of the parties (most important)

- Agreements between the parties

## Estates in Realty

Ownership under our allodial system evolved from the English feudal system, which ended in the 17th century. Freeholders in possession of real estate registered their ownership with appropriate government agencies established for the transfer of property into private hands, and the private property allodial system was established. These private ownerships were termed **freehold estates.**

**Freehold Estate.**   An estate in **fee simple absolute,** or fee simple ownership, designates the highest bundle of rights a person may enjoy in our allodial system and is for an indeterminable length of time. In the language of real estate, a person is said to own a "fee" in a property as the legal owner. The ownership is defined by the deed held. This fee is what an owner will pledge as collateral to back up the promise to repay a real estate loan.

A fee ownership may be divided into a number of entities. One person may own the fee in the land, another may own the minerals under the surface of the land, and another may own the water that flows over the land. Future ownership of the land may be held by remainder persons under the terms of a trust or a life estate.

Fee ownership also can be divided into time elements such as interval ownership or **time-shares.** Under time-shares, a fee owner can use property for a specified period, such as for one or two weeks a year, as in a vacation property time-share. Fee ownership can also pertain to a space within a cube in addition to an undivided ownership of certain common areas, as in a **condominium** project.

Most fee owners in California hold **legal title** to their properties. Others hold an **equitable title** on a land contract when property is purchased under a land sales contract. This equitable title changes to a legal title when the terms of the land sales contract are satisfied.

Legal and equitable titles may be held by individuals and corporations as sole and separate property or may be held by more than one entity in **concurrent ownership.** Concurrent ownership in California includes tenants in common, partnerships, community property, community property with a right of survivorship, and joint tenancy.

**Tenants in common** and **partnerships** own undivided equal or unequal inheritable shares in real property. These shares are passed on to the heirs of the owners by the terms of a will or, in the absence of a will, by the California distribution laws.

**Community property**, a carryover from the Spanish law, describes ownership that is limited to equal, undivided interests between husbands and wives of properties acquired after marriage with community funds. After the demise of either person, the deceased's one-half interest will be distributed according to the terms of the will. As of July 1, 2001, community property may also be held with the right of survivorship. Upon the death of the husband or the wife, the survivor automatically owns the entire property.

To avoid the probate of a will, property may be owned in **joint tenancy** where, upon the demise of one of the owners, this person's interest will vest automatically in the survivor(s)' name(s). Thus, in a two-party arrangement between a husband and a wife, the deceased husband's one-half interest vests immediately and automatically in his wife's name, giving her the whole legal ownership. In a three-party joint tenancy arrangement among a father, mother, and child, the death of one of the parties will raise the survivors' equal interests from one-third to one-half each.

Anyone may own in joint tenancy, although it is usually a family arrangement because joint tenants give up their inheritable estate through automatic survivorship. Joint tenancy is always held and distributed in equal shares.

**Leasehold Estate.**   An estate that is for a fixed length of time is called a **leasehold estate.** A leasehold estate is established when a landlord gives up possession of real estate to a tenant who acquires an *equitable* interest in the property according to the terms and conditions of the lease. The landlord retains legal fee, but the tenant has physical control of the leased property.

A leased property is sold subject to the terms of the existing lease. Thus, a tenant has the right to peaceful possession of the property for the term of the lease.

Freehold and leasehold estates are of primary interest in the field of real estate finance. A person's degree of ownership or control of real property will determine the amount and terms of the financing that will be available. That financing stems primarily from the savings of others.

**Real Estate Characteristics**

Real estate has certain properties that enhance its ability to qualify as collateral for financing purposes. These characteristics are generally grouped into three categories: physical, economic, and social.

**Physical.**   Real estate is considered to be fixed in place, although some shifting takes place under certain conditions, such as avulsion (when land is torn from its place by a devastating rush of waters) in the distorted wrenching of the earth in a sudden earthquake, or when people deliberately change the earth's topography. Nevertheless, the boundaries of the land remain clearly definable. This quality of *fixity* creates the security that lenders require in order to know that their collateral will be there in the morning if a defaulting borrower should disappear in the middle of the night.

Using the same reasoning, land is considered to be *indestructible*. Although the quality of land changes as it is used, it prevails permanently and can be rejuvenated. This quality of durability has made land a popular form of investment.

Furthermore, each parcel of land is *unique*. Legally, each parcel is individually definable according to its specific boundaries and ownership. Because property is readily identifiable, the legal enforcement of contractual promises pertaining to a certain property is made easier, which again provides the protection required by lenders.

**Economic.**   Land has an attribute of being *scarce*, but not in the aggregate sense. A virtually unlimited supply of land exists for expansion through more intensive use, but in the micro sense, there is a *relative scarcity*. People congregate in small areas of the world, usually in cities, where they find the employment and cultural activities that community living develops. As a result, increased demands upon the relatively fixed supplies of land in these small areas create a *value*, the economic consequence of buyers bidding against each other for the limited supply of land.

Also, the *fixity of the improvements* placed upon the land complements its unique position. Aside from minor improvements, most construction has a quality of longevity intrinsic in its design. Bricks and mortar, streets, and sewers all have a long life expectancy that, when coupled with the concept of scarcity, underwrites lenders' abilities to make loans.

In addition, land has a *locational characteristic* that affects its value in relation to similar parcels in the same area and enables lenders to identify its worth more accurately—an important input into the quantity and quality of the loans to be made.

**Social.**   Real property has an increasingly important third general characteristic, one that is currently being enlarged upon by promulgators of social consciousness. This characteristic adds a stimulating, but often frustrating, dimension to the definition of real estate. It is the *social characteristic*, defined as the rights of the public in the private property of the individual.

A private property owner's rights are defined by statute and common law. An owner's highest bundle of rights is limited by the government's **police powers,** which regulates the uses of property for the public welfare, and by **eminent domain,** which gives the government sovereign powers of **condemnation** over private property for the community's benefit. The use of police power does not normally require compensation to the property owner. However, the use of eminent domain, considered a "taking" of private property for public use, usually requires compensation according to fair market value.

The U.S. Supreme Court has rendered decisions in cases that significantly impact the concern for rights in real property. The first case, considered a landmark decision, is *First English Evangelical Lutheran Church of Glendale v. County of Los Angeles.* In this case, the county of Los Angeles denied the church the right to rebuild church camp buildings that were washed away by flooding in the Angeles National Forest in 1978. First English argued that the county's decision effectively took property away from it. The high court agreed that the extreme land-use regulations could be construed as an "illegal taking."

Another case, *Nollan v. California Coastal Commission,* concerns two Ventura County homeowners who requested permission to replace a small beachfront cottage with a significantly larger two-story home. The Coastal Commission required that the public be given access to walk across the beach in front of the home in exchange for the right to develop the land. The Nollans objected and challenged. The Supreme Court sided with the Nollans, maintaining that the right to build on a person's own property is not a privilege but a right that is subject only to *reasonable* regulation.

In 1994, the U.S. Supreme Court ruled in *Dolan v. Tigard* that the City of Tigard, Oregon, engaged in an uncompensated taking of private property when it refused to grant permission to Mrs. Dolan to pave the parking area around her store building without first dedicating a portion of the land for a public greenway.

On June 23, 2005, the Court ruled in favor of the City of New London, Connecticut, which wanted to condemn individually owned property for private economic development "for the greater good of the community." Congress is presently considering adopting the Private Property Protection Act to prevent government entities from seizing property for economic development. The California Community Redevelopment Law prevents such actions.

Currently, social limitations on private property rights are being expanded to include control of property use as it affects our environment. A major concern is the pollution of air, earth, and water as it affects our current well-being and the well-being of generations yet unborn. The imposition of social controls can seriously change property values and even inhibit community development in many areas of the country. The costs of these controls are reflected in the increasing prices of real estate.

## ■ CHARACTERISTICS OF REAL PROPERTY INVESTMENTS

Each parcel of real estate is unique and thus requires an individual investment analysis relevant to its specific locational attributes. However, all real property has certain common characteristics that affect its value. These characteristics include *fixity*, *longevity*, *permanence*, *risk*, and *market segmentation*.

**Fixity**

Real estate is fixed in location, which greatly restricts the scope of its marketability. As a result of this *fixity*, real estate values are acted on and are subject to any political and economic activities occurring in the immediate vicinity.

**Longevity**

Real estate is generally considered to be a long-term investment because of the durability of the improvements and the permanence of the land. This quality of *longevity* enables investors to estimate, with some degree of reliability, the present value of a future stream of income from their properties.

**Permanence**

The attribute of *permanence* of real estate forms the basis of our system of long-term mortgage-debt amortization. Investment in real estate, usually involves relatively large dollar amounts that require complex financial arrangements. These complexities, in turn, require the expertise of lawyers, accountants, brokers, property managers, real estate consultants, and other specialists.

**Risk**

Real estate investment is a relatively *high-risk venture* that reflects the uncertainties of a somewhat unpredictable market. In fact, there is no readily identifiable, organized national market for real estate, as there is for stocks and bonds. The realty market is a combination of local markets that react speedily to changes in local economic and political activities and somewhat more slowly to regional, national, and international events.

**Market Segmentation**

The fractured aspect of this unorganized and largely unregulated real estate market is further complicated by the lack of standardization of the product and the fact that most of the market's participants react intuitively, giving little attention to formal feasibility or marketing studies. However, the investor who seeks qualified help and takes advantage of available protective measures can often mitigate some of the risks.

Besides these inherent characteristics of real property, many government activities also directly or indirectly influence property values. At the federal level, income tax laws are often confusing and frustrating. So is the government's regulation and control of money. This power effectively dictates the extent of real estate activity through manipulation of the supply as well as the cost of mortgage money.

Our various levels of government also function in numerous other ways to affect real estate property values. Environmental controls and impact studies add time and costs to the development of land—costs that are inevitably paid by consumers. Local political attitudes regarding zoning and growth restrictions act to raise the prices of properties already developed, effectively creating a monopolistic position for their owners.

Fueling these political attitudes is the antigrowth philosophy of citizens in some areas where property taxes and other public costs are rising at an alarming rate to serve an ever-increasing population. "Not in my backyard" is becoming the slogan in these troubled cities.

## ■ PURPOSES OF INVESTING IN REAL ESTATE

**To Preserve Capital**

A primary reason for investing in real estate is the preservation and possible enhancement of the capital invested. Generally, owners have enjoyed rising property values over the years. Consequently, the capital value of the investment is preserved or increased by appreciation. It is precisely for this reason that real estate investments are described as hedges against inflation. Theoretically, the values of real estate fluctuate with local market cycles, but real estate values tend to rise over the long term.

A real estate investment may build up additional equity for its owner through reduction of the mortgage debt. The periodic repayments of the principal amounts owed on existing financing increase an equity in property. This increasing equity can be secured for reinvestment either by refinancing the mortgage or by selling the property, depending on the market. In fact, one of the more important benefits of investing in real estate is ability to reuse the capital through periodic, tax-free refinancing, while at the same time preserving the value of the investment. In addition, the owner's equity in an investment may be raised by increasing the amount of the *net operating income* (NOI), which invariably raises the total value of the investment.

Although the problems associated with tenants are legendary as well as endless, tenants often improve the properties they occupy to enhance their living environment. These betterments tend to increase a property's value and are invariably left behind when the tenant moves. This not only preserves an owner's capital investment but actually enhances it, sometimes substantially.

**To Earn a Profit**

Fundamentally, all investors in real estate seek a profit on the money they invest. By definition, an investment of any kind is a commitment of funds with the intention of preserving capital and earning a profit. For real estate investors, these profits assume two forms. The income stream from the tenants' rents should generate one kind of profit. The gross amount of rent should be adequate to pay for all the fixed and variable operating expenses of the property, with enough remaining to show a return on the investment. Thus, an investor anticipates that the *income* will provide a steady cash profit, while the invested capital remains protected over time. When the property is sold, this investment will be recovered intact, or better still, a gain will be made. This gain reflects the increase in the property's value during the time it was held and is the second form of profit that can be earned by a real estate investor.

Before committing any funds, an investor should carefully analyze the returns available from opportunities other than the purchase of real estate. For instance, a viable alternative to investing in a real estate venture is to deposit money into a government security that pays interest each year. The annual interest, or profit (before taxes), that would be earned on this investment becomes a benchmark against which to measure the anticipated profitability of an alternative investment. The principal can be withdrawn from this security at a specific time, so it meets the requirements of an investment: preservation of capital and generation of a profit.

If we analyze a real estate investment that shows an annual return (before taxes), with the possibility of recovering the full investment within some identifiable future time period, we see a situation that parallels the government security. However, unlike this security, a greater degree of risk is associated with real estate investments. This risk includes the likelihood of actually being able to collect the rents in the amounts and at the times anticipated and the chances of fully recovering the investment in the future. In addition, unforeseeable problems might occur over time.

Thus, the profit from a real estate investment should not be considered equal to this same profit from a government security. Something extra must be earned to offset the greater risks that are so much a part of realty ownership. In addition, to compensate for lack of liquidity, real estate investments must develop even larger returns. Unlike other investments, real estate is often difficult to sell at a specific point in time. Therefore, to be viable, a real estate investment should be designed to develop a relatively higher rate of return (profit) than is available from other safer, more liquid investment opportunities.

**To Enjoy Tax Relief**

Under the current income tax code, unlike many other investments, the income derived from rental real estate can be sheltered substantially to diminish the income tax liability and thus enhance the bottom-line return.

After all income from a rental property is accumulated for the year, the expenses incurred to develop this income may be deducted, effectively sheltering this amount from income taxes. These expenses include all operating costs, such as management fees, property taxes, utility expenses, repairs, maintenance, advertising, bookkeeping, and others, as required. In addition, the interest paid on existing real estate loans is deductible, as are allowable amounts of depreciation; thus, the gross income derived from rentals is effectively reduced to a net amount that is then subject to the imposition of income taxes at the taxpayer's bracket.

In addition, real estate tax investments are normally made for extended periods of time and, as such, enjoy the tax limitations available under long-term capital gains when the investment is sold for a profit.

The full ramifications of the current tax laws, as they apply to investment decision making, will be examined in later chapters.

**Advantages of Investing in Real Estate**

Any list of available avenues of investment includes stocks, bonds, savings certificates, life insurance policies, antiques, commodities, consumer merchandise, and real estate. The investment opportunities in real estate include open land, vacant lots, farm acreage, industrial properties, houses, apartment buildings, stores, shopping centers, office buildings, clinics, recreational projects, mineral deposits, securities, mobile-home parks, condominiums, and airspace. Competition for the dollars available for investment is high, and each opportunity has its own particular advantages and disadvantages. The general advantages of investing in real estate, however, include its relatively high-yield possibilities, leveraging opportunities, tax flexibilities, and the retention of a high degree of personal control over the capital invested.

**Relatively High Yields.**  Bottom-line yields in excess of 20 percent are not unusual for many real estate investments. Yields can even exceed this amount, reaching infinity, in those cases where 100 percent or more leverage—using borrowed funds to purchase property—has been achieved. More common, though, are realty investments that regularly develop 10 to 15 percent annual returns over the life of the investment. These profits reflect the opportunities that exist in real estate and, when compared with average yields on other types of investments, explain its popularity.

The return on a savings investment is the rate of interest paid by the bank or savings association. These rates currently range between less than1 percent and 4 percent, depending on the type and duration of deposit. These are *before-tax* yields, which are eroded by the taxes paid, in accordance with the investor's particular tax bracket. Stocks often pay dividends that average about 5 percent of the value of the investment; but unlike savings, for which the amount of the deposit remains constant over time, the value of the stocks fluctuates in the market. As a result, an element of *risk* is introduced for a stock investor who analyzes yield in terms of dividends received plus growth in value. If this growth is 5 percent per year and the shareholder receives 5 percent in dividends, the yield is 10 percent, before taxes.

Bond yields fluctuate, sometimes dramatically, as a function of the money market. A bond owner may earn 7 percent interest but may have to take a discount when selling in a market at more than 7 percent. Some bonds, such as municipals, are tax exempt, and their yields are commensurately lower, depending on the bond's rating.

It is axiomatic in real estate investment that high profits are positively correlated with high risk. Although yields on real estate investments do fluctuate from time to time and from property to property, there are guidelines on which objective decisions may be based. For instance, despite the fractured quality of the general real estate market, there are fairly definable submarkets. One such submarket is apartment projects. Depending on location, number of apartments in the complex, and their size and decor, an investor can usually find comparable projects, research competitive rents, and estimate the income possible from an anticipated investment. This analysis and others will provide data on which an objective decision concerning the profitability of the investment can be based. There are similar submarkets for houses, stores, office buildings, shopping centers, and other forms of real property.

**Leveraging Opportunities.**   Although stocks and bonds allow a purchaser to borrow up to 50 percent of the value of the securities, real estate offers an investor the highest leveraging opportunities of any investment alternative. Many realty transactions require 20 to 40 percent of a property's value as a cash down payment, while others have 10 percent, 5 percent, or even no down payment requirements. A few investors, after completing some highly sophisticated financing strategies, may even be able to enjoy the benefits of arranging their real estate investment portfolios with greater than 100 percent leverage and end up with cash in their pockets.

High-leverage situations include transactions involving carryback mortgages, land leases, subordination, joint ventures, syndication, sale-leasebacks, wraparound mortgages, participation mortgages, and other creative real estate ownership and financing arrangements. These concepts and their applications, among others, will also be examined in upcoming chapters.

**Income Tax Flexibility.**   Real estate allows its owners a high degree of tax flexibility, due in large part to the application of depreciation allowances and the ability to deduct the premises' operating costs from the gross income collected.

**High Degree of Personal Control.**   Real estate investments provide the opportunity for a high degree of personal control. Purchase terms can be designed to reflect specific financial circumstances. Often, rents can be arranged to anticipate changes in future realty cycles. Various bookkeeping techniques can be adopted to reflect individual needs as they change over time. Property can be periodically refinanced to capitalize on the equity accumulated. And the investor usually retains the power to decide when, how, and to whom the investment will be sold, under terms that satisfy personal economic requirements.

## ■ MORTGAGE LENDING ACTIVITIES

Underlying and forming the foundation for mortgage lending is the concept of savings. Savings are loaned to borrowers from whom additional earnings are produced for the lenders in the form of interest. These earnings are then used in part to pay interest to the savers on their deposits.

Most loans for real estate are made by financial institutions designed to hold individuals' savings until they are withdrawn. These institutions include the following, among others:

- Primary market

- Commercial banks

- Savings banks

- Life insurance companies

- Credit unions

- Secondary market

- Fannie Mae

- Freddie Mac

- Ginnie Mae

- Federal Home Loan Bank

The total amount of mortgage loans outstanding at the end of June 2012 was more than $13 trillion. More than 77 percent of all loans made are for one- to four-family residential properties, a dramatic testimony to the importance of housing in the real estate market.

The price of real estate fluctuates over time, depending on changing market conditions. Most buyers do not have the cash required for real estate purchases. They must borrow to complete their acquisitions. If the sources for these loans were to be limited to any large extent, fewer properties would be developed and fewer would be sold. Shortages of funds for mortgage lending affect every level of the construction industry, with serious ramifications throughout the total national economy.

In the early to mid-1980s, interest rates on real estate loans were at double-digit levels, as shown in Figure 1.1. This effectively eliminated a major portion of the participants in the real estate market. To meet this emergency, a broad range of creative financing arrangements was invented to allow market continuity. These arrangements included partnerships between lenders and borrowers (participation financing), variable-interest-rate loans, and variable-payment loans, all designed to relieve borrowers' burdens and permit lenders to stay in business. These financing techniques are still used today and will be described in later chapters.

As the decade progressed, interest rates fell almost as rapidly as they had risen and the demand for basic fixed-rate mortgages returned. This reduction in interest rates, to between 6 and 8 percent, resulted in a sharply increased demand for mortgage refinancing, and the focus of the lenders

**FIGURE 1.1**
**30-Year Fixed-Rate**
**Mortgage Interest Rates**

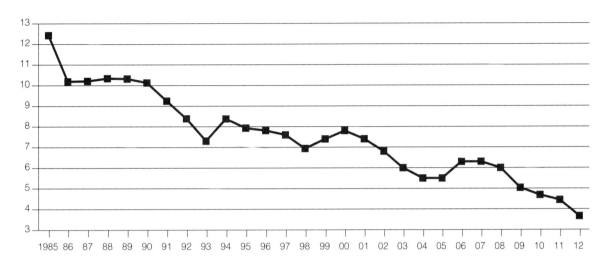

Source: *www.freddiemac.com*

shifted from loans for purchasing property to loans for refinancing existing high-interest, adjustable-rate, and fixed-rate loans. In addition, relatively low interest rates fueled a sharp rise in real estate activity.

In the late 1990s and early 2000s, the subprime market more than doubled offering higher qualifying ratios, hybrid adjustable-rate mortgages (ARMs) with artificially low initial payment schedules, and more liberal qualifying standards. Fannie Mae- and Freddie Mac-conforming loans also became available in many different forms using liberal qualifying standards and long-term risky loan products.

As the overall housing market boom began to decline in 2006, the subprime market was the first to crash, but by 2007, Fannie Mae and Freddie Mac were also in trouble. Borrowers found themselves unable to pay their sharply increased mortgage payments as adjustable-rate mortgages began to reset at higher rates. Refinancing was no longer an option because housing values were declining and the slow market made it very difficult to sell. By 2007, more than 1 percent of all households were facing foreclosure, with projections for at least 10 percent by 2010. In order to protect the safety and soundness of Fannie Mae and Freddie Mac, the agencies were placed under the supervision of a new agency, the Federal Housing Finance Agency (FHFA) and, in September 2008, were placed into conservatorship.

Significant changes continue to be made almost daily as the government and private industry work to recover from the financial crisis of 2008–2009.

On July 30, 2008, the federal Secure and Fair Enforcement for Mortgage Licensing Act of 2008 (SAFE Act) was passed. The purpose of the **SAFE Act** is to protect consumers, and it was designed to minimize the potential for fraudulent lending activities. It created the Nationwide Mortgage Licensing System (NMLS) and Registry for those in the residential mortgage business. There are specific requirements for those who make, arrange, or service loans secured by real property. These individuals are required to complete prelicensing courses, pass written qualifying tests at both federal and state levels, be subject to background checks, and take annual continuing education courses to meet annual licensing renewal requirements.

**Dodd-Frank Wall Street Reform and Consumer Protection Act (Dodd-Frank).** As a result of the economic distress within the real estate mortgage marketplace during the Great Recession of 2008, Congress enacted the **Dodd-Frank Wall Street Reform and Consumer Protection Act**, which became effective in 2010. The purpose of the act is to promote the financial stability of the United States by improving accountability and transparency in the financial system, to end "too big to fail" financial institutions, to protect the American taxpayer by ending bailouts, and to protect consumers from abusive financial services practices, among other provisions.

**Consumer Financial Protection Bureau (CFPB).** In 2011, another provision of Dodd-Frank created the **Consumer Financial Protection Bureau** and brought numerous other agencies and federal acts under its jurisdiction. By order of the CFPB, mortgage lenders are to focus on specific underwriting guidelines to verify and determine a borrower's ability to repay a home loan over the long term before extending credit. In January 2013, the CFPB issued a proposal whereby a category of loans called *qualified mortgages* cannot have risky features—for example, negative amortization—nor excessive fees. There is a presumption that these qualified mortgages have satisfied the requirements of the borrower's ability to repay. Among the many requirements is that consumers have a total debt-to-income ratio that does not exceed 43 percent of income. There may be more flexible requirements evaluated on an individual basis.

In addition to the requirements of the federal NMLS, California Senate Bill 36/SAFE Act, which went into effect on January 1, 2010, was intended to implement the federal act and has new filing requirements for licensees who conduct residential or commercial mortgage loan activities. It is important for those in the mortgage business to determine which requirements they must fulfill. For information regarding specific requirements, deadlines for compliance with federal and state laws, and penalties for nonconformance, refer to the following organizations:

- Nationwide Mortgage Licensing System:

  — 240-386-4444

  — *http://mortgage.nationwidelicensingsystem.org*

- California Department of Corporations: *www.doc.ca.gov*

**Credit System Economy**

We all recognize that our society is *credit oriented*. We postpone paying for our personal property purchases using credit cards and charge accounts. Credit expands our ability to own goods that enhance our lives.

The credit concept of enjoying the use of an object while still paying for it is the basis of real estate finance. Financing a real estate purchase involves large sums of money and usually requires a long time to repay the loan. Instead of revolving charge accounts or 90-day credit lines for hundreds of dollars, real estate involves loans of thousands of dollars for up to 40 years.

Real estate lending requires longevity, a quality that complements the holding profile of most of the major financial lenders. Furthermore, the systematic repayment of real estate loans, usually in regular monthly amounts, creates the rhythm that enables lenders to continue to collect savings and redistribute funds to implement continued economic growth. However, this rhythm can be interrupted when there is a prolonged **dis-intermediation,** that is, when individuals, seeking higher yields, remove more funds from financial institutions than are being deposited, resulting in a net loss of deposits. There is continuous competition for the use of money among individuals, industry, and government.

**Financing Relationships**

The nature of the real estate financing relationship can be described in three ways. In its simplest form, real estate finance involves pledging real property as **collateral** to back up a promise to repay a loan. A building and the land upon which it stands are pledged to a lender as the borrower's guarantee that the terms of a loan contract will be satisfied. If a borrower defaults on repayment promises, the lender is legally able to foreclose on the real estate and sell it to try to recoup the loan balance.

Another way to describe real estate finance is **hypothecation.** The borrower retains rights of possession and control, while the lender secures an underlying equitable right in the property. If the borrower repays the loan in accordance with its conditions, the lender will release the underlying interest, also called a **lien.** However, if the borrower defaults on the promise to pay, the lender will perfect the lien or equitable position into one of full ownership—a fee simple absolute.

Hypothecation is found in other situations. A tenant may pledge leasehold rights as collateral for a loan. A lender may pledge rights in a receivable mortgage, deed of trust, or land contract as collateral for another loan. Life tenants can mortgage their rights, as can remaindermen. A farmer may pledge unharvested crops as collateral for a loan. In each of these cases, and others of similar design, the borrower retains possession, control, and use of the collateral but capitalizes on its value by borrowing against it.

Leverage is the third way to describe real estate finance. **Leverage** is the use of a proportionately small amount of money to secure a large loan for the purchase of a property. People who borrow money to buy property are using other people's savings to help make the purchase. They invest a portion of their money as a down payment and then leverage by borrowing the balance needed toward the full purchase price.

The quality and quantity of leverage are important topics in this book. Some borrowers may leverage 100 percent of the purchase price under certain circumstances and not be required to invest any personal funds. Others may have to invest 5, 10, or even 20 percent of the total purchase price before they can be eligible to borrow the balance. The degree of leverage used depends upon the specific situation and the type of loan desired. As we shall discover, these varying cash requirements dramatically affect a buyer's ability to purchase property.

**Local Markets**

Real estate is fixed in place. It is impossible to move a parcel of land. As a result, any activities are done *to* and *upon* the property. A building is constructed *on* the lot. Utilities are brought *to* the property while taxes are imposed *upon* it. A real estate loan is made *upon* a property, usually by a local lender or the local representative of a national lender.

The activities of the local real estate market, especially as they influence property values, are of vital importance to the activities of the local real estate lenders. Although international, national, and regional economic and political events have an indirect effect on specific real property values, the immediate impact of *local* activities on individual properties most directly affects their value.

Police power decisions involving **zoning** regulations can dramatically raise property values, while just as dramatically lowering neighborhood property values. Political decisions concerned with community growth or no-growth policies, pollution controls, building standards, and the preservation of coastlines and wildlife habitats can significantly alter a community's economic balance and property values.

In times of economic distress, as evidenced by higher unemployment and/or interest rates, local financial institutions decrease their mortgage lending activities, which only adds to the downward cycle. In good times, their lending activities increase to serve the growing demand.

**National Markets**

When the demand for mortgage money is great, local lenders quickly deplete available funds. In an economic slump, these lenders may not have any safe outlets for their excess funds. A national mortgage market has developed to balance these trends.

Historically, the various banks and savings institutions have been local in their lending activities, with few opportunities to function outside their fixed geographical areas. Their independent ownership and inability to control large quantities of deposits limited their capacities for loan participation.

As indicated earlier, in the early 1980s, interest rates on real estate loans spiked at 15 percent or more, making it difficult for **savings associations** to attract and hold new depositors. The money market certificate was created to offer short-term flexible interest rates; however, major money market investors countered by developing high-yield securities without any restrictions, minimum balances, or withdrawal penalties. The result was a serious outflow of funds—disintermediation—from the nation's savings associations.

At the same time, the Federal Home Loan Bank Board deregulated mortgage interest rates, held constant under Regulation Q, allowing member associations the opportunity to include variable rates in their loan contracts and to charge whatever interest rate the market would accept.

Under **deregulation**, savings associations were able to establish interest-bearing checking accounts, issue credit cards and provide consumer loans to stem disintermediation.

Deregulation and the development of regional commercial banks, investment trusts, and a sophisticated secondary mortgage market increased the abilities of the local lenders to participate in a national market. Local institutions could buy and sell mortgages and deeds of trust originating from every part of the country while servicing their own local markets.

The bank holding companies allowed a more efficient regional distribution of member banks' funds from one locale to another as the market required. **Fannie Mae**, formerly the Federal National Mortgage Association (FNMA); **Freddie Mac**, formerly the Federal Home Loan Mortgage Corporation (FHLMC); and the Government National Mortgage Association (GNMA), also known as **Ginnie Mae**, were the major contributors to a viable national market for real estate mortgages. In this **secondary mortgage market**, where mortgages originated at the **primary market** and then were sold to second owners, these agencies acted directly to stabilize the market by making additional funds available to capital-deficient areas and by providing safe investments in inactive areas. Slow-growth, low-demand area lenders could invest their surplus funds by purchasing mortgages from these agencies. Fast-growth, high-demand area lenders could sell their mortgages in the secondary market in order to secure additional funds for loans. Thus, *savings were pooled on a local level* and then allocated according to needs on a national level. Activities in the secondary mortgage market are presented in Chapter 12.

## ■ REAL ESTATE CYCLES

The economic ups and downs of real estate activities are described as "real estate cycles." The word **cycle** implies the recurrence of events in a somewhat regular pattern. Real estate cycles can be short-term or long-term. Short-term cycles run from three to five years, while long-term cycles run from seven to ten years. Despite the fluctuations in real estate activities during the cyclical years, real estate values have always increased over time, never more dramatically than over the past few years. By studying past real estate markets activities, researchers can develop prognoses for future investment plans.

**Supply and Demand**

Real estate cycles are affected by many variables, all of which, either directly or indirectly, are influenced by the economic forces of supply and demand.

In the short-term cycle, the general business conditions that produce the earnings needed to create an effective demand usually trigger the real estate market's activity. In a growth area, where business is good and demand is higher than the available supply of real estate, the prices of properties available for sale increase. Naturally, this active demand encourages more building, and the supply of real estate will probably increase until there is a surplus. When the supply exceeds the demand, prices decrease. Therefore any new building in this environment becomes economically unsound. The cycle repeats itself as soon as the demand exceeds the supply again.

Another variable of the real estate cycle is the supply of money for financing. Tight money circumstances (high interest rates) develop when competitive drains on the money supply occur. The two largest competitors for savings are the federal government and its large budgetary commitments, and private industry, which taps the money markets to finance additional inventory and plant expansions. Continued huge deficits in government budgets force it into the borrowing market, reducing funds available for real estate finance. These money shortages push interest rates to high levels, depressing the housing market. In other words, when there is more demand for money than can be satisfied at present interest rates, the price of money (the interest rates) increases.

The hope that traditional real estate cycles can be moderated by better market information is currently being realized by increasing openness about real estate dealings, financing, and new construction. Four key groups are largely responsible for providing this important market information:

1.  Bond analysts and rating agencies, who submit highly detailed information to investors who participate in mortgage-backed securities, 14 percent of the real estate debt market

2.  Real Estate Investment Trust analysts, who provide full disclosure of the data in the field, which now controls about 40 percent of the commercial real estate

3.  Bank and insurance analysts publishing essential underwriting market data

**FIGURE 1.2**

**Factors That Affect Cycles of Real Estate**

Housing Supply

Supply of Money for Financing

Business Activities

Population Growth and Characteristics

IRS Tax Rules

Social Attitudes

4. The Internet, which acts as an important conduit of the vast amount of data available simultaneously

The factors that affect the real estate cycle are illustrated in Figure 1.2.

**Population Characteristics**

An important factor involved in making real estate development decisions is the makeup of this country's population and how it changes over time. Past census information revealed that 80 percent of U.S. households live in officially designated metropolitan areas, mostly in the suburbs. The median house consists of 1,688 square feet and has 5½ rooms, 2.6 of which are bedrooms; and more than a third have two or more bathrooms. Two-thirds of these households have no children younger than 18. About 22 million persons live alone.

The 2000 census predicted a substantial increase in the total population to 394 million in 2050, up from 255 million in 1992. As shown in Figure 1.3, people from Asia and the Pacific Islands will increase from 3 to 9 percent of the population, while as a percentage of the population, Hispanics will grow from 9 to 25 percent and African Americans from 12 to 16 percent.

Our population is also aging. The 78 million baby boomers born between 1946 and 1964 are creating a middle-age bulge in our population demographics. With fewer children being born and more people living longer, a higher proportion of the population is elderly. This creates a strong

**FIGURE 1.3**

**Projected U.S. Population in 2050**

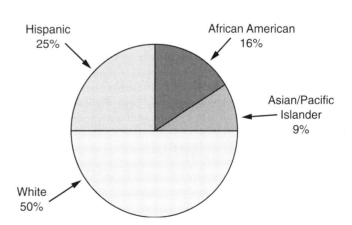

demand for nursing homes, congregate care centers, and other forms of housing for the elderly.

Our population is divided as follows (see *www.census.gov*):

- 25 percent, married couples with children at home

- 25 percent, single persons

- 30 percent, married couples without children

- 10 percent, single parents with children

- 10 percent, nonfamily households (institutions)

**Political Attitudes**

Changing political attitudes also influence both short-term and long-term real estate cycles. Historically, fast growth was the goal of many California communities. Local governments offered concessions to induce industries to move to new locations. Now, however, an attitude of planned growth prevails; local leaders are legally limiting new construction to satisfy voters' demands.

The effects of growth limitations can be seen in the prices of existing properties. The increase in property values has been great and reflects the quasi-monopolistic position present property owners enjoy.

The constantly changing federal income tax structure also affects real estate cycles. In 1986, Congress imposed dramatic restrictions on the use of excess losses from real estate investments to shelter other income under the **Tax Reform Act of 1986 (TRA '86)**. Special treatment for capital gains and excessive depreciation deductions were also introduced.

Effective May 7, 1997, Congress again fine-tuned the income tax laws by passing the **Taxpayer Relief Act of 1997 (TRA '97)**, providing homeowners with broad exemptions from capital gains taxes on profits made from the sale of personal residences. TRA '97 exempted up to $500,000 of profits from taxes for a married couple filing jointly (or up to $250,000 for a single person) who had lived in the property as a primary residence for more than two years in the five years previous to the sale.

TRA '97 eliminated the necessity to purchase another residence at a price equal to or higher than that of sold property. It also eliminated keeping records of repairs, additions, or other changes to the sold property's tax basis unless the gain from the sale exceeded the exemptions. These tax benefits may be taken every two years, and new Internal Revenue Service (IRS) regulations stipulate that if the property meets the entire exclusion, the transaction need not be reported at all. It is felt that TRA '97 stimulated increased activities in the national residential real estate market and effectively raised property values to new heights.

For 2013, the capital gains tax rate remains at 15 percent for lower-income earners. It increases to 20 percent for single taxpayers who earn $400,001 or more and for married persons who earn $450,001 or more and file their tax return jointly. Note that the property must be held a minimum of 12 months and one day. In addition, depreciation recapture is set at 25 percent. California has a top tax rate of 13.3 percent.

The Health Care and Education Reconciliation Act of 2010, a federal law, imposes a 3.8 percent Medicare surtax on net investment income for high-income earners. This applies to single taxpayers who earn $200,000 or more and to married persons who earn $250,000 or more and file their tax return jointly. It is important to consult with a tax professional when buying and selling all types of investment property in order to understand tax implications and to make informed decisions.

## ■ SUMMARY

Real estate is pervasive. Not only do we depend upon it for physical sustenance, but it also provides us with the materials for our economic well-being.

Millions of persons are involved in some form of activity related to real estate. When flourishing, the construction industry directly employs more than four million people with innumerable additional workers engaged in providing this industry its materials and peripheral services.

Most real estate activities are financed. Savings accumulated by banks, **thrifts**, life insurance companies, pension funds, and other financial intermediaries are loaned to builders and developers to finance their projects. Other loans are made to buyers of already existing structures, thus providing the financial institutions a continuing opportunity for investments of their entrusted funds. These investments produce returns and new funds available for loans to stimulate additional growth. By the end of June 2012, more than $13 trillion was outstanding in mortgage balances in the United States—quite a testimony to the scope and importance of real estate finance.

These financing activities are based on the premise of real estate being pledged as collateral to guarantee the repayment of a loan. Thus, an owner of a property will borrow money from a lender and execute a promise to repay this loan under agreed-upon terms and conditions. The real estate is pledged as collateral to back up this promise. The borrower continues to be able to possess and use the collateral real estate during the term of the loan.

The ability to maintain control of the property while borrowing against it is called hypothecation. It is also a manifestation of leverage, by which a small amount of money can provide the means for securing a large loan for the purchase of property. If the promise to repay the loan is broken, the lender can acquire the collateral and sell it to recover the investment.

Real estate is fixed in place and is subject to the changes of local economic, political, and social activities. Although international, national, and regional occurrences can affect the values of realty in a given area, local conditions are usually more important to property value fluctuations. Generally, the majority of loans on real estate are made by lenders in the primary market, using savings accumulated by persons in the community.

A national market for real estate finance has developed under the auspices of Fannie Mae, Freddie Mac, and Ginnie Mae. These agencies operate a secondary market for buying and selling mortgages on a national level and provide additional funds to mortgage lenders. Savings accumulated locally can be transferred from money-rich areas to money-poor areas. This lessens the impact of wildly fluctuating local real estate conditions.

The overall cycle of real estate economics and finance is modified by the forces of supply and demand. Excess demand will usually act to increase production until excess supply reverses the cycle. Mirroring these forces of supply and demand is the availability of money for financing at reasonable costs. Other variables that affect a real estate cycle include population changes in terms of numbers, age, and social mores, as well as changing political attitudes governing community growth policies.

Complementing the secondary market activities for balancing funds available for mortgage loans on a national level are the much broader controls exercised by the Federal Reserve and the U.S. Treasury. By controlling the amounts of money in circulation and the cost of securing these funds, these agencies attempt to balance the fluctuations of the national money markets.

Effective July 1, 2013, the California Department of Real Estate comes under the California Department of Consumer Affairs, and will be called the Bureau of Real Estate (BRE).

## ■ INTERNET RESOURCES

California Bureau of Real Estate   *www.bre.ca.gov* (as of July 1, 2013)

Department of Consumer Affairs   *www.dca.gov*

Fannie Mae   *www.fanniemae.com*

Freddie Mac   *www.freddiemac.com*

Ginnie Mae   *www.ginniemae.gov*

Internal Revenue Service   *www.irs.gov*

U.S. Census Bureau   *www.census.gov*

## ■ REVIEW QUESTIONS

1. The nature of the real estate financing relationship includes all of the following *EXCEPT*

   a. collateral.
   
   b. disintermediation.
   
   c. leverage.
   
   d. hypothecation.

2. In finance, leverage is applied to

   a. pay cash.
   
   b. use your savings.
   
   c. avoid payments.
   
   d. use others' savings.

3. Through June 2012, the total of U.S. mortgages outstanding on all types of property exceeded

   a. $1 trillion.
   
   b. $5 trillion.
   
   c. $10 trillion.
   
   d. $13 trillion.

4. All of the following qualities of real estate contribute to its being the perfect collateral for a loan *EXCEPT* its

   a. being fixed in place.
   
   b. permanent construction.
   
   c. salability.
   
   d. unique location.

5. Local real estate markets are *MOST* affected by

   a. oil embargoes.
   
   b. open-housing laws.
   
   c. zoning decisions.
   
   d. welfare payments.

6. Of all the loans outstanding on real estate in the United States, the largest total amount of money is loaned on

   a. one- to four-family residential properties.
   
   b. multifamily properties.
   
   c. commercial properties.
   
   d. farm properties.

7. All of the following participate in a national secondary market for real estate mortgages *EXCEPT*

   a. Federal Deposit Insurance Corporation.

   b. Ginnie Mae.

   c. Freddie Mac.

   d. Fannie Mae.

8. The secondary mortgage market is designed to

   a. issue new real estate loans.

   b. insure FHA loans.

   c. guarantee DVA loans.

   d. redistribute money nationally.

9. Real estate cycles are primarily reflections of

   a. supply and demand.          c. interest rates.

   b. international events.          d. the income tax code.

10. With increases in the age of the California population, in the number of single persons living alone, and in the number of large Asian American and Latin American families, all of the following housing markets will be in demand *EXCEPT*

    a. condominium projects.       c. affordable detached homes.

    b. luxury beach homes.         d. congregant living centers.

# ■ EXERCISES

1.  Investigate your local real estate market to determine its place in the cycle.

2.  Check with your local title companies and find out what percentage of recent home sales were made with junior and/or seller financing. Do you think such financing is an important aspect of the present California real estate finance market?

## CHAPTER TWO

# MONEY AND THE
# MONETARY SYSTEM

■ **KEY TERMS**

annual percentage
  rate (APR)
discount rate
discretionary income
disposable personal
  income
FDIC
Federal Reserve
  System (Fed)

federal funds rate
FHLB
FOMC
M1, M2, M3
nominal rate
Office of Thrift
  Supervision (OTS)
open-market
  operations

personal income
prime interest rate
Regulation Z
reserve requirements
U.S. Treasury
Treasury bills
Treasury bonds
Treasury notes

An understanding of real estate finance begins with the knowledge of how the mortgage market functions within our monetary system. The federal government is deeply involved in our financial systems, beginning with the creation and distribution of money. In addition, it provides a number of regulatory agencies to supervise the actions of financial institutions and their representatives in order to insure and protect a multitude of depositors.

The federal participants in the monetary system, which control to a great degree, the activities in the real estate financial markets, are the Federal Reserve System (**Fed**), the **U.S. Treasury**, and the Federal Home Loan Bank (**FHLB**) system. The format of these agencies will be reviewed in this chapter, as well as the Federal Deposit Insurance Corporation (FDIC).

## ■ WHAT IS MONEY?

Money allows us to convert our physical and mental efforts into a convenient method of exchange. Thus, money can be viewed as any or all of the following:

- A medium of exchange or means of payment

- A storehouse of purchasing power

- A standard of value

In primitive societies, money is anything that is accepted as a means of exchange, such as beads, salt, shells, and so on. Money can also be represented by coins, bills, checks, coupons, or stamps. Our present monetary system is based primarily on convenience, so paper money and coins are the acceptable representative means for exchanging value.

Before we can examine the impact of governmental bodies in relation to the supply and cost of money, it is important that we understand what money really is. Although some people seek to accumulate money for the sheer joy of possessing it, a la King Midas, most of us strive to acquire money for the goods and pleasures it can purchase. Our efforts to acquire money are directly related to satisfying our needs for the basic necessities of food, clothing, and shelter. Once these essentials are acquired, we then strive to accumulate money to satisfy our needs for security, pleasure, and/ or power, depending on individual motivations.

In more technical terms, **personal income** is earned from wages, salaries, commissions, interest, and profits from businesses or investments. From this amount, the deduction of taxes, rent, and other nontax payments leaves **disposable personal income.** To the extent that these funds are spent for personal consumption, what is left are savings. And, depending on how much of these savings are allocated for short-term reserves, there are funds for investment, called **discretionary income**.

■ **EXAMPLE**

| | |
|---:|---|
| $49,500 | Personal income from all sources |
| − 25,000 | Taxes, rent, payments |
| 24,500 | Disposable personal income |
| − 20,000 | Personal consumption |
| 4,500 | Funds available |
| − 2,500 | Short-term reserves and savings |
| 2,000 | Discretionary income |

**The Use of Paper Money**

The use of paper money dates back to the days of goldsmiths who issued receipts for the deposits of gold and other valuables placed in their safes. It became more convenient for the depositors to exchange these paper receipts for specified amounts than to continually withdraw and redeposit the gold itself. The holders of the receipts always expected to be able to withdraw the same amount of precious metal as the stated face amount of the receipts when they needed it. In other words, the goldsmiths' paper money was backed by something of value—in this case, gold. Gold was one of the first metals used as a value for exchange of goods or services, and throughout recorded history, people have considered it to be precious.

Until 1933, the U.S. monetary system was based on a gold standard. One dollar of paper money represented 23.22 grams of pure gold. Any person wishing to exchange money for the equivalent quantity of gold could do so without restriction. Other than those interested in working with gold, such as jewelers and artisans, few persons pursued this alternative because handling the metal was an inconvenient means of exchange. It was much simpler to write a check or use paper or coins as money.

The Gold Reserve Act of 1934 changed the standards of that monetary system. As a result of a severe worldwide depression and an international competitive devaluation of existing currencies, the gold standard was replaced by the gold exchange standard—the system still in effect today. The 1934 Gold Reserve Act stipulated that 13.71 grams of pure gold was considered sufficient to back up each dollar, and the privilege of exchanging coins or paper for gold was eliminated. The government ruled that only licensed dealers could purchase gold from the U.S. Treasury—and then only for domestic, industrial, medical, or artistic use—and requested the return of all gold coins then in circulation. All other forms of money in use in 1934, such as paper, silver coins, and bank notes, were declared legal tender for paying all public and private debts. They could be redeemed for another metal then in abundance—silver.

Although no money could actually be redeemed for gold after 1934, gold was supposed to be on deposit in federal repositories in sufficient quantities to back each dollar in circulation up to the 13.71 grams specified. Since 1960, dollars have not been able to be redeemed for silver either. Silver certificate notes have been replaced by Federal Reserve notes. Essentially, today's monetary system is based on confidence. As long as the public can exchange symbolic paper money for commodities of like value, the system works. When that confidence is shaken, as in countries suffering economic or political turmoil, the ability of money to command commodities of like value diminishes.

**The Supply and Cost of Money**

Economic stability is directly linked to the supply and cost of money. As shown in Figure 2.1, the larger the *supply of money* available, the greater the economic activity. When the economy is infused with more spendable cash, the possibility for an increase in spending activity is enhanced, complemented by concurrent demands for increased production to replenish depleted inventories. With increased production come more jobs. More people are employed and spending money.

If this economic cycle is true, then the reverse condition, the withdrawal of funds from circulation, should result in a slowdown of economic activity. Money doesn't disappear in the literal sense of being consumed. Our economic activities are influenced not only by the quantity of available money but also by how quickly this "permanent" asset is circulated. Thus,

**FIGURE 2.1**

**The Supply of Money and Economic Activity**

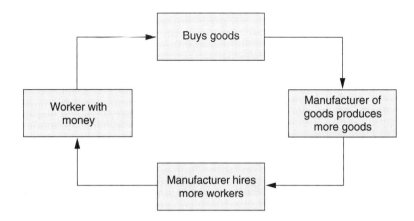

its effective quantity is a function of both the measured aggregate and the velocity of its circulation.

The basic money supply is described as follows:

- **M1**   Cash in public hands, private checking accounts at commercial banks, credit union share accounts, and demand deposits at thrift institutions

- **M2**   All of M1 plus money market mutual fund shares as well as savings deposits and time deposits of less than $100,000 at all depository institutions

- **M3**   All of M2 plus large time deposits at all depository institutions

National monetary policy has undergone a dramatic transition from emphasis on fine-tuning the economy by specifying interest rates to controlling the money supply. In other words, interest rates are now being established primarily by marketplace realities rather than by governmental edicts.

All depository institutions have developed the ability to "create" money through credit. Joining the banks and savings institutions are the brokerage houses, mutual fund managers, insurance companies, and credit card services that now can offer checking accounts or electronic fund transfers through sophisticated computer programs. These creators of money can affect the quantity of money available for mortgages.

Considering the *cost of money* in terms of the interest charged for borrowed funds, it would appear that the higher the cost, the lower the borrowing activity and the slower the economic activity. The reverse situation, the lowering of interest rates, should raise the demand for borrowed funds and produce increased economic activity. Theoretically, then, manipulations of the supply and cost of money should result in economic balance.

## ■ THE FEDERAL RESERVE SYSTEM (FED)

The *Federal Reserve System*, as this nation's "monetary manager," is charged with the maintenance of sound credit conditions to help counteract both inflationary and deflationary movements and with a role in creating conditions favorable to high employment, stable values, internal growth of the nation, and rising levels of consumption. The Fed keeps the public informed of its activities through its web site as shown in Figure 2.2.

The **Federal Reserve System (Fed)** was established in 1913 when President Woodrow Wilson signed the Federal Reserve Act. Although its original purpose was to establish facilities for selling or discounting commercial paper and to improve the supervision of banking activities, its full impact on our monetary system has broadened over time to influence the availability and cost of money and credit (interest rates).

As the nation's central bank, the Federal Reserve attempts to ensure that money and credit growth over the long run is sufficient to provide a rising standard of living for all. In the short run, the Federal Reserve seeks to *adapt* its policies in an effort to combat deflationary or inflationary pressures as they arise. And as a lender of last resort, it is responsible for utilizing available policy instruments in an attempt to forestall national liquidity crises and financial panics.[*]

**Organization**   The Fed is a central banking system composed of 12 federal reserve districts, each served by a district Federal Reserve bank. Each is coordinated

---

[*]   *Purpose and Functions* (Washington DC: Federal Reserve System, Board of Governors, September 1974), p. 2.

**FIGURE 2.2**

**www.federalreserve.gov**

and directed by the seven-member board of governors in Washington DC, who are appointed by the president with the consent of the Senate. These districts and their branch territories are delineated in the map shown in Figure 2.3. The Federal Reserve banks are not under the control of any government agency, but each reserve bank is responsible to a board of nine directors representing their Federal Reserve district. (See Figure 2.4.)

All nationally chartered commercial banks must join the Federal Reserve System, and some state-chartered banks also are members. Each member bank is required to purchase capital stock in its district Federal Reserve bank in an amount up to 6 percent of its paid-in capital and surplus. Currently, most members hold only about 3 percent of this required stock, but the Fed can call for the additional purchases whenever necessary.

Member banks are required to maintain sufficient monetary reserves to meet the Fed's requirements and to clear checks through the system. In addition, they, and now also nonmember banks, must comply with various rules and regulations imposed by the Fed for governing loans and main-

**FIGURE 2.3**

**The Federal Reserve System (Boundaries of Federal Reserve Districts and Their Branch Territories)**

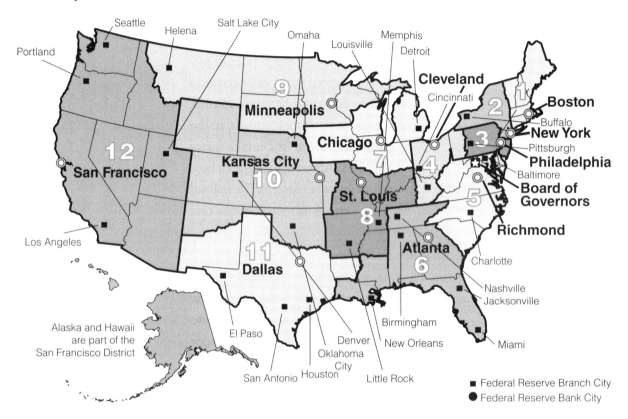

Source: Federal Reserve Board

**FIGURE 2.4**

**Organization of the Federal Reserve System**

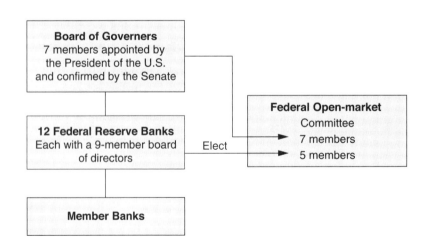

taining the stability of our monetary system. Member banks may borrow money from their district Federal Reserve bank when in need of funds, share in the informational systems available, and engage in all banking activities under the protective umbrella of the Federal Reserve System.

**Functions**

The Fed has numerous functions, among which are issuing currency in the form of Federal Reserve notes (examine the paper money you have in your possession), supervising and regulating member banks, clearing and collecting their checks, administering selective credit controls over other segments of the economy, acting as the government's fiscal agent (in holding the U.S. Treasury's principal checking accounts), and assisting in the collection and distribution of income taxes. However, the five functions most closely related to real estate finance are the Fed's regulation of the amount of its member banks' reserves, determination of the discount rates, establishment of the federal funds rate, open-market operations, and supervision of the Truth in Lending Act (Regulation Z).

**Reserve Requirements.**   Each of the Fed's individual member banks is required to keep reserve funds equal to a specified percentage of the bank's total funds on deposit with its federal district bank. The **reserve requirements** are designed to protect bank depositors by guaranteeing that their funds will be available when they need them. But even more important than this security for the banks' depositors is the Fed's ability to effectively "manage" the national money market by adjusting the *amount* of reserves required from time to time. By raising the reserve requirements and thereby limiting the amount of money available to the member banks for making loans, the Fed can frequently cool down a "hot" money market and slow the economic pace. By lowering the reserve requirements, the Fed can permit more money to enter a sluggish economy. Member banks can retain a larger percentage of their total assets, allowing more money to become available for loans. Managing the reserve requirements is one way the Federal Reserve System serves its purpose of balancing the national economy.

The amounts of reserves vary from 3 to 22 percent of the member banks' deposits, depending on the types of deposits and the location of the member banks. For instance, more reserves are required for checking accounts than for savings, reflecting the short-term quality of the former. In addition, more reserves are required from a city bank than from a country bank because of the increased banking activities expected from numerous urban depositors as opposed to a smaller number of rural depositors. The passage of the Deregulation Act of 1980 strengthened the Fed's control over *non-member* banks giving the Fed authority to require them to meet the reserve requirements.

**Discount Rates.**   Commercial banks operate primarily to finance personal property purchases and short-term business needs. The loans they issue are called *commercial paper*. When it was established in 1913, the Federal Reserve System primarily provided its member banks with facilities for selling or discounting their commercial paper. The Fed operates a market for selling this paper at a discount, providing member banks with additional funds for continued lending activity.

Although discounting commercial paper may appear to have little significance for real estate finance, the process enables member banks to expand their lending activities. The banks actually *borrow* funds from their district Federal Reserve bank and pledge their commercial paper as collateral. In effect, the Fed charges the borrowing bank *interest* on its loan, interest that is considered to be the **discount rate**, which can also be interpreted as the cost of borrowed funds to the borrower bank. The individual bank has a basic or **prime interest rate** against which it can measure the interest it must charge its borrowers. Thus, a borrower of funds from a bank dealing with the Fed will be required to pay a higher rate of interest than the bank is paying for its funds. Now the implications for real estate finance become clearer. The higher the Fed's discount rate charged to the bank, the higher the rate of interest charged by the bank to the real estate borrower.

In real estate finance, these discount or prime rates establish the base interest charges for short-term mortgage loans. Borrowers, depending on their credit standings, can expect to pay the prime rate or higher, as circumstances dictate.

■ **EXAMPLE**  Many construction loans are secured from commercial banks at "two points above prime" or "2 percent above the prime rate." If the prime rate is 5 percent when the construction loan is made, the interest rate charged under this formula would be 7 percent. Thus, by adjusting the rate of its discount, the Fed can exert a modicum of control over the amount of money or credit available throughout the system.

When the Fed wants to slow the economy, it raises its discount rate, and member banks slow their sales of commercial paper and obtain less additional funds. Therefore, less credit becomes available at the local level, and the economy is slowed. To jump-start the economy again, the discount rate is lowered. The Fed's discount rate can be found daily in most metropolitan newspapers.

**Federal Funds Rate.**  The Fed also lends money to its member banks without requiring collateral. These loans usually are made for short periods of time, and the rate of interest that is charged to the borrowing banks is known as the **federal funds rate.** This rate is published daily in financial journals and becomes another benchmark against which the banks can base interest charges to their customers.

**Open-Market Operations.**  The Fed relies on its **open-market operations** as another important tool to achieve its goal of balancing the economy. These activities involve the purchase or sale of government securities in lots, which consist primarily of U.S. Treasury issues but also include securities issued by federally sponsored housing and farm credit agencies such as the Federal Home Loan Bank System, the Federal Housing Administration, and the Government National Mortgage Association, to name just a few.

Open-market bulk trading in securities generally averages several billion dollars per day. Special dealers authorized to handle these transactions "over the counter" manage the purchase and sale of these securities. Dealers and their customers are linked by a national system of telephone and wire services that facilitate the transfer of tremendous quantities of securities.

The Fed's open-market operations are directed and regulated by the system's **Federal Open-Market Committee (FOMC)**, which meets once a month to decide on current policies. This committee is composed of 12 members. All 7 members of the Federal Reserve's board of governors serve on FOMC, giving them the majority. The president of the Federal Reserve Bank of New York and four other district reserve bank presidents are elected to serve one-year terms on a rotating basis.

A decision by FOMC to buy or sell securities has an immediate and important impact on the availability of money for economic activities. When FOMC sells securities, the economy slows as money available for credit is withdrawn from the market. When FOMC buys securities, it is, in effect, pumping money into the economic system, thereby encouraging growth and expansion. Because of these activities, FOMC is considered one of the most powerful committees in the U.S. government. The impact of these procedures on the availability of money for real estate is obvious and is quite similar to the impact caused by raising or lowering the discount rate.

**Truth in Lending Act (Regulation Z).**   The Federal Reserve is responsible for supervising the Truth in Lending Act (TILA), Title I of the Consumer Protection Act of 1968. The Fed's board of governors was given the responsibility at that time to formulate and issue a regulation, called **Regulation Z**, to carry out the purpose of this act. Although enforcement of Regulation Z is spread over other federal agencies, mainly the Federal Trade Commission, the Fed retains supervision over these agencies as part of its primary role as regulator of the U.S. national credit level.

Each of the following loans is covered by the act if the loan is to be repaid in more than four installments or if a finance charge is made:

- Real estate loans

- Loans for personal, family, or household purposes

- Consumer loans for $25,000 or less

Regulation Z requires that lenders inform their borrowers in writing of all the costs involved in securing a loan. In addition, lenders must reveal the loan's actual **annual percentage rate (APR)**. This is not an interest rate per se, but simply a rate that will reflect the effective rate of interest on a loan, which can then be used by the borrower as a standard to shop the market for the best rate and terms available.

■ **EXAMPLE**   Consider a loan of $1,000 for one year at 8 percent interest, the **nominal rate** or the actual rate on the loan. If, at the end of the year, the borrower repays the $1,000 plus $80 interest, the APR and the interest rate will be the same ($80 ÷ $1,000 = 8%). However, if the lender charged a $50 service fee paid in advance, the borrower would receive $950 instead of the $1,000 and pay $130 instead of $80. The APR would be calculated as follows: $130 ÷ $950 = 13.7%, which is the true interest rate on the loan.

A summary view of the interrelationships of the credit policy tools of the Federal Reserve System is shown in Figure 2.5.

**FIGURE 2.5**
**Federal Reserve System**

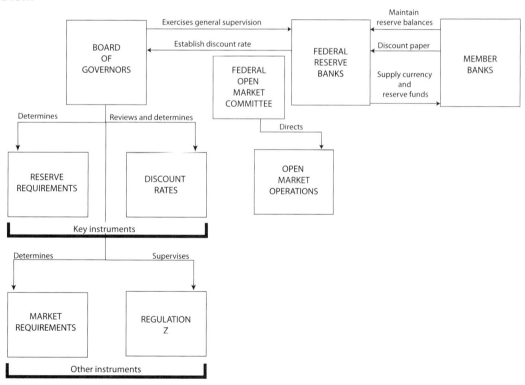

Source: Federal Reserve Board

# ■ THE U.S. TREASURY

Although the Federal Reserve System regulates money and credit, the U.S. Treasury is also involved in maintaining the nation's economic balance. Whereas the Fed determines monetary policies, the Treasury acts as the nation's fiscal manager and is responsible for controlling the daily operations of the federal government, including the management of the enormous federal debt and the supervision of the banking system through the FDIC. How effectively the Treasury balances the government's income against its long-term and short-term debt instruments has a direct effect on the monetary and credit climate of the country.

**Nation's Fiscal Manager**

The Treasury collects funds for government operating expenses from federal income tax payments, Social Security receipts, and other sources. These receipts are held on deposit in Federal Reserve banks and other insured domestic and foreign banks. Employers regularly send their payroll deductions for income tax and Social Security withholding tax to the nearest federal bank.

When federal revenues do not keep pace with federal spending, in either volume or timing, a deficit occurs. Often, the amount of government funds on deposit in the nation's banks is not sufficient to make the payments required to keep federal agencies in operation, and the Treasury has to borrow money to offset these shortages.

From time to time, short-term or long-term debt instruments, called *securities*, may be issued and sold by the Treasury to generate the cash it requires. These securities are guaranteed by the full faith and credit of the U.S. government, whose financial stability is backed by its taxing power. Thus, it is not so much the total amount of the national debt that is the measure of our economic health as it is the willingness of our citizens to pay for the debt by buying government security issues.

As of March 13, 2013, the national debt was over $16.7 trillion and is composed of smaller components of varying denominations, drawn at different interest rates and due at various times. The Treasury's long-term debt instruments, called **Treasury bonds**, run from 5 to 30 years; its intermediate-length obligations, for 2 to 5 years, are called **Treasury notes**;

and its short-term securities are called **Treasury bills**. As existing debt instruments become due, they are either repaid, reducing the balance of the overall debt, or refinanced by a new issue of certificates, notes, and/ or bills. At the same time, Treasury officials must meet their continuing regular fiscal obligations, which include federal payrolls and Social Security payments.

**The Treasury's Role**

The Treasury mixes its issues of short-term and long-term debt instruments to repay or refinance the securities periodically coming due, which keeps the government in funds. How this is done directly influences the money supply and indirectly affects sources of funds for real estate finance. Theoretically, issuing more securities should remove money from a "hot" economy and act to slow it down by increasing interest rates, just like the selling operations for the FOMC. Likewise, repaying some securities issues as they become due should pump more money into a sagging economy.

Sometimes, because of purely fiscal pressure, the Treasury's efforts run counterproductive to the Fed's goals. For instance, in an attempt to speed up a sluggish economy, the Fed reduces its reserve requirements and discount rates to pump money into the economy. Simultaneously, the Treasury floats a huge securities issue to meet unusually large deficits. By removing funds from the market, the Treasury is counteracting the Fed. Finally, the Treasury's historical and continuing role as supplier of funds for practically all the federal agencies makes it a primary contributor to the success of many important national programs for real estate financing. The Treasury's participation in establishing Fannie Mae, Freddie Mac, and Ginnie Mae created an indispensable national secondary mortgage market. Furthermore, the Treasury's funding of the Farm Credit System has been of immeasurable and sustained help to farmers. Further discussion of the various roles of the Treasury Department may be explored on *www.treasury.gov*.

**The Office of the Comptroller of the Currency (OCC)**

Established in 1863 to develop a national currency, the OCC charters, regulates, and supervises all U.S. banks. It is funded from assessments on the national banks and income from its investments in U.S. Treasury securities (see *www.occ.treas.gov*).

**The Federal Deposit Insurance Corporation**

The Federal Deposit Insurance Corporation (FDIC) was created by the Banking Act of 1933 to add stability to the failing U.S. bank system during the Great Depression. Its primary goal was to help reinstate the public's confidence in the commercial banking system by insuring the safety of deposits. Initially, insurance covered up to $5,000 for each account. This coverage climbed steadily. The FDIC insures all accounts in member depository institutions, including both banks and thrifts.

On May 20, 2009, the insurance amounts for deposits at FDIC institutions increased up to at least $250,000 per depositor through December 31, 2013. On January 1, 2014, the standard insurance is presently scheduled to return to $100,000 per depositor for all accounts except for individual retirement accounts (IRAs) and certain other retirement accounts, which will remain at $250,000 per depositor.

The FDIC is administered by a board of governors consisting of two permanent members—the Office of the Comptroller of the Currency (OCC) and the director of the Office of Thrift Supervision—and three U.S. citizens appointed by the president, with the consent of the Senate, to serve for a maximum of six years. No more than three members of the board may be from the same political party. The chair and vice-chair are designated from the three appointed members. Members so designated may not serve more than five years in either capacity. The FDIC supervises its member banks and thrifts by conducting regular examinations of their operations.

The FDIC is appointed receiver or conservator for the purpose of reorganizing or liquidating failed banks or thrifts. When acting in either of these capacities, the FDIC is not subject to the direction or supervision of any other agency or department of the United States or any state.

If a bank or savings institution fails, the FDIC can take any of the following actions to put the insured depository institution in a sound and solvent position:

■ Appropriate funds to carry on the business of the failing institution

■ Conserve its assets and property

- If necessary, place the insured depository institution in liquidation and proceed to dispose of its assets, having due regard for the conditions of credit in the locality

- Organize a new federal savings association to take over such assets or liabilities

- Merge the insured deposits of the failed institution with those of another insured depository organization

- In the event of a liquidation, the payment of insured deposits will be made by the FDIC as soon as possible, either by cash or by a transferred deposit into another insured depository institution

**Office of Thrift Supervision**

Another important bureau under the Treasury is the **Office of Thrift Supervisions (OTS)**. Similar to the way the OCC charters, regulates, and supervises the national banks, the OTS charters and regulates the nation's thrift associations. The OTS is funded by assessments and fees charged to the thrifts it regulates.

In 1996 Congress gave thrifts increased flexibility in offering consumer loans. As a result, many of the new charters approved by OTS were issued to nonbanks, such as insurance companies and other large financial entities. A federal charter from OTS preempts state laws and allows the chartered entity to operate in all 50 states without needing to be licensed in each state. In 2011, the OTS merged with the Office of the Comptroller of the Currency (OCC). For more details, see *www.occ.gov.*

**The Bureau of Engraving and Printing**

The Bureau of Engraving and Printing (BEP) produces security documents along with billions of Federal Reserve notes for delivery to the Federal Reserve System each year. These notes are produced at facilities in Washington DC and Fort Worth, Texas. In addition to U.S. currency, the BEP also produces portions of U.S. passports, materials for the Department of Homeland Security, military identification cards, and the Department of Immigration and Naturalization certificates.

**The United States Mint**

Congress created the United States Mint in 1792. Its primary mission is to produce an adequate volume of circulatory coinage for the nation to conduct its trade and commerce. Its recent activities include producing up to 20 billion coins annually, in addition to maintaining physical custody and protection of the nation's billions of dollars of gold and silver assets.

The mint also produces commemorative coins and medals for the general public as well as selling platinum, gold, and silver bullion coins. It has production and storage facilities in Denver, Colorado; Philadelphia, Pennsylvania; San Francisco, California; West Point, New York; and Fort Knox, Kentucky.

## ■ THE FEDERAL HOME LOAN BANK SYSTEM (FHLB)

Organized in 1932 to bring stability to the nation's savings associations, the Federal Home Loan Bank **(FHLB)** was designed to provide a central credit clearing facility for all member savings associations and to establish rules and regulations for its members.

**Organization**

Patterned after the Fed, the FHLB includes 12 regional federal home loan district banks; see Figure 2.6. These district banks are distributed throughout the states. The FHLB, now regulated by the Federal Housing Finance Agency, has been praised for remaining stable and profitable during the period of financial crisis. See *www.fhlbanks.com*.

**Activities**

A major function of the FHLB is to provide its members a national market for their securities. Although member associations may borrow money directly from their district home loan banks for up to one year *without* collateral, the longer-term loans necessary for real estate finance must have collateral pledged by the borrowing association. Acceptable collateral may include government securities or established real estate mortgages held in the association's investment portfolio. If thrifts capitalize on their stock in trade, real estate mortgages, they can obtain additional funds to expand their activities, just as commercial banks can discount their commercial paper with their Federal Reserve district banks.

The thrifts throughout this country play an important role in the single-family home loan market while also participating in other forms of real estate loans. The intensity of their lending activities depends on the amount of accumulated savings, as well as reserve requirements set by the FHLB.

The FHLB purchases loans from its member banks and provides strong competition in the secondary market. In terms of total financial assets, the FHLB ranks second in the country, behind Fannie Mae.

# ■ CALIFORNIA FINANCIAL AGENCIES

The following agencies regulate the state's savings and loan associations, banks, insurance companies, credit unions, and mortgage companies.

**Department of Savings and Loans**

The Department of Savings and Loans regulates state savings and loan associations by regular examination of the books and records of each institution. Many state savings and loan associations have converted to federally chartered savings and loan associations.

**California Housing Finance Agency**

The California Finance Agency (CalHFA) does the following:

■ Provides real estate loans for low-income families through approved lenders who agreed to participate in this plan

■ Obtains funds for the purchase of these loans by the sale of tax-free bonds

**FIGURE 2.6**
**Federal Home Loan Bank Districts**

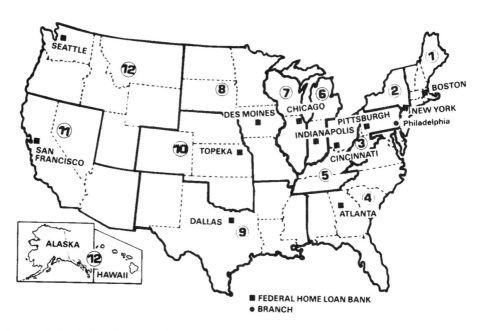

Source: Federal Home Loan Bank

The approved lenders actually make the loan, which is then sold to the California Housing Finance Agency. The Sacramento office can provide a list of approved lenders and information.

## Department of Financial Institutions

The Department of Financial Institutions (DFI) does the following:

- Oversees the secure operation of approximately 700 state-licensed financial institutions

- Is responsible for administering state laws regulating banks, credit unions, industrial banks, trust companies, offices of foreign banks, issuers of travelers checks, money orders, money transmitters, and premium finance companies

The department also administers the Local Agency Security Program, which ensures that public deposits in California financial institutions that exceed the federal deposit insurance limit are secured by pledged assets.

## Department of Insurance

The Department of Insurance does the following:

- Regulates various types of insurance companies by examining records to monitor financial stability

- Regulates insurance companies to judge their rating and underwriting procedures for compliance with the Open Competition Rating Law of California

- Issues Certificates of Authority for companies to operate in California

- Administers the examination for agents' licensing

## Department of Corporations

The Department of Corporations (DOC) does the following:

- Handles securities transactions

- Deals with franchising of businesses

- Licenses thrift and loan companies, credit unions, money order issuers, escrow companies, and broker dealer investments

- Conducts periodic audits of these organizations

The department is involved in licensing, regulating, and providing surveillance and control of companies engaged in the business of lending money and/or selling securities or commodities or advising or receiving funds from the public in a fiduciary capacity. (The corporation commissioner regulates real estate syndications.)

**Bureau of Real Estate**

Effective July 1, 2013, the California Department of Real Estate comes under the California Department of Consumer Affairs and is called the Bureau of Real Estate (BRE), often known as *the Bureau*. The Bureau does the following:

- Enforces provisions of the real estate law to achieve maximum protection for purchasers of real property and persons dealing with real estate licensees

- Investigates complaints against licensees

- Regulates subdivisions, nonexempt franchises, and real property securities

- Screens and qualifies applicants for license

- Requires endorsements by the Bureau for mortgage loan originators

- Investigates nonlicensees allegedly doing business for which a real estate license is required

The Real Estate commissioner does not have authority to settle or litigate commission disputes or to give legal advice.

**Office of Real Estate Appraisers**

The Office of Real Estate Appraisers (OREA) was created to implement the requirements of FIRREA regarding appraisals of real property. Anyone other than a state-licensed or certified appraiser is prohibited by FIRREA from conducting an appraisal for federally related real estate transactions.

# ■ SUMMARY

Our monetary system is based primarily on confidence—rather than on gold or silver. Money is identified as a medium of exchange, with its value being largely its ability to command the purchase of goods and services. When money is available at relatively low interest rates, the economy booms. The reverse is also true.

The federal government's role in real estate finance permeates every phase of financial activity. The federal agencies charged with determining the quantity of funds circulating in our monetary system and, as a result, the amount of credit available and the rates of interest in effect are the Federal Reserve System and the U.S. Treasury. The Federal Reserve System functions as a "manager" of money. Created in 1913 to stabilize the commercial banking system, the Fed is charged with regulating its member banks' reserves, determining discount rates, operating in the open market for buying and selling government securities, supervising the Truth in Lending Act, and regulating and controlling all facets of the U.S. commercial banking system. The Fed attempts to anticipate the changes in the U.S. economy and tries to balance the supply of money in the system with the demand for funds to minimize inflationary or deflationary trends. Fluctuations in the money supply affect the cost of borrowed funds. Because real estate finance depends on the availability of money and credit, the actions of the Federal Reserve have a very strong influence on the number and dollar amounts of mortgage loans made.

The U.S. Treasury also plays an important role in real estate finance. The Treasury's primary purpose is to manage the national debt and balance the federal budget. Budget deficits often are offset by issuing and selling government securities to raise funds. The number of Treasury securities for sale determines to a large degree the quantity and costs of money available for other investments, such as mortgages.

In addition, the Treasury is now involved in supervising the U.S. depository institutions through the administrations of the FDIC and the Office of the Comptroller of the Currency (OCC).

The FHLB System, operating similarly to the Federal Reserve System, is designed to regulate U.S. savings and loan associations. The FHLB determines its members' reserve requirements and provides them an important secondary source of funds.

The California financial supervising agencies include the Department of Savings and Loans, the California Housing Finance Agency, the Department of Financial Institutions, the Department of Insurance, the Department of Corporations, the Bureau of Real Estate, and the Office of Real Estate Appraisers.

## ■ INTERNET RESOURCES

Federal Deposit Insurance Corporation   *www.fdic.gov*

Federal Home Loan Bank System   *www.fhlbanks.com*

The Federal Reserve   *www.federalreserve.gov*

Office of the Comptroller of Currency   *www.occ.treas.gov*

# ■ REVIEW QUESTIONS

1. We can view money as all of the following *EXCEPT*

   a. as a medium of exchange.

   b. as a measurement of inflation.

   c. as a storehouse of purchasing power.

   d. as a standard of value.

2. Our present monetary system is based on a

   a. gold standard.                    c. gold reserve standard.

   b. silver standard.                  d. standard of confidence.

3. Discretionary income is money that is used for

   a. rent.                             c. taxes.

   b. investment.                       d. food.

4. The FDIC is involved in all of the following activities *EXCEPT*

   a. insuring commercial bank deposits up to $250,000.

   b. insuring savings association deposits up to $250,000.

   c. being appointed receiver for failed banks and thrifts.

   d. insuring and guaranteeing FHA and DVA bank loans.

5. When a bank fails, the FDIC can take all of the following actions *EXCEPT*

   a. liquidating the bank and its assets.

   b. merging the failed bank with another insured depository organization.

   c. reimbursing depositors up to $250,000 for each account.

   d. closing the failed bank's operations for six months to reorganize.

6.  The Federal Reserve System is designed to

    a.  issue checks.                 c.  guarantee DVA loans.

    b.  insure FHA loans.            d.  manage the economy.

7.  When the Fed sells securities, it tends to

    a.  stimulate a slow economy.

    b.  increase the money supply.

    c.  lower interest rates.

    d.  slow a "hot" economy.

8.  The Fed's open market includes the sale and purchase of

    a.  government savings bonds.

    b.  blue-chip stocks.

    c.  foreign debentures.

    d.  U.S. Treasury issues.

9.  The U.S. Treasury is this nation's

    a.  fiscal manager.              c.  monetary policy maker.

    b.  stockbroker.                 d.  international financier.

10. The Office of Thrift Supervision

    a.  is under the FDIC.

    b.  replaced the FSLIC.

    c.  is under the Comptroller of the Currency.

    d.  has been eliminated by Congress.

## ■ EXERCISES

1. Find the prime rate for real estate loans in your area. Is it relatively high or low and how does it affect the number of loans being made?

2. Check the activities of the California Bureau of Real Estate. Have the annual number of licenses issued to salespersons and brokers increased over the past five years? Have licensee censures increased over the past five years? Why or why not?

## CHAPTER THREE

# INSTITUTIONAL LENDERS FOR REAL ESTATE FINANCE

## ■ KEY TERMS

| | | |
|---|---|---|
| credit union | financial intermediary | participation financing |
| equity loan | interim financing | underwrite |

Most responsible **financial intermediaries**, banks, thrifts, and life insurance companies take a conservative approach to real estate finance—some more conservative than others. In every instance, however, they are all concerned with preserving the money entrusted to them, while at the same time trying to invest these funds to make the profits necessary for their own continuity. In any discussion of the major financial institutions and their attempts at investing for profit, it is axiomatic that the word *profit* carries with it the implied element of *risk*. Any investment is risky, and usually the higher the profit, the higher the risk.

Being rational investors, lenders spend a lot of time, money, and energy managing their risks. They invest in government securities, blue-chip stocks and bonds, insured and guaranteed mortgages, and other "safe" investments, as well as real property and conventional mortgage loans. In estimating the feasibility of a real estate loan, lenders carefully investigate the value of the collateral at the same time they examine and analyze the financial responsibility and capability of the borrower. They have access to the most sophisticated tools of financial analysis, including computerized statistical data on a national level. By using advanced mathematical analyses, they can identify and measure the most significant variables and the ways they might affect the success or failure of a particular loan.

In the final analysis, decisions of these lenders will be influenced by steps taken to protect their position against risks. This "protection" is built into each transaction, sometimes indirectly but always as a prerequisite for making the loan. Origination fees, discount points, interest rates, prepayment penalties, lock-in clauses, due-on-sale conditions, assumption fees, and variable interest rates, all of which are discussed in later chapters, are an integral part of financing agreements. All are designed to protect and enhance the yields of the lenders.

Due to the highly leveraged nature of real estate finance, the money available from the various financial institutions is a strong factor in determining the amount of construction activity, what is built, and where it is located. This chapter examines the various financial organizations that invest much of their capital in loans secured by real property.

## ■ COMMERCIAL BANKS

Commercial banks are designed to act as safe depositories and lenders for a multitude of commercial activities. Although they have other sources of capital, including savings accounts, loans from other banks, and the equity invested by their owners, commercial banks rely on demand deposits, better known as *checking accounts*, for their basic supply of funds.

**Origins**

Banking history began in ancient times. However, our present system evolved from the banking industry established in England in the 17th century. Originally, British merchants deposited their funds with the monarch's treasurer for safekeeping. When substantial misappropriations of these funds were discovered, the merchants sought the aid of the various local goldsmiths who had huge safes and could hold deposits of bullion and cash until they were needed.

An interesting phenomenon took place when the goldsmiths observed the deposit and withdrawal habits of their new customers. They discovered that depositors withdrew only a portion of their money from time to time, resulting in certain sums of money remaining in the goldsmiths' safes. Although the goldsmiths were already charging depositors a service fee for guarding the money, they designed an additional source of revenue based on lending out the reserve monies—those that remained in their safes. Goldsmiths then became *money lenders* as well as *money holders* and charged their borrowers interest for the use of funds.

At this point, the goldsmiths became commercial banks because they loaned money to other merchants for short periods of time to finance their commercial activities. Thus, money left on deposit by some customers was lent to others and the "bankers" profited doubly in these activities. Before long, some bankers realized that the more money they had on hand, the more profits they could make. They began soliciting for depositors and borrowers. In many cases, the loaned funds found their way back into the bankers' safes after going through many hands.

Inevitably, it became burdensome for the bankers to continually distribute and redistribute the actual coins, paper money, and bullion held in their safes, so bank notes and receipts were designed to be used in lieu of the actual precious metals being held. In this way, the checking system was created.

Now, a depositor could simply exchange a check for goods or services that would be honored at the bank on which it was drawn. This technique was gradually expanded so that various banks accepted each others' checks to exchange later among themselves—the forerunner of a central banking system.

The advent of the checking system increased the bankers' ability to retain larger amounts of reserve funds and afforded them the opportunity to expand their lending activities. Depending on depositors not to withdraw all of their funds at the same time, a banker could lend money to borrowers who would repay these loans on demand or over some prescribed short time period. The amount of liquid assets that these demand and short-term loans required to be held in reserve depended on the integrity and financial capabilities of the borrowers.

Early in the history of banking, those charged with the responsibility for issuing loans developed the procedures and skills necessary to qualify a borrower and determine acceptable collateral to insure, or **underwrite**, the safe return of the funds loaned. If the borrowers did not repay their loans when due or the depositors withdrew their funds heavily at the same time, then *the banker had to make up any deficiencies* in order to maintain a fiduciary responsibility to the customers and continue in business.

**Organization and Operation**

Until the passage of the National Bank Act in 1863, commercial banking in the United States developed in a haphazard manner. Banks could operate without liquid assets or reserves of any kind, and many issued worthless securities to raise funds. Wildcat banking was rampant in the early 1800s, and the nation was flooded with worthless paper. After the passage of the National Bank Act, federally chartered banks were organized under the regulatory administration of the Comptroller of the Currency.

Today, the supervision is shared with the Federal Reserve System. Federally chartered banks operate side by side with state-chartered banks, and all function primarily to satisfy the banking needs of their commercial customers.

Although the National Bank Act permitted national banks to make loans on real estate as well as on personal property, the law was quickly amended to prohibit any direct loans on real property. As a result, many *nationally* chartered banks did not participate in real estate lending until the Federal

Reserve Acts of 1913 and 1916 allowed them this opportunity, although on a very limited basis.

Insured or guaranteed government loans were exempt from these limitations. Banks could not lend more than 70 percent of their total savings deposits as real estate loans. Loans made to their commercial customers were not considered real estate loans, even though such loans might include real property as collateral. *State*-chartered banks, on the other hand, have always had more freedom in their lending activities and can participate more actively in real estate finance.

The Garn-St. Germain Act in 1982 removed virtually all statutory restrictions on real estate lending by national banks. Real estate lending policies are now controlled and limitations set by the Comptroller of the Currency.

There is a growing trend to locate branch banks in supermarkets. Numerous branch banks are located in neighborhood shopping markets, with more in the offing.

**Mortgage Loan Activities**

Primarily, the real estate financing activities of the commercial banks, as handled by their mortgage loan departments, include construction loans (also known as **interim financing**) home improvement loans, and loans on manufactured homes. These loans are all relatively short term and match the bank's requirements, especially because they are high-yield loans.

Construction loans run from three months to three years, depending upon the size of the project. Home improvement loans may run up to five years and include financing the cost of an addition, modernization, swimming pool construction, or other similar improvements.

Manufactured home loans are usually carried for 10 years, but many have been extended to 15 years to serve the increasing demand for this form of housing. These longer loans usually include insurance from the Federal Housing Administration (FHA) or guarantees from the Department of Veterans Affairs (DVA).

To meet increasing competition, commercial banks have increased their participation in the conventional single-family home loan market and the secondary money market. Commercial banks also make loans to farmers for the purchase or modernizing of their farms or for financing farm operations.

Commercial banks participate actively in the **equity loan** market. Loans to borrowers based on the equity in their homes have always been available, but they have been given greater emphasis as a result of the TRA '86. This act eliminated deductions for interest paid on consumer finance but preserved the deductions for interest paid on home loans. Thus, banks are competing vigorously for the equity loan business as consumers continue to pay off consumer debt using their equity in real estate.

Commercial banks also participate in real estate financing through at least three other avenues: by operation of their *trust departments*, by action as *mortgage bankers*, and by direct or indirect ownership of *other lending businesses*.

Commercial bank trust departments supervise and manage relatively large quantities of money and property for their beneficiaries. They act as

- executors or co-executors of estates;

- conservators of the estates of incompetent persons;

- guardians of the estates of minors;

- trustees under agreements entered into by individuals or companies for specific purposes;

- insurance proceeds trusts;

- escrow agents in the performance of specific escrow agreements;

- trustees for corporations in controlling their bonds, notes, and stock certificates; and

- trustees for company retirement or pension funds.

In keeping with their fiduciary responsibilities to obtain maximum yields at low risk, trust departments usually practice an ultraconservative attitude when making investments with funds left in their control. Primarily, the role of the trustees is to preserve the basic integrity of the value of the property entrusted to their management. Real estate loans made from these trust accounts are only one possibility in a long list of investment opportunities.

In addition to acting as originating and servicing agents for their own mortgages, many commercial bank mortgage loan departments originate and service loans for other lenders. Acting as mortgage brokers, commercial banks represent life insurance companies, real estate investment or mortgage trusts, or even other commercial banks seeking loans in a specific community. In this capacity, a mortgage loan department will secure an origination fee and a percentage fee for servicing the new account, adding earnings to its bank's overall profit picture.

Finally, some commercial banks participate, either directly or indirectly, as owners of real estate mortgage trusts or as members in a regional bank holding company. This participation generates both additional real estate lending opportunities and greater profits. These expanded investment opportunities add great flexibility to the real estate mortgage loan activities of commercial banks. Some of the larger banks make loans on commercial real estate developments, such as apartment projects, office buildings, or shopping centers. These larger loans are usually placed through bank holding companies or subsidiary mortgage banking operations.

Despite a movement toward the consolidation of banks, there is a countermovement of small-bank start-ups. These banks are mostly organized by bankers who have lost their jobs through mergers. They are seeking business from the customers generally overlooked by the larger banks— small-business owners, elderly depositors, and persons disenchanted with large-bank anonymity. On November 12, 1999, the Financial Services Modernization Bill, also known as the Gramm-Leach-Bliley Bill, was signed into law.

It ended the severe banking restrictions imposed by the 1933 Glass-Steagall Act, which prohibited banks from marketing a range of financial products, a practice many believed led to the severity of the Great Depression. The new law allows banks to market annuities, stocks and bonds, and title insurance in addition to certificates of deposit and other financial services. The bill prohibits banks from acting as real estate brokers, although this prohibition is being challenged to the chagrin of the realty brokerage industry.

The banking world is fighting for the right to conduct general real estate brokerage business, arguing that brokerage falls within the definition of "financial services." Real estate practitioners are disputing this claim, and federal legislation may be required to clarify the issue.

## ■ SAVINGS AND LOAN ASSOCIATIONS/THRIFTS

Legend recounts that the savings and loan associations, now known as savings banks or thrifts, were born when ten friends got together, each of them contributing $1,000 into a pot. Each contributor then drew a number from a bowl, with 1 having the use of the $10,000 for a prescribed time period, then 2 and so on. This legend is not too far from the truth because the early institutions were established as building and loan associations, having as their specific purpose the provision of loans to their depositors for housing construction.

**Origins and Development**

Historically, the first associations were designed as *self-terminating trusts*, with beneficial shares offered for sale to the public. When the subscription limits were met, the beneficiaries/depositors could then borrow available money. Profits from the interest on those loans were distributed to the shareholders. Once all the beneficiaries had satisfied their requirements, the association would cease to function, redistributing the assets to its shareholders. Some of the earliest of these terminating building societies paid no interest on savings deposits and charged no interest on loans, based on the nonprofit "friendly societies" of the 17th century. Members obtained loans by ballot or lottery. Eventually these organizations evolved into permanent building societies.

As noted in the *Appraisal Briefs* of February 25, 1976, published by the Society of Real Estate Appraisers (Chicago), "The first house in the United States to be financed by a savings and loan association was purchased with a $375 mortgage, payable at $4.90 per month, of which $1.90 represented interest and $3 principal. The Philadelphia house, built in 1831, was estimated to have been sold for $750.

The early self-terminating trusts slowly evolved into more permanent organizations called *serial associations* in which each new group of beneficial interests was identified in series. Gradually, the original purpose of providing loans only to members faded, and loans began to be made to other qualified persons as well. The organizational emphasis shifted from a borrower orientation to one of serving depositors. Changing from *building* and loans to *savings* and loans, these associations vigorously promoted the positive attributes of thrift. By applying compound interest to customers' accounts, sometimes on a daily basis, they began attracting savers in ever-increasing numbers—savers who anticipated high earnings on their deposits while their money remained safe and available when needed. Based on these dual concepts of thrift and liquidity, the savings and loan associations offered their depositors a safe repository for their excess funds while, at the same time, *paying these depositors interest on their money.* The functions of the savings and loan associations have expanded from those of neighborhood friends groups to those of full-line banking services. Still, the organizational profile of these associations remains predominantly one of financing owner-occupied, single-family homes.

**Organization**

Savings and loan associations, known as thrifts, were relatively free from any public regulation until the creation of the Federal Home Loan Bank System in 1932. All thrifts must be chartered, either by the federal government or by the state in which they are located. All chartered thrifts are required to participate in the FDIC program, with deposits insured up to $250,000 per account.

**Mortgage Lending Activities**

Of all the financial institutions, thrifts have the most flexibility in mortgage lending operations. Although some limitations are imposed by federal or state regulating agencies, thrifts can make conventional mortgage loans for up to 100 percent of a property's value. More commonly, however, savings associations' loans are based on an 80 percent loan-to-value ratio.

Any limitation on the area in which loans can be made has virtually been eliminated by the ability of the savings associations to participate in the national mortgage market through Fannie Mae and Freddie Mac. They also participate in the FHA/DVA loan market, but only to a limited extent.

The major source of funds for most savings institutions is savings deposits made by individuals. Savings plans vary from the short-term passbook account to long-term arrangements, described as certificates of deposit (CDs).

**California-Chartered Savings and Loan Associations**

State-chartered associations in California are regulated by the California Department of Financial Institutions. They are authorized to participate in the market to the full extent of national laws, including issuing savings accounts, demand deposits, and savings certificates of various amounts and duration and making loans on real and personal property.

With regard to real estate loans, state-chartered associations may lend up to 100 percent of the appraised value of the collateral, provided the loan is financially sound and the loan instrument clearly becomes a lien or claim against the real estate securing the loan. These loans may be made at fixed or adjustable interest rates and may be placed on one- to four-residential unit properties. For property consisting of more than four residential units or for nonresidential properties, the loan term may not exceed 30 years for amortizing loans, 5 years for nonamortizing loans, and 6 years for construction loans. The total amount that may be invested in nonresidential real estate loans may not exceed 40 percent of the total assets of the association.

State-chartered associations may also make secured or unsecured loans for agriculture, business, corporate, commercial, personal, family, or household purposes. In addition, they may invest in, sell, or hold commercial paper or corporate debt securities, subject to certain limitations. Most state-chartered savings associations have converted to federal charters.

# ■ LIFE INSURANCE COMPANIES

A large portion of the U.S. public's savings is in the hands of life insurance companies. Until the meteoric rise of the thrifts, life insurance companies were the most important depositories of institutional savings in the United States. Today, they control about 12 percent of all savings, second only to the thrifts, and predominate in the area of large commercial realty loans.

Historically, life insurance companies have played a major role in the real estate mortgage market. Approximately 20 to 30 percent of their assets are invested in all types of real estate loans. California is the repository of the largest dollar volume of insurance company real estate loans, followed closely by Texas. The rest of the states fall far behind.

Life insurance companies are less concerned with liquidity than with the safety and long-term stability of an investment. Therefore, they display a desire to finance the larger real estate projects, leaving the smaller loans to other lenders. Today, however, they are taking a more active role in financing single-family homes. Many of these smaller loans are made through the services of mortgage brokers and bankers.

Many life insurance companies try to enhance the profitability and safety of their positions by insisting on equity positions in any major commercial project they finance. As a condition for such a loan, the company will require a partnership arrangement with the project developer. This type of financing is called **participation financing,** and it serves to expand the life insurance companies' investment portfolios. Another type of real estate mortgage investment made by life insurance companies is the purchase of blocks of single-family mortgages or securities from the secondary mortgage market.

The average cost of funds to life insurance companies is generally lower than the cost of funds to the savings associations because dividends to participating policyholders are usually paid at a lower rate than the interest paid on savings accounts. Also, term insurance provides life insurance companies with billions of dollars upon which they do not pay dividends. This allows these companies to participate competitively in the real estate mortgage market, and life insurance companies have come to play an indispensable role in providing funds for real estate developments.

## ■ PENSION AND RETIREMENT PROGRAMS

Born in the late 1800s with a retirement program designed by the American Express Company for its employees, the pension plan idea found immediate favor with railroad corporations and utility companies. General interest in the pension plan concept increased dramatically in the 1930s with public acceptance of the federal Social Security program. At this time, many businesses and public agencies also inaugurated sophisticated retirement programs wherein the employers matched, in varying degrees, the contributions made by their employees. Currently, more than 250 million persons are covered by some form of public or private pension plan.

Countless stories of abuses involving pension plan management—ranging from dismissal of employees prior to their retirement to fraud and theft of pension funds—emerged. A federal investigation launched in the early 1970s was to determine how the rights of pensioners had been violated and could be protected. This congressional investigation resulted in passage of the Employment Retirement Income Security Act in 1974 to regulate pension fund operations. These laws specifically define the fiduciary responsibilities of fund managers, require clear and precise record keeping, and prohibit pension loan managers from making loans to themselves or to companies in which they have an interest. Often, such fraudulent loans were not repaid or the value of the collateral involved was misrepresented. Occasionally, no collateral was pledged at all—a gross breach of the fiduciary responsibility of the fund managers.

The money being held in pension funds is similar to the premiums collected and held by life insurance companies. Pension money is collected routinely, usually from payroll deductions, and is held in trust until needed at retirement. The money is then distributed in regular payments, usually monthly. This gives fund managers a continuous flow of money into pension fund accounts, with the opportunity to invest these assets.

Historically, pension money was invested in government securities and corporate stocks and bonds, with little going into real estate finance. Since the advent of the secondary mortgage market, pension fund managers have participated by buying blocks of mortgage-backed securities.

Today, pension funds constitute about 24 percent of the total real estate equity market. Some funds participate in joint ventures with other large lenders, and a few place loans on more specific projects, such as student housing, senior living facilities, and self-storage projects.

## ■ CREDIT UNIONS

Created in 1970 under the National Credit Union Administration (NCUA), **credit unions** in the United States are financial organizations into which members deposit their savings, usually through payroll deductions. The attraction of these organizations is their ability to pay higher interest rates on deposits than conventional savings associations. In addition, they offer their members a wide variety of loans at interest rates often below the competition. Credit union members may borrow money on their personal property, such as autos and furniture. Real estate equity loans may be used for home improvements and the purchase of real estate.

Until recently, court rulings prohibited credit unions from reaching out for new members beyond their existing membership base. Congress reversed this ban with the Credit Union Membership Access Act, effective January 1999. Now, credit unions may solicit new memberships. In addition, the NCUA board of directors expanded membership eligibility to household occupants of existing members.

These changes have allowed small-business groups to join credit unions as well as any persons who reside in a member's household, including unmarried couples, live-in housekeepers, nursing care professionals, or anyone who contributes support to the household. Moreover, all immediate family members may also be eligible to join, greatly expanding credit union growth potential.

Credit unions are serious competition to the banking industry. They generally are not governed by federal, state, or local banking regulations, which provides them great flexibility in making loans. They have been aggressively marketing their equity and real estate loans and hold an increasing share of the mortgage loan market.

Although credit unions specialize in personal property loans, it is expected that they will continue to expand their participation in real estate finance because they offer highly competitive interest rates and relatively low placement fees. Credit unions are also involved in the secondary markets by pooling their mortgage loans into various real estate mortgage conduits (REMC).

## ■ SUMMARY

Most of the money available for real estate finance originates with savings. The organizations designed to hold savings are called institutional lenders. The major California lenders are commercial banks, thrifts, life insurance companies, pension and retirement funds, and credit unions.

Commercial banks participate in real estate finance mainly as short-term lenders, preferring to maintain their liquidity while, at the same time, maximizing their earnings by trading in commercial paper. Through their mortgage loan departments, however, commercial banks are active in construction loans, home improvement loans, and manufactured home mortgages—all relatively short-term investments. In addition, through their trust departments, mortgage banking facilities, and ownership of real estate investment trusts, commercial banks participate to some degree in long-term real estate investments.

Savings banks are designed to participate extensively in the realty mortgage market. Savings by definition have a long-term nature, and these institutions are able to make those long-term loans, predominantly in real estate finance.

The advent of the money market certificate has changed the deposit profile of thrifts. Most deposits have shifted from short-term passbook savings into a variety of longer-term savings certificates. This change has precipitated a number of new loan arrangements, and the traditional fixed-interest-rate loan is being replaced to some extent by variable-rate mortgages.

Savings institutions participate actively in their local mortgage markets because they are receptive to single-family, owner-occupied residential mortgages. Some savings institutions also participate in regional and national mortgage markets by buying and selling blocks of securities from and to the secondary market. Others join holding companies to expand their investment opportunities.

Life insurance companies have a great impact on the national mortgage market. They accumulate large reservoirs of money to be held for long periods of time, and their real estate investments complement this profile and include mortgages on major national commercial and industrial real estate developments. Although life insurance companies invest only one-third of their total assets in real estate finance, the huge dollar amounts of these assets make their contribution to real estate financing and the success of large-scale construction projects indispensable.

Pension and retirement funds have increased their assets and have the potential to become a source of real estate finance similar to insurance companies. However, in the past, pension funds have not been active in realty finance because their funds have primarily been invested in government and corporate securities. It is anticipated that as these pension and retirement programs continue to grow in assets, legitimacy, and stature, they will begin to take a more active role in financing real estate.

Another type of financial fiduciary that participates to an increasing degree in real estate finance is the credit union. Although primarily involved in financing their members' personal property purchases, many credit unions also finance long-term mortgage loans.

# ■ INTERNET RESOURCES

National Credit Union Administration   *www.ncua.gov*

Office of Thrift Supervision   *www.ots.treas.gov*

# ■ REVIEW QUESTIONS

1. Commercial bank trust departments act as all of the following *EXCEPT*

   a. executors.              c. lenders.

   b. conservators.           d. guardians.

2. Which of the following institutional lenders is the leading lender for one- to four-family loans?

   a. Commercial banks        c. Life insurance companies

   b. Thrift institutions      d. Pension funds

3. Which of the following is *NOT* an institutional lenders?

   a. Savings bank            c. Pension fund

   b. Credit union            d. Mortgage broker

4. Which type of property has the highest total of mortgage loans outstanding against it?

   a. One- to four-family      c. Commercial

   b. Multifamily             d. Farm

5. Commercial banks participate in real estate finance through all of the following *EXCEPT*

   a. trust departments.       c. secondary markets.

   b. interim loans.          d. mutual companies.

6. MOST commercial banks create long-term, fixed-rate real estate loans for

    a. their own portfolio.

    b. sale in the secondary market.

    c. the FHA.

    d. the DVA.

7. Of the following categories, which is the MOST active in the multi-family loan market?

    a. Savings associations

    b. Commercial banks

    c. Life insurance companies

    d. Federally supported agencies

8. When making nonamortized real estate loans, state-chartered banks in California are limited to which maximum percentage of the property's appraised value?

    a. 60 percent

    b. 75 percent

    c. 80 percent

    d. 100 percent

9. Life insurance companies

    a. make loans on large real estate projects.

    b. are concerned with safety and long-term stability.

    c. make participation loans.

    d. all of the above.

10. California state-chartered savings banks are permitted all the following activities EXCEPT

    a. make loans of up to 100 percent of appraised value.

    b. invest in speculative real estate.

    c. make nonresidential loans to 40 percent of their total assets.

    d. issue checking accounts.

# ■ EXERCISES

1.  Are insurance companies making real estate home loans in your community? If not, how are buyers financing their purchases?

2.  Compare the costs for securing a real estate loan from a credit union with those of a local bank or thrift. Are there significant differences?

## CHAPTER FOUR

# NONINSTITUTIONAL LENDERS

## ■ KEY TERMS

balanced trust
balloon payment
blue-sky provision
combination trust
correspondent
cosigners
debenture
equity trust
general obligation
  bond
general partner

industrial revenue
  bonds
investment conduit
limited liability
  company (LLC)
limited partner
line of credit
mortgage banker
mortgage broker
mortgage companies
mortgage revenue
  bonds

municipal bonds
noninstitutional
  lenders
real estate investment
  trust (REIT)
real estate mortgage
  trust (REMT)
syndicate
Truth in Lending
warehousers
zero coupon bonds

The second general source of funds for real estate finance is a group known as **noninstitutional lenders**. This heterogeneous group is composed of real estate mortgage brokers and bankers, real estate mortgage and investment trusts, real estate bond dealers, endowment fund managers, private loan companies, and individuals. Some arrange mortgages between the institutional lenders and borrowers, while others make direct loans using their own funds.

Unlike banks, thrifts, life insurance companies, pension funds, and credit unions, which are directly responsible to their depositors and premium payers, the noninstitutional lenders are removed from a first-person fiduciary relationship. Although they are expected to invest entrusted funds with sound judgment, no guarantee is given that the money will be returned dollar for dollar, as is the case with the primary lenders. This distinction allows the noninstitutional lenders to take more risks than the primary lenders.

# ■ MORTGAGE BROKERS AND BANKERS

Financial intermediaries sometimes lack the capacity to expand beyond their local markets. However, various commercial and savings banks do accumulate assets that exceed local needs. When this occurs, these institutions look to the regional and national mortgage markets provided by Fannie Mae, Freddie Mac, and Ginnie Mae for expanded investment opportunities. These institutions will also use the services of mortgage brokers and mortgage bankers.

Likewise, life insurance companies and pension fund managers enlist the aid of mortgage bankers to originate and service some of their real estate loans on a local level, rather than maintain an expensive network of branch offices. Similarly, investment trusts, endowment fund managers, and individuals make mortgage loans with the aid and services of these local mortgage brokers and bankers. The SAFE Act requires all mortgage loan originators (MLOs) to be licensed under the Nationwide Mortgage Licensing System (NMLS). California MLOs also require an endorsement from the Bureau of Real Estate.

## Mortgage Brokers

Mortgage brokers are scrappy entrepreneurs and sales representatives who match up borrowers and lenders on roughly seven out of every ten new mortgages. It is estimated that they will collect some $33 billion from their share of a projected $2.8 trillion in new home mortgages. The rise of the mortgage brokers as the retail arm of the mortgage industry was spurred by the decline of the savings and loan companies and by the growth of Fannie Mae and Freddie Mac.

Much as a stockbroker or a real estate broker acts to bring buyers and sellers together to complete a transaction for which the broker is compensated, a **mortgage broker** joins borrowers with lenders for a real estate loan. The successful completion of the loan entitles the mortgage broker to earn a placement fee. Usually a borrower seeks the services of a mortgage broker to help secure the appropriate financing for a specific realty property.

■ **EXAMPLE**  The mortgage broker charges the borrower a small percentage of the loan secured, about 1 percent, as a fee. The successful placement of a $1 million loan at a 1 percent fee would result in the mortgage broker's earning $10,000. Because the larger the loan, the larger the broker's fee, mortgage brokers generally seek loans for large commercial realty projects.

Unlike the major institutional lenders, mortgage brokers seldom invest capital in a loan and most do not service a loan beyond its placement. After a loan "marriage" is completed, specific arrangements are designated for the collection of the required payments. Usually, these payments are made directly to the lender, but often they are collected by a local collection service. Most mortgage brokers' obligations are fulfilled when the loan is completed.

It is important that mortgage brokers assume a large part of the responsibility for qualifying borrowers and investigating the soundness of an investment. In fact, their very business lives depend upon the quality of the loans recommended. Thus, mortgage brokers conscientiously qualify loans before submitting them to lenders.

A borrower seeking the services of a mortgage broker depends upon the broker's access to the major lending institutions. A mortgage broker's success is really a function of two things—accessibility to the offices of the major real estate lenders and ability to "sell" the loan to these lenders. If the loan initially appears to be a poor risk, a broker would be destroying long-run effectiveness with a recommendation.

The National Association of Mortgage Brokers, based in Washington DC, is the trade organization for this group. Emphasizing adherence to a strict code of ethics, this association promulgates a full range of educational programs for its members. In addition, it promotes the licensing in all states of mortgage brokers and bankers.

The scope of mortgage brokerage activities ranges from the plush offices of the large national firms, to the commercial banks' mortgage loan departments, which often originate loans for other lenders, to the real estate broker, who arranges a loan between a property buyer and a lender. Some people say that a computer, phone, fax machine, state lending license, and a few months' rent is essentially all that is needed to become a broker. However, regardless of the operation's size, if the intermediary receives a fee for mortgage placement services, he or she is acting as a mortgage broker.

Because of the continuing demand for housing in California, the mortgage business has expanded to serve the increasing need for financing and refinancing. The California Association of Mortgage Brokers (CAMB) was established in 1990 by mortgage professionals. Mortgage brokers are consumer advocates in the mortgage selection process, helping borrowers to prequalify, select a mortgage loan, and complete escrow. By linking with banks, other financial institutions, and private lenders, mortgage brokers offer consumers access to a wide range of choices as they select the right mortgage for their needs.

**Mortgage Bankers**

Many lenders seek to make real estate loans on properties located far from where they can personally supervise the loans. Because it is desirable to observe carefully the physical condition of the collateral, as well as to be available in the event of loan collection difficulties, mortgage lenders, also known as *investors*, seek the services of local **mortgage bankers** (also called **mortgage companies** by the California Bureau of Real Estate). These intermediaries, also known as **correspondents,** not only originate new loans, but also collect payments, periodically inspect the collateral, and supervise a foreclosure, if necessary. Thus, mortgage bankers actually *manage real estate loans*.

**Development.** It is speculated that mortgage banking was born when an individual, maybe a lawyer or, perhaps, a real estate broker, arranged to lend money to a client to enable a real estate transaction to be closed. This loan originator then sold the mortgage to another client who desired such an investment. By repeating the process frequently over time, the loan originator became known in the community as a source of money for real estate loans. Soon there were other loan originators lending their own monies to borrowers, keeping some loans for their own investment portfolios and selling other loans to people and businesses interested in the profits provided by such investments.

Starting in the 1900s, mortgage banking grew rapidly but somewhat haphazardly, developing mainly short-term mortgages at relatively high rates of interest. Small farm and home loans were issued at about 50 percent of the property's value for three-year to five-year terms. These mortgage loans usually were designed so only the interest would be paid, on either a monthly or an annual basis, with the entire amount of principal due in full as a **balloon payment** at the end of the period. These payoff obligations were usually met by refinancing the property with a new mortgage loan under similar terms. This refinancing process allowed the lender an opportunity to take another look at the borrower's financial position, reinspect the physical condition of the collateral property, adjust the interest to current market rates, and charge a new loan placement fee.

Business continued to prosper in the early 1920s, and appraisers became optimistic about the continuing increase in property values. Many loans were made on properties having unrealistically high appraised values. The dangers inherent in overestimating property values for loan placement purposes were overlooked because the inflationary spiral resulted in increasing prices with each sale, thus seeming to validate the exaggerated appraisals. However, during the depression years of 1929 to 1934, borrowers could not find the funds required to satisfy their short-term mortgage loans as they became due. Many borrowers had difficulty making the interim interest payments on mortgage amounts based on highly inflated prices. The results were numerous foreclosures and a rapid decline in the acceptability of real estate as an investment or as security for a mortgage loan. A situation very similar to the present real estate market.

At this point in U.S. history, the federal government undertook a series of economic projects designed to turn the tide of the depression. One successful project was the formation of the Federal Housing Administration (FHA) in 1934. The FHA mortgage insurance program removed many of the risks previously involved in lending money for real estate mortgages. By advancing a system of standardized criteria to be used in estimating the value of a property and the credit ability of a borrower, the FHA encouraged hesitant lenders to reenter the real estate field. To be eligible to receive an FHA-insured mortgage loan, which was extremely desirable to the borrower because it reduced the required down payment to a minimum amount, an applicant had to prove the ability to repay the loan and the collateral property had to meet minimum standards of acceptability. These credit and appraisal standards are still used today.

In addition to new standards for qualifying borrowers and collateral, the FHA instituted a plan for long-term payback arrangements. Rather than refinance a mortgage loan every five years, the FHA designed a 25-year payback system whereby the borrower was allowed to make regular monthly payments over a long period of time. Each payment included a portion for repayment of the amount borrowed as well as interest on the amount owed. This system enabled the borrower to afford the property. These innovations strengthened the qualities of a mortgage and, when coupled with the federal government's guarantee to back up the value of the loan, created an investment market for individual mortgages. FHA-insured mortgages could now be created by local financial lenders, then bought and resold in a national market by individuals and businesses seeking such financial investments.

Only approved mortgage lenders were eligible to service the new FHA-insured loans, and the mortgage bankers were ready, willing, and able to conform to the new FHA standards for loan originators. Investors in mortgages were reluctant to purchase these FHA-insured loans until the system proved itself successful, which it did by encouraging many people to purchase more and better housing by providing them with the opportunity to pay for this housing with affordable monthly payments. Once initial investor reluctance was overcome, the mortgage banking industry flourished again and, to this day, has remained a major source for real estate financing.

**Operation.**  Mortgage banking is not banking in the traditional sense. There are no tellers, cashiers, checking accounts, savings accounts, safe deposit boxes, or depositors. Mortgage bankers are real estate loan administrators. Although some banks and bank holding companies own subsidiary mortgage banking companies to expand their latitude in creating and servicing their loans, most mortgage banking companies are privately owned. As private entrepreneurs, they derive income from fees received for originating and servicing real estate loans. The more loans they place in their books, the greater their income. Thus, the mortgage banker is under continual pressure to secure new business with which to earn substantial origination fees and to increase service collection accounts.

**Servicing a Loan.**  Once a loan is closed, arrangements must be made to service it. Principal and interest payments need to be collected in a timely manner and accurate records must be kept. Some loan payments include amounts for property taxes and insurance. The servicing agent must not only place these funds in a proper escrow account but must also take responsibility for their payment, promptly and in the proper amounts. These activities are repetitious and continuing, usually on a monthly basis for many years.

Servicing duties are usually accepted by mortgage bankers and other lenders as an opportunity to earn money. Most payment collectors charge their lenders a fee for these services. A few weeks after closing the loan, the borrowers will receive information in the mail as to how and where to make their payments.

**Assignment of Loan.**  For many years, the servicing of real estate loans by financial institutions was the task of the lenders themselves because they maintained ownership of the securities. This relationship has changed as the originators of loans have found it more expedient to sell these securities in the secondary market. When these loans are sold (assigned), the originators often retain the servicing responsibility under a contract with the new owners. Using this technique, loan originators can build a substantial loan collection business.

These loan servicing companies collect the payments and keep records for borrowers and lenders. They provide a property tax service, checking the records of the county for the amounts due and paying the taxes on time. Servicing companies are also billed directly by insurance companies for premiums due on the various hazard policies placed on the collateral properties. Probably most importantly, they maintain a watchful eye on the timely receipt of loan payments.

When a payment is late, the collection manager is alerted to watch for a check. If it is not forthcoming, a letter is sent to the borrowers that notifies them of the consequences of a default. If no payments are received, the manager notifies the lender and follows instructions to foreclose on the property.

Under the loan servicing transfer provisions included in the October 1990 Federal Housing Law:

- lenders must give 15-day advance notice that a loan is changing hands;

- both the old and the new owners of the loan must give toll-free numbers and the names of persons empowered to handle borrower inquiries; and

- waivers of up to 60 days after the loan has been assigned must be given for late fees in the event that the borrowers sent in a payment on time but to the wrong lender.

**Activities.**    Most mortgage bankers maintain a high community profile, taking active roles in social, political, and humanitarian efforts within their geographic regions. They also cultivate friendships with local land developers, builders, and real estate brokers in order to establish reciprocally beneficial associations. At the same time, they associate with mortgage loan investment companies, which they represent in a specific locale. Thus, the mortgage banker assumes the role of an intermediary—

searching out and developing new mortgage business, originating loans, selling the loans to investors, and then collecting the payments on the loans for the benefit of the investors. Some of the larger mortgage banking companies maintain hazard insurance and escrow departments in addition to their loan origination and servicing divisions. Some also write life insurance and act as real estate brokers, appraisers, and investment counselors.

Although the mortgage banking industry is regulated under specific state laws, it is less regulated than banks because, in effect, mortgage bankers are not lending depositors' monies. Most often, mortgage bankers lend their own monies from borrowed funds to place new loans, which are then grouped into homogeneous "packages" that satisfy the requirements of specific loan investors as to loan amounts and property locations. Such packages are then sold to these investors, while the mortgage banker retains the servicing contract.

Mortgage bankers are involved with every type of real estate loan and they can finance every stage of a real estate development—from providing funds to a developer to purchase, improve, subdivide the land, and construct buildings thereon, to providing the final, permanent, long-term mortgages for individuals to buy these homes. In fact, a mortgage banker provides the expertise, money, and commitments necessary for the success of many real estate projects, both residential and commercial. Some of their business comes from the origination of conventional, FHA-insured, and DVA-guaranteed, owner-occupied, single-family home loans.

The mortgage banker's financial participation is based largely upon the investors' commitments as to the quantity and required yields of mortgages to be placed in a particular community.

■ **EXAMPLE** Metropolitan Life Insurance Company may wish to invest $50 million in multiunit apartment projects in a specific community.

The company may specify a certain interest rate and that no single mortgage may be less than $10 million or more than $20 million. Its representative mortgage banker would then seek to loan these funds on economically feasible projects to qualified borrowers.

The mortgage banker in this example typically might begin by making a commitment to a builder for a permanent loan on the apartment buildings to be built. This commitment would be based upon the value of the property, as estimated from the builder's plans and specifications, and the banker would stipulate a certain sum of money to be loaned under the specific terms and conditions of payment, interest, and time.

On the strength of this commitment, the builder would be able to obtain a construction loan from an institutional lender, usually a commercial bank. This construction loan would be repaid from the permanent loan proceeds when the project is completed. When the total number of these loans satisfied the $50 million commitment of Metropolitan Life, they would be sold as a package to this investor, who would then reimburse the mortgage banker. The banker would often retain the responsibilities of collecting and supervising the loans.

Mortgage bankers generally lack the financial capacity to directly loan the monies necessary to develop a "package" for their final investors. They will usually seek the aid of a commercial banker who will establish a **line of credit**. These short-term loans fit perfectly into the commercial bank's requirements and, essentially, these banks become **warehousers** for mortgage money. Now the mortgage banker can draw down on the committed warehouse of funds until the final funding from the investor satisfies the total commitment. Thus, the financial participants complement each other's activities.

Substantial and constant competition is ever present in the mortgage lending business. Depending to a great degree upon the status of the money markets, the mortgage bankers compete with local thrifts, commercial banks, real estate investment trusts, and other mortgage bankers for a share of the market.

## ■ REAL ESTATE TRUSTS

Real Estate Trusts are designed to provide vehicles by which real estate investors can enjoy the special income tax benefits granted to mutual funds and other regulated investment companies. Unlike regular corporations, whose earnings are taxed at the corporate level and again at the individual level when distributed as dividends to stockholders, the real estate trusts act as **investment conduits**, with only a single tax being imposed at the beneficiary level. There are three types of real estate trusts: the **real estate investment trust (REIT)**, also known as an **equity trust**; the **real estate mortgage trust (REMT)**; and the **combination trust**, which is called a **balanced trust** in California.

To qualify, a trust must meet the following basic requirements:

- The trust must not hold property primarily for sale to customers in the ordinary course of business.

- The trust must be owned beneficially by at least 100 investors.

- The trust must not have fewer than five persons who own more than 50 percent of the beneficial interest.

- The trust's beneficial interests must be evidenced by transferable shares or certificates of interest.

- Ninety-five percent of the trust's gross income must be derived from its investments.

- Seventy-five percent of the trust's gross income must be derived from real estate investments.

- No more than 30 percent of the trust's gross income may result from sales of stocks and securities held for less than 12 months or from the sale of real estate held for less than four years.

- Ninety-five percent of the trust's gross income must be distributed in the year it is earned.

- All trust income must be considered passive by the IRS.

In California, each share or certificate of interest must carry with it an equivalent vote in determining trust policy. This condition is one that many believe restricts this state's development of trusts.

Real estate trusts' investment decisions are generally entrepreneurial in design. As with a mutual fund in the stock market where the value of the stock is primarily a reflection of the success of the fund's managerial decisions, so also is the value of a beneficial interest in an investment trust the profitability function of that enterprise. If the investment trust is a successful entity, the beneficiaries profit accordingly. However, if the investment trust fails, as many have over time, the beneficiaries' investments are lost.

**Real Estate Investment Trusts (REITs)**

Designed to deal in equities, REITs are owners of improved income properties, including apartments, office buildings, shopping centers, and industrial parks. As an equity trust, the REIT can offer small investors an opportunity to pool their monies to participate as owners of larger and, they hope, more efficient and profitable real estate investments.

The REIT's income is derived from the rents secured from specific properties owned by it and the capital gains made when these properties are sold. The REITs are subject to income tax only at the participant's level.

**Real Estate Mortgage Trusts (REMTs)**

More significant to real estate finance are the *REMTs*. Attracting millions of dollars through the sale of beneficial shares, REMTs expand their financial bases with strong credit at their commercial banks and make mortgage loans on commercial income properties.

Many of these are properties constructed for the investment portfolios of the REITs. In fact, many REMTs are owned by either a parent company REIT or a commercial bank.

The REMT's main sources of income are mortgage interest, loan origination fees, and profits earned from buying and selling mortgages. Although these trusts participate in long-term permanent financing, they are more inclined to invest in short-term senior and junior loans, where higher potential profits prevail.

*Balanced trusts* combine the REIT with the REMT, thus earning profits from rental income and increased property values as well as mortgage interest and placement fees.

# ■ CALIFORNIA SYNDICATION

A **syndicate** is an organization of investors pooling capital for real estate investment. Syndicates can take the form of a corporation, a full partnership, or, the most popular, a limited partnership. A typical syndicate combines the money of the individual investors with the management expertise of a sponsor, known as the **general partner**, and follows a three-step-cycle: acquisition, operation, and disposition.

Syndicates are considered to be investment conduits that pass profits and losses to investors in proportion to their ownership shares. Any tax liabilities are imposed at the investors' level. Intrinsic in the design is the investors' liability for debts of the partnership, which are usually limited to their investment. The income from these syndicates, or limited partnerships, is considered passive by the IRS.

In reaction to past misrepresentations and fraudulent profits claimed by some syndicate promoters, when a syndicate is marketed nationally, the Securities and Exchange Commission (SEC) requires full disclosure of all the risks involved in the investment, the **blue-sky provision**.

In California, the Department of Corporations regulates control of syndicates. Under the Corporations Code, Section 25000, real estate brokers may engage in the sale of real estate syndicate security interests without obtaining a special broker-dealer license. However, all such sales must be made under strict adherence to the full disclosure provisions of the California Uniform Partnership Act. In addition, the California Corporations Code, Section 15507, states that a **limited partner** may become liable for the *total* debts of the partnership if the limited partner takes an active role in management.

Unlike the C corporation, which charges taxes at both the company and shareholder levels, the popular **limited liability company (LLC)**, combines the single-level tax benefit of a partnership with the organizational structure and limited liability of limited partnerships and corporations. Members of an LLC can participate in running the organization without becoming personally liable for business obligations.

In California, an "articles of organization" form must be filed with the Secretary of State to establish the LLC. The LLC format may incur higher fees and taxes than general or limited partnerships.

# ■ REAL ESTATE BONDS

Bonds can be used to secure funds for financing real estate projects in two distinct ways. One is the issuance and sale of mortgage bonds by business firms, usually *corporations*, as a means of raising capital. The other is the issuance and sale of municipal, county, or state bonds for purposes of financing community improvements, such as schools, parks, paving, sewers, and renewal projects. Bonds in the latter group are collectively termed **municipal bonds**.

The administration of funds raised by a bond sale is left in the hands of a *trustee*, who acts as an intermediary between the borrower (issuer) and the bond owners (purchaser-lenders). The trustee supervises the collection of payments from the borrower and makes disbursements to the appropriate bondholders.

If the borrower defaults on a real estate bond, the trustee files a notice with the borrower that the entire balance and the interest to date are immediately due in full. At the same time, upon declaration that the borrower cannot or will not satisfy the debt, the trustee may enter the property, dispossess the borrower, and manage or sell it. All income or sales proceeds will inure to the benefit of the bond owners.

**Nature of Bonds**

Corporate bonds are credit instruments used to raise long-term funds. When these bonds are backed by a mortgage on specifically described real property, they are called *secured bonds*. When a company issues bonds that are a claim against its general assets, they are called *unsecured bonds* or **debentures**.

Corporate bonds are also classified according to their method of payment. *Coupon bonds* have interest coupons attached, which are removed as they become due and are cashed by the bearer. Interest is paid to the person possessing the coupon, so these bonds are also called *bearer bonds*. *Registered bonds* are issued to a specific owner and cannot be transferred without the owner's endorsement. Under this form of bond, interest is paid to the last registered owner. *Registered coupon bonds* have only the face amount of the bonds, the principal amount, registered.

Bonds can be further classified as to the nature of the issuer—for instance, railroad bonds, industrial bonds, or corporate bonds. They are often described by the nature of their security, such as mortgage bonds, income bonds, or guaranteed bonds, or by their *maturity* date, as in long-term, short-term, or perpetual bonds. In addition, bonds may be classified by their type of termination—for instance, convertible, redeemable, serial, or sinking fund bonds. Finally, they may be classified by their purpose—for example, refunding, construction, equipment, or improvement bonds.

The issuance of corporate bonds as a means of raising funds for capital improvements to real estate, such as plant expansion or new equipment acquisition, is a relatively costly approach when compared to the use of mortgages. To float a new bond issue, a corporation must secure the services of an investment banker or broker, print bonds (usually in $1,000 denominations), and pay fees in advance to the appropriate regulating agencies as well as to the issuing brokerage house. The success of a new bond issue is usually underwritten by the investment company because, in effect, it promises to buy all the bonds not sold. The effectiveness of a bond sale depends upon the yields designated to be paid to the purchasers as well as the available supply of investment money. Underlying the entire process are the financial credibility of the issuing company and the value of the collateral property involved.

A large company could easily float a debenture or unsecured bond issue, while smaller companies would have difficulty even in issuing secured bonds. The investment broker is responsible for advising which bonds to market, what interest rates to pay, and what prices the bonds should be, according to specific money market conditions.

After the bonds are sold, their values fluctuate with the money market. For instance, if market interest rates rise, the value of the bonds issued at a lower interest rate decreases accordingly. In order to compete with higher market interest rates, the face value of these bonds would be discounted if the bond owner wished to sell them. The reverse is also true. When market interest rates drop below those being paid on existing bonds, their value increases above their face amount. Thus, bonds may be worth 95 percent of their face value at one time and 105 percent at another, depending upon market conditions. This effectively changes the yield on bonds that are sold before maturity to more or less than the stated rate of interest, depending upon the bond's sales price.

Bonds are rated according to the financial security of their issuers. Investment rating services, such as Moody's, Fitch, and Standard and Poor's, constantly watch the major companies and report their financial conditions as they reflect upon the companies' ability to pay their debts when due. Bonds with the highest ratings are considered by buyers to be safe investments and, thus, are not discounted to any major degree. Bonds with lower ratings are usually traded at greater discounts to reflect their higher risks.

## Uses for Bond Issues

Real estate bonds were used widely in the United States in the 1920s. Designed to attract small investors into large investment pools, bonds were issued to finance office buildings, apartment projects, and commercial developments. The bonds were repaid from the flow of rents coming from these income properties and were a popular form of investment. They generated relatively safe and high yields for their owners.

The depression of the 1930s quickly changed the existing euphoric attitude enjoyed by the bondholders into one of harsh reality. In many instances, the total amount of the bonds issued exceeded reasonable estimates of the value of the collateral. Consequently, when property values declined, even by a small amount, the bondholders were wiped out.

As a result, the use of bonds as a device to finance corporate capital projects faded and has never recaptured its former popularity. Mortgages are used today as one method of raising corporate funds, but many companies continue to use debenture bonds as a source for raising long-term funds. Because the debenture bond is an unsecured general lien against all of a company's assets, financial managers can effectively balance their company's overall debt by establishing the proper mix of short-term notes, longer-term individual property mortgages, long-term debenture bonds, and equity participation through preferred and common stock sales.

**Municipal and Private Bonds**

A more popular use for real estate bonds is to finance municipal improvement projects. By issuing **general obligation bonds** guaranteed by the taxing power and the full faith and credit of the community, governments can raise funds for financing schools, street improvements, sewer installations, park developments, and other civic improvement projects.

For years, municipal bond owners enjoyed a special tax privilege under a federal government statute exempting the interest income earned on state and local securities from federal income tax. Buyers of municipal bonds do not have to declare their interest earnings as taxable income. This acts to reduce the cost of improvements to state and local governments and is an added incentive for purchasers. However, on April 20, 1988, in *South Carolina v. Baker*, 56 U.S.L.W., 4311, the U.S. Supreme Court ruled that the federal government may tax the interest earned on state and local bonds. This decision, as yet, has had no impact on the marketing of tax-free bonds, but the possibility exists that future legislation would seek to tax such interest income to increase federal tax revenues.

A variation on this theme is the issuance of *revenue bonds* to fund a specific community improvement project. The bonds are repaid from the revenues generated by the improvement. For instance, a toll bridge could be constructed using the money raised from the sale of revenue bonds and the repayment of the bonds would be designed to match the revenue secured from tolls collected.

A dramatic illustration of the role of such revenue bonds in real estate finance is their possible use in developing employment centers for a community. For instance, a city could float revenue bonds to develop an industrial park or to construct buildings that might be leased to commercial tenants. These bonds are known as **industrial revenue bonds.** The rental income from the buildings would be adequate to repay the bonds over a long period of time. By this process, new jobs are created, new taxes are generated, and, generally, an impetus of growth occurs in the community. Additional revenue bonds and other incentives can then be used by these growth-oriented communities to attract more businesses to industrial parks.

**Industrial Development Bonds**

Unlike industrial revenue bonds, which are issued by a municipality for public improvements, *industrial development bonds* are designed to allow private investors an opportunity to finance apartment and commercial developments by using tax-exempt, and, thus, relatively inexpensive, funds. The developer prepares an application for approval by a local city or county Industrial Development Authority (IDA). This application includes the plans for the apartment or commercial development and a statement describing the need for these units as an enhancement of the community's welfare. The bond attorney for the IDA reviews the application and makes a recommendation to an all-volunteer board. If approval is secured, the developer hires a bond broker who floats a new issue. The interest rate is determined by the broker as a function of the market with the earnings exempted from federal and, often, state income taxes.

**Mortgage Revenue Bonds**

**Mortgage revenue bonds** are a form of industrial development bond. The bond issue is tax-exempt because it is offered by state and local governments through their housing financing agencies.

The government agency transfers the proceeds of the bond sale to the lender, who then makes a mortgage loan to the developer of the project. Because of the tax exemption on income derived by the bondholders, interest to the borrower is lower than market rates, and rents can be lowered accordingly. In addition, one-fifth of the units must be allocated for low-income renters for ten years or half the life of the loan, whichever is longer.

**Zero Coupon Bonds**

Also known as zero treasuries, **zero coupon bonds** represent an old approach to bond buying that has been reintroduced into the money market. Patterned after World War II savings bonds, which were sold for $18.75 and redeemed after ten years for $25, tax-deferred zero bonds are designed to postpone the interest income tax liability until the bonds are redeemed. A buyer writes a check for a bond at a discounted price and holds this bond until maturity or until sold. Interest compounds regularly, and the buyer pays tax on the earnings after cashing in the bond. Taxable bonds, on the other hand, require the holders to report the interest income as it accrues each year.

**Mortgage Loan Bonds**

Some states issue income-tax-free bonds to secure funds for relatively low-cost mortgage loans. These loans are available to eligible persons to help them acquire homes and condominium apartments. The interest income from these bonds is tax-exempt at both the federal and state levels, so their purchasers can buy them at lower rates than would be required on other, taxable investments. These savings are passed along to the borrowers, who will pay slightly higher interest rates on their loans than are paid to the bondholders to cover operational costs. Thus, although the entire program is designed to be self-supporting, it does pass the subsidizing effect over the entire country and the state involved through the loss of income tax revenue. California issues Cal-Vet Bonds to finance eligible veterans' homes. See Figure 4.1 for a review of bonds used in mortgage lending.

**California Bonds**

In California, Community Redevelopment Agencies (CRAs) are authorized under the Community Redevelopment Law (Health and Safety Code, Section 33000) to carry out redevelopment programs at the local level. CRAs can finance projects by issuing general obligation bonds. In addition, CRAs can finance residential and limited commercial developments by issuing tax-exempt *mortgage revenue bonds*. The bond proceeds may be used to make below-market interest rate loans to qualified developers of low-income and medium-income residential projects.

California law also permits savings associations an opportunity to issue mortgage-backed bonds. The association pledges a mortgage pool as collateral to the trustee to back up the sale of these bonds to investors. The monies from the sale are used to create more mortgages, creating an almost perpetual supply of funds for real estate finance.

## ■ ENDOWMENT FUNDS

In the financial sense, *endow* means to provide with a permanent fund or source of income. A myriad of educational institutions and research foundations enjoy the earnings from endowment funds established by generous donors. The basic quality of an endowment is its permanence, with a specific requirement being the preservation of the value of the invested capital while the recipient benefits from its income. Managers of endowment funds are charged with maximizing earnings as well as protecting the integrity of the principal.

**FIGURE 4.1**
**Bonds Used in Mortgage Lending**

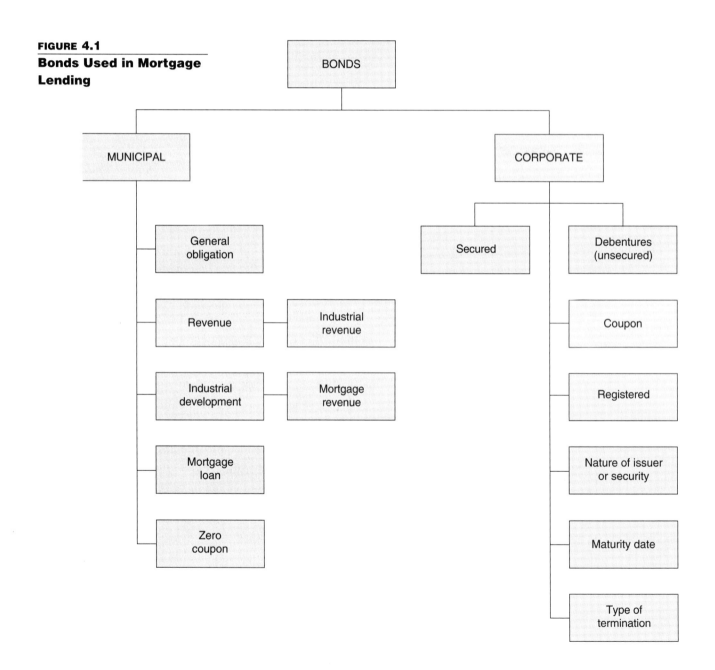

Donations to educational institutions and nonprofit research foundations are tax-deductible, and donors usually place few restrictions upon the investment of endowment funds. The permanent quality of these funds complements the acquisition of long-term investment portfolios, but investment decisions are complicated by the need to preserve the basic values of the funds. Many endowment funds are not large enough to support a full-time investment staff; the management is usually assigned to an investment counselor, to a trust company, or to members of the institution's or foundation's board of trustees.

These managers must select investments that will safely generate relatively high levels of income for long periods of time. Although it would seem that sound real estate mortgages fit this description, endowment fund managers have not as yet pursued these investment alternatives to any significant extent. However, a new entity resulting from TRA '86 is the Real Estate Mortgage Investment Conduit (REMIC) that may be the vehicle for motivating these endowment managers to pursue real estate loans aggressively as an investment alternative. (See REMIC in Chapter 12.)

## ■ PRIVATE LOAN COMPANIES

Privately owned loan companies are found throughout the United States. Ranging from large national companies with branches in almost every city to individual entrepreneurs who may personally buy and sell loans, these private lenders deal primarily in junior financing arrangements, such as second deeds of trust that utilize a borrower's equity in real property as collateral. This type of financing is often used to raise funds for consumer purchases, such as automobiles, furniture, and other "big ticket" consumer items.

Although the consumer goods financing companies technically can participate in real estate finance, their activities are too peripheral and sporadic to make them important in this field. However, there are numerous other private loan companies designed to deal exclusively in real estate finance. These companies make loans from their own funds or monies borrowed from their commercial banks, act as mortgage brokers in arranging loans between other lenders and borrowers, and buy and sell junior financing instruments.

In this latter capacity, these private real estate loan companies help create a market for investment in junior loans. TRA '86 disallowed interest deductions on consumer loans but permitted deductions for interest paid on home loans, making investment in junior loans more prevalent.

Private real estate loan companies usually charge more than other lenders. They attempt to offset the risks inherent in their junior lien position by charging the maximum interest rates allowable by law and by imposing high loan placement fees.

California has laws regulating the activities of private lenders. The state requires loan companies to obtain licenses and performance bonds. Limits are imposed on the fees these lenders can charge for their services.

Regulation Z of the **Truth in Lending** portion of the 1968 Consumer Protection Act requires lenders to reveal what the final effects of the various charges will be on the overall cost of a loan. This revelation does not prohibit a borrower from completing a loan transaction. It only reveals the total costs involved and allows a borrower up to three business days to cancel the loan arrangement. Known as *rescission*, this right applies only to loans for refinancing.

## ■ CALIFORNIA REAL PROPERTY LOAN LAW

Under Article 7, Chapter 3 of the California Real Estate Law, a real estate broker or mortgage broker is limited in the amount of commission and fees that can be charged for making or arranging a hard money loan. A hard money loan is an equity loan and not a purchase loan. Commission and cost limitations are:

■ First trust deed loans of LESS than $30,000

— 5 percent of principal if term of loan is less than three years

— 10 percent if term of loan is three years or more

■ Junior trust deed loans of LESS than $20,000

— 5 percent of principal if term is less than two years

— 10 percent of principal if term is at least two years but less than three years

— 15 percent of principal if term is three years or more

■ Expenses of making the loan include appraisal fees, notary fees, escrow fees, credit report fees, and others. They are not to exceed the following:

— Loans from $0 to $7,800: actual costs or $390, whichever is less

— Loans from $7,801 to $14,000: actual costs or 5 percent of the loan amount, whichever is less

— Loans over $14,000: actual costs but not more than $700

■ **EXAMPLE**   The cost for borrowing $19,500 on a junior trust deed equity loan for three years is $3,625:

$19,500
× 15%
2,925   Broker's Commission
+ 700   Maximum Closing Expenses
$3,625

Balloon payments are not allowed on hard money loans of less than three years, nor on a hard money loan of six years or less for owner-occupied dwellings. If the borrower does not disclose to the broker any and all liens against the property being offered as security for the loan, the borrower may be liable for payment of all costs and one-half of the broker's commission if the new loan cannot be completed.

The borrower cannot be required to purchase credit life or disability insurance as a condition of the loan. A mortgage loan disclosure statement must be given and a copy kept for four years. Any late charges are limited to 10 percent (with a $5 minimum) of the principal and interest part of the installment. No late charge can be assessed for a payment received within ten days of the due date. Any listing agreement between the borrower and the broker authorizing a broker to find a loan of $2,000 or less cannot be for more than 45 days. Interest cannot begin until the funds have been made available to the borrower. Concerning a loan on an owner-occupied dwelling, the following applies:

■ Up to 20 percent of the principal can be paid off during any 12-month period without penalty.

■ The maximum allowable prepayment penalty is 6 months' interest on the balance after 20 percent payment.

■ No prepayment penalty can be imposed after seven years from the date of the loan.

If a real estate broker expects to deal with 20 or more loans or negotiates loans worth more than $2 million in any one-year period, the broker must notify the Bureau of Real Estate within 30 days and will be obligated to comply with additional requirements.

Exempt from the California Real Property Loan Law are institutional lenders, such as banks, credit unions, savings associations, and finance companies. Also exempt are first trust deed loans of $30,000 or more, junior trust deeds loans of $20,000 or more, and seller carryback purchase money transactions.

## ■ INDIVIDUALS

**Sellers as Lenders**

Sellers participate in the finance market by financing a portion of the sales price with carryback loans. Using junior loans, land contracts, wraparounds, and other creative financing devices (to be described in later chapters), sellers frequently agree to help finance some of the property's sales price rather than lose the deal.

Recently, there has been a significant increase in the variety of loan products available to qualified borrowers. Lenders are offering senior loans at up to 100 percent of appraised value coupled with appropriate junior loans, lessening the need for seller financing.

■ **EXAMPLE** A property sells for $750,000 with a 5 percent cash down payment ($37,500), a 15 percent junior loan ($112,500), and a new senior loan for 80 percent ($600,000).

■ **EXAMPLE** A home sells for $550,000 with an existing loan balance of $350,000. The buyer makes a 20 percent cash down payment ($110,000) and the seller agrees to carry back a second deed of trust for $55,000. The buyer then obtains a new senior loan for $385,000 to pay off the existing loan.

The secondary market for the sale of real estate loans will be examined in Chapter 12.

**Families as Lenders**

Family members also participate as lenders on real estate. Frequently, they provide the cash necessary for the down payment and closing costs toward the purchase of a residence or investment property. Sometimes, to allow the buyer to secure the loan, family members are required to **cosign** the loan documents to include their financial resources as additional collateral.

Based on the 2013 tax law, which now allows anyone to make an annual tax-free gift of $14,000, some parents can aid their children in purchasing a home. A married couple could accept up to $56,000 in tax-free gifts; $14,000 from each parent to each of the children.

**Other Lenders**

Various foreign sources of funds for real estate financing activities in our country have not yet been clearly identified. The oil-producing countries of the Middle East and North Africa have billions of dollars on deposit in U.S. banks. Although these monies substantially increase the capacity of these banks to enlarge their loan portfolios, the quality of these funds is still unknown. If they turn out to be relatively short-term funds, they will have little impact on the real estate financial market. But if these funds are left on deposit for longer periods of time, they may have a profound effect upon the monies available for real estate finance.

Foreign investors participate in about seven percent of the U.S. equity market. A decline in the Euro causes many European investors to sell rather than buy U.S. real estate. Dutch investors usually buy REITs while Australians prefer their U.S. holdings in New York City, San Francisco, Boston, and Washington DC.

# ■ SUMMARY

Mortgage brokers act as catalysts in the process of matching borrowers and lenders, a service for which they earn a finder's fee. Once a loan is finalized, the broker's responsibilities are usually completed.

Mortgage bankers, on the other hand, not only generate new mortgage loans between the major lenders and individual borrowers but also continue to function as intermediaries by collecting the mortgage payments, inspecting the condition of the collateral, counseling delinquent borrowers, and foreclosing, when necessary. In addition, mortgage bankers often invest their own funds or borrow money from their banks to finance site acquisitions, land improvements, and construction costs and issue permanent mortgages in order to complete a full development program. Mortgage bankers also serve as representatives or correspondents for large real estate mortgage investors, such as major insurance companies, who rely upon these bankers to place new loans and group them into packages, which are then sold to the investors while the bankers retain the service contracts. Thus, the mortgage bankers provide a vehicle for the national distribution of mortgage money.

The real estate trusts, much like the stock market's mutual funds, are depositories for small investors who pool their monies for greater investment flexibility. The investors take a passive role in management and allow the trust's directors to decide on the investment policy.

Some real estate trusts are involved exclusively in equity holdings. These equity trusts are described as real estate investment trusts (REITs) and they purchase property for its income and potential growth in value. Other real estate trusts, identified as real estate mortgage trusts (REMTs), invest primarily in short-term real estate mortgage loans. Some real estate trusts are hybrids that combine equity participation and mortgage investments.

The issuance and sale of real estate bonds is an additional source of funds for financing real estate. Corporations issue bonds to secure money for plant expansion, equipment purchases, and operational expenses. Various government bodies issue bonds to raise funds for improvements, such as schools, parks, streets, industrial developments, and sewage plants, to name just a few. The administration of funds raised by a bond sale is left in the hands of a trustee, who supervises the collection of payments from the borrower/issuer and the distribution of dividends to the investors/purchasers.

Corporation bonds can be either secured bonds backed by specific pledges of real property or debenture bonds secured by all of a company's general assets. Some municipal and state bonds are designed to be repaid by property taxes—general obligation bonds. Others are paid from rents and tolls collected from the improvements—revenue bonds. Often the interest received by municipal bondholders is exempt from federal and state income taxes, which encourages more investment in these financing instruments and, thus, more public improvements. Industrial development bonds have been designed to allow private investors an opportunity to finance their apartments and commercial developments using tax-exempt funds. Mortgage revenue bonds are issued by state and local governments to finance their housing agencies' activities. Tax-deferred zero coupon bonds allow the holders to postpone paying tax on the interest income until the bonds mature. Mortgage loan bonds are issued to aid low-income and middle-income families to secure relatively low-cost home financing.

Endowment funds consist of monies contributed by donors to educational institutions and research foundations. The principal is invested; the recipient institutions use only the profits from the investments. The bulk of the assets of these endowment funds is invested in government and private securities, such as stocks and bonds, and only indirectly do these assets find their way into real estate finance, either from purchasing properties or from providing funds for mortgages secured by real property.

Although private lenders occupy a minor position in relation to the major institutional lenders in terms of money loaned, they are a recognizable segment of real estate financing sources.

The private lenders, both companies and individuals, often provide the funds required to close many real estate transactions. Without their ability to make independent decisions and to take extra risks, many real estate transactions would be impossible to complete.

# ■ REVIEW QUESTIONS

1. Mortgage brokers do all of the following *EXCEPT*

   a.  arrange mortgages.

   b.  collect payments.

   c.  collect placement fees.

   d.  act as noninstitutional lenders.

2. The success of a mortgage broker depends upon all of the following *EXCEPT*

   a.  underwriting ability.

   b.  the number of defaulted loans.

   c.  continuing relationship with investors.

   d.  continuing supervision of the loan.

3. Mortgage bankers do all of the following *EXCEPT*

   a.  accept savings deposits.      c.  arrange discounts.

   b.  collect payments.            d.  lend their own money.

4. Mortgage bankers are usually described as all of the following *EXCEPT* as

   a.  investors.                   c.  noninstitutional lenders.

   b.  correspondents.              d.  intermediaries.

5. When a mortgage banker establishes a line of credit with a commercial bank, the bank is acting as the mortgage banker's

   a.  investor.                    c.  correspondent.

   b.  warehouser for funds.        d.  mortgage broker.

6. Real estate investment trusts are all of the following *EXCEPT*

    a. corporations.

    b. partnerships.

    c. investment conduits.

    d. owned by 100 or more investors.

7. Tax-free bonds are issued to provide funds to finance houses for

    a. unemployed workers.

    b. investors.

    c. low-income and middle-income homebuyers.

    d. municipal housing agencies.

8. Real estate bonds are issued for all of the following purposes *EXCEPT* to finance

    a. industrial park developments.

    b. the sale of subdivision lots.

    c. municipal improvements.

    d. subdivision offsite improvements.

9. Unsecured bonds are called

    a. coupon bonds.              c. registered bonds.

    b. bearer bonds.              d. debenture bonds.

10. When a bond is paid from property taxes, it is a

    a. railroad bond.             c. general obligation bond.

    b. revenue bond.              d. corporate bond.

# ■ EXERCISES

1. Compare the points, discounts, and interest rates charged by private loan companies, banks, and savings associations when issuing new real estate loans. Which loan type issued is the least expensive?

2. Investigate the impact of foreign ownership of property in your community.

## CHAPTER FIVE

# CONVENTIONAL, INSURED, AND GUARANTEED LOANS

## ■ KEY TERMS

adjustable-rate mort-
gage (ARM)
automatic rate
reduction (ARR)
loan
buydowns
Cal-Vet
certificate of eligibility
certificate of reason-
able value (CRV)
coinsurance
conventional loan
Department of
Veterans Affairs
(DVA)
direct endorsement
program

entitlement
Federal Housing
Administration
(FHA)
FHA 203(k)
fixed-rate loan
funding fee
graduated payment
mortgage (GPM)
home equity loan
housing ratio
interest-only loans
loan-to-value (LTV)
ratio
mortgage insurance
mortgage insurance
premium (MIP)

negative amortization
novation
National Housing Act
partial entitlement
piggy-back loan
predatory lending
private mortgage
insurance (PMI)
rehabilitation loan
release of liability
split loan
streamline refinance
subprime loans
substitution of
entitlement
tax-exempt bonds
total obligation ratio

There are three general types of real estate loans in California: conventional, government insured (FHA), and government guaranteed (DVA). A **conventional loan** has no third-party guarantor unless it is insured by a private mortgage insurance company. The FHA ensures lenders that they will receive the balance of monies owed them in the event of a foreclosure. The DVA guarantees lenders a sum of money if their loans are foreclosed. This chapter will examine each of these loan types and the requirements necessary to secure them.

# ■ CONVENTIONAL LOANS

It is important to note that most of the real estate loans made today are conventional loans. Moreover, most originators of conventional loans do not keep them for their own portfolios but sell them in the secondary market. They do keep the collection responsibilities and the commensurate fees. To sell these loans, the lenders adhere to the guidelines established by Fannie Mae and Freddie Mac.

## Fixed-Rate Loans

Conventional loans have traditionally been designed as **fixed-rate loans** in which the interest rate remains constant over the term of the loan (although other variable features can be included in the loan contract). Fixed-rate loans may be amortized over a specific number of years in equal monthly payments, including principal and interest. The favorite fixed-rate loan is the 30-year mortgage where the payment is predictable, and the opportunity always exists to pay the balance of the loan down or off, depending on the borrower's financial circumstances and the opportunity to refinance at a lower rate.

### ■ EXAMPLE

30-Year Fixed-Rate Self-Amortizing Loan for $100,000 at 7 percent interest:

| Month | Fixed Payment | Interest | Principal | Balance |
|---|---|---|---|---|
| 0 | | | | $100,000.00 |
| 1 | $665.31 | $583.33 | $81.98 | 99,918.02 |
| 2 | 665.31 | 582.85 | 82.46 | 99,835.56 |
| 3 | 665.31 | 582.37 | 82.94 | 99,752.62 |
| 4 | 665.31 | 581.89 | 83.42 | 99,669.20 |
| 5 | 665.31 | 581.40 | 83.91 | 99,585.29 |

etc., to 360

Fixed-rate loans for 15 years are becoming increasingly popular. Lenders like them because of their relatively short amortization time, and they market these loans on the basis of the borrower's being able to save significant amounts of interest, compared with the 30-year loan. Moreover, 15-year loans are usually offered at 25 to 50 basis points below market rates. (There are 100 basis points in 1 percent, so 25 basis points equal one-fourth of 1 percent, and 50 basis points equal one-half of 1 percent.) However, the monthly payment required on the 15-year loan is approximately 20 percent higher than the payment on the 30-year loan, which inhibits many borrowers.

### ■ EXAMPLE

15-Year Fixed-Rate Self-Amortizing Loan for $100,000 at 7 percent interest:

| Month | Fixed Payment | Interest | Principal | Balance |
|---|---|---|---|---|
| 0 | | | | $100,000.00 |
| 1 | $898.83 | $583.33 | $315.50 | 99,684.50 |
| 2 | 898.83 | 581.49 | 317.34 | 99,367.16 |
| 3 | 898.83 | 579.41 | 319.42 | 99,047.74 |
| 4 | 898.83 | 577.77 | 321.06 | 98,726.68 |
| 5 | 898.83 | 575.90 | 322.93 | 98,403.75 |

etc., to 180

## Interest Only Loans

With residential real estate prices reaching new highs, qualifying borrowers for higher mortgage payments on larger loans has become a serious problem. In order to reduce monthly payments, the use of **interest-only loans** has emerged as a viable alternative to solve these problems.

When you examine the 30-year fixed-rate loan payment schedule in the first amortization example, the regular monthly payment of $665.31 includes an amount for principal and interest and is designed to pay the debt of $100,000 at 7 percent in full over the 30-year time period.

To reduce this payment, the only portion that can logically be waived is the principal amount of $81.98 reducing the payment to $583.33, interest only. To reduce this payment any further would be paying *less than interest only*, and that would result in the loan balance *increasing* each month by the difference, resulting in **negative amortization**.

When establishing an interest-only loan, the participants must decide how and when the principal owed will be paid. One alternative is to establish a five-year stop date when the entire balance will be due as a balloon payment. These monies can be received from refinancing the property, which, hopefully, will have retained or increased its value over time. Another plan might be to establish a series of smaller balloon payments over time to gradually whittle the balance down to zero.

The interest-only loan is being employed as a financing device on loans that equal or exceed the purchase price of the collateral property, creating risky portfolios. As long as the housing market enjoys an inflationary movement, these lenders can be safe. Any significant downturn will result in many loan defaults.

With the current real estate market collapse, lenders with portfolios of interest-only loans are experiencing difficulty in remaining viable as their collateral properties values drop below the balance amounts of their existing loans. Inters-only loans are not currently available in the real estate finance market.

## Private Mortgage Insurance

**Private mortgage insurance (PMI)** is required on conventional loans when the **loan-to-value (LTV)** ratio is in excess of 80 percent as stated in the Fannie Mae and Freddie Mac guidelines. The insurance covers the amount of the loan in excess of the 80 percent LTV ratio. Some private mortgage insurance companies require first-time home buyers to pursue a course of education on the responsibilities of home ownership prior to securing their loan. Private mortgage insurance programs can vary in the need for coverage and amount of coverage required. Rates can also vary depending on the private mortgage insurance carrier.

**Mortgage insurance** is issued to protect the lender in case the borrower defaults on the loan payments. If a property is foreclosed, the insurance company either pays the lender in full and acquires the property or pays the lender in accordance with the terms of the insurance plan plus expenses, and the lender acquires the property.

Although some borrowers may choose to pay part or all of the private mortgage insurance at closing, it is more common today for the annual renewal fee to be paid monthly and added to the PITI payment. The annual premium is calculated as a percentage of the loan amount (generally ranging from 0.65 to 0.90 percent depending on the amount of the down payment) divided by 12 and added to the monthly mortgage PITI payment, as seen below.

| **$100,000 fixed rate, 30-year loan with 10 percent down (90 percent LTV)** | |
| --- | --- |
| Premium: | 0.75 percent of loan amount |
| Calculation: | $100,000 × 0.75 = $750 annual premium |
| | $750 ÷ 12 = $62.50 added to monthly PITI payment |

There are also PMI payment plans in which the costs are financed. This is accomplished by adding the lump sum premium amount to the loan balance to be repaid over the life of the loan. There is also a plan where the lender pays the PMI, but the borrower pays a higher interest rate on the PMI portion of the loan. The advantage to the borrower is that all of the interest is deductible. The disadvantage is that the higher interest rate remains for the life of the loan.

PMI premiums continue until the lender releases the coverage, which depends not only on the increased equity position of the borrower, but on the payment history as well. Once the LTV ratio reaches 80 percent, the insurance company is no longer liable for any losses due to default by the borrower and the insurance premium payments should stop. Usually the borrower must initiate the release. Under current tax laws, the PMI premiums are deductible for persons earning $100,000 adjusted gross income or less annually.

Under the Home Owners Protection Act of 1999, PMI premiums must be terminated automatically when the LTV ratio is scheduled to reach 78 percent of the property's original value, not its current market value. Termination is required only if the loan payments are current. Borrowers may also request to have the PMI canceled when the LTV ratio reaches 80 percent, if their recent payment history is unblemished and there is no other debt on the property. If the borrower is current, under no circumstances can PMI be required beyond the midpoint of a loan's amortization period.

Fannie Mae and Freddie Mac require that mortgage lenders and servicers doing business with them automatically terminate PMI premiums on all *existing* loans that are halfway through their term. They also require lenders to drop the PMI once a homeowner reaches 20 percent equity. They calculate this figure by including the value of the home improvements and market appreciation. However, this approach is not automatic. The borrower must have a record of timely payments and formally request such an action.

Because of the high values of California real estate, one way for a borrower to totally *avoid* paying a PMI premium is to create a **split loan** or a **piggy-back loan**, involving a first and second mortgage executed simultaneously. Thus, an arrangement can include an 80/10/10 split, or an 80/15/5 split, or even an 80/20/0 split. In each case the first mortgage remains at 80 percent LTV, which requires no PMI. The second number represents a second mortgage that is held by the same lender but at a slightly higher rate and shorter term. The last number represents the down payment. The actual monthly payment is usually less than it would have been with a 95 percent or 97 percent LTV, and all of the interest is deductible. Piggy-back loans have become difficult to obtain under present market conditions.

PMI companies have expanded their coverages from basic residential insurance, which is presently the bulk of their business, into commercial and industrial mortgage and lease guarantee insurance. For example, the Mortgage Guaranty Insurance Corporation (MGIC) insures the top portion of loans on multifamily, commercial, and industrial properties. It owns a subsidiary company, the Commercial Leasehold Insurance Corporation (CLIC), which insures commercial tenants' lease payments and loans issued for leasehold improvements. These special policies are normally written for five years, and the insurance premiums can be either a percentage of the loan as a one-time charge or an agreed-upon annual premium. A renewal fee is charged at the end of the five-year term if the insurance is extended. Figure 5.1 lists the members of the Mortgage Insurance Companies of America.

**FIGURE 5.1**

**Members of the Mortgage Insurance Companies of America**

**AIG Unitod Guaranty Residential Insurance Co.**
230 North Elm Street
Greensboro, NC 27401
800-334-8966
*www.ugcorp.com*

**Genworth Financial**
6601 Six Forks Road
Raleigh, NC 27615
800-334-9270
*www.genworth.com*

**Mortgage Guaranty Insurance Corp.**
250 East Kilbourn Avenue
Milwaukee, WI 53202
800-558-9900
*www.mgic.com*

**PMI Mortgage Insurance Co.**
3003 Oak Road
Walnut Creek, CA 94596
800-288-1970
*www.pmigroup.com*

**Republic Mortgage Insurance Co.**
190 Oak Plaza Blvd.
Winston-Salem, NC 27105-4470
800-999-7642
*www.rmic.com*

**Triad Guaranty Insurance Corp.**
101 South Stratford Road
Winston-Salem, NC 27104
800-451-4872
*www.tgic.com*

## Permanent/Temporary (Escrow) Buydown Plan

A **buydown** is money paid by someone (seller, builder, employer, buyer) to a lender in return for a lower interest rate and monthly payment. This buydown payment may lower the borrower's payments for the entire loan term (a permanent buydown) or for a lesser period of time, usually one year to three years (temporary or escrow buydown).

■ **EXAMPLE**  Assume a $100,000 loan for 30 years at 8 percent interest. To *PERMANENTLY* buy down this interest rate to 7.75 percent would cost approximately 6 points, or 6 percent of the loan amount ($6,246).

| | |
|---|---|
| $100,000 @ 8% for 30 years | $733.77 PI per month |
| $100,000 @ 7.75% for 30 years | <u>716.42</u> PI per month |
| Difference | 17.35 per month × 360 months |
| Buydown Costs | $6,246 |

Depending on market conditions for a particular area, it might be possible to lower an interest rate from 8 to 7.75 percent by paying as little as one and one-half to two points, which would be much less than the calculated buydown cost.

■ **EXAMPLE** Assume a $100,000 loan for 30 years at 8 percent. To apply a *TEMPORARY* buydown of 2-1-0 would cost $2,432.04, or approximately two and one-half points.

| Payment | Rate | Reg. P&I | Effective Rate | P&I | Difference |
|---------|------|----------|----------------|-----|------------|
| Year 1 | 8% | $733.77 | 6% | $599.56 | $134.21 |
| Year 2 | 8% | 733.77 | 7% | 665.31 | 68.46 |
| Year 3 | 8% | 733.77 | 8% | 733.77 | 0.00 |
| Etc. | | | | | |

| | |
|---|---|
| Buydown Cost Year 1 | $134.21 × 12 = $1,610.52 |
| Buydown Cost Year 2 | $68.46 × 12 = 821.52 |
| Total Buydown Costs | $2,432.04 |

**Borrower's Qualifications**

The following four Fannie Mae and Freddie Mac guidelines are generally used to qualify borrowers for conventional loans. (It is important to know that loan underwriters have flexibility in applying these guidelines in specific cases and that the rules can be changed from time to time.)

■ Rule 1 Principal, interest, taxes, property insurance, private mortgage insurance, and any applicable condominium or homeowner association fees shall not exceed 28 percent of the borrower's gross monthly income.

■ Rule 2 All of the above plus monthly debts shall not exceed 36 percent of the borrower's gross monthly income.

■ Rule 3 The borrower must have good credit.

■ Rule 4 The borrower must have stable employment.

■ **EXAMPLE 1**   The borrowers have a combined gross monthly income of $8,500 per month. The loan amount applied for is $275,298 at 6 percent for 30 years payable at $1,651 per month, principal and interest. The monthly obligations are property taxes $387, insurance $129, PMI premium $115, and the neighborhood association fee is $90. In addition, the borrowers have a monthly installment of $70, child care expenses of $400 per month, a revolving charge of $25 and an auto loan payment of $175. They have stable jobs and good credit. Do they qualify under Rules 1 and 2?

| Combined Monthly Gross Income | $8,500 |
|---|---|
| Payment P and I | $1,651 |
| Property Taxes | 387 |
| Hazard Insurance | 129 |
| PMI Premium | 115 |
| Association Fee | 90 |
| Total | 2,372 |

Rule 1 ratio: 2,372 / 8,500 = 28%

| Installment Payment | 70 |
|---|---|
| Child Care | 400 |
| Revolving Charges | 25 |
| Auto Loan Payments | 175 |
| Total | 670 |
| Plus Housing Expenses | 2,372 |
| Grand Total | 3,042 |

Rule 2 ratio: 3,042 / 8,500 = 36%

The borrowers meet both requirements.

■ **EXAMPLE 2** A single parent's gross monthly income is $4,000. The loan amount applied for is $121,000 at 6.5 percent for 30 years with a monthly principal and interest payment of $765. The property taxes are $133 per month, insurance $53, PMI $50, installment obligations $150, auto loan $195, and child care is $250.

| | |
|---|---|
| Monthly Gross Income | $4,000 |
| Housing Expenses | 765 |
| Property Taxes | 133 |
| Hazard Insurance | 53 |
| PMI | 50 |
| Total | 1,001 |

Rule 1 ratio: 1,001 / 4,000 = 25% O.K.

| | |
|---|---|
| Installment Payment | 150 |
| Auto Loan | 195 |
| Child Care | 250 |
| Total | 595 |
| Plus Housing Expenses | 1,001 |
| Grand Total | 1,596 |

Rule 2 ratio: 1,596 / 4,000 = 40%

The borrowers meet requirement 1 but not requirement 2.

## Jumbo Loans

Anything exceeding the current Fannie Mae/Freddie Mac conforming loan limits is considered a *jumbo* loan. Each lender is free to set its own qualifying standards, although the Fannie Mae/Freddie Mac guidelines are often used. Jumbo loans may be up to $1 million with as little as 5 percent down or more depending on the particular lender.

## Home Equity Loans

When the Tax Reform Act of 1986 eliminated the tax deduction for interest paid on everything except home mortgages, the **home equity loan** became an important financing tool for many Americans. In most cases, the interest paid is tax deductible and the funds may be used for any purpose. A home equity loan is usually made at a lower rate of interest than credit card or other short-term financing and can be either a fixed-rate or adjustable-rate loan. The amount that can be received is based on a percentage of the equity in the home and is currently limited to a combined loan-to-value (CLTV) ratio of the first mortgage plus the equity loan of usually 80 percent. The home equity loan is a second mortgage and closing costs can be included in the loan. An obvious disadvantage of the home equity loan is that the borrower is using up the equity established in the home which will reduce the amount to be received upon a future sale of the property. Many lenders have suspended issuing home equity loans until the economy improves.

**Automatic Rate Reduction**

The **automatic rate reduction (ARR)** loan provides the borrowers with the option to lower their interest rate when the adjustment rate (based on the Fannie Mae Index) drops as little as $1/4$ percent plus the guarantee that the new lower rate will never go back up. The borrower must have excellent credit and no late payments in the previous 12 months. Closing costs are minimal, ranging from nothing to an amount to buy new title insurance and record the new mortgage or deed of trust. The ARR may be a good option when considering refinancing. The ARR may start at a rate slightly higher than the current market rate.

**Subprime Loans**

In the financial world, mortgage loans are designated as A, B, C, or D *paper*. Ideally, all borrowers would be rated "A." There are cases, however, where the loan is considered "B" quality—showing definite credit problems; "C" quality—indicating borrowers with very marginal or poor credit; or even "D" quality—indicating a very high risk on the loan. Lenders who provided loans or even specialized in the B, C, or D paper are called *subprime lenders*.

**Subprime loans** were credited with making home ownership possible for many immigrants, first-time homebuyers, and those suffering from temporary financial setbacks and were a contributing factor to the current financing crisis.

Although the terms *subprime* and *predatory* are sometimes considered to be synonymous, in fact they are not. Subprime loans are made to persons with less-than-perfect credit ratings and usually carry higher interest rates and fees than the *prime* loans offered to applicants with no credit problems.

Subprime loans are now identified as "higher priced" loans which are

- first trust deeds having rates which are 1.5 percent or higher than the prevailing market rate, or

- second trust deeds having rates which are 3.5 percent or higher than the prevailing market rate.

The guidelines covering this new class of loans require the lender to have the borrower fully document and verify income and assets. Additionally, the lender must underwrite the loan based on the borrower's ability to make the monthly payments from income sources only.

Another provision became effective April 2010, which requires borrowers obtaining these higher-rate loans to have property taxes and insurance premiums impounded for the first 12 months.

**Predatory Lending**

In California the term **predatory lending** encompasses a variety of home mortgage lending practices. Predatory lenders often try to pressure consumers into signing loan agreements they cannot afford or simply are not in the consumers' best interest. Also, through the use of false promises and deceptive sales tactics, borrowers are convinced to sign a loan contract before they have had a chance to review the paperwork and do the math to determine whether they can truly afford the loan.

Predatory loans carry high up-front fees that are added to the balance, decreasing the owner's equity. Loan amounts are usually based on the borrower's home equity without consideration of the borrower's ability to make the scheduled payments. When borrowers have trouble repaying the debt, they are often encouraged to refinance the loan into another unaffordable, high-fee loan that rarely provides economic benefit to the consumer. This cycle of high-cost loan refinancing can ultimately deplete the borrower's equity and result in foreclosure.

Predatory lending practices specifically prohibited by law include

- flipping—the frequent making of new loans to refinance existing loans,

- packing—the selling of additional products without the borrower's informed consent, and

- charging excessive fees.

Homeowners in certain communities, particularly the elderly and minorities, are especially likely to be targets of predatory lending but almost anyone can fall prey to abusive lending practices. You can protect yourself by knowing what you can afford; choosing a reputable, licensed broker/lender; understanding the loan application and contract; and being aware of commonly used predatory lending tactics.

According to the Center for Responsible Lending, more than $25 billion is lost by consumers every year due to predatory mortgages, payday loans, and other lending abuses, such as overdraft loans, excessive credit card debt, and tax refund loans. HUD, DVA, Fannie Mae, Freddie Mac, the Mortgage Bankers Association, the National Association of Mortgage Brokers, and the major subprime lenders in this country are all working very hard to combat the prevalence of predatory lending. Unfortunately, the predatory lender may be someone well-known and trusted by the potential borrower. It is suggested that a borrower check out any lender being considered with the local chamber of commerce, the Better Business Bureau, or either the Mortgage Bankers Association or the Association of Mortgage Brokers. The problem is especially difficult when the borrowers do not speak English and are literally being preyed upon by a lender of their particular ethnic group.

In communities across America, borrowers have lost their homes because of the actions of predatory lenders, appraisers, mortgage brokers, and home improvement contractors. Other predatory lending practices include

- lending on properties for more than they are worth using inflated appraisals;

- encouraging borrowers to lie about their income, expenses, or cash available for down payment;

- knowingly lending more money than a borrower can afford to repay;

- charging high interest rates to borrowers based on their race or national origin;

- charging fees for unnecessary or nonexistent products and services;

- pressuring borrowers to accept higher risk balloon or interest-only loans, or loans with steep prepayment penalties or possible negative amortization;

- *stripping* homeowners' equity from their homes by convincing them to refinance again and again when there is no benefit to the borrower;

- using high pressure sales tactics to sell home improvements and single-premium mortgage insurance; and

- steering the borrower into a subprime mortgage when they could have qualified for a mainstream loan: Fannie Mae has estimated that up to one-half of borrowers with subprime mortgages could have qualified for loans with better terms.

Two types of loans that are not necessarily predatory but could be if the borrower does not understand the implications of the loan are the following:

- Balloon loan requiring full payment at the end of the initial term

- Interest-only loan with balance of principal plus interest due at end of term

**Home Ownership and Equity Protection Act of 1994**

Some protection against predatory lending exists under the Home Ownership and Equity Protection Act of 1994 (HOEPA). This law addresses certain deceptive and unfair practices in home equity lending. The law was recently strengthened by the Federal Reserve with an amendment to the Truth in Lending Act (TILA) in Section 32 of Regulation Z, the implementing regulation of TILA. Under this amendment, home loans are covered if the annual percentage rate exceeds the rate of Treasury securities of comparable maturity by more than 8 percentage points (10 percent for second mortgages) or the fees and points paid by the borrower exceed $510 including the cost of credit insurance and other debt protection products paid at closing. (The $510 figure is for year 2005; this amount is adjusted annually by the Federal Reserve Board, based on the Consumer

Price Index.) The rules also tighten the prohibition against extending credit without regard to the borrower's repayment ability. For more information on the types of loans covered, required disclosures, and prohibited practices, go to the Federal Trade Commission Web site at *www.ftc.gov* and click on "For Consumers."

## Refinancing Existing Conventional Loans

With mortgage interest rates at relatively low levels, many homeowners have considered refinancing their existing loans as a method for saving money by lowering their monthly payments. The amount of this saving may not be cost-effective for everyone, however. The costs of refinancing are unregulated and vary dramatically among lenders. A new loan may require an application fee, title insurance, an appraisal, an attorney, and probably some discount charges in the form of points where one point equals 1 percent of the loan amount. Thus, it is important to determine the total costs before making a decision to refinance.

For example, assume a balance exists on a 30-year amortizing loan of $100,000 at 8 percent with a monthly payment of $733.77, including principal and interest. To refinance this amount with a new 30-year loan at 7 percent interest will require a monthly payment of $665.31, a savings of $68.46 per month. If the cost of securing this new financing total is $3,500, it will take about 51 months to recover the costs ($3,500 ÷ $68.46 = 51.12 months). It is generally accepted that a rule to use in analyzing the advisability of refinancing is that the costs of the new loan should be recovered over a two-year to three-year period. Thus, when the owner continues to occupy the property for a longer period of time, a savings will be achieved.

Some persons are better off not refinancing their home loans. Before making the decision, it is important to discuss a loan modification with the existing lender. Although some lenders may not be willing to modify their existing loan structures, many large mortgage companies have created customer retention programs to keep their best customers on the books. They may offer a lower interest rate with minimal transaction fees eliminating the need for refinancing.

## Electronic Real Estate Loan Services

There are sites on the World Wide Web offering real estate loans and related services. A borrower can arrange for a loan on the computer without the necessity of a face-to-face interview with the lender. It still requires the filing of a loan application and the probable submission of ancillary documents such as bank statements and annual income tax reports.

Applicants should be aware that the companies offering loans on the Internet are not regulated, and it is possible for some scam artists to offer loans for a fee and then disappear. It is also difficult for federal agencies to enforce their rules of disclosure under various settlement requirements.

The Home Affordable Refinance Program (HARP) may be of help to those who remain employed and are not behind on mortgage payments but cannot obtain traditional refinancing because of the home's decline in value. HARP refinancing may be available for loans held by Fannie Mae or Freddie Mac. For details, contact your mortgage servicer, Fannie Mae, or Freddie Mac.

By offering a loan modification, the Home Affordable Modification Program (HAMP) may assist a borrower who is employed but struggling to make the mortgage payments. For eligibility and criteria, contact your mortgage servicer.

For more information on both HARP and HAMP, visit *www.making-homeaffordable.gov*.

## ■ FEDERAL HOUSING ADMINISTRATION (FHA)

Established under the provisions of the National Housing Act of 1934, the **Federal Housing Administration (FHA)** was organized to stimulate new jobs by increasing activities in the construction industry. It was also designed to stabilize the real estate mortgage market and to facilitate the financing of repairs, additions, and sales of existing homes and other properties. A system of mortgage loan insurance is used to accomplish these goals. In this system the credit of the U.S. government is placed squarely behind the credit of an individual borrower. The FHA insures against losses on real estate loans made by private lending institutions. Since its inception, the FHA has enlarged and expanded its scope of operations to include rent programs, interest subsidy programs, and a myriad of other mortgage lending activities that have a special social emphasis. It has insured millions of home loans since it began.

Today, FHA operates entirely from its self-generated income through the proceeds of mortgage insurance premiums paid by borrowers. Although the variety of attractive conventional loan programs available today have lowered the FHA share of the mortgage market substantially, it is still important for first-time homebuyers, borrowers with credit issues who may have trouble qualifying for a conventional loan, and for the purchase of manufactured housing.

**Organization and Requirements**

Since 1965, the FHA has operated under the direction of the Department of Housing and Urban Development (HUD) with headquarters in Washington DC, and regional centers located throughout the country. Each region is divided into area offices located in almost every major city. Through these offices, the FHA closely supervises the issuance of mortgage loans bearing its insurance.

Any lender participating in the FHA insurance program must grant long-term, self-amortizing loans at interest rates established in the marketplace. There is no limit on the number of points that may be paid by the borrower, although they must be reasonable. The FHA designates qualified lenders to underwrite loans directly without submitting applications to the FHA. These lenders participate in the direct endorsement program.

Every loan application is reviewed to determine the borrower's financial credit and ability to make payments. In addition, a comprehensive written appraisal report is made on the condition and value of the property to be pledged as collateral for the loan. All property must meet certain minimum standards of acceptability. After qualifying the borrower and the property, the FHA issues a conditional commitment for mortgage insurance to the lender reflecting the value of the property. This commitment is valid for six months on existing property and for nine months on new construction.

Since September 1999, FHA requires appraisers evaluating property for FHA-insured loans to be state licensed or certified and to pay detailed attention to the physical defects of homes they examine. A seven-page *valuation condition* disclosure form must be completed to reveal any defects that do not meet minimum standards. This report is to be delivered to the borrower prior to the close of escrow. It must include the statement that "this review is not a physical inspection of the house and there is no guarantee that the property is free of any defects." The report also advises that the borrower may wish to have the house inspected by a professional inspector. The disclosure form also requires appraisers to indicate whether they recommend inspections on the home's structural features, heating and cooling systems, plumbing, roofing, electrical, environmental factors, and pest control success. Under the FHA rules, any obvious property defects must be corrected before the mortgage closing.

Every FHA borrower is required to receive and sign a form entitled, "For Your Protection: Get a Home Inspection." (This is HUD form 92543-CN.)

## Program Summary

The FHA is designed as a program of mortgage insurance so it does *not* make direct loans to borrowers, except in very special circumstances involving the resale of properties acquired by the FHA as a result of foreclosure. Even under these circumstances, the FHA usually expects a buyer of a foreclosed property to secure financing elsewhere and pay the FHA cash for the property. Although FHA lenders are required to make every effort to offset a possible foreclosure, in the event of a default and subsequent foreclosure, an insured lender will look to the FHA to recover the unpaid balance of the mortgage and any costs involved in the foreclosure action.

By designing a program of mortgage insurance funded by mortgage insurance premiums, the FHA has reduced the down payment obstacle for cash-short buyers. By insuring 100 percent of the loan amount, the insurance program eliminates lenders' risks by ensuring that lenders will not lose any money on loans they make to eligible borrowers. This insurance helps stabilize the mortgage market and develops an active national secondary market for FHA insured mortgage loans.

## Existing FHA Programs

The **National Housing Act** of 1934 provided for Title I and Title II insurance programs that are still in use today, along with additional sections that have been added to reflect consumer needs and market conditions.

**Title I**   Title I, Section 2 provides insurance for loans to finance light or moderate rehabilitation of properties, including the construction of nonresidential buildings. Loans on single-family homes may be used for alterations, repairs, and site improvements. Loans on multifamily structures may only be used for building alteration and repairs.

Maximum Loan Amount:

- Single-family house—$25,000

- Manufactured house on permanent foundation—$17,500

- Manufactured house (classified as personal property)—$7,500

- Multifamily structure—average of $12,000 per unit up to $60,000

Maximum Loan Term:

- Single-family house—20 years

- Manufactured house on permanent foundation—15 years

- Manufactured house (classified as personal property)—12 years

- Multifamily structure—15 years

The interest rate is based on the common market rate and is negotiable between lender and borrower. Any loan over $7,500 must be secured by a mortgage or deed of trust on the property. The structure must have been completed and occupied for at least 90 days.

Since 1969, Title I, Section 2 has provided insurance loans used for the purchase or refinancing of a manufactured home, a developed lot on which to place a manufactured home, or a combination of lot and home.

Under the FHA Manufactured Housing Loan Modernization Act of 2008, maximum loan limits have been increased as follows:

- Repairs/improvements—$25,090

- Manufactured home only—$69,678 (20-year term)

- Manufactured home lot—$23,226 (15-year term)

- Manufactured home and lot—$92,904 (20-year term)

- Multi-section manufactured home and lot (25-year term)

MIP upfront premiums may not exceed 2.25 percent; annual premiums not to exceed 1.0 percent.

Manufactured homes must comply with the National Manufactured Home Construction and Safety Standards and have a suitable homesite that meets local standards and has adequate water supply and sewage disposal facilities.

Borrowers must provide a 5 percent down payment, be able to demonstrate adequate income to make the payments, and use the home as a principal residence. Built-in appliances, equipment, and carpeting may also be financed.

**Title II** Title II originally established two basic mortgage insurance programs: Section 203 for one-family to four-family homes, and Section 207 for multifamily projects such as rental housing, manufactured home parks, and multifamily housing projects. Many additional programs have been added over the years. Changes to FHA programs under H.R. 3221 (Housing and Economic Recovery Act of 2008) are reflected in the following list. The most frequently used Title II insurance programs are described in more detail later in the chapter.

- Section 203(b)—Mortgage Insurance for One-Family to Four-Family Homes

- Section 203(h)—Mortgage Insurance for Disaster Victims (100 percent financing available; must file within one year after declaration of disaster)

- Section 203(k)—Rehabilitation Mortgage Insurance

- Section 221(d)(2)—Mortgage Insurance for Low- and Moderate-Income Buyers

- Section 223(e)—Mortgage Insurance for Older, Declining Areas

- Section 234(c)—Mortgage Insurance for Condominium Projects (Individual condominium units are insured under the 203(b) program.)

- Section 251—Insurance for Adjustable-Rate Mortgages

- Section 811—Supportive Housing for Persons with Disabilities (provides direct funding to nonprofit organizations to support housing for low-income adults with disabilities)

- Section 255—Home Equity Conversion Mortgage (reverse mortgage)

- Section 257—Pilot program to establish a process for providing alternative credit rating information for borrowers with insufficient credit history

**Special HUD/FHA Programs**

Special programs to assist buyers and homeowners are available through HUD/FHA, including the following.

**Energy Efficient Mortgage (EEM).** The EEM can be used to finance the cost of adding energy-efficient features to new or existing houses in conjunction with a Section 203(b) or 203(k) loan. It can also be used with the Section 203(h) program for victims of presidential-declared disasters. The cost of the energy-efficient improvements that are eligible for financing is the greater of 5 percent of the property's value (not to exceed $8,000) or $4,000. The money for the improvements is placed in an escrow account at closing and released after an inspection verifying that the improvements are installed and that energy savings will be achieved.

**Home Equity Conversion Mortgage (HECM).** FHA's mortgage insurance makes this HUD *reverse mortgage* program less expensive and more attractive for homeowners 62 and older who wish to borrow against the equity in their home. No monthly payments are required, and there are no asset or income requirements or limitations. Homeowners may receive a percentage of the value of the equity in the home in a lump sum, on a monthly basis (either for life or for a fixed term), or as a line-of-credit. No repayment of the loan plus interest and other fees is due until the surviving homeowner leaves the home. The FHA insurance provides the assurance that the funds will continue as long as one surviving member remains in the home—in the event that the eventual sale does not cover the balance due the lender, there will be no debt carried over to the estate or heirs.

In 2008, provisions were added that provide for:

- seniors to purchase and obtain a HECM as long as the home is to be a primary residence;

- applicants for a HECM loan to receive adequate counseling from an independent third party not related to the transaction. FHA uses a portion of the mortgage insurance premiums to fund such counseling;

- lenders being prohibited from requiring the borrower to purchase insurance, an annuity, or other additional product as a requirement or condition of eligibility for a HECM loan. (Exceptions are title insurance, hazard, flood, or other peril insurance);

- HECM origination fees to be limited to 2 percent of the total claim amount up to $6,000;

- cooperatives to be insured under the HECM program (condominiums were already allowed); and

- single loan limits of $417,000 applied nationwide up to $625,500 in high-cost areas.

**Good Neighbor Next Door.**   The Officer Next Door program has been expanded to include law enforcement officers, pre-kindergarten through 12th grade teachers, firefighters, and emergency medical technicians. Under this program, HUD offers a discount of 50 percent from the list price of the home with a down payment of $100. The borrower must commit to live in the property for at least 36 months. Available homes are listed by state on the Internet. If more than one person makes an offer on a property, selection is made by a random lottery. If the property needs repairs, a 203(k) mortgage may be used.

**Homeownership Vouchers.**   The Housing Choice Voucher program, formerly known as Section 8, has expanded its rental assistance program to allow participants to use Homeownership Voucher funds to assist in meeting monthly homeownership expenses such as mortgage payments, real estate taxes and insurance premiums, utilities, maintenance costs, and repairs. Applicants must be first-time homeowners, have at least one member of the family employed, and meet minimum income requirements. Interested applicants should contact their local public housing authority for more information.

**Native American Housing.**   Under Section 184 Indian Housing Loan Guarantee Program, HUD offers homeownership and housing rehabilitation opportunities for Native American individuals, families, and tribes.

**Underwriting Guidelines**

Like Fannie Mae and Freddie Mac, the FHA has its own set of guidelines to qualify eligible borrowers for acceptable loans. These requirements include all of the following elements.

**Maximum Loan Limitations.**   The FHA establishes maximum limitations on mortgages it will insure. These limitations vary by geographic area and are adjusted each October as a calculation of a percentage of the Fannie Mae and Freddie Mac conforming loan limits. Maximum FHA loan limits are set at 95 percent of the median house price for a metropolitan statistical area up to the limits shown in Figure 5.2.

**Down Payment Requirements.**   FHA has greatly simplified its formula for calculating the down payment required on its insured loans. As of January 1, 2009, the purchaser must provide 3.5 percent of either the sales price or appraised value (whichever is less) either from their own funds, a family gift, or a grant from local, state, or nonprofit down payment

**FIGURE 5.2**
**2009 Maximum FHA Loan Limits**

| Type of Property | Standard | High Cost Area |
| --- | --- | --- |
| Single Family | $271,050 | $ 625,500 |
| Duplex | 347,000 | 800,775 |
| Triplex | 419,425 | 967,950 |
| Four Units | 521,250 | 1,202,925 |

*All limits are 150 percent higher in Alaska, Guam, Hawaii, and the U.S. Virgin Islands.*

*The maximum loan amounts for your geographical area may be found on the Internet at www.hud.gov/buying/index.cfm, click on "FHA Mortgage Limits."*

assistance program that does not receive any financial benefit from the transaction. In most cases this is applied as the down payment. For some special programs that allow for a higher LTV (loan to value) ratio, a part of the 3.5 percent may go towards approved closing costs.

**Borrowers' Income Qualifications.** The FHA qualifies borrowers based on two ratios (the borrowers must qualify under *both ratios*):

1. The **housing ratio** of 31 percent. A borrower's total monthly housing expenses may not exceed 31 percent of the total gross monthly income. Included in these expenses are mortgage principal and interest, property taxes, home insurance premiums, mortgage insurance premiums, and homeowners or condominium association fees, if applicable.

   The housing ratio may be raised if the borrowers have certain compensating factors, such as

   ■ low long-term debt;

   ■ a large down payment;

   ■ minimal credit use;

   ■ excellent job history;

   ■ excellent payment history for amounts equal to or higher than new loan payment; or

   ■ additional income potential.

2. The **total obligations ratio** of 43 percent. A borrower's total monthly obligations may not exceed 43 percent of the total monthly gross income. Included in these obligations are monthly housing expenses plus monthly debt payments. Debts that will be paid in full within ten months generally are not included. Alimony and child support payments are deducted from monthly gross income before calculating the qualifying ratio.

For borrowers who qualify under FHA's Energy Efficient Homes, the ratios may be *stretched* to 33 percent for housing and 45 percent for total obligations.

■ **EXAMPLE** Assume that borrowers want to qualify for a $200,000 FHA-insured home loan at 6 percent interest for 30 years. The upfront MIP of 1.75 percent is added to the loan amount. The principal and interest plus MIP payment is $1220 per month; property taxes are $300 per month, hazard insurance premium is $30 per month, and the monthly MIP payment is $83. The borrowers pay $600 per month on other long-term debt.

| | |
|---|---|
| $1,220 | Principal and Interest + MIP ($200,000 + $3350 = $203,350 @ 6%) |
| 300 | Property Taxes |
| 30 | Hazard Insurance |
| + 83 | Monthly MIP |
| 1,633 | Housing Costs divided by 0.31 = $5,268 |
| + 600 | Other Debts |
| $2,233 | Total Obligations divided by 0.43 = $5,193 |

To qualify for this loan, the borrowers would need to earn at least $5,268 in combined gross monthly income.

**Non-Traditional Credit.** FHA allows a lender to develop a non-traditional mortgage credit report (NTMCR) to document a borrower's payment history in cases where a credit bureau score cannot be derived. A 12-month history of timely payments for rent, utilities, telephone and cellular phone services, and cable television is preferred. Additional sources that may be given consideration include insurance coverage (medical, auto, or life insurance), childcare payments, and other documented history of payments or savings.

**Mortgage Insurance Premium (MIP).** When the FHA issues an insurance commitment to a lender, it promises to repay the balance of the loan in full if the borrower defaults. This guaranty is funded by imposing a **mortgage insurance premium (MIP)** that must be paid by the borrower when obtaining an FHA-insured loan. It can be paid in cash or financed even if the loan plus the MIP exceeds the maximum loan limit. For a brief period in 2008, FHA implemented a risk-based premium for mortgage insurance. This was placed in a one-year moratorium by the Economic and Housing Recovery Act effective through September 30, 2009.

The upfront MIP premium is as follows:

- Purchase Money Mortgages and Qualifying Refinances = 1.75 percent

- Streamline Refinances (all types) = 1.50 percent

- *FHASecure* (Delinquent Mortgagors) = 3.00 percent

- There is no upfront MIP charged on condominium loans.

FHA borrowers must also pay an annual premium of 0.5 percent for a 30-year loan or 0.25 percent for a 15-year loan, payable monthly and included in the regular PITI payment. This MIP premium applies to all types of FHA loans and is subject to periodic change. See *www.hud.gov* for updates.

The upfront MIP premium is as follows:

- LTV less than 95%        30-year loan        0.5%
- LTV greater than 95%     30-year loan        0.55%
- LTV less than 90%        15-year loan        none
- LTV greater than 90%     15-year loan        0.25%

FHA monthly insurance payments will be automatically terminated under the following conditions:

- For mortgage terms of more than 15 years, the annual MIP premium will be canceled when the loan-to-value ratio reaches 78 percent, provided the mortgagor has paid the annual premium for at least five years.

- For mortgage terms of 15 years or less and with original loan-to-value ratios of 90 percent or greater, annual premiums will be canceled when the loan-to-value ratio reaches 78 percent, regardless of the amount of time the mortgagor has paid premiums.

- Mortgages with terms of 15 years or less and with loan-to-value ratios of 89.99 percent and less will not be charged any annual premiums.

**Allowable Closing Costs.**   The FHA has strict guidelines defining allowable closing costs that may be charged to a borrower. The amounts may differ by geographic area but must be considered to be reasonable and customary. All other costs in the transaction are generally paid by the seller when purchasing a new home or by the lender in the case of a refinance.

The seller may contribute for the borrower up to 6 percent of the sales price to cover discount points and other allowable closing costs.

The allowable closing costs are

- appraisal fee and any inspection fees;

- actual costs of credit reports;

- lender's origination fee;

- deposit verification fee;

- home inspection service fees up to $200;

- cost of title examination and title insurance;

- document preparation (by a third party not controlled by the lender);

- property survey;

- attorney's fees;

- recording fees, transfer stamps, and taxes; and

- test and certification fees, water tests, and so on.

The allowable costs in a refinance are

- courier fees,

- wire transfer fees,

- fees to pay off bills, and

- reconveyance fees.

**Second Mortgages/Buydowns.** The FHA will allow a second mortgage to be acquired on the collateral property. There are certain conditions, however, including the following:

- The total of the first and second mortgages must not exceed the allowable maximum LTV ratio.

- The borrower must qualify to make both payments.

- There can be no balloon payment on the second mortgage if it matures before five years.

- The payments on the second mortgage must not vary to any large degree.

- The second mortgage must not contain a prepayment penalty.

The FHA allows mortgage buydowns when the borrower or seller can make an advance cash payment to lower the interest rate for a period of time. This effectively reduces the corresponding monthly payments. The FHA also allows the borrower the advantage of qualifying for the loan at the *bought-down* interest rate, not the contract interest rate.

**Assumptions.** FHA loans originated prior to December 1989 are generally assumable without qualifying, but the original borrower retains some responsibility in the event of a default. For FHA loans originated after December 1989, all sellers are released from liability under an assumption. Buyers have to qualify under the current 31 percent and 43 percent rule and must occupy the property. The FHA currently prohibits the assumption of loans by investors.

**Frequently Used
FHA Loans**

The most frequently used FHA loans are described as follows.

### Section 203(b) One-Family to Four-Family Mortgage Insurance.

This mainstay of the FHA single-family insurance programs remains an important financing option for first-time homebuyers, persons who may have trouble qualifying for a conventional loan, or those living in underserved areas. The low down payment, higher total debt ratio, and consideration of compensating factors may make it possible for owner-occupants to achieve their dream of homeownership.

### Section 234(c) Mortgage Insurance for Condominium Units.

Similar to the 203(b) program, the 234(c) is specifically for the purchase of a unit in a condominium building that must contain at least four dwelling units and can be detached, semidetached, row house, walk-up, or elevator structure. Down payment, loan limits, and borrower qualifying are the same as for the 203(b), but there is no up-front mortgage insurance premium required for condominiums.

### Section 251: Insurance for Adjustable-Rate Mortgage.

The FHA adjustable-rates mortgages (ARMs) are available to owner-occupants of one-family to four-family dwelling units. The down payment, maximum loan amount, and qualifying standards are the same as for 203(b) and may be written for 30 years. *Hybrid* five-year adjustable-rate loans that carry popular 2 percent annual rate-increase limits and 6 percent life-of-the-loan limits are available with a 3 percent down payment. They allow first-time buyers to lock in a relatively low fixed rate for the initial five years of the mortgage.

The FHA ARMs are fully assumable and buydowns are permitted. When qualifying at the buydown rate of interest, it is possible for the borrower to afford a larger loan amount.

### Section 203(k): Rehabilitation Mortgage Insurance.

The Section 203(k) loan makes it possible for the purchaser to obtain a single long-term loan (either fixed or adjustable rate) to cover both the acquisition and rehabilitation of a property. The 203(k) is also available for refinancing a property that is at least one year old. The value of the property is limited by the FHA mortgage loan limits for the area and is determined by either

- the value before rehabilitation plus the cost of rehabilitation, or
- 110 percent of the appraised value after rehabilitation, whichever is less.

Other features of the rehabilitation loan **FHA 203(k)** include the following:

- Rehab costs must be at least $5,000.
- Prospective buyers can add $5,000 to $15,000 to the loan amount for renovations to meet FHA minimum standards.
- The borrower pays only taxes and insurance during the first six months.
- The rehab funds are paid to the borrower in draws.
- The rehab costs and installation time must be approved by the lender before the loan can be granted.
- Basic energy efficiency and structural standards must be met.
- The FHA 203(k) program is not available to investors.

A list of the types of improvements that may be made under 203(k) financing and other information regarding eligible properties and applicants may be found on the HUD Web site.

**Streamline Refinance.** Since 1980, FHA has permitted insured mortgages to be *streamline* refinanced. The amount of documentation and underwriting is greatly reduced, although closing costs will still apply. These costs can be included in the new mortgage amount with sufficient equity in the property as determined by an appraisal. The basic requirements for a **streamline refinance** are:

- the mortgage must already be FHA insured;
- the mortgage must be current, not delinquent;

■ the refinance must result in lowering of monthly principal and interest payment; and

■ no cash may be taken out.

**Direct Endorsement and Coinsurance**

Under the **direct endorsement program**, applications for FHA's single-family mortgage insurance programs can be underwritten by an approved lender that certifies the mortgage complies with applicable FHA requirements. The lender performs all appraisal duties and analyzes the borrower's credit. Direct endorsement leaves FHA with the risk of loss from default but gives it control through its ability to remove the lender from the program. Direct endorsement has become increasingly popular with lenders. The majority of all FHA mortgage insurance applications are now being processed under its format. Lenders who avoided FHA insurance because of the delays and red tape now use direct endorsement as an alternative to private insurance.

Under **coinsurance**, an approved lender both processes and underwrites qualified mortgages. The coinsuring lender shares losses with the FHA in the event of a default.

**Advantages of the FHA Mortgage**

Using the FHA mortgage provides the following advantages:

■ *The loan-to-value (LTV) ratio is high.* In many cases an FHA mortgage may be obtained with as little as 1.25 percent down payment.

■ *Different types of loans are available.* The FHA has loan structures to meet a variety of borrowers' needs. There are fixed-rate or adjustable-rate loans. The FHA also insures loans for low-income housing, subsidized interest loans, and manufactured home purchases.

■ *There is no due-on-sale clause.* The original terms of the loan can remain the same and cannot be changed because of a sale. Most FHA loans are fully assumable with qualification.

■ *There is no prepayment penalty.* The absence of a prepayment penalty allows the borrower to increase the monthly payment or prepay the loan.

**FHA Contributions to Real Estate Finance**

Every financier recognizes the significance of the FHA's major contributions to the stabilization of the real estate mortgage market. These contributions are summarized as follows:

- *The FHA instituted basic standards for qualifying borrowers.* Because credit applications and borrower credit ability criteria are standardized, all lenders who issue FHA-insured loans use the same basic language and tools.

- *The FHA instituted standards for appraising property.* Minimum construction standards are established that must be met before a property can qualify for an FHA-insured loan. These standards apply to both new and used buildings, and they are measured by an FHA appraisal of the potential collateral.

- *The long-term amortized loan was devised.* Prior to the FHA's long-term amortization design, in which a borrower has from 15 years to 30 years to repay a loan in equal monthly payments, most mortgage loans had to be paid in full or refinanced approximately every five years. This created hardships for both borrowers and sellers, and contributed to the many foreclosures during the Depression years. Currently the FHA monthly payments include an amount for principal, interest, property taxes, hazard insurance, and, if required, property improvement assessments and FHA mortgage insurance premiums.

- *The FHA lending standards and amortization design provided the foundation for a national market in mortgage securities.* By developing reliability and safety in mortgage loan investments, the FHA enables financial investors from all over the world to trade in these securities.

## ■ THE U.S. DEPARTMENT OF VETERANS AFFAIRS REAL ESTATE LOAN GUARANTEE PROGRAM

It long has been the custom in the United States to acknowledge the needs of the men and women who serve in the armed forces. They and their dependents receive special consideration in terms of educational opportunities, medical care, and housing allowances. The **U.S. Department of Veterans Affairs (DVA)** supervises a network of programs designed to aid U.S. war veterans.

Special finance programs have been established to provide funds to eligible veterans, reservists, and members of the National Guard to enable them to purchase homes, farms or ranches, and to improve these properties.

In 1944, shortly before the end of World War II, Congress passed the Serviceman's Readjustment Act, more commonly known as the GI Bill of Rights. This program was designed to provide returning veterans medical benefits, bonuses, and low-interest loans to help them readjust more easily to civilian life. This act is divided into six parts, or titles. Title III concerns guarantees to the lenders making real estate loans to eligible veterans that these loans will be repaid regardless of any borrower default.

Originally the guarantee was for 50 percent of the loan's balance, not to exceed $2,000. In 1945, Congress increased the guarantee to 60 percent against $4,000 and has gradually increased these limits. The conforming loan limit is adjusted each year by the Federal Housing Finance Agency (FHFA). In 2006 the VA-guarantee is $104,250, or 25 percent of the current Freddie Mac loan limit of $417,000. (See Figure 5.3.)

Because the lender regards this guaranteed amount the same as a 25 percent down payment, the lender will loan four times the guaranty

**FIGURE 5.3**
**DVA Loan Guarantees**

| | |
|---|---|
| December 28, 1945 | $ 4,000 |
| July 12, 1950 | 7,500 |
| May 7, 1968 | 12,500 |
| December 31, 1974 | 17,500 |
| October 1, 1978 | 25,000 |
| March 1, 1988 | 36,000 |
| December 20, 1989 | 46,000 |
| October 13, 1995 | 50,750 |
| January 1, 2002 | 60,000 |
| January 1, 2005 | 89,912 |
| January 1, 2006 | 104,250 |

*The maximum loan amount is 50 percent higher in Alaska, Hawaii, Guam, and the U.S. Virgin Islands.*

for a single-family home. Thus, a lender would be willing to loan a qualified veteran borrower up to $417,000, four times the entitlement.

**Program Application**

In general, the DVA is concerned with guaranteeing loans made by institutional lenders, such as commercial banks, thrift organizations, life insurance companies, and mortgage bankers and brokers. It tries to eliminate any risks taken by these lenders when they make loans on real estate to eligible veterans. If a veteran cannot continue to meet the required payments, the lender is compensated by the DVA for any losses incurred in the foreclosure and subsequent sale of the property, up to the limit of the guarantee.

The operations of the DVA real estate loan guarantee program are managed by 11 regional centers located throughout the country. The program is not designed to be used indiscriminately. Each loan application is reviewed carefully to determine the veteran's eligibility, credit history, and ability to pay. The value of the property is firmly established by an appraisal, and assurances are secured that the veteran will occupy the premises as the major residence. Poor risks are denied loans and are referred to other programs. The DVA guarantees about 200,000 loans per year.

Several veterans, related or not, may purchase one-family to four-family homes as partners, as long as they intend to occupy the property. A veteran and a nonveteran who are not married may purchase a home together as coborrowers, although the DVA will not guarantee the nonveteran's portion of the loan. However, the DVA does qualify common-law marriages without reduction of the loan guarantee for the nonveteran, as long as proper documentation has been supplied.

**Eligibility/Entitlement.**   A veteran's eligibility or **entitlement** to participate in the program is derived from the following active-duty criteria:

■ More than 90 days of continuous active duty; or discharge because of a service-connected disability; or separation under other than dishonorable conditions during any of the following wartime periods:

| | |
|---|---|
| World War II | September 16, 1940, to July 25, 1947 |
| Korean Conflict | June 27, 1950, to January 31, 1955 |

> Vietnam War          August 5, 1964, to May 7, 1975
>
> Persian Gulf War     August 2, 1990, to undetermined date

- More than 180 days of continuous active duty for other than training purposes; or discharge because of a service-connected disability; or separation under other than dishonorable conditions during the following peacetime periods:

  > Post-World War II     July 26, 1947, to June 26, 1950
  >
  > Post-Korean Conflict  February 1, 1955, to August 4, 1964
  >
  > Post-Vietnam War      May 8, 1975, to August 1, 1990

- For enlisted personnel, two years of continuous active duty or separation under other than dishonorable conditions during the peacetime period from 1980 to the present. For officers, two years of continuous active duty or separation other than dishonorable discharge during the peacetime period from 1981 to the present.

- At least six years of continuous active duty as a reservist in the Army, Navy, Air Force, Marine Corps, or Coast Guard, or as a member of the Army Air National Guard (in effect until September, 2009).

Active duty service personnel are eligible after serving 90 days of continuous activity. When an ending date is established for Persian Gulf War service, a minimum of 181 days of continuous active duty will be required.

Unremarried spouses of veterans may be eligible for DVA loans if the veteran died of a service-connected injury or illness or is listed as missing in action.

**Certificate of Eligibility.**   One of the most important documents needed for a loan application by a veteran is a **certificate of eligibility**. To receive this certificate, the veteran must secure forms to determine eligibility as well as an available loan guarantee entitlement. These forms must be accompanied by evidence of military service. At present, veterans receive their certificate of eligibility with their discharge from service.

There is no time limit on the entitlement, and it remains in effect until completely used up. This loan guarantee must be used in the United States, its territories, and its protectorates. A certificate may be requested on DVA Form 26-1880 and submitted along with the DD Form 214 (Certificate of Release or Discharge) through the local DVA office. Detailed information is available on *www.va.gov*. After using the DVA guarantee for a real estate loan, the veteran may gain the restoration of eligibility when the loan is paid in full and the property has been conveyed to another owner. (There is a one-time exemption of the conveyance requirement.)

**Partial Entitlement.**   Veterans who have used their benefits in the past may be eligible for another DVA loan if they have any remaining entitlement. With a **partial entitlement**, a veteran may pay cash down to the maximum loan amount and still benefit accordingly.

To determine any remaining entitlement, examine Figure 5.3 and subtract the amount used previously from the amount currently in effect. This is the amount available for the guarantee. Finally, to determine the maximum DVA loan allowed under a partial entitlement, take 75 percent of the appraised value and add the remaining entitlement amount.

■ **EXAMPLE** *(See Figure 5.3.)* Consider a veteran who purchased a house in 1989 using the entitlement of $46,000. In 1999, the veteran decided to purchase a new house but wanted to keep the original residence for an income property. With the new house appraised for $150,000, a new VA loan of $117,250 was acquired using the following process:

| | |
|---|---:|
| Maximum 1999 entitlement | $50,750 |
| 1989 entitlement | −46,000 |
| Remaining entitlement | 4,750 |
| 75 percent of $150,000 | +112,500 |
| | $117,250 |

To complete the transaction, the veteran paid $32,750 as a cash down payment.

**Certificate of Reasonable Value (CRV).**   The DVA requires a certified real estate appraiser to submit a formal estimate of the value of the property to be financed. The appraiser issues a **certificate of reasonable value (CRV)**, stating the amount of the appraisal. This CRV is valid for

6 months for existing properties and 12 months for new construction. It may not be extended.

If a sale is made subject to a CRV and the appraisal comes in at *less* than the sale price, the following may occur:

■ The buyer can make up the difference in cash.

■ The seller can accept the lower amount as the sale price.

■ The buyer and seller can compromise.

■ The transaction can be canceled.

In the purchase of a home in excess of the maximum guaranteed DVA loan amount with no money down, the difference is required to be paid in cash. The DVA reserves the right to approve the source of the cash. This is to ensure that the veteran is not borrowing an additional amount that would adversely affect the total debt ratio.

**Interest.**   In the past, the DVA specified the interest rate the lender could charge the veteran. Now, however, the DVA allows the borrower the opportunity to shop the marketplace and negotiate the best rate available. Thus, all types of mortgage loans are competitive as to interest rates, leveling the financing market.

**Income Qualifying Requirements.**   The DVA utilizes only one ratio to analyze a borrower's ability to qualify for the loan payment. This ratio is 41 percent of the borrower's gross monthly income and includes principal, interest, taxes, insurance, utilities, maintenance, repairs, and other monthly obligations. The DVA publishes information pertinent to maintenance, repair, and utility estimates for various regions in the United States. This information is based on a property's square footage and age, and whether the property has a pool, air-conditioning, or evaporative cooling. For example, one regional office allocates $76 per month for maintenance and repairs to a house more than three years old, consisting of 1,600 square feet, including a pool and air-conditioning. Furthermore, it allocates $214 per month for the utilities at this property.

■ **EXAMPLE**  A veteran applies for a DVA loan of $100,000 at 7 percent interest for 30 years. The monthly principal and interest payment is $665. Other monthly costs include $70 for taxes, $15 for insurance, $214 for utilities, $76 for maintenance, and $200 for other obligations. The veteran's total gross monthly income will have to be at least $3,024, or $36,288 per year, to qualify for this loan.

| | |
|---|---:|
| Principal and Interest | $665 |
| Property Taxes | 70 |
| Hazard Insurance | 15 |
| Utilities | 214 |
| Maintenance | 76 |
| Other Payments | 200 |
| Total Obligations | 1,240 |
| VA Income Ratio | ÷ 0.41 |
| Gross Monthly Income Required | 3,024 |
| | × 12 |
| Gross Annual Income Required | $36,288 |

**Closing Costs.**   *Closing costs may not be included in DVA loans* and must be paid in cash at closing. The only costs that may be charged to the veteran include:

- ■ 1 percent of the loan amount charged by the lender as a loan origination fee;

- ■ discount points as determined by the market;

- ■ DVA funding fee; and

- ■ reasonable and customary charges for: appraisal; credit report; recording fees; taxes and/or assessments chargeable to borrower; initial deposit for tax and insurance escrow accounts; hazard insurance including flood insurance; survey if required; and title examination and title insurance.

The seller may pay all of the borrower's closing costs plus an additional 4 percent of the loan amount to be used for the funding fee or to pay off borrower's debt to allow borrower to qualify for the loan.

**Funding Fee.**   The DVA charges a **funding fee**, which may be paid in cash or *included in the loan amount*, even in excess of the CRV. However, the addition of the funding fee to the original loan amount may not exceed the maximum allowable loan. The funding fee is required on all DVA loans *except*: from veterans receiving compensation for service-connected disabilities; from veterans receiving retirement pay in lieu of disability compensation; from spouses of veterans who died in service or died from service-connected disabilities; and in some transactions in which a large down payment is made. (See Figure 5.4.)

■ **EXAMPLE** The funding fee charged on a $100,000 DVA loan where the veteran makes no down payment is $2,150:

$$\begin{array}{r} \$100,000 \\ \times\ 0.0215 \\ \hline \$2,150 \end{array}$$

■ **EXAMPLE** The funding fee charged on a $100,000 DVA loan where the veteran makes a 10 percent down payment is $1,250:

$$\begin{array}{r} \$100,000 \\ \times\ 0.0125 \\ \hline \$1,250 \end{array}$$

■ **EXAMPLE** The funding fee charged on a $100,000 DVA loan secured for refinancing is $500:

$$\begin{array}{r} \$100,000 \\ \times\ 0.005 \\ \hline \$500 \end{array}$$

**FIGURE 5.4**

**Schedule of Funding Fees for DVA Loans**

| Category | First Time Use | Subsequent Use | Reservist/ National Guard | Subsequent Use Reservist/ National Guard |
|---|---|---|---|---|
| 0 to 5% down | 2.15% | 3.30% | 2.40% | 3.30% |
| 5.1 to 9.9% down | 1.50% | 1.50% | 1.75% | 1.75% |
| 10% or more down | 1.25% | 1.25% | 1.50% | 1.50% |
| Cash-Out Refinance | 2.15% | 3.30% | 2.40% | 3.30% |

***First Time or Subsequent—all categories of service***

| | |
|---|---|
| *Assumptions* | *0.50%* |
| *Rate Reduction Refinancing* | *0.50%* |
| *Manufactured Home* | *1.00%* |

**Second Mortgages.** The DVA will allow second mortgages to be placed on the collateral property under the following conditions:

- The second mortgage document must be approved by the DVA legal department prior to loan closing.

- The total of the first and second mortgage liens may not exceed the value of the property.

- The interest rate on the second mortgage may not exceed the interest rate on the first.

- The second mortgage may not have a prepayment penalty or a balloon payment.

- The second mortgage must be amortized for at least five years.

**Buydowns.** Buydowns are allowed only on DVA loans issued with level payments. A **buydown** is an amount of money paid in advance, accepted by the lender, to reduce the interest rate on the loan. The buydown fee may be paid by the seller, the buyer, or family members. The borrower must qualify at the first year's payment rate.

**Assumptions.** Prior to March 1988, DVA loans were fully assumable without prior lender approval of the buyer's credit. For DVA loans made after this date, the buyer's credit must be approved by the lender prior to the assumption of an existing loan. Any unauthorized assumption may trigger a technical default and the loan balance can be called in full. In any approved assumption, the loan interest rate will not be changed.

**Release of Liability/Novation.** The original makers of a DVA loan remain liable until it is paid in full or the veteran receives a release of liability or a **substitution of entitlement** from a cooperating buyer. The release of liability relieves the veteran-seller of the responsibility for repayment and any deficiencies resulting from a default on the loan.

Although it is unusual for a veteran to have more than one DVA loan in effect at any one time, it is not unusual for a veteran to secure a complete release from the liability of a previous DVA loan and a restoration of eligibility for a new maximum guarantee. General requirements for restoration of entitlement by the DVA call for the veteran to sell the property and repay the debt in full. A recent change allows for a one-time only provision for restoration of entitlement with repayment of the debt without having to dispose of the property. In addition, a veteran can qualify to ask the DVA for a substitution of entitlement if the home is sold to another qualified veteran willing to assume the loan.

In cases in which a veteran's loan is assumed by a purchaser who is not a veteran, the DVA will not allow the seller-veteran to regain maximum entitlement. The purchaser, however, can agree to assume the veteran's liability to reimburse the DVA in case of default, and the buyer and seller can then petition the DVA to release the veteran from all obligations. This full substitution technique is called **novation**. If the new buyers meet the credit requirements of the old lender, the DVA may accept them in lieu of the veteran and release the veteran's liability on the loan. Note, however, that release of a veteran's liability does not restore eligibility for the maximum guarantee amount. It will not be restored until the loan is finally paid off by the purchaser.

**DVA Adjustable-Rate Mortgage (ARM)**

The Veteran's Benefits Act of 2004 reinstated the **adjustable-rate mortgage (ARM)**. Following are the key features of this program:

- Annually adjusted interest rate

- Interest rate adjustments limited to increase or decrease of 1 percent per year

- Interest rate adjustments not to exceed 5 percentage points over life of the loan

- Requirement that ARM loan be underwritten at 1 percent above initial rate

The Act authorized the DVA to guarantee hybrid ARM loans through September 30, 2008. The Veteran's Benefits Improvement Act of 2008 extended the DVA's authority to guarantee new hybrid ARM loans through September 30, 2012. If the initial contract interest rate is fixed for less than five years, the initial adjustment is limited to a maximum increase or decrease of 1 percent, and 5 percent for the life of the loan. If the initial contract interest rate is for more than five years, the adjustment is limited to 2 percent and 6 percent over the life of the loan.

The provisions of the 2004 and 2008 act do not affect existing DVA ARMs, which remain subject to the terms in affect at the time of origination.

**Additional DVA Loan Guarantee Programs**

The DVA also guarantees loans for condominiums, cooperatives, manufactured housing, and mobile homes. Three types of refinance programs are available to veterans:

1. *DVA Streamline Refinance*—Interest Rate Reduction Refinancing Loan (IRRRL): refinance for a lower interest rate with no out-of-pocket closing costs, no appraisal required, and no income or credit check needed. There is a 0.5 percent funding fee.

2. *Cash Out Refinance*—refinance using existing equity to take out cash or pay off debts up to 90 percent of the value of the property. Funding fee is required.

3. *Conventional to DVA Mortgage*—refinance into a DVA mortgage from a conventional loan. Funding fee is required but may be financed. There is no private mortgage insurance required, no out-of-pocket closing costs, and new interest rate may be lower.

# ■ CALIFORNIA VETERANS HOME AND FARM PURCHASE PROGRAM (CAL-VET)

Originated in 1921, the California Veterans Home and Farm Purchase Program, also known as **Cal-Vet**, was created by the state legislature to assist qualified veterans to acquire California home or farm properties at low financing costs. The state Department of Veterans Affairs provides the funds and administers the loans until they are paid. State laws governing the program are contained in Division 4, Chapter 6 of the Military and Veterans' Code.

**Funding and Title**

Monies for the program are secured primarily through the sale of revenue bonds collateralized by the Cal-Vet loan portfolio. Funds are also raised through the sale of general obligation bonds, the issuance of which must be approved by both the legislature and the voting public. Both types of bonds are **tax-exempt bonds** at both the federal and state level.

The amount loaned to each borrower is repaid at a low interest rate sufficient to cover the costs of the bond issue and the costs of the program's administration, involving no expense to taxpayers.

The department purchases the subject property from the sellers, takes legal title, and then resells it to the veteran who acquires an equitable interest in the real estate under a land contract. The veteran has full use of the property, as long as it is a personal residence, and secures full legal title when the Cal-Vet loan is repaid.

**Eligibility Requirements**

To qualify for the Cal-Vet program, all veterans are eligible and must meet the following criteria:

- At least 90 days active service or prior discharge due to service-connected disability, or eligible to receive a U.S. campaign or expeditionary medal, or were called to active duty from the Reserves or National Guard due to a Presidential Executive Order.

- Honorable discharge

- Active service within these periods:

| | |
|---|---|
| World War I | April 6, 1917 – November 11, 1918 |
| World War II | December 7, 1941 – December 31, 1946 |
| Korean Conflict | June 27, 1950 – January 31, 1955 |
| Vietnam War | August 5, 1964 – May 7, 1975 |
| Gulf War | August 2, 1990 – present |

- A veteran receiving approved medals during peacetime may also qualify.

In addition, unremarried spouses of veterans killed in active duty or missing in action may qualify. Veterans with more than one qualifying period may be eligible for more than one loan, but only one loan may be active at any time. Proof of eligibility lies with the veteran. Further information may be found online at *www.cdva.ca.gov* or by calling 1-800-952-5626.

**Qualifying Procedures**    Properties that qualify for Cal-Vet financing are:

- Single-family homes, condos, townhouses, and mobile homes on owned lots to $521,250

- Manufactured homes in approved parks up to $175,000

- Self-supporting farms and ranches up to $625,500

There may be additional loan amounts available for homes equipped with solar heating devices, based on Cal-Vet's requirements. The down payment for a Cal-Vet loan differs depending on the type of loan. For example, for qualified borrowers, the Cal Vet/DVA loan requires no down payment. The Cal-Vet 97 program requires 3 percent down. The Cal-Vet 80/20 program requires 20 percent down. The funding fee ranges from 1.25 to 3.3 percent. There is a 1 percent origination fee on all Cal-Vet loans.

Most loans are established on a 30-year amortization schedule except for manufactured homes in a park, which run from 15 to 20 years.

The interest rates on Cal-Vet loans fluctuate as new bond issues are created. The existing and new loans acquire a weighted average rate over time; however, the interest rates are usually below market. Cal-Vet also provides adjustable-rate loans.

A Cal-Vet loan may be satisfied at any time without any prepayment penalty.

A minimal application fee is required. Prorations of property taxes and insurance premiums will be paid at closing. Borrowers must meet normal credit requirements, including an acceptable credit history.

Borrowers are required to purchase special hazard insurance against floods and earthquakes. They also must purchase life and disability insurance to provide for full repayment of the loan in the event of death or disability.

**Special Conditions**

**New Construction.**   The Department does make construction loans and offers permanent financing for eligible properties. Prior approval must be secured before entering into a contract for a new building.

**Funds for Refinancing.**   The Department does not provide funds for refinancing existing loans except: to provide permanent financing for an approved construction loan or if money is not available at the time of commitment and the veteran has to secure an interim loan for not more than two years.

**Junior Financing.**   The Department may consent to additional financing that would be in junior position to the Cal-Vet loan if the combined total does not exceed 90 percent of the appraised value of the property.

**Occupancy.**   The veteran must occupy the property within 60 days of closing a Cal-Vet contract and must maintain residency until the loan is satisfied. An exception is made for farm and ranch properties if the veteran personally cultivates the land and harvests the crops or tends the livestock.

The subject property may be rented under prior approved circumstances, but not longer than a total of four years throughout the contract.

**Others.**   The rental, sale, assignment, or encumbrance of Cal-Vet property is prohibited without the prior consent of the Department. The veteran may borrow against equity with approval.

Veterans who must move may qualify to have their Cal-Vet loan transferred or may qualify for a second loan contract.

Some veterans may be eligible for special Cal-Vet loans. These include a *deferred principal payment loan* for low-income applicants and a *conditional commitment loan* for property in need of rehabilitation.

# ■ SUMMARY

This chapter examined conventional, insured, and guaranteed loans.

Most of the real estate loans made in the market today are conventional loans. When issuing a conventional loan, a lender is accepting risks of loss. Thus, a certain amount of equity is required, usually up to 20 percent of the collateral's value, to act as a cushion to protect the lender's position.

This relatively high down payment prevents many potential property buyers from participating in the housing market. To relieve this problem a system of insured and guaranteed loans has been developed.

Private insurance companies, such as the Mortgage Guaranty Insurance Corporation (MGIC), insure the top portion of a conventional loan, usually 10 to 15 percent, so a borrower qualified to make the payments may be able to secure up to 95 percent of the value of a property as a new loan. If the borrower defaults, the insurance agency will reimburse the lender in an amount appropriate to reduce the risk to the acceptable 80 percent level.

Established during the crisis of the Great Depression under the provisions of the National Housing Act of 1934, the Federal Housing Administration (FHA) is now under the jurisdiction of the Department of Housing and Urban Development (HUD).

The FHA is an insurance program that puts the credit of the U.S. government behind the credit of the individual borrower. With FHA insurance, a lender may rely on the government to reimburse funds loaned to a defaulted borrower.

The FHA provides standards for qualifying borrowers and appraising property. The FHA designed the long-term, self-amortizing loan, enabling borrowers to secure affordable monthly payments.

Under FHA insurance, borrowers enjoy low down payments, a variety of loan arrangements, no due-on-sale clauses, assumable loans, no prepayment penalties, and market interest rates.

Insurance premiums are required and these premiums constitute the reserves from which the FHA pays the lenders for defaulted loans.

The FHA provides insurance for loans on single-family dwellings, one-family to four-family apartment units, medical clinics, and hospitals. The FHA also provides special subsidized programs to pay interest or rent for low-income and moderate-income families.

One FHA program is the **graduated payment mortgage (GPM)** under Section 245. This program allows first-time homebuyers an opportunity to qualify under less-than-interest-only payments (negative amortization) in anticipation of increased earnings over time. The payments rise gradually to match the increasing financial capabilities of the borrowers.

Past criticisms of the time-consuming FHA process have been diminished by efficient direct endorsement and coinsurance programs. Now loan originators can issue loans directly, eliminating unnecessary red tape.

The U.S. Department of Veterans Affairs real estate loan guarantee program eliminates lender risks on loans made to eligible veterans. A lender is compensated by the DVA for any losses incurred in a foreclosure and subsequent resale of a subject property, up to the amount of the guarantee.

A veteran's eligibility for this program requires at least 90 consecutive days active duty during war time, 181 days continuous active duty during peacetime, or two years of continuous active duty from September 8, 1980, to the present.

There are several benefits to a DVA loan. These include: that no down payment is required on full entitlement loans, that the seller can pay all closing costs, that there is no mortgage insurance premium, and that the loans are fully assumable.

A DVA appraisal is known as a Certificate of Reasonable Value (CRV) and is valid for six months for existing property and for 12 months for proposed construction. Closing costs may not be included in the loan amount. A funding fee is required on most DVA loans, and the discount points must be paid by someone other than the veteran. Interest rates are established in the marketplace.

Although it is unusual for a veteran to have more than one DVA loan in effect at one time, it is not unusual for a veteran to secure a complete release from the liability of a previous DVA loan. This release restores the veteran's eligibility for a new maximum loan guarantee. In cases where a veteran's loan is assumed by a purchaser who is not a veteran, the DVA does not allow the seller-veteran to regain maximum entitlement until the old loan is satisfied. The purchaser, however, can agree to assume the veteran's liability and petition the DVA to release the veteran of all obligation. This full substitution is called novation.

One of the more important documents needed for a veteran's loan application is the Certificate of Eligibility. Once the veteran submits proof of eligibility and the entitlement is determined, the loan process may proceed.

The California Veterans Farm and Home Purchase Program, also known as Cal-Vet, was created to assist eligible veterans to acquire California farm or home properties at low financing costs. The program is funded with tax-free revenue bonds that allow lower-than-market interest rates to be applied on Cal-Vet loans. The Department of Veterans Affairs purchases the subject property and resells it to the veteran on a land contract. The entire cost of the program is covered by the loan payments.

# ■ INTERNET RESOURCES

Department of Housing and Urban Development, FHA   *www.hud.gov*

Department of Veterans Affairs   *www.va.gov*

# ■ REVIEW QUESTIONS

1. A straight conventional loan includes

   a. FHA insurance.

   b. a DVA guaranty.

   c. a private mortgage insurance agreement.

   d. no third party insurance or guarantees.

2. All of the following relationships are correct *EXCEPT*

   a. DVA L/V ratio = 100 percent.

   b. FHA L/V ratio = 95 percent.

   c. conventional-guaranteed L/V ratio = 90 percent.

   d. conventional L/V ratio = 90 percent.

3. Private mortgage insurance companies usually charge the borrower a premium as a percentage of the

   a. entire amount of the loan.

   b. bottom 75 to 80 percent of the loan.

   c. top 10 to 15 percent of the loan.

   d. balance of the loan.

4. The FHA is a

   a. loan insurance agency.

   b. loan origination agency.

   c. secondary market agency.

   d. loan guaranty agency.

5. FHA loans made after December 1989

   a. are assumable by investors.

   b. require qualification ratios of 31 percent and 43 percent.

   c. are generally assumable without qualifying.

   d. do not release sellers from liability.

6. Which of the following is the MOST that an eligible veteran may pay for a home under the current DVA loan formula?

   a. $60,000                    c. $417,000

   b. $104,260                   d. No maximum limitation

7. Interest rates on an FHA-insured loan is established by the

   a. Fed.                       c. market.

   b. FNMA.                      d. FHA.

8. The interest rates on a DVA-guaranteed loan is established by the

   a. Fed.                       c. market.

   b. FNMA.                      d. DVA.

9. The DVA loan guarantee program protects the

   a. seller.                    c. veteran.

   b. lender.                    d. broker.

10. A qualified veteran with full entitlement wishes to purchase a home with a $417,000 CRV. Which of the following is the correct down payment?

    a. $0                        c. $83,400

    b. $20,850                   d. $104,250

# ■ EXERCISES

1. Explain why most home foreclosures are against DVA, FHA, or owner-carryback loans.

2. Investigate the effects of the increased costs of securing FHA and DVA loans as to the numbers of loans issued. Are more borrowers securing conventional loans?

3. Explore how an employed borrower having difficulty making mortgage payments might find some help with the federal Home Affordable Modification Program (HAMP). See *www.makinghomeaffordable.gov*.

4. Look into how the federal Home Affordable Refinance Program (HARP) might help refinance loans on those homes that have lost value. See *www.makinghomeaffordable.gov*.

6

# FINANCIAL AGENCIES AND LENDING PROGRAMS

## ■ KEY TERMS

Community Reinvestment Act (CRA)

Equal Credit Opportunity Act (ECOA)

Farm Credit System (FCS)

Farmer Mac

Garn-St. Germain Bill

good-faith estimate (GFE)

Home Mortgage Disclosure Act

Housing Choice Voucher Program

HUD (Department of Housing and Urban Development)

HUD-1 settlement statement

Interstate Land Sales Full Disclosure Act

moratorium

mortgage revenue bonds

mortgage servicing disclosure statement

open-end mortgages

Proposition 13

Real Estate Settlement Procedures Act (RESPA)

redlining

tax-increment financing

Truth in Lending Act (Regulation Z)

urban renewal

USDA Rural Development Program

usury

In addition to its roles as controller of money and credit, insurer of deposits and loans, and operator in the secondary market, the government is active in agricultural lending, public housing, and regulating local participants' real estate financial activities.

# ■ AGRICULTURAL LENDING

Farm loans have special cyclical requirements. The values of farm and ranch lands depend on productivity, and productivity in turn depends on management expertise and climatic conditions. Although management skills can be evaluated based on past experience, nobody can estimate the influence of nature on each season's crops, and farm and ranch loans acquire a unique risk factor.

Agricultural loans have to be designed with as much flexibility as possible. Rather than following a rigid payment pattern, their design must allow the farmer-borrowers the opportunity to pay when they can. It is essential, for instance, that the principal amount not come due in a bad crop year. The terms of the loans need to be lengthened, up to 40 years in some cases, to allow for those years when crops may fail and no payments can be made. Farmer-borrowers also need an opportunity to pay larger portions of the principal, in addition to the interest required, during a good year so that they can repay their loans in full over the longer time period.

Farmer-borrowers need to be able to extend, expand, and otherwise adjust their loans depending on unforeseen circumstances. The extension and expansion techniques designed to satisfy the special problems of the farmers are defined as **open-end mortgages**. As a last resort for a distressed farmer-borrower, a **moratorium** on payments occasionally is used to offset imminent foreclosures brought on by situations outside the borrower's control. Open-end mortgages and moratoriums will be discussed later in this book.

# ■ THE FARM CREDIT SYSTEM (FCS)

The **Farm Credit System (FCS)** was created by Congress in 1916 to provide American agriculture with a source of sound, dependable credit at competitive rates of interest. This nationwide network of borrower-owned financial institutions provides loans to farmers, ranchers, producers and harvesters of aquatic products, rural homeowners, agricultural cooperatives, rural utility systems, and agribusinesses.

Five banks (AgFirst, AgriBank, CoBank, Farm Credit Bank of Texas, and U.S. AgBank) plus ninety-three local, direct-lending associations provide credit and other financial services to agricultural producers and farmer-owned cooperatives. The FCS banks do not take deposits. The funds used for lending are raised through the sale of bonds and notes in national capital markets. The Federal Farm Credit Banks Funding Corporation manages the sale of systemwide debt securities. Purchasers of these securities are assured of timely payment of principal and interest by the Farm Credit System Insurance Corporation (FCSIC).

Long-term mortgage loans are generally made by Farm Credit Banks, Federal Land Bank Associations, or Federal Land Credit Associations. Short-term and intermediate-term loans are usually made by Production Credit Associations. In some cases, these entities have combined to form Agriculture Credit Associations that provide both long- and short-term loans. See *www.fca.gov* for more information on the Farm Credit System.

**Farm Credit Administration (FCA)**

The Farm Credit Administration (FCA) is an independent federal regulator responsible for examining and ensuring the soundness of all FCS institutions. See *www.fca.gov*.

**Federal Agriculture Mortgage Corporation (Farmer Mac)**

The Federal Agriculture Mortgage Corporation, known as **Farmer Mac**, was created by Congress to provide a secondary market for agricultural and rural housing mortgage loans. By purchasing qualified loans from agricultural mortgage lenders, Farmer Mac replenishes their source of funds to make new loans. See *www.farmermac.com*.

**The U.S. Department of Agriculture Rural Development Program (USDA Rural Development)**

The activities of the Farm Credit System are complemented by the USDA Rural Development agency. This governmental unit was created in 1994 to combine the Farmers Home Administration, the Rural Development Administration, the Rural Electrification Administration, and the Agricultural Cooperative Service.

The **USDA Rural Development Program** forges new partnerships with rural communities to reverse the downward spiral of rural job losses, out-migration, and diminishing services. The program funds projects that bring housing, community facilities, utilities, and other services to rural areas. The USDA also provides technical assistance and financial backing for rural businesses and cooperatives to create quality jobs in rural areas.

## ■ U.S. DEPARTMENT OF HOUSING AND URBAN DEVELOPMENT (HUD)

Under President Johnson, the **Department of Housing and Urban Development (HUD)** was given cabinet status in 1965. It consolidated a number of older federal agencies.

HUD is the federal agency responsible for national policy and programs that address America's housing needs, improve and develop U.S. communities, and enforce fair housing laws. HUD's mission is to help create a decent home and suitable living environment for all U.S. citizens.

As illustrated in Figure 6.1, HUD's primary activities include

- supervising the Federal Housing Administration (FHA);

- directing Ginnie Mae;

- directing development block grants;

- enforcing fair housing and RESPA regulations;

- managing the Housing Choice Voucher Program (formerly Section 8 Housing);

**FIGURE 6.1**

**The Primary Supervisory Activities of HUD**

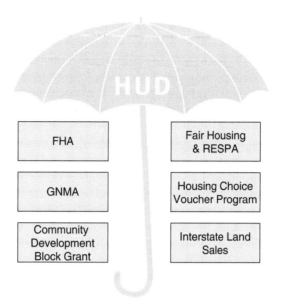

regulating interstate land sales registration, urban renewal, and rehabilitation programs; and

as part of the Housing and Economic Recovery Act of 2008 (HERA), HUD has authorized a Neighborhood Stabilization Program designed to reduce sources of abandonment and blight. Funds are provided to acquire and redevelop foreclosed properties.

One of the important functions of HUD is to provide information on home ownership to the public. The HUD Web site (*www.hud.gov*) is a tremendous resource for the public and for real estate practitioners. The introductory page, "Homes and Communities," guides the visitor to numerous other pages offering detailed information on home mortgage lending, FHA loan guidelines, and sources for home ownership education and counseling.

The HUD Strategic Plan for 2006–2011 emphasizes the following strategic goals:

Increase home ownership opportunities

Promote decent affordable housing

Strengthen communities

- Ensure equal opportunity in housing

- Embrace high standards of ethics, management, and accountability

**Other Programs**

HUD also provides funds for public housing agencies to develop and operate housing for low-income families. HUD has more than 3,500 public and American Indian housing authorities that provide public housing and services to more than 1.5 million households.

HUD helps finance public housing agency projects to integrate public housing into surrounding communities and to provide residents the skills to contribute to their communities. It offers monetary support to state and local governments and to nonprofit organizations to assist homeless individuals and families to move from the streets to temporary shelters to supportive housing and, ideally, back into the mainstream of American life. HUD also helps fund cooperative housing for low-income persons, housing for the elderly, mortgage interest subsidies, relocation assistance, college housing, disaster area reconstruction, urban renewal, and housing in isolated areas.

**Urban Renewal.**   HUD sponsors urban renewal projects that encompass entire neighborhoods as well as specific properties. Neighborhood renewal involves large-scale planning, including site acquisition, site clearance, construction, and disposition. Urban renewal originates at the community level, where a workable plan is developed and then sent to HUD for approval and sponsorship.

In addition to providing funds for slum clearance, HUD makes loans and grants to owners and tenants in depressed areas for rehabilitating their properties. Grants are also available to demolish structures unfit for habitation.

**Subsidized Housing.**   The HUD subsidized housing program assists low-income households with rental subsidies in the private sector through the **Housing Choice Voucher Program** (formerly Section 8). Families seeking assistance apply through their local public housing agency. Tenants have the freedom to select housing where they want to live within a standard rent range. The rent subsidies are paid to owners and consist of the difference between what the tenant can pay and the contracted rent.

Under legislation passed in year 2001, individual public housing authorities (PHAs) now have the option to use a portion of their housing choice vouchers to assist first-time homebuyers. Each PSA makes the determination of how much of their funding they wish to allocate to this Home Choice Voucher Program. FHA sets minimum income and employment requirements, but other eligibility requirements are set by the PHA. For example, recipients must attend a home ownership and housing counseling program.

**Community Development Block Grants (CDBG).**   The Community Development Block Grants (CDBG) program helps communities with economic development, job opportunities, and housing rehabilitation. CDBG funds have been used to construct and improve public facilities such as water, sewer, streets, and neighborhood centers; to purchase real property; and to assist private businesses.

CDBG funds are split between states and *entitlement communities*, defined as metropolitan cities with populations of at least 50,000 and urban counties with populations of at least 200,000. States distribute to nonentitlement communities. Seventy percent of CDBG funds must benefit low-income and moderate-income families.

Under the Section 108 loan guarantee component of the CDBG program, communities can obtain financing for economic development, housing rehabilitation, and large-scale physical development projects.

**Public Housing.**   HUD provides financial assistance to local authorities for acquisition and operation of properties for public housing programs. This assistance includes grant monies, housing subsidies, and other means of support. As discussed in Chapter 5, HUD provides a program called Neighbors Next Door. Under this program HUD provides qualified teachers and police officers with second mortgages of 40 percent of the purchase price to be used for down payments and closing costs. The second mortgage payments are deferred for three years with no payments and no interest accrual. At the beginning of the fourth year, payments are required at a rate of 2 percent.

**The Real Estate Settlement Procedures Act (RESPA)**

In July 2011, the administration of the **Real Estate Settlement Procedures Act (RESPA)** came under the Consumer Financial Protection Bureau (CFPB) and is designed to protect the participants in a real estate transaction by providing closing cost information so they better understand the settlement procedures. RESPA covers the sale of residential properties and the acquisition of mortgage loans, including home equity loans, second mortgages, and refinancing loans on residential properties.

Violators are subject to severe penalties such as triple damages, fines, and even imprisonment. RESPA covers almost every service provider involved in the purchase of a home including

- real estate brokers and agents,

- mortgage brokers and mortgage bankers,

- title companies and title agents,

- home warranty companies,

- hazard insurance agents,

- appraisers,

- flood insurers and tax service suppliers, and

- home and pest inspectors.

Real estate brokers or agents are prohibited from receiving anything "of value" for referring business to another real estate service provider or from splitting fees received for settlement services unless the fee is paid for an actual service. Exemptions from the referral restrictions are

- promotional and educational activities,

- payment for goods provided or service performed, and

- affiliated business arrangements.

For a detailed description of each of the exempt categories and to see examples of permissible activities and payments, see *www.hud.gov*.

**Disclosures under RESPA.**   In order to protect participants in a real estate transaction, RESPA requires all service costs to be disclosed at various times during the process. Disclosures must be made during the time of a loan application, before settlement, at settlement, and after settlement.

***Disclosure at the Time of a Loan Application.***   At the beginning of the mortgage loan process, the lender must provide the borrower the following three items:

1. A special information booklet containing information on real estate settlement services

2. Within three business days, a **good faith estimate (GFE)** of settlement costs listing the charges the borrower is likely to pay at closing and indicating whether the borrower has to use a specific settlement service

3. A **mortgage servicing disclosure statement** informing the borrower whether the lender intends to keep the loan or transfer it to a different lender for servicing in addition to information on how the borrower can resolve complaints

***Disclosures before Settlement Closing.***   Prior to settlement, the lender must inform the borrower whenever a settlement service refers the borrower to a firm with which the servicer has any connection, such as common ownership. The service usually cannot force a borrower to use a connected firm. A preliminary copy of a **HUD-1 settlement statement** is required if the borrower requests it 24 hours prior to closing. This form estimates all settlement charges that must be paid by the participants. Prior to closing, the borrower must also receive a copy of a truth-in-lending statement that discloses the annual percentage rate and total costs of credit involved in the transaction.

***Disclosures at Settlement.***   The HUD-1 settlement statement is distributed at closing and shows the *actual* charges incurred by the participants. In addition, an initial escrow statement is required at closing or within

45 days of closing. This statement itemizes the estimated taxes, insurance premiums, and other charges that must be paid from the escrow account during the first year of the loan. It is now federal law to include a lead-based paint disclosure on all properties built before 1978.

***Disclosures after Settlement.***   After settlement the loan servicer must deliver an annual escrow loan statement to the borrower. This document enumerates all escrow deposits and payments during the past year. It indicates any shortages or surpluses in the escrow account and informs the borrower how to remedy them. If the loan service is transferred to another servicer, a servicing transfer statement is delivered to the borrower.

For example, consider Sam Smith who recently represented Ann Jones as her buyer agent for the purchase of a new town house. Sam recommended three different loan officers for Ann to contact regarding obtaining a home mortgage loan. Ann picked Jim Brown and was very happy with him until this morning when she received a truth-in-lending statement in the mail. She immediately called Sam, obviously very upset, saying: "You and Jim both assured me that I was getting a 6.5 percent loan and that I was going to be able to borrow $200,000. Today I get this statement in the mail saying that the interest rate will be 6.82 percent and that I am only borrowing $194,000! Now I don't know what or who to believe!"

This is not an uncommon reaction to receipt of a truth-in-lending statement. Fortunately, Sam has dealt with this many times before and was quickly able to calm Ann down. He then explained to her that the Truth in Lending Act requires the lender to disclose exactly how much they are earning on the loan, including any loan fees and discount points that may have been charged. Because there were three points on this $200,000 loan the lender only sends a check for $194,000 to the settlement table (they receive the other $6,000 in points, paid by the buyer, seller, or both). When the discount points and additional loan fees of $500 are calculated, the lender's actual yield becomes 6.82 percent.

## The Federal Equal Credit Opportunity Act (ECOA)

The **Equal Credit Opportunity Act (ECOA)** is Title VII of the Consumer Protection Act. It prohibits lenders from discriminating against credit applicants on the basis of race, color, religion, national origin, sex, marital status, age, or dependency on public assistance. The basic provisions of the act include the following:

- The lender may not ask if the applicant is divorced or widowed. However, the lender may ask if the borrower is married, unmarried, or separated. The term *unmarried* denotes a single, divorced, or widowed person and, in a community property state, is of particular interest to local lenders.

- The lender may not ask about the receipt of alimony or child support unless the borrower intends to use such income to qualify for the loan. The lender may ask about any obligations to pay alimony or child support.

- The lender may not seek any information about birth control practices or the childbearing capabilities or intentions of the borrower or coborrower.

- The lender may not request information about the spouse or former spouse of the applicant unless that person will be contractually liable for repayment or the couple lives in a community property state.

- The lender may not discount or exclude any income because of the source of that income.

- The lender must report credit information on married couples separately in the name of each spouse.

- The lender may ask about the race or national origin of the applicant, but the borrowers can refuse to answer without fear of jeopardizing their loan.

The ECOA also prohibits lenders from discriminating against credit applicants who exercise their rights under the truth-in-lending laws. In addition, lenders and other creditors must inform all rejected applicants in writing of the principal reasons why credit was denied or terminated. The focus of the ECOA is to ensure that all qualified persons have equal access to credit.

Both the Justice Department and HUD are charged with protecting borrowers from discrimination in lending practices under the fair housing laws and ECOA. An example of ECOA's effectiveness is the case against the Chevy Chase Federal Savings Bank in Washington DC, which was accused of violating the racial discrimination standards. The bank denied all allegations but agreed to invest $11 million to open at least one new branch in an African American area of the city. The bank also agreed to provide eligible borrowers discounted interest rates and grants equaling 2 percent of the loan down payments.

**Interstate Land Sales**

The **Interstate Land Sales Full Disclosure Act**, passed by Congress in 1968, established criteria for the dissemination of vital information to potential buyers of residential land. Designed to reduce fraud in the sales of land, the law requires that anyone selling or leasing 25 or more lots of unimproved land as part of a common plan in interstate commerce must comply with the Act's provisions. The exceptions include subdivisions of five acres or more, cemetery land, commercial and industrial land, and any residential subdivision being marketed exclusively in the state where it is located.

A developer must provide HUD *a statement of record* that includes explanations and descriptions of existing and proposed encumbrances, improvements, utilities, schools, recreation areas, roads, and all services to be provided for the residents' use. A *property report* must be delivered, evidenced by a signed receipt for same, *prior* to the purchase of the property. If a property report is received within 48 hours prior to signing, the buyers have the right to change their minds within three days, cancel their contract, and receive a return of any deposits made. However, if the report is not received within the allotted time, the buyers can rescind their contract at any time.

# ■ FEDERAL LEGISLATION

In the past, real estate transactions were virtually unregulated, and each party was assumed to be knowledgeable of the true facts and conditions surrounding the sale and financing of the property. As the marketplace evolved and became more complex, it became apparent that many purchasers or sellers were not well informed. As a result, some significant federal legislation was passed that has become standard practice in every real estate transaction.

**Fair Housing Act**

The rules and regulations of the Civil Rights Act (Title VIII—Fair Housing) effective December 31, 1968, and amended, are of significance to finance students.

Upheld by the U.S. Supreme Court decision in *Jones v. Mayer* (392 U.S. 409 88 S.C.T.2186 20 L.Ed.2d 1189), this act is designed to eliminate discrimination in the sale or rental of housing based on race, color, sex, or national origin. Single-family homes sold without the services of a real estate broker or single-family homes rented by an owner who does not own more than three such houses at the same time—as well as rooming houses for not more than four families where the owner resides on the property—are exempt from the provisions of the act. These exemptions do not indicate that the government sanctions discrimination under any circumstances.

The 1989 amendments expanded the act to include protection against discrimination of the handicapped and families with children. The law now extends fair housing protection to both the mentally and physically handicapped. However, it specifically excludes persons who would pose a direct threat to the health and safety of others.

The law stipulates that apartment buildings with four or more units and public buildings are to be made accessible to persons in wheelchairs. In buildings with no elevators, only first-floor units are covered by the provisions. All doorways and hallways in the building, as well as individual units, must be wide enough to allow passage by wheelchairs. Light switches, electrical outlets, and other controls also must be wheelchair accessible. Bathroom walls must be reinforced to accommodate the installation of grab bars, and kitchens and bathrooms must be designed to allow free mobility for the handicapped.

The law also extends fair housing coverage to families with children younger than 18, including pregnant women. As a result of this expansion of the law, all-adult communities are banned except

- those that operate specifically for the elderly under state or federal programs,

- projects in which all residents are at least 62, and

- retirement housing in which at least 80 percent of the units are occupied by at least one resident who is 55 and if special services and facilities are provided for the elderly.

Although the Fair Housing Act is a federal law and under the jurisdiction of HUD, its implementation is generally left to the individual states that have inaugurated their own open housing regulations. These state laws are usually broader in scope than the federal law, and many include prohibitions against discrimination in the financing and appraising of property as well as in leasing and selling.

When a problem occurs under the open housing laws, a complaint is filed with the local commissioner, who investigates accordingly. The commissioner attempts to solve the problem amicably and without litigation. If a suit is necessary, it is initiated by the complainant in the appropriate state or federal court. In addition, the U.S. Attorney General's office may bring an action for injunctive relief in the federal court having jurisdiction over the dispute.

A complainant can generally expect an answer to a locally filed action within 30 days. If filed at the federal court level, an answer will be presented within 100 days.

Violators who refuse to obey the orders of the court are held in contempt and fined or sent to prison for up to six months. Persons found guilty of bringing false charges or complaints with "willful intent" to falsify are subject to five years imprisonment or a fine.

**Unruh Civil Rights Act**   The Unruh Civil Rights Act (Civil Code Section 51) requires the elimination of discrimination in "accommodations, facilities and services in all business establishments of every kind whatsoever..." Discrimination applies to sex, race, color, religion, ancestry, national origin, and, more recently, persons with disabilities and families with children.

The validity of this act has been upheld in the courts and it applies to all real estate activities in the state. Thus, real estate brokers and their salespersons who deny full and equal representation to clients and customers are liable for the offense and must remit actual damages suffered plus a fine.

The California Fair Employment and Housing Act (Government Code Section 12900), which is an expanded version of the Rumford Act, parallels the Unruh Act. The provisions of this act apply not only to some private owners of businesses and real estate, but also to real estate brokers and their salespersons, other agents, and financial institutions.

This law prohibits discrimination in supplying housing accommodations as rentals, sales, leasing, or financing. Complaints should be directed to the Department of Fair Employment and Housing, and actions are brought in the Superior Court. If a violation is declared, the commissioner, acting for the court, may order the sale or rental of the accommodations or like accommodations, if available. In addition, the commissioner may order payment of punitive damages. The law exempts only rentals to one roomer or boarder in a single-family house.

The California Bureau of Real Estate under its Business and Professional Code, Section 10177(1), specifies a cause for disciplinary action to be the inducement to panic selling, also known as *steering*, by the "solicitation or inducement of the sale, lease or listing for sale or lease of a residential property on the grounds, wholly or in part, of loss in value, increase in crime or decline in the quality of the schools due to the present or prospective entry into the neighborhood of a person or persons of another race, color, religion, ancestry or national origin."

## Community Reinvestment Act

The **Community Reinvestment Act (CRA)** was passed by Congress in 1977 to ensure that financial institutions expand their responsibilities to meet both the deposit and the credit needs of every member of the communities in which they are chartered. Each institution is required to delineate their community, specify the types of credit services they offer, post a public notice stating that the institution is being reviewed by a federal supervisory agency, and prepare a community reinvestment statement to be made available to the public.

The Act provides that an appropriate *federal supervisory agency* assess the institution's record in meeting the credit needs of the community, including low-income families. The Act covers the majority of U.S. financial institutions because the term *federal supervisory agency* includes the Comptroller of the Currency, Board of Governors of the Federal Reserve System, Federal Deposit Insurance Corporation, and the Office of Thrift Supervision.

When assessing an institution's compliance with the Community Reinvestment Act, this agency must prepare a written evaluation that includes a section for filing in the records and a section that will be made public. The public portion will include the agency's rating of the institution, ranging from "outstanding" to "substantial noncompliance" in meeting community credit needs.

## The Home Mortgage Disclosure Act

Under the **Home Mortgage Disclosure Act**, all mortgage originators are required to report information to the Federal Reserve relating to income levels, racial characteristics, and gender of mortgage applicants. This includes loans originated as well as applications rejected. However, under ECOA, this data may not be used to discriminate.

## Truth in Lending Act (Regulation Z)

The **Truth in Lending Act (Regulation Z)** is administered by the Federal Reserve and enforced by the Federal Trade Commission. It requires that all costs involved in securing a loan be revealed to the borrower in advance with an effective annual percentage rate clearly specified. This allows the borrower to shop the market more intelligently with a common cost reference as a comparison.

While the Truth in Lending Act does not set limits on interest rates or other finance charges, it regulates the way lenders disclose these items. A lender must make these disclosures when credit or funds are offered to borrowers and when credit terms are advertised to potential customers.

The following loans are covered by the act if the loan is to be repaid in more than four installments or if a finance charge is made:

- Real estate loans and loans for personal, family, or household purposes

- Consumer loans for $25,000 or less

The disclosure statement must include the creditor's identity, the amount financed, the number, amount and due dates of the payments, the notice of the right to receive an itemization of the amount financed, the late payment and prepayment provisions and penalties, a description of the security, and whether the loan can be assumed by a subsequent purchaser.

**Advertising.** Prior to the passage of the Truth in Lending Act, residential real estate lenders and arrangers of credit frequently included only the favorable loan aspects in advertisements, thus distorting the actual cost of obtaining credit. Now, advertising is strictly regulated by the law and advertisers are required to disclose all financing details if one item is disclosed. The advertising requirements apply to newspapers, TV, handbills, and signs.

Advertising terms that would require complete disclosure include "Only 5% down!"; "Why pay the landlord when you can own for $550 per month?"; "30-year financing available"; or "Assume a 9.5% VA loan." Advertising terms that would not require complete disclosure include "Low Down"; "Easy monthly payments"; "10% APR loans available"; or "FHA and VA loans."

**Right of Rescission.** Under Regulation Z, if a consumer obtains a loan (refinancing, remodeling, equity) that is secured by a principal residence, the borrower has the right to rescind the transaction up to three business days following the loan transaction or delivery of the disclosure statement, whichever comes later. Because borrowers have the three-day rescission period, lenders usually do not release funds until the rescission period has passed.

A major exception to the right of rescission applies to a loan that is used for the purchase or initial construction of the borrower's principal residence. Consequently, there is no right of rescission in a typical residential real estate purchase.

Any lender or arranger of credit who intentionally violates the requirements of the Truth in Lending Act is subject to a fine of up to $5,000 and/or imprisonment for up to one year. However, if the lender or arranger of credit unintentionally violates the law, the lender or arranger could be liable to the borrower for actual and punitive damages equal to twice the finance charge, up to a maximum of $1,000.

**Usury Laws**

**Federal Usury Laws.** Usury is defined as the charge of an excessive rate or amount of interest. Historically, the Church of England established usury rates above which it was unconscionable to charge for a loan. When early banking regulations were established in the United States, this awareness for citizens' interests was adopted by many of the states. Some placed specific limitations on interest for real estate loans. Others allowed the rates to float freely in the marketplace, conditions that continued for decades.

Those that stipulated ceilings that were less than market rates found that they were hurting the very people whom they were trying to help. In order to make loans at low interest rates, lenders were forced to charge high placement fees and points at a loan's inception to raise the yields to acceptable levels. This placed heavy cash burdens on the borrowers. When some legislatures blocked this effort to raise yields by including front-end charges in the interest rate, the monies left those states with low usury rates to find more profitable areas for investment.

To relieve this problem, Congress passed the Deregulation Act in 1980 and the **Garn-St. Germain Bill** in 1982 that stipulated that the laws of any state limiting the rate of interest would *not* apply to loans issued for purchasing a house, condominium, cooperative apartment, or a manufactured home. These loans would have interest rates set by the market. Most states have followed the lead established by this bill and have updated their usury laws.

**California Usury Laws.** On November 6, 1979, Proposition 2 of a special statewide election passed and became effective the next day. Proposition 2 amended California's constitutional usury law and acted primarily to exempt any loan made by a real estate broker and secured by real property from any interest rate limitation. Under the California laws, the following are *exempt* from usury ceilings:

- Loans made by banks and savings associations

- Loans made by credit unions

- Loans made by personal finance companies and pawnbrokers

- Loans secured by liens on real property made by licensed real estate brokers

The current interest limits depend on the purpose of the loan. For *business* loans, the interest rate ceiling is equal to the Federal Reserve discount rate plus 5 percent. Thus, if the discount rate is 7 percent, the maximum interest that can be charged for a business loan is 12 percent.

For *consumer* loans, if the purpose is related to the purchase, construction, or improvement of real property and is to be received from anyone other than those listed above as exempt, the maximum interest rate is the same as that for business loans. However, if the loan is for something other than real estate and is received from someone other than those listed as exempt, the maximum interest that can be charged is 10 percent.

## ■ STATE FINANCING AGENCIES

Various California agencies provide financial assistance at the community level for special real estate developments. These agencies are grouped into two categories—one to assist local communities in attracting new industry and the other to improve the housing of its citizens.

**Industrial Development Agency**

Under enabling legislation from the state government, communities have organized industrial development agencies empowered to purchase and improve land for industrial and office parks. These activities are funded by revenue bonds backed by a state's bonding credit. Some funds are also raised through voluntary contributions from those citizens interested in expanding the economic base of their communities.

Community growth is the ultimate goal behind the development of industrial land. By offering preplanned industrial park sites, as well as other amenities and incentives, a community can attract new industrial activities that will offer new jobs and generally create more commercial activity in the local area, with commensurate increases in profits for businesses and tax revenues for the community. Theoretically, these additional revenues would offset much of the bond costs, although the primary sources for monies to repay the bonds would be building rentals and sales of the improved industrial sites.

**Community Redevelopment Agency (CRA)**

Authorized under the California Community Redevelopment Law, local governments may establish community redevelopment agencies (CRAs) for expansion of the supply of low-income housing. These agencies are supervised by city council members and can acquire property by eminent domain. Any building program must agree to allocate 30 percent of the rental units for low-income tenants before it can be approved. Replacement housing must be provided within or outside the redevelopment area for every person displaced by the project.

**Tax-Increment Financing.** CRA projects are funded in large part with **tax-increment financing**. This technique allocates the increased property tax revenues derived from the redevelopment to pay the debts incurred in improving the area. It requires that property taxes be frozen as of the date of the adoption of the redevelopment plan. After the debts have been satisfied, the taxes may rise to current levels, offsetting additional community costs brought about by the improvements. Tax-increment monies may be applied directly to satisfy the debts or be used as security for the sale of bonds.

**Mortgage Revenue Bonds.** Some CRA projects are financed by issuing tax-exempt mortgage revenue bonds. The proceeds are utilized to make below market interest rate loans to developers in the project area.

**Special Assessments.**   As an exception to **Proposition 13**, which passed in 1978 and limited property tax increases to 2 percent per year, the state legislature allows cities and counties the right to make special assessments on property. This provides a means to make up any shortfall in taxes that may diminish the effectiveness of tax-increment financing.

## ■ CALIFORNIA HOUSING FINANCE AGENCY (CALHFA) FORMERLY KNOWN AS CHFA

**CalHFA Programs**

Established in 1975, CalHFA was chartered as the state's affordable housing bank to make low interest rate loans through the sale of tax-exempt bonds for eligible first-time homebuyers. Periodically they also offer down payment assistance programs. A completely self-supporting state agency, bonds are repaid by revenues generated through mortgage loans, not taxpayer dollars.

CalHFA's loan requirements include:

- Be a first-time homebuyer (not having owned and occupied a home in the past three years)

- Live in a targeted area: census tracts in which 70 percent or more of the families have incomes at or below 80 percent of the state median family income or are in a Federally designated "Target Area"

- Have an annual household income within CalHFA's guidelines for the county the home is located (see Figure 6.2)

- Purchase a home within CalHFA's price limits based on family size and  county home is located (see Figure 6.3)

- Occupy the home as primary residence

- Meet credit and income requirements of the CalHFA lender and the mortgage insurer

- Citizen or other national of the United States or a qualified alien

- Complete a homebuyer education counseling course through an approved organization

**FIGURE 6.2**

## Homeownership Program Income Limits 2011 (Effective 6/30/2011)

| COUNTY NAME | EXISTING RESALE ($) | | NEW CONSTRUCTION ($) | |
|---|---|---|---|---|
| | 1 or 2 Persons | 3+ Persons | 1 or 2 Persons | 3+ Persons |
| Alameda | 110,760 | 129,220 | 110,760 | 129,220 |
| Alpine | 84,720 | 98,840 | 84,720 | 98,840 |
| Amador | 80,160 | 93,520 | 80,160 | 93,520 |
| Butte | 70,400 | 81,060 | 70,400 | 81,060 |
| Calaveras | 81,120 | 94,640 | 81,120 | 94,640 |
| Colusa | 70,400 | 80,960 | 70,400 | 80,960 |
| Contra Costa | 110,760 | 129,220 | 110,760 | 129,220 |
| Del Norte | 70,400 | 80,960 | 70,400 | 80,960 |
| El Dorado | 90,120 | 105,140 | 90,120 | 105,140 |
| Fresno | 70,400 | 80,960 | 70,400 | 80,960 |
| Glenn | 70,400 | 80,960 | 70,400 | 80,960 |
| Humboldt | 70,400 | 80,960 | 70,400 | 80,960 |
| Imperial | 70,400 | 80,960 | 70,400 | 80,960 |
| Inyo | 75,840 | 88,480 | 75,840 | 88,480 |
| Kern | 70,400 | 80,960 | 70,400 | 80,960 |
| Kings | 70,400 | 80,960 | 70,400 | 80,960 |
| Lake | 70,400 | 80,960 | 70,400 | 80,960 |
| Lassen | 72,041 | 82,847 | 72,041 | 82,847 |
| Los Angeles | 102,480 | 119,560 | 102,480 | 119,560 |
| Madera | 70,400 | 80,960 | 70,400 | 80,960 |
| Marin | 128,160 | 149,520 | 128,160 | 149,520 |
| Mariposa | 70,440 | 82,180 | 70,440 | 82,180 |
| Mendocino | 70,400 | 81,060 | 70,400 | 81,060 |
| Merced | 70,400 | 80,960 | 70,400 | 80,960 |
| Modoc | 70,400 | 80,960 | 70,400 | 80,960 |
| Mono | 85,320 | 99,540 | 85,320 | 99,540 |
| Monterey | 81,360 | 94,920 | 81,360 | 94,920 |
| Napa | 102,000 | 119,000 | 102,000 | 119,000 |
| Nevada | 85,920 | 100,240 | 85,920 | 100,240 |
| Orange | 110,760 | 129,220 | 110,760 | 129,220 |
| Placer | 90,120 | 105,140 | 90,120 | 105,140 |
| Plumas | 70,680 | 82,460 | 70,680 | 82,460 |

**FIGURE 6.2** (CONTINUED)

## Home Ownership Program Income Limits 2011 (Effective 6/30/2011)

| COUNTY NAME | EXISTING RESALE ($) | | NEW CONSTRUCTION ($) | |
|---|---|---|---|---|
| | 1 or 2 Persons | 3+ Persons | 1 or 2 Persons | 3+ Persons |
| Riverside | 78,600 | 91,700 | 78,600 | 91,700 |
| Sacramento | 90,120 | 105,140 | 90,120 | 105,140 |
| San Benito | 93,960 | 109,620 | 93,960 | 109,620 |
| San Bernardino | 78,600 | 91,700 | 78,600 | 91,700 |
| San Diego | 98,880 | 115,360 | 98,880 | 115,360 |
| San Francisco | 128,160 | 149,520 | 128,160 | 149,520 |
| San Joaquin | 78,480 | 91,560 | 78,480 | 91,560 |
| San Luis Obispo | 89,280 | 104,160 | 89,280 | 104,160 |
| San Mateo | 128,160 | 149,520 | 128,160 | 149,520 |
| Santa Barbara | 93,240 | 108,780 | 93,240 | 108,780 |
| Santa Clara | 124,320 | 145,040 | 124,320 | 145,040 |
| Santa Cruz | 120,960 | 141,120 | 120,960 | 141,120 |
| Shasta | 70,400 | 81,480 | 70,400 | 81,480 |
| Sierra | 76,680 | 88,869 | 76,680 | 88,869 |
| Siskiyou | 70,400 | 80,960 | 70,400 | 80,960 |
| Solano | 97,800 | 114,100 | 97,800 | 114,100 |
| Sonoma | 97,800 | 114,100 | 97,800 | 114,100 |
| Stanislaus | 73,320 | 85,540 | 73,320 | 85,540 |
| Sutter | 70,400 | 82,040 | 70,100 | 02,040 |
| Tehama | 70,400 | 80,960 | 70,400 | 80,960 |
| Trinity | 70,400 | 80,960 | 70,400 | 80,960 |
| Tulare | 70,400 | 80,960 | 70,400 | 80,960 |
| Tuolumne | 75,120 | 87,640 | 75,120 | 87,640 |
| Ventura | 105,720 | 123,340 | 105,720 | 123,340 |
| Yolo | 90,960 | 106,120 | 90,960 | 106,120 |
| Yuba | 70,400 | 82,040 | 70,400 | 82,040 |

**FIGURE 6.2** (CONTINUED)

## Homeownership Program Income Limits 2011 (Effective 6/30/2011)

| | USE FOR RECAPTURE/LOAN ASSUMPTIONS/TARGETED AREAS | | | |
| --- | --- | --- | --- | --- |
| | NON-TARGETED AREAS ($) | | TARGETED AREAS ($) | |
| COUNTY NAME | 1 or 2 Persons | 3+ Persons | 1 or 2 Persons | 3+ Persons |
| Alameda | 110,760 | 129,220 | 110,760 | 129,220 |
| Alpine | 84,720 | 98,840 | 84,720 | 98,840 |
| Amador | 80,160 | 93,520 | 84,480 | 98,560 |
| Butte | 70,400 | 81,060 | 84,480 | 98,560 |
| Calaveras | 81,120 | 94,640 | 84,480 | 98,560 |
| Colusa | 70,400 | 80,960 | 84,480 | 98,560 |
| Contra Costa | 110,760 | 129,220 | 110,760 | 129,220 |
| Del Norte | 70,400 | 80,960 | 84,480 | 98,560 |
| El Dorado | 90,120 | 105,140 | 90,120 | 105,140 |
| Fresno | 70,400 | 80,960 | 84,480 | 98,560 |
| Glenn | 70,400 | 80,960 | 84,480 | 98,560 |
| Humboldt | 70,400 | 80,960 | 84,480 | 98,560 |
| Imperial | 70,400 | 80,960 | 84,480 | 98,560 |
| Inyo | 75,840 | 88,480 | 84,480 | 98,560 |
| Kern | 70,400 | 80,960 | 84,480 | 98,560 |
| Kings | 70,400 | 80,960 | 84,480 | 98,560 |
| Lake | 70,400 | 80,960 | 84,480 | 98,560 |
| Lassen | 72,041 | 82,847 | 84,480 | 98,560 |
| Los Angeles | 102,480 | 119,560 | 102,480 | 119,560 |
| Madera | 70,400 | 80,960 | 84,480 | 98,560 |
| Marin | 128,160 | 149,520 | 128,160 | 149,520 |
| Mariposa | 70,440 | 82,180 | 84,480 | 98,560 |
| Mendocino | 70,400 | 81,060 | 84,480 | 98,560 |
| Merced | 70,400 | 80,960 | 84,480 | 98,560 |
| Modoc | 70,400 | 80,960 | 84,480 | 98,560 |
| Mono | 85,320 | 99,540 | 85,320 | 99,540 |
| Monterey | 81,360 | 94,920 | 84,480 | 98,560 |
| Napa | 102,000 | 119,000 | 102,000 | 119,000 |
| Nevada | 85,920 | 100,240 | 85,920 | 100,240 |
| Orange | 110,760 | 129,220 | 110,760 | 129,220 |
| Placer | 90,120 | 105,140 | 90,120 | 105,140 |
| Plumas | 70,680 | 82,460 | 84,480 | 98,560 |

**FIGURE 6.2   (CONTINUED)**

## Home Ownership Program Income Limits 2011 (Effective 6/30/2011)

| | USE FOR RECAPTURE/LOAN ASSUMPTIONS/TARGETED AREAS | | | |
|---|---|---|---|---|
| | **NON-TARGETED AREAS ($)** | | **TARGETED AREAS ($)** | |
| **COUNTY NAME** | **1 or 2 Persons** | **3+ Persons** | **1 or 2 Persons** | **3+ Persons** |
| Riverside | 78,600 | 91,700 | 84,480 | 98,560 |
| Sacramento | 90,120 | 105,140 | 90,120 | 105,140 |
| San Benito | 93,960 | 109,620 | 93,960 | 109,620 |
| San Bernardino | 78,600 | 91,700 | 84,480 | 98,560 |
| San Diego | 98,880 | 115,360 | 98,880 | 115,360 |
| San Francisco | 128,160 | 149,520 | 128,160 | 149,520 |
| San Joaquin | 78,480 | 91,560 | 84,480 | 98,560 |
| San Luis Obispo | 89,280 | 104,160 | 89,280 | 104,160 |
| San Mateo | 128,160 | 149,520 | 128,160 | 149,520 |
| Santa Barbara | 93,240 | 108,780 | 93,240 | 108,780 |
| Santa Clara | 124,320 | 145,040 | 124,320 | 145,040 |
| Santa Cruz | 120,960 | 141,120 | 120,960 | 141,120 |
| Shasta | 70,400 | 81,480 | 84,480 | 98,560 |
| Sierra | 76,680 | 88,869 | 84,480 | 98,560 |
| Siskiyou | 70,400 | 80,960 | 84,480 | 98,560 |
| Solano | 97,800 | 114,100 | 97,800 | 114,100 |
| Sonoma | 97,800 | 114,100 | 97,800 | 114,100 |
| Stanislaus | 73,320 | 85,540 | 84,480 | 98,560 |
| Sutter | 70,400 | 82,040 | 84,480 | 98,560 |
| Tehama | 70,400 | 80,960 | 84,480 | 98,560 |
| Trinity | 70,400 | 80,960 | 84,480 | 98,560 |
| Tulare | 70,400 | 80,960 | 84,480 | 98,560 |
| Tuolumne | 75,120 | 87,640 | 84,480 | 98,560 |
| Ventura | 105,720 | 123,340 | 105,720 | 123,340 |
| Yolo | 90,960 | 106,120 | 90,960 | 106,120 |
| Yuba | 70,400 | 82,040 | 84,480 | 98,560 |

**FIGURE 6.3**

## Homeownership Program Sales Price Limits (Effective 4/19/2009)

| COUNTY | EXISTING RESALE ($) | | NEW CONSTRUCTION ($) | |
|---|---|---|---|---|
| | Non-Targeted | Targeted | Non-Targeted | Targeted |
| Alameda | 637,645 | 779,344 | 637,645 | 779,344 |
| Alpine | 478,397 | None | 478,397 | None |
| Amador | 387,742 | None | 387,742 | None |
| Butte | 349,514 | 427,183 | 349,514 | 427,183 |
| Calaveras | 404,126 | None | 404,126 | None |
| Colusa | 347,329 | None | 347,329 | None |
| Contra Costa | 637,645 | 779,344 | 637,645 | 779,344 |
| Del Norte | 271,965 | None | 271,965 | None |
| El Dorado | 506,795 | None | 506,795 | None |
| Fresno | 333,130 | 407,159 | 333,130 | 407,159 |
| Glenn | 258,690 | None | 258,690 | None |
| Humboldt | 344,052 | 420,509 | 344,052 | 420,509 |
| Imperial | 283,979 | 347,086 | 283,979 | 347,086 |
| Inyo | 382,281 | None | 382,281 | None |
| Kern | 322,208 | 393,809 | 322,208 | 393,809 |
| Kings | 283,979 | 347,066 | 283,979 | 347,086 |
| Lake | 350,606 | 428,519 | 350,606 | 428,519 |
| Lassen | 258,690 | None | 258,690 | None |
| Los Angeles | 637,645 | 779,344 | 637,645 | 779,344 |
| Madera | 371,358 | 453,883 | 371,358 | 453,883 |
| Marin | 637,645 | None | 637,645 | None |
| Mariposa | 360,436 | None | 360,436 | None |
| Mendocino | 447,814 | 547,329 | 447,814 | 547,329 |
| Merced | 412,863 | 504,610 | 412,863 | 504,610 |
| Modoc | 258,690 | None | 258,690 | None |
| Mono | 504,878 | None | 504,876 | None |
| Monterey | 637,645 | 779,344 | 637,645 | 779,344 |
| Napa | 637,645 | None | 637,645 | None |
| Nevada | 491,504 | None | 491,504 | None |
| Orange | 637,645 | 779,344 | 637,645 | 779,344 |

**FIGURE 6.3   (CONTINUED)**

## Homeownership Program Sales Price Limits (Effective 4/19/2009)

| COUNTY | EXISTING RESALE ($) | | NEW CONSTRUCTION ($) | |
|---|---|---|---|---|
| | Non-Targeted | Targeted | Non-Targeted | Targeted |
| Placer | 506,795 | None | 506,795 | None |
| Plumas | 356,252 | None | 358,252 | None |
| Riverside | 436,892 | 533,979 | 436,892 | 533,979 |
| Sacramento | 506,795 | 619,416 | 506,795 | 619,416 |
| San Benito | 637,645 | None | 637,645 | None |
| San Bernardino | 436,892 | 533,979 | 436,892 | 533,979 |
| San Diego | 609,465 | 744,902 | 609,465 | 744,902 |
| San Francisco | 637,645 | 779,344 | 637,645 | 779,344 |
| San Joaquin | 427,062 | 521,965 | 427,062 | 521,965 |
| San Luis Obispo | 600,727 | 734,222 | 600,727 | 734,222 |
| San Mateo | 637,645 | None | 637,645 | None |
| Santa Barbara | 637,645 | 779,344 | 637,645 | 779,344 |
| Santa Clara | 637,645 | 779,344 | 637,645 | 779,344 |
| Santa Cruz | 637,645 | None | 637,645 | None |
| Shasta | 370,266 | 452,547 | 370,266 | 452,547 |
| Sierra | 258,690 | None | 258,690 | None |
| Siskiyou | 258,690 | 313,713 | 256,690 | 313,713 |
| Solano | 487,135 | None | 487,135 | None |
| Sonoma | 578,882 | None | 578,882 | None |
| Stanislaus | 370,266 | 452,547 | 370,266 | 452,547 |
| Sutter | 371,358 | 453,883 | 371,358 | 453,883 |
| Tehama | 273,058 | None | 273,058 | None |
| Trinity | 258,690 | 298,155 | 258,690 | 298,155 |
| Tulare | 283,979 | 347,086 | 283,979 | 347,086 |
| Tuolumne | 382,281 | None | 382,281 | None |
| Ventura | 637,645 | 779,344 | 637,645 | 779,344 |
| Yolo | 506,795 | 619,416 | 506,795 | 619,416 |
| Yuba | 371,358 | 453,883 | 371,358 | 453,883 |

On May 4, 2009, CalHFA announced it would continue programs that offer down payment assistance to first-time homebuyers and support local communities to promote affordable housing. They offer the California Homebuyer's Down Payment Assistance Program, which provides loans of up to 3 percent of a home's value to assist with down payment and/or closing costs. Conditional grants for buyers of new construction are available through the School Facility Fee Down Payment Assistance Program.

Additionally, they have made commitments to the Residential Development Loan Program, which provides local communities with funds to promote infill development for affordable, owner-occupied housing.

CalHFA does not lend money directly to consumers. CalHFA works through and uses approved private lenders to qualify consumers and to make all mortgage loans. CalHFA then purchases closed loans that meet CalHFA's requirements. The fees consumers pay could be different depending on the lender and the program.

For more information, visit *www.CalHFA.ca.gov*.

**City of Los Angeles Home Mortgage Program**

Los Angeles's Single-Family Home Mortgage Revenue Bond Program provides mortgage loans to low-income and moderate-income first-time homebuyers who wish to purchase from selected new homes and condominiums.

To qualify, the annual income of a household cannot exceed $46,900 for one or two people or $56,280 for three or more people. Qualified persons who have not owned a home within the last three years are eligible.

Buyers must deposit at least 3.5 percent as a down payment and agree to occupy the home for at least two years. Loans may be assumed by new buyers with certain limitations related to income and price restrictions.

**The Housing Financial Discrimination Act of 1977 (Holden Act)**

The goals of the Holden Act are to offset the illegal practice of **redlining**, which is the marking of certain neighborhoods as undesirable for making loans, and to ensure the adequate supply of financing for safe and decent housing for creditworthy buyers in low-income areas of California.

The Holden Act prohibits lending discrimination on the basis of race, color, religion, sex, marital status, national origin, or ancestry. Financial assistance cannot be denied because of ethic composition, conditions, characteristics, or expected trends in the neighborhood surrounding the subject property. The act encourages increased lending in areas where, in the past, financing has been unavailable.

## ■ CALIFORNIA PUBLIC EMPLOYEES' RETIREMENT SYSTEM (CALPERS)

CalPERS provides retirement and health benefits to California public employees, public agency employers, retirees, and their families. It also offers a Member Home Loan Program, which includes both adjustable and fixed-rate loans as well as special loan programs. For more information, visit *www.calpers.ca.gov.*

## ■ SUMMARY

This chapter examined the federal agencies involved with agricultural financing, HUD, and federal legislation that protects borrowers in a real estate financing transaction. In addition, industrial development and community redevelopment agencies were described.

The Farm Credit System serves the credit needs of farmers, ranchers, rural homeowners, cooperatives, and rural water systems. The Farm Credit Banks make direct real estate loans through their various affiliated associations with funds provided by the Farm Credit Funding Corporation and Farmer Mac through their secondary market operations.

The USDA Rural Development Program provides funds to reverse the downward spiral of rural job losses and outmigration. In addition, they make loans to farmers and ranchers unable to secure credit from other sources.

The Department of Housing and Urban Development (HUD) also participates actively in real estate finance. HUD regulates interstate land sales and finances and promotes the various urban renewal, rehabilitation, open-space, and model-city programs. Among its other socially oriented housing activities are public housing programs, cooperative housing for low-income persons, mortgage interest subsidies, relocation aid, disaster area construction, and isolated area housing.

Legislation involved in financing real estate includes: the federal Equal Credit Opportunity Act (ECOA), which prohibits lenders from discriminating against credit applicants on the basis of race, color, religion, national origin, sex, marital status, age, or dependency on public assistance; the Community Reinvestment Act, which requires all federally regulated financial institutions to expand their responsibilities to meet the needs of all citizens of a community; the Truth in Lending Act (Regulation Z), which requires information on the costs of financing be imparted to the borrowers prior to their executing a loan; and the Real Estate Settlement Procedures Act (RESPA), which is designed to provide buyers and sellers with the estimated costs of closing a real estate transaction before closing to avoid any last-minute shocks.

Finally, California has established financing agencies to aid both in the industrial development of various communities and in providing the means for enhancing the housing requirements of their citizens. These agencies usually use bond issues to raise funds for their programs, many of which are repaid through tax increments.

## ■ INTERNET RESOURCES

California Housing Finance Agency   *www.calhfa.ca.gov*

Department of Housing and Urban Development   *www.hud.gov*

Fannie Mae   *www.fanniemae.com*

Farm Credit Administration   *www.farmcredit.com*

Farm Credit System Insurance Corporation   *www.fcsic.gov*

Federal Agricultural Mortgage Corporation   *www.farmermac.com*

Freddie Mac   *www.freddiemac.com*

Ginnie Mae   *www.ginniemae.gov*

U.S. Department of Agriculture   *www.usda.gov*

# ■ REVIEW QUESTIONS

1. Financing for farms and ranches depends on all of the following categories *EXCEPT*

    a. productivity of the land.

    b. management skills.

    c. environmental restrictions.

    d. climactic conditions.

2. The Farm Credit System includes all of the following participants *EXCEPT* the

    a. Federal Credit Banks.

    b. Federal Reserve Banks.

    c. Production Credit Associations.

    d. Farmers Home Administration.

3. The City of Los Angeles Mortgage Program provides mortgage loans for

    a. industrial redevelopment.

    b. eligible first-time homebuyers.

    c. slum clearance.

    d. low-rent housing.

4. The California Housing Finance Agency provides loans for all of the following purposes *EXCEPT*

    a. low-rent apartment projects.

    b. refinancing term loans.

    c. first-time homebuyers.

    d. down payment assistance.

5. HUD has direct responsibility for all of the following categories *EXCEPT*

    a. GNMA.

    b. FHA.

    c. interstate land sales.

    d. zoning regulations.

6. ECOA is a

    a. special form of title policy.

    b. state financing agency.

    c. state environmental agency.

    d. law prohibiting discrimination in lending.

7. The federal Truth in Lending Act (Regulation Z)

    a. prohibits discrimination in lending.

    b. establishes maximum interest rates.

    c. provides borrowers with a comparative percentage rate.

    d. prohibits bank redlining.

8. RESPA is designed to

    a. eliminate discrimination in lending.

    b. establish maximum interest rates.

    c. fund Cal-Vet loans.

    d. provide borrowers with closing cost information.

9. The Holden Act prohibits discrimination in lending on the basis of all the following reasons *EXCEPT*

    a. existing neighborhood conditions.

    b. national origin.

    c. financial ability.

    d. neighborhood ethnic composition.

10. Under California usury laws, loans made by all of the following participants are exempt from usury ceilings *EXCEPT*

   a. banks.

   b. credit unions.

   c. pawnbrokers.

   d. individuals.

## ■ EXERCISES

1. Secure a report on a land sale that took place in a subdivision under the jurisdiction of HUD's Interstate Land Sales Act. Review it for access, utilities, underlying liens and their relationship to the buyer's finance contract and subdivision restrictions, if any.

2. Find a government subsidized low-rent housing project in your community. Is it compatible with surrounding developments, or has it lowered neighborhood property values?

# CHAPTER SEVEN

# JUNIOR LOANS IN REAL ESTATE FINANCE

## ■ KEY TERMS

| | | |
|---|---|---|
| carryback | junior loans | senior loan |
| cross-defaulting clause | lifting clause | yield |
| equity loans | piggy-back loans | |

When special problems or needs arise in the financing of real estate, junior financial instruments are often used as part of the solution. The senior loan forms can also be used for junior loans. Generally, when a mortgage or deed of trust is used as a second encumbrance, the loan involves a higher risk.

To distinguish between senior and junior loans: first trust deeds are typically made in larger amounts than junior liens, and first trust deeds usually carry lower interest rates than subordinate financing due to lower risk in the event of a default. However, there are no litmus tests to determine whether or not a loan is a first or junior lien. The only thing that definitely sets the liens apart are the time and date of recording and in the event the two liens are recorded simultaneously, the document with the lowest sequential number at the county has priority.

Under normal conditions, most real estate sales are finalized when a buyer secures a new first deed of trust from a financial fiduciary to cover the major portion of a property's purchase price. The balance, if any, is usually paid in cash as a down payment. Frequently, however, a buyer who has insufficient cash for the entire amount of the required down payment will make an offer to purchase a property based upon the condition that the seller **carryback** a portion of the sale price in the form of a junior encumbrance. A seller might be asked to accept a purchase-money second mortgage or deed of trust (trust deed) for the amount needed to complete the transaction.

Thrifts and commercial banks sometimes participate as junior financiers in an effort to enhance their earnings. They offer combinations of first and second mortgages, known as **piggy-back loans**, to allow the borrower to avoid paying mortgage insurance premiums. Examples of these programs are: 80/10/10; 75/15/10; and 80/20; with the first mortgage remaining at 80 percent or less, a second mortgage of 10 percent or 15 percent and the remainder as a down payment.

In addition, mortgage brokers, mortgage bankers, and various small loan companies operating on direct lines of credit from commercial banks will arrange junior loans. Some companies buy and sell these so-called second securities on a regular basis. This activity has diminished substantially in the current market.

In addition to commercial and residential properties, junior financing often provides funds for land developers to pay for offsite improvements such as streets, sidewalks, sewers, and other utility installations. A lender would advance the funds necessary for these improvements and accept a lien on all of the property involved. Such a lien would usually be in second priority position behind a developer's purchase-money loan, which had been given as part of the purchase price of the land in its raw form. Once the land was subdivided, improved, built upon, and sold, the underlying first lien and the junior lien for improvements would be replaced by individual conventional or guaranteed loans executed by the buyers of the buildings constructed on the developed land.

There are also third deeds of trust in California. An example of a third-position loan would be one that wraps around existing first and second loans (see Chapter 8 on wraparounds).

## ■ ANATOMY OF A SECOND MORTGAGE/DEED OF TRUST

As its name implies, a second mortgage or deed of trust is a lien on real property that is second or junior in position behind an existing first lien. Just as a senior loan requires the execution of a note specifying the terms and conditions of the promise to pay, so also does the junior loan form call for such a promissory note. The property that is described as collateral for the junior loan will be the same property that is pledged as collateral for the existing senior loan.

Because the second mortgage is in a subordinate position, the junior lienholder is in a relatively high-risk position. If the senior encumbrance is not paid according to its terms and conditions, the senior lienholder may foreclose on the collateral property and sell it in order to recover as much of the outstanding senior debt as possible. This foreclosure process could effectively eliminate the junior lienholder's position in the subject property without commensurate compensation. After costs, the proceeds from the sale would be allocated to the senior lienholder first, and then to the junior lienholders, according to their priority positions. If the property did not sell for a price sufficient to satisfy the senior lender, there would be no funds left to distribute to the junior lienholder(s).

In the event of a default, a senior lender, knowing of the existence of a junior lien, will usually give the junior lender a chance to step in and make the delinquent payments. Then the junior lender will foreclose against the collateral property. But the primary lender must be protected and will pursue any legal means available to maintain the value of the investment.

**Clauses**

Certain provisions can be incorporated into a junior lending instrument to protect the junior lienholder's position against that of the senior lender. A clause can be included that grants the junior lender the right to pay property taxes, insurance premiums, and similar charges for a borrower who is not making these payments. These charges can then be added to the total debt in anticipation of foreclosure. Another clause can allow the junior lender to pay into escrow the funds for taxes and insurance and make any delinquent senior loan payments to offset any possible default. The junior lender can also reserve the right to cure any default on the senior loan. Another junior loan provision includes the requirement of a borrower's personal guarantee to be liable for any possible deficiencies in case of a default and subsequent foreclosure. Still another prohibits the junior borrower from amending the terms of the existing first loan without the written permission of the junior lender. Some junior loans include a **lifting clause** that allows a borrower to replace a senior loan without disturbing the status of the junior loan, but the amount of the new senior loan cannot exceed the specific amount of the original senior loan outstanding at the time the second loan was established. Finally, if a **cross-defaulting clause** is included in the junior loan provisions, a default on the senior loan will automatically trigger a default on the junior loan.

## Junior Loan Risks

Higher risks are involved in the use of junior financing than with senior financing. The greater the risk, the greater the possibility of being unable to secure the full balance of both the first and second loans at a public sale in the event of a foreclosure. Although the senior lender is generally protected by a reasonable cash down payment, or by some insurance or guarantee, the junior lender is usually self-insured. The second lender is generally financing the difference between the amount of the first loan, the borrower's down payment, and the property's sale price. In other words, a junior loan helps to fulfill the down payment requirement to a first loan, and the second lender assumes the full risk for the *top portion* of a collateral property's value.

Although junior financing is sometimes employed after high down payments, it is most often utilized in low down payment transactions. Occasionally, after the expiration of some agreed-upon time period, usually five years, a borrower will merge a junior loan with an existing senior loan by increasing the senior loan by an amount sufficient to satisfy the balance of the junior loan.

**Junior Loan Interest Rates and Usury**

It would appear that interest rates would be high on loans that are in a high risk position, such as second and third. In many instances this is correct. The high interest rates offset, to some degree, the possibility of losses due to defaults. Although junior loans secured from mortgage brokers and bankers, institutional lenders and small loan companies usually do carry relatively high interest rates, it is interesting to observe that junior carryback loans issued by sellers intent on completing the sales of their properties often include interest rates that are at or below market rates.

This phenomenon stems from the different motivations of these various lenders. On one hand, those that are in the lending business seek to maximize their profits by charging as much interest as the law and the borrower will accept. Other persons are trying to sell their properties, especially when prices are high, and are often forced to carry back junior financing at low interest rates in order to actually complete a sale. Their goal is the sale of the property, not the yield on the loan.

As a practical matter, there can never be an effective legal limitation on the amount of interest that can be charged on a loan. If the law stipulates a specific maximum interest rate, a lender can circumvent it by charging points or by raising the principal amount to reach a desired effective **yield**. Thus, a charge of four points on a $100,000 loan will result in the borrower's receiving only $96,000 in actual proceeds, raising the effective yield on a ten-year loan about a half percent. The alternative is to add the $4,000 to the loan's balance, creating the same effect.

## ■ HOME EQUITY LOANS

Primed by the Tax Reform Act of 1986, which eliminated interest deductions on consumer finance but allowed them on home loans, junior financing is being used with greater frequency by owners who have accumulated measurable equity in their property. This equity, acquired through a paydown of the first mortgage balance or through an inflationary rise in a property's value, or both, is being pledged as collateral to secure funds over short-term periods of up to five years. When these **equity loans** become due, the borrowers invariably refinance the entire property to secure a new first trust deed adequate to pay all liens in full.

Many lenders actively solicit for home equity loans. The relatively short-term quality of these loans affords the lenders the opportunity to control the interest rates and periodically check the value of the collateral and the credit of the borrowers. The modern day equity loan is a throwback to the real estate finance of the 1930s when five-year rollover loans were the norm.

Some equity lenders offer lower-than-market interest rates. The borrowers should be aware that these lower rates may prevail for only a short period of time before the contract specifies their rise to market or even higher rates. Some lenders offer to waive the first month's interest charge while others offer different incentives to encourage borrowers to make these loans. Some of these incentives include zero placement or origination fees, or guaranteed renewals, but at adjusted interest rates and fast processing to provide instant cash.

Home equity loans face significant defaults when the economy slows. Particularly at risk are the high yield loans amounting to more than 100 percent of the value of the collateral. Interest on these loans is well above standard rates. Because most of these loans are pooled into residential-backed mortgage securities, the risks are being spread to a wide group of investors.

Owners also pledge their equity to secure funds for home improvements. Improvement loans are somewhat safer than other types of junior financing because they are secured not only by the equity pledged but also by the enhanced value of the improved property. Therefore, improvement loans may have longer terms of repayment than other forms of junior finance—some for as long as 20 years.

Responding to changing economic conditions, many homeowners improve their properties rather than re-enter the housing market. Freddie Mac has a program for the purchase of secured home improvement loans, allowing lenders to leverage into additional business.

## ■ SUMMARY

When a prospective buyer does not have enough cash to satisfy the down payment required in a purchase of real property, a second mortgage or a second deed of trust may be carried back by the seller to finance the difference. Owners who have developed equity in their property also use junior mortgages, pledging their equity as collateral for new loans for home improvements or personal needs.

A second or third mortgage or trust deed is junior in priority to an existing senior loan issued by a financial fiduciary. Being in second position, a junior financier anticipates certain risks and charges appropriate interest rates to offset these risks. However, economic conditions limit the amount of interest that can be charged on loans between individuals.

## ■ REVIEW QUESTIONS

1. All of the following encumbrances are considered junior loans *EXCEPT* a(n)

    a.  equity loan.

    b.  wraparound contract for deed.

    c.  second mortgage.

    d.  note and first deed of trust.

2. The use of junior finance through owner carrybacks increases when

    a.  market interest rates are high.

    b.  money is readily available.

    c.  the realty cycle is up.

    d.  market interest rates are low.

3. Junior finance is often utilized for all of the following *EXCEPT*

    a.  land improvements.           c.  DVA-guaranteed loans.

    b.  home improvements.          d.  low down payment purchases.

4. In the event of a default of the priority senior loan, a junior lender can usually do all of the following *EXCEPT*

    a.  pay the senior loan balance in full.

    b.  bid at the foreclosure sale.

    c.  foreclose against the junior borrower.

    d.  change the terms of the junior loan.

5. Creating a junior loan at the same time as a senior loan is known as

    a.  predatory lending.           c.  refinancing.

    b.  piggy-back lending.         d.  subordination.

6. When traded in the market, junior loans are usually sold at

   a. par.

   b. a premium.

   c. a discount.

   d. face value.

7. Lenders may increase their yields on real estate loans by using all of the following techniques *EXCEPT*

   a. raising the interest rate.

   b. decreasing the loan term.

   c. charging origination fees.

   d. adding a discount amount to the principal owed.

8. Interest rates on junior loans carried back by *home sellers* are usually

   a. equal to or lower than market rates.

   b. higher than market rates.

   c. variable over the life of the loan.

   d. fixed at 10 percent by the usury laws.

9. Interest rates on real estate loans are established by

   a. the Federal Reserve.

   b. the State of California.

   c. agreement between the lender and borrower.

   d. the lender.

10. A cross-defaulting clause in a junior loan

   a. automatically triggers a default on the junior loan.

   b. voids a senior loan foreclosure.

   c. cancels the junior loan.

   d. cancels the senior loan foreclosure.

## ■ EXERCISES

1.  In many urban areas of California where property prices are high, the use of junior finance is probably the only way real estate can be sold. Interview a mortgage loan broker to discover how properties are financed in your neighborhood.

2.  Problem: The buyers can just afford to make the payments on the existing first and second encumbrances on the house they wish to buy. They do not have enough money to cash the seller out. Help them engineer a financing plan that may enable them to purchase the house.

**CHAPTER EIGHT**

# LOAN TERMS AND NOTE PAYMENTS

■ **KEY TERMS**

| | | |
|---|---|---|
| adjusted book basis | credit loan | package mortgage |
| amortization | draws | purchase-money mort- |
| balloon payment | exchange | gage |
| blanket mortgage | hard-money mortgage | recognition clause |
| blends | installment sale | reverse annuity mort- |
| boot | Internal Revenue | gage (RAM) |
| bridge loan | Code Section 1031 | right of first refusal |
| completion bond | leasehold mortgages | sale-leaseback |
| condominium | lease-option | security agreements |
| construction mortgage | manufactured home | stop date |
| construction/perma- | loans | term loan |
| nent loan | mortgage participation | two-step mortgage |
| convertible loan | open-end mortgage | wraparound encum- |
| cooperative | option to buy | brance |

Real estate loans can be as flexible and adaptable as needed to satisfy market demands. Contemporary financing techniques offer an opportunity to

provide for most contingencies by varying one or more of the three basic characteristics of a real estate loan—the principal amount, the interest rate, and the payment schedule. Each loan lends itself to a number of variations, limited only by the imaginations of those involved. This chapter examines the alternative lending techniques once thought innovative that today are accepted as standard.

## ■ INTEREST

From a borrower's point of view, *interest* can be described as *rent paid for the use of money*. A lender views interest as *money received or earned from a loan investment*. Thus, just as rent is paid and received for the use of an apartment, house, office, or store under the special conditions of a lease, real estate finance can be considered the process by which interest and principal are paid and received under the terms and conditions of a loan agreement. Money is borrowed (leased) at a certain interest rate (rent) for a specified time period during which the amount borrowed is repaid.

The amount of rent that a landlord can charge for the use of property depends on the rental market for that particular type of real estate. Similarly, the rate of interest that a lender can charge depends on the money market as it affects that particular type of loan. A rational borrower will not pay a lender more interest than the lowest interest rate available on a specific loan at a particular time.

**Simple Interest**

Most real estate loans are established at a simple rate of interest. *Simple interest* is *rent* that is paid only for the amount of principal still owed. When money is repaid to the lender, rent for that money stops.
The formula for computing simple interest is:

$$I = PRT$$

where:

$I$ = interest,
$P$ = principal,
$R$ = rate,
$T$ = time

■ **EXAMPLE** Using this formula, the interest on a $1,000 loan to be repaid in one year at 8 percent is $80.

$$I = PRT$$
$$I = \$1,000 \times 0.08 \times 1$$
$$I = \$80$$

This simple interest formula is incorporated into the following types of repayment plans.

## Term Loan

Also known as a straight loan or bullet loan, a **term loan** requires payments of interest only with the entire principal being repaid at a specified time, called the **stop date**. The loan is then paid in full with a **balloon payment** of the principal plus any interest still owed.

■ **EXAMPLE** Consider a term loan of $10,000 at 8 percent per annum, payable interest only monthly, to be paid in full in three years.

| | |
|---|---:|
| Loan Amount | $10,000 |
| Interest Rate | × .08 |
| Annual Interest | 800 |
| Pro Rata Months | ÷ 12 |
| Monthly Interest Payment | 66.66 |
| Final Principal Payment | 10,000 |
| Balloon Payment | $10,066.66 |

## Amortization

The most common payment format for a real estate loan is a system of regular payments made over a specified period. These payments include portions for both principal and interest, the process is called **amortization**. Amortization tables are available that have the level monthly payments precalculated when the loan is established under a fixed rate of interest (see Figure 8.1).

**FIGURE 8.1**

**Monthly Payment Required to Amortize a $1,000 Loan**

| Years | 5% | 5.5% | 6% | 6.5% | 7% | 7.5% | 8% |
|---|---|---|---|---|---|---|---|
| 5 | 18.88 | 19.11 | 19.34 | 19.57 | 19.81 | 20.04 | 20.28 |
| 10 | 10.61 | 10.86 | 11.11 | 11.36 | 11.62 | 11.88 | 12.14 |
| 15 | 7.91 | 8.18 | 8.44 | 8.72 | 8.99 | 9.28 | 9.56 |
| 25 | 5.85 | 6.15 | 6.45 | 6.76 | 7.07 | 7.39 | 7.72 |
| 30 | 5.37 | 5.68 | 6.00 | 6.33 | 6.66 | 7.00 | 7.34 |

*To compute the monthly principal and interest, multiply the number of thousands in the loan by the appropriate factor.*

■ **EXAMPLE**  Consider a loan of $90,000 at 7 percent for 30 years. The monthly payment of principal and interest is $599.40.

| | |
|---|---|
| Number of Thousands | 90 |
| Payment Factor (Figure 8.1) | × 6.66 |
| Monthly Payment P&I | $599.40 |

Note that there may be a few pennies difference in various amortization tables due to rounding.

## Distribution of Principal and Interest

Intrinsic in the amortization design is the distribution of the level payments into proportionate amounts of principal and interest.

■ **EXAMPLE**  Consider the $90,000 loan at 7 percent interest for 30 years with a monthly principal and interest payment of $599.40.

| Payment No. | Balance | Interest | Principal |
|---|---|---|---|
| 1 | $90,000.00 | $525.00 | $74.40 |
| 2 | 89,925.60 | 524.57 | 74.83 |
| 3 | 89,850.77 | 524.13 | 75.27 |
| 4 | 89,775.50 | 523.69 | 75.71 |
| 5 | 89,699.79 | 523.25 | 76.15 |
| etc. to 360 | | | |

The schedule in the example can be extended for the full period of 360 months to show the complete distribution of principal and interest and the remaining balance of the loan at any time. These amortization schedules can be prepared on computer printouts and are often presented by lenders to borrowers so they can follow the progress of their payments. (See Chapter 15.)

# ■ VARIATIONS IN PAYMENTS AND INTEREST RATES

In a fixed-rate mortgage instrument two basic characteristics do *not* change throughout the life of the loan: the interest rate and the repayment term. In addition to the principal and interest, the lender often collects monthly amounts needed to pay annual taxes and insurance. These amounts, referred to as *impound funds* or *escrow funds*, are determined by dividing the total amounts due each year by 12. Although the principal plus interest payment remains constant over the life of the loan, the amount needed to pay the taxes and insurance may vary, resulting in a change in the total monthly payment. The accrued interest due on the loan is always paid first, with the balance of the payment allocated to principal, taxes, and insurance accordingly. The result of this payment format is that the borrower begins to build equity with the first monthly payment.

Traditionally most loans are fairly standard in their payment schedules, requiring a certain sum to be paid at regular intervals over a prescribed time period. However, some real estate loans are designed to vary the required payments and interest to reflect more accurately the financial capabilities of a borrower, as well as the current state of the economy.

These alternative mortgage instruments allow a lender's return to keep pace with prevailing interest rates while simultaneously providing a borrower the opportunity to qualify for larger mortgage amounts.

**Graduated-Payment Mortgage (GPM)**

A graduated-payment mortgage is designed with lower payments in the early years of a loan. These payments increase gradually until they are sufficient to amortize the loan fully. Thus, buyers are able to obtain home loans with affordable payments while the lenders earn the desired interest rate over the loan term. A GPM may specify less-than-interest-only early payments. This results in *negative amortization* or *deferred interest*, and the principal amount owed increases over time by the amount of the deficiency. As the monthly payments are increased each year, however, the situation is reversed and the loan is amortized.

**Adjustable-Rate Mortgage (ARM)**

In an adjustable-rate mortgage (ARM) the interest rate is adjusted in accordance with a prearranged index. The ARM usually includes an annual interest rate cap to protect the borrower from volatile interest rate fluctuations. In addition, there usually is an overall interest rate cap over the entire term of the loan.

Fannie Mae continually revises its ARM plans. These plans are designed to give the consumer the protective features they desire. Consider the following when selecting an adjustable-rate or variable-rate mortgage.

**Adjustment Periods.**   This indicates the frequency of interest rate adjustments with concomitant payments. For example, the interest of a one-year ARM will change every year, while the interest of a three-year ARM will change every three years.

**Initial Rate.**   Sometimes called the *teaser rate*, it will always be below the market rate in order to attract borrowers to this type of loan.

**Note Rate.**   The note rate or the calculated rate is the adjusted rate, index plus margin, imposed from time to time at the adjustment period.

**Qualifying Rate.**   Because ARM interest rates fluctuate from time to time, the rate at which to qualify a borrower often creates problems. If the initial loan rate is low but is expected to increase in the near future, the borrower may not be able to make the higher payments. Freddie Mac has an underwriting rule concerning the method by which borrowers can qualify for an ARM. Those with a less than 20 percent down payment must qualify at the maximum second-year rate. However, all interest rate adjustments on the loan will be made from the initial loan rate.

Borrowers should be cautious about incentives offered by some lenders. Lenders sometimes advertise below-market rates for a limited time period. At the end of the initial period, the interest rate is automatically increased. For example, an initial rate of 5 percent results in monthly payments of $429.46 on an $80,000, 30-year loan, but payments will increase to $702.06 at 10 percent.

**Index.**   The index is the starting point to adjust a borrower's applicable interest rate. Lenders must use an index that is readily available to the borrower but beyond the control of the lender. Some indexes are more volatile than others. Those most frequently used are:

- the six-month, three-year, and five-year Treasury rates;

- the Eleventh District Federal Home Loan Bank cost of funds;

- the national average contract interest rate on conventional home loans;

- the national median cost of funds to federally insured savings institutions;

- the new CD-ARMs by Fannie Mae tied to the average certificate of deposit interest rate; and

- the London Interbank (LIBOR) interest rates.

**Margin.**   Each lender adds a certain margin percentage amount to the index at every adjustment period to derive the new rate. Individual lenders set different margins based on their estimated expenses and profit goals. Fannie Mae's interest rate adjustments for its ARMs fall between 1.5 and 3 percent, depending on the market. Thus, an initial rate of 6 percent will increase to 9 percent with an index adjustment of 1 percent and a margin of 2 percent.

**Interest Rate Caps.**   Most variable rate loans include an *annual cap* applied to the adjusted interest rate. This cap limits interest rate increases or decreases over a stated period of time and varies from lender to lender and ranges from 1 to 2 percentage points per year. Some lenders also include a *life-of-the-loan* interest cap ranging up to 6 percent. This combination of caps provides the borrower protection against debilitating payment increases.

**Payment Caps.**   Some lenders will use annual payment caps instead of interest rate caps. The most common payment cap is 7.5 percent of the initial payment. This is equivalent to 1 percent change in the interest rate. This means a payment of $750 per month, principal and interest, could not vary up or down more than $56.25 per month in one year's time. These payment caps are also combined with life-of-the-loan caps in some plans.

Most variable-rate loans do not need to include a prepayment penalty. Without this penalty, a borrower can more easily refinance to a fixed-rate mortgage. Some lenders also include a **convertible loan** feature that allows a variable-rate loan to be changed to a fixed-rate loan after the initial adjustment periods have been completed. A copy of the Fannie Mae adjustable-rate note appears in Figure 8.2.

All ARM originations from federally insured lending institutions must comply with disclosure regulations. Under an amendment to Regulation Z, the borrower must receive:

- a descriptive ARM brochure;

- details of the specific loan program; and

- an illustrative example, based on a $10,000 loan, showing how the payments and loan balance have been affected by historical changes in the index.

## ■ INNOVATIVE PAYMENT PLANS

In addition to varying the payments and interest in a real estate loan, alternative types of loans can be arranged to satisfy the borrower's specific needs. Following are a few popular alternative loan plans.

**The 15-Year Mortgage**

The 15-year mortgage has become very popular. It constitutes about 33 percent of Freddie Mac's loan portfolio. The attraction of this relatively short-term real estate loan is the amount of interest that can be saved when compared with a 30-year loan. The major inhibiting quality of the 15-year loan is the higher amount required for monthly principal and interest.

**Reverse Annuity Mortgage (RAM)**

This plan is based on a borrower's ability to capitalize on accumulated equity and is designed to enhance the income of the elderly. Many senior

**FIGURE 8.2**

**Adjustable-Rate Note**

**FIXED / ADJUSTABLE RATE NOTE**

(30 Year Fannie Mae Index -- Rate Caps)

**THIS NOTE PROVIDES FOR ONE CHANGE IN MY INTEREST RATE AND MY MONTHLY PAYMENT.  THIS NOTE LIMITS THE AMOUNT MY INTEREST RATE CAN CHANGE AND THE MAXIMUM RATE I MUST PAY.**

_____    _____    _____
[Date]                          [City]                        [State]

_____
[Property Address]

**1. BORROWER'S PROMISE TO PAY**

In return for a loan that I have received, I promise to pay U.S. $_____(this amount is called "principal"), plus interest, to the order of the Lender. The Lender is _____.    I understand that the Lender may transfer this Note. The Lender or anyone who takes this Note by transfer and who is entitled to receive payments under this Note is called the "Note Holder."

**2. INTEREST**

Interest will be charged on unpaid principal until the full amount of principal has been paid. I will pay interest at a yearly rate of _____ %. The interest rate I will pay will change in accordance with Section 4 of this Note.  The interest rate required by this Section 2 and Section 4 of this Note is the rate I will pay both before and after any default described in Section 7(B) of this Note.

**3. PAYMENTS**

(A) Time and Place of Payments

I will pay principal and interest by making a payment every month.

I will make my monthly payment on the _____day of each month beginning on _____ I will make these payments every month until I have paid all of the principal and interest and any other charges described below that I may owe under this Note. Each monthly payment will be applied as of its scheduled due date and will be applied to interest before principal. If, on _____ , I still owe amounts under this Note, I will pay those amounts in full on that date, which is called the "maturity date."

I will make my monthly payments at _____
_____or at a different place if required by the Note Holder.

(B) Amount of My Initial Monthly Payments

Each of my initial monthly payments will be in the amount of U.S. $_____ . This amount may change.

(C) Monthly Payment Change

Change in my monthly payment will reflect changes in the unpaid principal of my loan and in the interest rate that I must pay. The Note Holder will determine my new interest rate and the changed amount of my monthly payment in accordance with Section 4 of this Note.

**4. INTEREST RATE AND MONTHLY PAYMENT CHANGE**

(A) Change Dates

The initial fixed interest rate I will pay may change on _____which is called the "Change Date."

(B) The Index

At the Change Date, my interest rate will be based on an Index.  The "Index" is Fannie Mae's posted yield on 30 year mortgage commitments (priced at Par) for delivery within 30 days for standard conventional fixed-rate mortgages as published in the money section of the _Wall Street Journal_.  The Index figure published in the Wednesday edition 42 to 48 days before the Change Date is called the "Current Index".

If the Index is no longer available, the Note Holder will choose a new index which is based upon comparable information.  The Note Holder will give me notice of this choice.

(C) Calculation of Changes

Before the Change Date, the Note Holder will calculate my new interest rate by adding _____ (%) to the Current Index. The Note Holder will then round the result of this addition up to the next one-eighth of one percentage point (0.125%). Subject to the limits stated in Section 4(D) below, this rounded amount will be my new interest rate until the Maturity Date.

The Note Holder will then determine the amount of the monthly payment that would be sufficient to repay the unpaid principal that I am expected to owe at the Change Date in full on the maturity date at my new interest rate in substantially equal payments. The result of this calculation will be the new amount of my monthly payment.

(D) Limit on Interest Rate Change

The interest rate I am required to pay at the Change Date will not be greater than _____ %.

(E) Effective Date of Changes

My new interest rate will become effective on the Change Date. I will pay the amount of my new monthly payment beginning on the first monthly payment date after the Change Date.

(F) Notice of Change

The Note Holder will deliver or mail to me a notice of any change in my interest rate and the amount of my monthly payment before the effective date of any change. The notice will include information required by law to be given me and also the title and telephone number of a person who will answer any question I may have regarding the notice.

**5. BORROWER'S RIGHT TO PREPAY**

I have the right to make payments of Principal at any time before they are due. A payment of Principal only is known as a "Prepayment". When I make a Prepayment, I will tell the Note Holder in writing that I am doing so. I may not designate a payment as a Prepayment if I have not made all the monthly payments due under the Note.

I may make a full Prepayment or partial Prepayments without paying a Prepayment charge. The Note Holder will use my Prepayments to reduce the amount of Principal that I owe under this Note. However, the Note Holder may apply my Prepayment to the accrued and unpaid interest on the Prepayment amount, before applying my Prepayment to reduce the Principal amount of the Note. If I make a partial Prepayment, there will be no changes in the due date or in the amount of my monthly payment unless the Note Holder agrees in writing to those changes.

MULTISTATE FIXED/ADJUSTABLE RATE NOTE

**FIGURE 8.2** **(CONTINUED)**
## Adjustable-Rate Note

**6. LOAN CHARGES**

If a law, which applies to this loan and which sets maximum loan charges, is finally interpreted so that the interest or other loan charges collected or to be collected in connection with this loan exceed the permitted limits, then: (i) any such loan charge shall be reduced by the amount necessary to reduce the charge to the permitted limit; and (ii) any sums already collected from me which exceeded permitted limits will be refunded to me. The Note Holder may choose to make this refund by reducing the principal I owe under this Note or by making a direct payment to me. If a refund reduces principal, the reduction will be treated as a partial prepayment.

**7. BORROWER'S FAILURE TO PAY AS REQUIRED**

**(A) Late Charge for Overdue Payments**

If the Note Holder has not received the full amount of any monthly payment by the end of 15 calendar days after the date it is due, I will pay a late charge to the Note Holder. The amount of the charge will be 5% of my overdue payment of principal and interest. I will pay this late charge promptly but only once on each late payment.

**(B) Default**

If I do not pay the full amount of each monthly payment on the date it is due, I will be in default.

**(C) Notice of Default**

If I am in default, the Note Holder may send me a written notice telling me that if I do not pay the overdue amount by a certain date, the Note Holder may require me to pay immediately the full amount of principal which has not been paid and all the interest that I owe on that amount. That date must be at least 30 days after the date on which the notice is mailed to me or delivered by other means.

**(D) No Waiver By Note Holder**

Even if, at a time when I am in default, the Note Holder does not require me to pay immediately in full as described above, the Note Holder will still have the right to do so if I am in default at a later time.

**(E) Payment of Note Holder's Costs and Expenses**

If the Note Holder has required me to pay immediately in full as described above, the Note Holder will have the right to be paid back by me for all of its costs and expenses in enforcing this Note to the extent not prohibited by applicable law. Those expenses include, for example, reasonable attorneys' fees.

**8. GIVING OF NOTICES**

Unless applicable law requires a different method, any notice that must be given to me under this Note will be given by delivering it or by mailing it by first class mail to me at the Property Address above or at a different address if I give the Note Holder a notice of my different address.

Any notice that must be given to the Note Holder under this Note will be given by delivering it or by mailing it by first class mail to the Note Holder at the address stated in Section 3(A) above or at a different address if I am given a notice of that different address.

**9. OBLIGATIONS OF PERSONS UNDER THIS NOTE**

If more than one person signs this Note, each person is fully and personally obligated to keep all of the promises made in this Note, including the promise to pay the full amount owed. Any person who is a guarantor, surety or endorser of this Note is also obligated to do these things. Any person who takes over these obligations, including the obligations of a guarantor, surety or endorser of this Note, is also obligated to keep all of the promises made in this Note. The Note Holder may enforce its rights under this Note against each person individually or against all of us together. This means that any one of us may be required to pay all of the amounts owed under this Note.

**10. WAIVERS**

I and any other person who has obligations under this Note waive the rights of presentment and notice of dishonor. "Presentment" means the right to require the Note Holder to demand payment of amounts due. "Notice of dishonor" means the right to require the Note Holder to give notice to other persons that amounts due have not been paid.

**11. UNIFORM SECURED NOTE**

This Note is a uniform instrument with limited variations in some jurisdictions. In addition to the protections given to the Note Holder under this Note, a Mortgage, Deed of Trust or Security Deed (the "Security Instrument"), dated the same date as this Note, protects the Note Holder from possible losses which might result if I do not keep the promises which I make in this Note. That Security Instrument describes how and under what conditions I may be required to make immediate payment in full of all amounts I owe under this Note. Some of those conditions are described as follows:

**Transfer of the Property or a Beneficial Interest in Borrower.**

If all or any part of the Property or any Interest in the Property is sold or transferred (or if Borrower is not a natural person and a beneficial interest in Borrower is sold or transferred) without Lender's prior written consent, Lender may require immediate payment in full of all sums secured by this Security Instrument. However, this option shall not be exercised by Lender if such exercise is prohibited by federal law.

If Lender exercises the option to require immediate payment in full, Lender shall give Borrower notice of acceleration. The notice shall provide a period of not less than 30 days from the date the notice is given in accordance with Section 15 within which Borrower must pay all sums secured by this Security Instrument. If Borrower fails to pay these sums prior to the expiration of this period, Lender may invoke any remedies permitted by this Security Instrument without further notice or demand on Borrower.

_[Sign Original Only]_

citizens own their homes free and clear but often face the problem that their incomes are fixed and relatively low. Thus, the **reverse annuity mortgage (RAM)** allows them to utilize their equities, with the *lender* paying the *borrower* a fixed annuity.

The property is pledged as collateral to a lender, who may provide funds to the borrower in one of the following three ways:

1. Regular monthly checks to the borrower until a stipulated balance has been achieved with no cash payment of interest involved. The increase in the loan balance each month represents the cash advanced, plus interest on the outstanding balance.

2. An initial lump-sum payment.

3. A line of credit on which checks may be drawn. When the maximum loan amount is reached, the borrower is obligated to start repayment. In some cases this requires the sale of the property.

Under the HUD reverse mortgage program, known as the Home Equity Conversion Mortgage (HECM), the monthly payments continue for as long as the borrowers live in the home with no repayment required until the property is sold. Any remaining value is distributed to the homeowners or their survivors. If there is any shortfall, HUD pays the lender. The size of the reverse mortgage loan is determined by several factors: the age of the borrower (must be at least 62); the interest rate; and the value of the property. There are no asset or income limitations on the HUD RAM.

HUD will insure loans taken out by owners 62 years of age or older and offers three mortgage plans:

1. A tenure mortgage, under which the lender makes monthly payments as long as the owner occupies the residence

2. A term mortgage, under which the payments are made for a specific number of years

3. A line-of-credit mortgage, under which the owner can draw against the credit as long as the cumulative draws plus accrued interest are less than the principal loan limit

For example, consider Sam and Sarah Jones who are both in their late 70s. They have lived in their home for 35 years and paid off the original mortgage loan many years ago. Unfortunately, Sam's health has been deteriorating over the past two years and he is no longer able to tend his rather extensive garden. The garden not only provided Sam with a great deal of pleasure but it provided an extra source of income during the spring and summer months. Sarah has been famous for years for her scrumptious baked goods. During the long winter months she filled the house with the smells of her breads and muffins, which she delivered to local restaurants in exchange for cash to supplement their Social Security checks.

Although Sam's condition does not require him to be hospitalized, he cannot work in the garden anymore, nor can he deliver Sarah's baked goods to the restaurants. In fact, Sarah finds that with the additional care Sam needs, she really does not have the time (or the energy) to spend long hours in the kitchen baking. The loss of this additional income has made it very difficult for the Joneses. They realize, sadly, they will probably have to sell their home of 35 years and move into a small apartment. Is there a better solution for Sam and Sarah?

Fortunately, Sam noticed an article in the *AARP Modern Maturity* magazine about the benefits of a reverse annuity mortgage (RAM). He contacted a local lender and learned that under this plan, the Joneses will be able to secure a mortgage on the house where the bank sends them a check every month. The loan will be repaid when the property is eventually sold, the Joneses will have enough cash to meet their monthly expenses, and—most important—Sam and Sarah can stay in the home they love!

**Fannie Mae Senior Housing Opportunities Program**

Fannie Mae has a special program available to Americans 62 years old or older that offers four financing options:

1. An accessory apartment, which is a private living unit in a single-family home, allowing independence and privacy with an assurance of help nearby

2. A cottage housing opportunity, which is a separate, self-contained unit built on the lot of an existing home, generally the home of a relative, offering privacy and proximity

3. Home sharing within a single-family home converted into up to four living units according to Fannie Mae standards

4. A **sale-leaseback** arrangement allowing a senior the opportunity to sell the home to an investor, perhaps a member of the family, and then lease it back

To qualify, a regular salary is not essential, but income from part-time work, pensions, Social Security, interest, dividends, and other sources must be sufficient to meet Fannie Mae's usual requirements. The monthly mortgage payments must not exceed 28 percent of the borrower's monthly gross income and the borrower's total debt, including monthly payments, may not exceed 36 percent of the gross income.

**Fannie Mae's Two-Step Mortgage Plan**

Fannie Mae, in its continual efforts to introduce new products to enhance its activities, has available a **two-step mortgage**, a hybrid between a fixed-rate and an adjustable-rate loan. The two-step requires a 10 percent down payment and offers interest rates at least three-eighths of 1 percent lower than the market rates for a 30-year fixed-rate loan. The lower rate remains in effect for seven years and is then adjusted automatically *once* for the balance of the loan period. The new rate is based on the ten-year Treasury bond rate but has a maximum 6 percent cap. No additional fees are charged when the two-step is converted.

# ■ VARIATIONS IN FORMATS

The deed of trust, note and mortgage, and contract for deed are flexible and therefore adaptable to many situations by using creative design. Almost every realty financing contingency can be solved to the satisfaction of all the participants. Not only can specific terms and conditions be designed to meet particular requirements, but special forms of these three lending instruments can also be developed to finance unique real estate situations.

**Open-End Mortgage**

An **open-end mortgage**, also known as a *mortgage for future advances*, allows a borrower to secure additional funds from a lender under terms specified in the original mortgage. Thus, an open-end mortgagee can advance funds to a mortgagor on an existing mortgage—funds that, in many instances, represent the principal already paid by the borrower. This allows a mortgage to stay alive for a longer period of time and can in some cases save the borrower the time and much of the expense of refinancing. The funds advanced by this process are repaid by either extending the term of the mortgage loan or increasing the monthly payments by the amount appropriate to maintain the original amortization schedule. The interest rate can also be adjusted accordingly, and appropriate fees can be charged.

Open-end mortgages have become useful financial tools for single-family home loans. Mortgagors are allowed to borrow funds for personal property purchases made after the original loan is recorded. These amounts are added to the principal owed, and the payments are increased to accommodate the new balance. If the personal property becomes part of the loan's collateral, along with the real property, the open-end mortgage is converted into a package mortgage, which will be described later in this chapter.

Open-end mortgages are often used by farmers to raise funds to meet their seasonal operating expenses. Similarly, builders use the open-end mortgage for their construction loans in which advances are made periodically while the building is being completed. In addition, many private loan companies are offering customers an opportunity to draw down on a line of credit backed by the collateral of their home equity.

A basic legal problem associated with open-end financing is one of securing future advances under an already existing debt instrument and, at the same time, preserving its priority against any possible intervening liens. In most states an obligatory future advance under the terms of an existing mortgage is interpreted as having priority over intervening liens. For example, an advance made under a construction mortgage that sets forth a specific pattern of draws is interpreted to have priority over a construction (mechanic's) lien that may have been filed in the period prior to the last advance.

On the other hand, nonobligatory future advances do not have priority over intervening liens, according to most state laws. In other words, the legal security of the advances to be made in the future under an already existing mortgage may not be enforceable against debts incurred by a borrower in the intervening time period.

If the terms of a mortgage do not obligate a mortgagee to make *specific* future advances, the mortgagee is well advised to protect the priority of the lien by searching the record for intervening liens prior to making any advances. Prevailing practice does not require a title search, but merely binds a mortgagee to any liens of which there has been outside notice. A few states require a title search and actually reduce the mortgagee to a junior position against any recorded intervening liens. A search of the records can only be to the advantage of the original mortgagee.

In addition, under the laws of those states that have adopted the Uniform Commercial Code, any personal property **security agreements** for the purchase of goods that become fixtures on the collateral property have a priority lien over future advances made under an original mortgage. Suppose a homeowner signs a financing contract with the ABC Appliance Company to purchase and install a central air-conditioning system in June, and the agreement is recorded. In December the owners secure an advance on their open-end mortgage to build an addition to their home. Because the central air-conditioning system is now a fixture, the appliance company's lien will take priority over any future advances made by the original mortgagee.

Not all states allow open-end mortgages. Texas, for example, does not allow open-end mortgages or lines of credit loans for residential properties under their Home Equity Loan Legislation.

**Construction Mortgage**   A **construction mortgage**, also called an *interim financing agreement*, is a unique form of open-end mortgage. It is a loan to finance the costs of labor and materials as they are used during the course of constructing a new building. An interim mortgage usually covers the period from the commencement of a project until the loan is replaced by a more permanent form of financing at the completion of construction. This financial format is unique because the building pledged as part of the collateral for the loan is *not in existence* at the time that the mortgage is created. The value of the land is the only available collateral at the loan's inception, a condition that requires the lender to seek some form of extra protection.

The procedure for protecting the lender is both logical and practical. Although the full amount to be loaned is committed at the start of construction, the funds are distributed in installments as the building progresses, not as a lump sum in advance. The outstanding loan balance is matched to the value of the collateral as it grows.

**Application and Requirements.**  To obtain a construction loan, the borrower submits plans and specifications for a building to be constructed on a specific site to a loan officer for analysis. Based on the total value of the land and the building to be constructed thereon, a lender will make a commitment for a construction loan, usually at the rate of 75 percent of the property's total value.

Hence a $250,000 project would be eligible for a $187,500 construction loan. This amount normally would be adequate to cover most, if not all, of the costs of construction, with the $62,500, or 25 percent equity, representing the value of the free and clear lot. Construction mortgages usually are secured from financial institutions that normally require that the lot be lien-free in order to preserve the first priority position of the construction loan. In a case where the lot is encumbered by an existing mortgage or lease, the mortgagee or the landlord must subordinate that interest to the lien of the construction mortgage before the loan can be granted.

Construction loans are available for projects of all sizes, from the smallest home to the largest shopping center, and the basic loan format is similar in each case. The charges imposed for securing a construction loan are usually based on a one-time 1 percent placement fee paid at the loan's inception, plus interest at about two points above the prime rate charged to AAA-rated borrowers. Thus, based on a prime rate of 6 percent and a 2 percent overcharge, a $187,500 construction loan would be placed for a front-end fee of $1,875 plus 8 percent interest on the funds disbursed from time to time. Interest rates and placement fees fluctuate as a function of business cycles, borrowers' credit ratings, and individual situations.

**Pattern of Disbursements.**   Disbursement of funds under a construction loan usually follows either of two basic patterns. A construction loan may be designed to include a schedule for disbursing funds in a series of **draws** as construction progresses. In a five-stage plan, an interim financier distributes 20 percent of the funds each time the building reaches another one-fifth of completion.

In the $187,500 example, $37,500 is distributed to the builder when the first stage is accomplished, with subsequent $37,500 draws until completion, when the final draw is paid. This final $37,500 might be withheld pending the full payment of all labor and materials as evidenced by lien waivers from each of the contractors and subcontractors of the job, receipt of a *certificate of completion and approval for occupancy* issued by a building inspector, or expiration of the statutory time to file a construction lien.

Interest is charged on these monies only after they are disbursed following each inspection of the work's progress. Careful records are kept of the interest as it begins from each disbursement date, and the accumulated interest charges and the entire construction loan principal are paid in full within some relatively short period of time after the completion of the project. Usually a construction loan is replaced by a permanent, long-term senior encumbrance for which the builder has arranged in advance.

Another pattern of disbursement under a construction loan requires the borrower to submit all bills for subcontracted labor and materials to the lender, who then pays these bills and charges the loan account accordingly. This plan gives the lender greater control over the possibility of intervening construction liens.

The pattern of disbursement, in the form of either draws to the builder or direct payments from the lender, effectively matches the value of the collateral to the amount of the loan outstanding at a particular time. If there is a default at any point during construction, the lender can foreclose and recover the collateral in its unfinished condition. It can then be sold *as is* or completed to recover the investment.

**Lender Protection.**   There are no insurance plans for guaranteeing the payments on construction loans. As additional protection, many construction financiers insist their borrowers-builders secure a **completion bond** from an insurance company, naming the lender as the primary beneficiary. The bond is drawn in the amount of the total construction cost and is exercised only if the builder is unable to complete the construction. Under this circumstance the lender can step in and use the bond proceeds to pursue the completion and subsequent sale of the property to recover the interim loan funds. Often small building companies cannot qualify for bonding and must pledge other assets as additional collateral for a construction loan.

Construction loans are drawn for relatively short time periods—six months to a year for a house and up to three years for larger projects. The interim lender needs to be paid in full at the end of these periods and is vitally concerned with making provisions *in advance* for the security and satisfaction of the construction loan. The borrower is equally concerned with this payback and is eager to be relieved of the heavy interest burden imposed during the construction period. Therefore, provisions for a permanent, long-term mortgage are made prior to the origination of the construction loan, to satisfy or *take out* the interim financier at the completion of construction.

In most cases the standby commitment for a takeout permanent loan will be exercised after the construction is completed to the satisfaction of this final lender. The builder must submit a set of plans and specifications to the long-term lender. When the application is approved, a written agreement of the standby commitment is delivered to the interim financier, enabling the construction loan to be placed. The interim lender can then rely on being paid in full at the expiration of the contract.

**Sources of Funds.** The relatively short-term nature of construction loans closely matches the investment profile of commercial banks, which take an active role in this form of financing. However, some fiduciaries that generally deal in long-term loans also participate in interim financing. For example, some lenders will provide money for construction and then simply convert these interim mortgages to permanent mortgages for eligible borrowers. In other words, these lenders have created an in-house loan package, called a **construction/permanent loan.**

While construction loans are tailored to the investment needs of commercial banks, permanent long-term takeout loans match the investment designs of thrift institutions and life insurance companies. Thus, all types of investment groups can participate in the various stages of construction financing.

An expedient way to orchestrate the activities of these various participants is through the services of a mortgage banking company, which often has all of these various lenders as investors. A developer can have a mortgage banker process the entire construction procedure in a "one-stop loan shop."

## Blanket Mortgage

Depending on the terms of a specific transaction, a lender may require a borrower to pledge *more than one* parcel of property as collateral to back up a mortgage. The debt instrument used in this situation is called a **blanket mortgage** and can take any of the financing forms discussed previously. On occasion the federal government secures a *blanket lien* against all of the properties of a person who has failed to pay income tax. When the properties encumbered by a blanket mortgage or federal blanket lien are located in more than one county, the debt instrument must be reproduced and recorded at the courthouse in each county where a subject property is located.

## Release Clauses

When two or more properties are pledged as collateral for one loan, it is often necessary to provide some means for relinquishing an individual parcel as payments are made. Such a tool is called a *release clause*. In exchange for some action, such as a designated amount of repayment, a specific property or portion of a property can be freed from the lien of a blanket mortgage.

Blanket mortgages are often used to purchase large tracts of land for development, and a release clause usually is incorporated into these financing instruments. The absence of a release clause requires the payment in full of the entire balance due before any portion of the land can be sold lien free. The alternative is to sell a portion of the land *without* satisfying the underlying blanket mortgage or contract for deed. This latter technique could create many difficulties for the buyer of a small parcel. If the payments on the underlying encumbrance are not made on time by the developer, the small parcel owner may be wiped out in a foreclosure. Unfortunately, some land promotion developments in this country were designed on this non-release basis, with concurrent losses to individual buyers.

**Recognition Clause.**   Most responsible land developers secure a special **recognition clause** from their underlying financiers that protects individual small-parcel owners. This clause specifies that, in the event of a default and a resultant foreclosure, the underlying financier will recognize and protect the rights of each individual lot owner. Many states require not only full disclosure of the physical attributes of the land involved in such a development but also a description of all financing terms. These state disclosure laws closely parallel those of the federal government for interstate land sale promotions.

## Leasehold Mortgage

*Tenants* are able to pledge their leasehold interests as collateral for **leasehold mortgages**. Some of these mortgages are eligible for FHA and VA insurance and guarantees, and national banks have been authorized to make such loans provided that the lease term extends for a sufficient interval after the expiration of the leasehold mortgage. For instance, the VA guarantees leasehold loans that will be repaid 15 years prior to the expiration of the ground lease, and the FHA insures leasehold mortgages issued on 99-year leases.

The major sources of funds for leasehold mortgages are life insurance companies, mutual savings banks, and commercial banks. Any lender must be in first priority lien position so that full title to the collateral property may be secured in the event of a default. Thus a leasehold mortgage arrangement usually includes the *landlord's pledge* of the legal fee in the property as well as the *tenant's pledge* of the improvements as collateral for the loan. The landlord's pledge of the fee simple legal rights in the land is called *subordination*.

As a consequence, if a loan default occurs that necessitates a foreclosure action, a lender will be protected by having the legal right to recover both the land and the building. Most leasehold mortgages are designed to include both land and buildings as collateral, requiring the landlord's subordination of the legal fee to the new lien.

**Credit Loans.**   There are some rare exceptions to the landlord's pledging the land or subordinating the legal fee to the lender. Such exceptions involve tenant-developers whose credit is strong enough to make consideration of the collateral's value almost incidental to the loan transaction. If a company such as Target or J.C. Penney wants to secure financing to construct stores or warehouses, it could obtain any needed funds simply through its signature alone and the pledge of the leasehold interests if the company was building on leased land. The landowner would not be required to participate in such a financial arrangement. This form of finance, in which a mortgage is issued strictly on the financial strength of a borrower without much regard for the value of the collateral, is called a **credit loan**.

## Package Mortgage

Often real estate purchases include items of personal property in the transaction. Generally expensive items of personal property are encumbered by a security agreement. The security agreement format involves filing a financing statement with the secretary of state in which the personal property purchase takes place. Some local filing may also be required at a county recorder's office for special types of collateral, such as farm equipment or crops. Subsequent filings must also be made properly at the place or places of the original filing to provide proper notice on a continuing basis. Such documents could include statements of continuation, termination, release, assignment, and amendment. A financing statement is effective for a specified period of time, usually five years, and must be renewed if necessary, or it will automatically lapse.

When personal property is included with the sale of real estate, however, it is possible to use a single financing instrument. This form of financing is called a **package mortgage**. It includes as collateral not only the real estate but certain fixtures attached to the property and/or other items of personal property described in the mortgage document. Most installations, such as heating units, plumbing fixtures, and central air systems, when attached to the real estate become real property and are automatically included under the lien. However, other fixtures not normally considered real property, such as ranges, ovens, refrigerators, freezers, dishwashers, carpets, and draperies, may be included in a home purchase financing agreement to attract buyers. This inclusion will enable homebuyers to stretch the payments for these items over the entire term of the mortgage, as opposed to the shorter term of a consumer installment loan.

The use of the package mortgage is increasing in popularity throughout the United States because it offers the added attraction to the buyer of not making separate cash down payments for these items. Moreover, having the payments for these purchases lowered substantially from the relatively high interest rate structure of the usual short-term personal property financing pattern is another attraction. An additional incentive to use the package loan is that the interest on a home loan is tax deductible whereas the interest on a consumer loan is not. Many commercial rental properties, including condominiums, apartment rentals, office buildings, and clinics, are specifically designed to include package financing.

**Manufactured Home Mortgages**

HUD reports that manufactured and mobile homes account for over one-third of all new single-family homes. There are about 7.2 million such homes with an average price exceeding $50,000, according to the Manufactured Housing Institute, an industry trade group.

Fannie Mae has expressed concern about rising loan delinquencies and foreclosures in this area of real estate and has required a minimum down payment of 10 percent for 30-year loans on such homes, plus an upfront fee of one-half of 1 percent of the loan amount. They also offer a 20-year loan with 5 percent down at higher monthly payments.

The problem in describing the unique quality of a loan for a manufactured home is in the definition of the collateral. Is a manufactured home real property or personal property? This definition determines the type of finance instrument necessary.

There is little doubt that a travel trailer attached by a hitch to an automobile or set onto the bed of a pickup truck or a van-type travel home is clearly identifiable as personal property. They pose no problem of definition and are financed by a personal property debt instrument. However, some difficulty arises in classifying trailers that are larger than travel units but also attach easily to a hitch and are parked temporarily at rental trailer parks. These smaller mobile homes are also generally financed as personal property.

More pertinent to real estate finance are the larger homes manufactured as factory-built housing units. Many are legally transportable only by professional home movers. These units are permanently attached to lots in rental parks that cater to long-term tenancies or are installed on property purchased by the owner of the manufactured home. When long-term leases are involved or a manufactured home owner has title to the lot on which the unit is permanently affixed, real estate financing is possible.

All forms of financial instruments are applicable to a manufactured home and its lot, but the repayment terms of these encumbrances would sometimes be for a shorter period of time than for other forms of real estate. Although the quality of the construction of most manufactured homes is increasingly more durable, the lending institutions are still reluctant to place long-term loans on this type of collateral. The depreciation on manufactured homes is severe in the first years of their lives, and, as a result, **manufactured home loans** are usually established for a 15-year period, as compared to conventional home loans of up to 30 years' duration. Nevertheless, some of the larger units are being financed for up to 20 years. Many of these loans are eligible for FHA or DVA financing.

## Purchase-Money Mortgage

A **purchase-money mortgage** is created when a seller carries back a portion or all of the sales price as a loan to a buyer. A purchase-money mortgage can be either a senior or junior lien on the property.

## Hard-Money Mortgage (Equity Mortgage)

Unlike a mortgage given to finance a specific real estate *sale*, a **hard-money mortgage** is one given by a borrower in exchange for actual money received, *cash out*. A first mortgage executed in exchange for cash funds is described as a hard-money mortgage. Frequently a hard-money mortgage will take the form of a junior loan given to a private mortgage company in exchange for cash needed by the borrower to purchase an item of personal property or solve some personal financial crisis. The borrower usually will pledge the equity in the property as collateral for this hard-money mortgage.

## Bridge Loan

A **bridge loan** is an equity loan designed to serve a specific purpose, usually for a relatively short period of time. For example, owners of one property wishing to purchase another might seek a short-term bridge loan on their equity to raise enough funds to close the purchase. This loan will be satisfied when the old property is sold or at a specified time, whichever came first. The bridge loan is usually an interest-only junior term loan, requiring a balloon payment at its conclusion. (For example, consider a $100,00 junior loan payable monthly at 7 percent interest-only, due in full in three years.)

**Wraparound Encumbrance (Wrap)**

A **wraparound encumbrance**, also known as an *all-inclusive encumbrance*, is a special instrument created as a junior financing tool that encompasses an existing debt. Adopting any of the three basic financing forms, these encumbrances are used in circumstances where existing financing cannot be prepaid easily due to a lock-in clause or a high prepayment penalty. They are also used where the low interest rate on the existing mortgage allows a lender to secure a higher yield by making a wrap loan.

■ **EXAMPLE**  The sale of a $100,000 property with a $10,000 cash down payment and an assumable first mortgage balance of $70,000 can be financed by a seller who would carry back a new wraparound loan for $90,000. This wraparound would require the purchaser-mortgagor to make payments on the $90,000, while the seller-wraparound-mortgagee would retain responsibility for making the required payments on the undisturbed existing $70,000 first mortgage.

The use of the wrap has diminished dramatically as most of the existing real estate loans cannot be easily assumed. Nevertheless, some individuals still use this type of financing to sell their properties. Lenders also use the wrap to enhance their yields. For example, some lenders offer their borrowers an opportunity to secure additional funds on the equities in their properties at less-than-market interest rates by arranging to wrap the existing loans at a one-point or two-point override. These loans are also known in some areas as **blends.**

**Mortgage Participation**

There are three types of **mortgage participation**. One is a partnership among several mortgagees, a second includes the teaming of several mortgagors, and a third establishes a partnership between a mortgagee and a mortgagor.

**Partnership of Mortgagees.**   In the first type of mortgage participation, more than one mortgagee is the owner of the instrument designed to finance a real estate project. It is used in large project financing. Several mortgagees join together, each advancing a proportionate share of the monies required and receiving a commensurate share of the mortgage payments.

The format of the Ginnie Mae mortgage pooling operation is in contrast to a simple partnership involving two or more mortgagees in a single mortgage. Many individual investors, large and small, may purchase shares in a designated group, or pool, of mortgages, and Ginnie Mae guarantees the repayment of principal and interest on these shares. Here we see that mortgage-backed securities are in reality a form of mortgage participation.

In addition to the private partnerships among several mortgagees on a single loan and the Ginnie Mae mortgage-backed securities program, real estate mortgage trusts (REMTs) also offer opportunities for mortgage partnerships. Trusts are formed where investors purchase beneficial shares under special terms. Using the pool of monies acquired by the sale of these beneficial interests, mortgage trust managers invest in real estate mortgages and distribute the profits according to a prearranged formula. The private ownership quality of REMTs allows them to invest in high-risk loans such as junior loans or construction financing. Sometimes, as a result of adverse financial conditions, REMTs are inadvertently converted to REITs (real estate investment trusts) when they foreclose on their delinquent mortgagors and end up *owning* the properties they financed.

**Partnership of Mortgagors.**   The second type of mortgage participation involves several mortgagors sharing responsibility for a single mortgage on a multifamily property, called a cooperative.

A cooperative vests ownership in a corporation that issues stock to all purchasers, giving them the right to lease a unit from "their" corporation. This *proprietary lease* is drawn subject to the rules and restrictions established by the corporation, and management is in the hands of a board of directors elected by the stockholders. The major weakness of the cooperative form of mortgage participation is that each cooperative participant is dependent on the other owners to prevent a default of the mortgage. A financially irresponsible tenant or units that remain unsold for long periods create a financial strain on the remaining tenants who are still liable for making the total mortgage payments.

The **condominium** has replaced the cooperative in most states. The condominium is designed to have each unit owner pay cash or get an individual mortgage loan eliminating any reliance on other owners in the condominium project.

**Partnership of Mortgagees and Mortgagors.**   The third type of participation, called a *participation mortgage*, is engendered when a mortgagee becomes a partner in the ownership of a project on which a loan will be placed. When a developer requests a commitment for a participation mortgage on a substantial commercial real estate project, a lender may accept a higher loan-to-value ratio, lower the interest rate, or make other concessions in return for a percentage of the project's ownership as a condition for issuing the loan commitment. These mortgagee ownerships range from 5 to 50 percent or more and simultaneously make the lender a partner in the development as well as its financier.

## ■ TAX-DEFERRED MORTGAGE LENDING

In addition to the variations in mortgage payment formats discussed to this point, there are special aspects of real estate that can be served through creative finance.

**Installment Sales**

A special financing tool designed to postpone capital gains income taxes on properties that do *not* qualify for special exemptions available under the income tax laws is called an **installment sale** plan.

A gain on an installment sale is computed in the same manner as is the net capital gain on a cash sale: gross sales price minus costs of sale minus **adjusted book basis** equals net capital gain. However, under an installment sale the seller can elect either to pay the total tax due in the year of the sale or to spread the tax obligation over the length of the installment contract.

The installment sale provision in the tax law was originally intended as a relief provision for owners who could sell their property only by agreeing to accept payments in installments. Such a seller might receive less cash in the year of the sale than the tax required on the total gain. The law allows tax payments to be made as installment payments are received.

Sellers soon realized that under a progressive tax system the total tax could well be less if paid in installments, because much of the gain could be paid later when the seller would be in a lower tax bracket and also because of the time value of money. Thus, an installment sale became a desirable end in itself.

■ **EXAMPLE** Consider a property that is sold for $100,000 net. The buyer pays $40,000 cash and assumes an existing loan balance of $60,000. The adjusted book basis on the date of the sale is $80,000. Given these facts, a cash transaction would result in a 28-percent-bracket taxpayer paying $5,600 tax on this property in the year of the sale ($100,000 – $80,000 = $20,000 capital gain × 0.28 = $5,600).

An installment sale can be designed to postpone portions of the seller's tax liability. For instance, the sale can be structured to require $8,000 as a cash down payment and $32,000 as a junior loan back to the seller. The buyer then assumes the $60,000 existing loan. The installment contract is payable in four equal annual principal payments plus interest at an agreed rate.

Computation of the seller's tax liability under the installment contract first requires a determination of the *installment factor* (gain divided by equity) to identify what portion is return of the equity buildup.

■ **EXAMPLE** In this case, the seller's gain is $20,000 ($100,000 - $80,000) while the equity is $40,000 ($100,000 - $60,000). Therefore, the installment factor is 50 percent ($20,000 gain ÷ $40,000 equity = 0.50).

The seller's annual tax liability is $1,120 ($8,000 × 0.50 = $4,000 × 0.28 = $1,120), for a total of $5,600 over five years ($1,120 × 5 = $5,600). This is exactly the same total tax that would be paid if the property were sold for cash. The installment treatment allows the seller to pay this sum over the term of the contract as the principal is received. All interest received by the seller is declared as portfolio income. The computations are as follows:

| | | | |
|---|---|---|---|
| Sale Price | $100,000 | Sale Price | $100,000 |
| Down Payment | - 8,000 | Adjusted Basis | - 80,000 |
| | 92,000 | Capital Gain | 20,000 |
| Second Mortgage | - 60,000 | Sale Price | 100,000 |
| First Mortgage | 32,000 | First Mortgage | - 60,000 |
| | | Equity | 40,000 |

Taxes (28 Percent Bracket) Sale Year:

| | | |
|---|---|---|
| $8,000 × 0.50 = | $4,000 | Gain ÷ Equity = $\frac{20,000}{40,000}$ = 0.50 |
| $4,000 × 0.28 = | 1,120 | |

Years 2 Through 5:

| | |
|---|---|
| $4,000 × 0.28 × 4 = | 4,480 |
| Total Tax | $5,600 |

The installment plan allows a seller to pay tax in amounts proportionate to the gain collected each year. A seller whose tax bracket *decreases* over the term of an installment contract will pay *less* tax than if he had elected to pay the full tax in the year of the sale. This arrangement is particularly advantageous to a seller nearing retirement age who will enter a lower tax bracket during the term of the installment contract. On the other hand, there is the possibility that a seller's tax bracket could rise over the installment term, which would lead to the payment of *more* tax. Consequently, a seller is allowed to pay the full amount of tax due on a capital gain whenever it becomes expedient during the installment contract period.

## Option to Buy

An **option to buy** gives the buyer, also known as the optionee, the absolute right (but not the obligation) to acquire certain real estate during the option period, provided the option payments are kept current.

## Lease with Option to Buy

A variation of the option to buy is a **lease-option** to buy. In this case, the buyer agrees to purchase the property at a price negotiated within the lease. Often, a portion of the rent is applied to the purchase price as an incentive for closing the transaction. It is rare for these agreements to be completed as written. More often, new negotiations are entered into at the time of the lease expiration, primarily as a result of changing economic circumstances. Contemporary lease-options include a **right-of-first-refusal** clause instead of an outright option. Here, the price is not fixed at the outset; market conditions dictate the final value to be accepted by both parties.

**Exchanges**

Another method often employed to postpone tax on capital gains is the property **exchange** technique. **Internal Revenue Code Section 1031** provides for the recognition of gain to be postponed under the following conditions:

- Properties to be exchanged must be held for productive use in a trade or business or for investment.

- Properties to be exchanged must be of like kind to each other; that is, their nature or character must be similar. *Like kind* is only limited to another income-producing property. A rental condo could be exchanged for a delicatessen, a rental town house could be exchanged for a gas station or marina. One property may be exchanged for several properties; it is not limited to one.

- Properties must actually be exchanged.

Property held for productive use in a trade or business may include machinery, automobiles, factories, and rental apartments. Property held for investment may include vacant land and antiques. Like kind includes a machine for a machine or real estate for real estate. Improvements on the land are considered to be differences in the *quality* of the real estate, not in the type. Thus, a vacant lot can be exchanged for a store property. Often unlike property, called **boot**, is included in an exchange and must be accounted for separately.

There are at least six basic mathematical computations involved in the exchange process:

1. Balancing the equities

2. Deriving realized gains

3. Deriving recognized gains

4. Determining tax impacts

5. Reestablishing book basis

6. Allocation of new basis

These computations are illustrated by the two-party exchange recorded in Figure 8.3.

It is rare to make a straight two-party exchange. More frequently, there are three-party exchanges or more, as well as *delayed* (Starker) exchanges requiring definite time limits, 45 days to select and 180 days to settle.

Generally, the investor who is trading up benefits by not being required to pay taxes, while the downside exchanger is taxed on gains. A prudent investment program provides for trading up during an investor's acquisition years and trading down after retirement, when tax brackets are lower.

## ■ SUMMARY

The scope of activities in the real estate finance market is broadened by many modern variations on loans. Variable-rate mortgage loans (VRMs) and variable-payment-plan loans, such as a graduated-payment mortgage (GPM), allow lenders and borrowers to tailor specific interest and payment variations to meet their needs.

Under a reverse annuity mortgage (RAM) a borrower, usually a senior citizen, pledges a property as collateral and secures monthly payments from the lender until a maximum amount has been reached. Then the loan must be repaid. A convertible loan allows a borrower to switch from an adjustable-rate loan to a fixed-rate loan to offset fears of an unaffordable high payment.

An open-end mortgage is designed to allow for future advances under terms specified in the original contract. The construction mortgage is the most commonly used open-end form.

A construction loan is designed to finance the cost of labor and materials during the course of constructing a building. It matches the amount of money loaned to the growing value of the collateral building. A system of

**FIGURE 8.3**

**Two-Party Exchange**

**Step 1. Balancing Equities**

| Property A | | Property B |
|---|---|---|
| $100,000 | exchange price | $150,000 |
| – 60,000 | existing mortgage | – 80,000 |
| 40,000 | owner's equity | $70,000 |
| + 30,000 | cash required | |
| $70,000 | | |

**Step 2. Deriving Realized Gain**

| | | |
|---|---|---|
| $100,000 | exchange price | $150,000 |
| – 70,000 | adjusted basis | – 90,000 |
| $30,000 | realized gain | $60,000 |

**Step 3. Deriving Recognized Gain**

(Recognized gain equals the sum of unlike properties.)

| | | |
|---|---|---|
| –0– | cash received | $30,000 |
| –0– | boot | –0– |
| –0– | mortgage relief | + 20,000 |
| –0– | recognized gain | $50,000 |

**Step 4. Determining Tax Impact**

(Taxable income is the realized gain or the recognized gain whichever is *less*.)

| | | |
|---|---|---|
| $30,000 | realized gain | $150,000 |
| –0– | recognized gain | 50,000 |
| –0– | taxable gain | $50,000 |

(Note: B will pay income tax on $50,000. A will pay no tax.)

**Step 5. Reestablishing Book Basis**

| | A | B |
|---|---|---|
| Old Basis | $70,000 | $90,000 |
| New Mortgage | 80,000 | 60,000 |
| Cash and Boot Paid | 30,000 | –0– |
| Recognized Gain | + –0– | + 50,000 |
| Total: | $180,000 | $200,000 |
| Less | | |
| Old Mortgage | $60,000 | $80,000 |
| Cash and Boot Received | + –0– | + 30,000 |
| Total: | $60,000 | $110,000 |
| New Basis | $120,000 | $90,000 |

**Step 6. Allocating New Basis**

Each party will decide which portions of the new basis to allocate to land and to improvements in order to establish new depreciation schedules.

draws is scheduled, with the builder collecting proportionate sums from the lender during the various stages of construction.

Blanket mortgages include more than one property as collateral. Release clauses are incorporated into the format to allow portions of the collateral to be released as needed. One type of partnership financing establishes ownership between two or more mortgagees in a single mortgage. Another involves several mortgagors sharing the responsibility for a single mortgage, such as in a cooperative apartment structure. Participation finance is created when a mortgagee acts as financier and receives part ownership at the same time. Leasehold mortgages include the pledging of a tenant's leasehold interest in a property in exchange for financing the improvements to be built thereon.

A manufactured home loan can be insured by the FHA or guaranteed by the DVA. A purchase-money mortgage is created when a seller carries back a portion of a property's sales price as a loan to the buyer. A hard-money mortgage is a cash loan to a borrower. Usually a property owner pledges equity as collateral to a private mortgage company for a second mortgage and receives cash needed to purchase some item of personal property. A wraparound encumbrance is a special form of junior financing designed to encompass an already existing financial instrument.

When investment property is sold, a taxpayer has various alternatives to postpone taxes on the net gain. Property sellers may defer their taxes by using an installment sale or by *trading up* through an exchange.

## ■ INTERNET RESOURCES

Department of Housing and Urban Development, Home Equity Conversion Mortgage   *www.hud.gov*

Internal Revenue Service, Section 1031   *www.irs.gov*

U.S. Treasury Department, ARM Index   *www.treasury.gov*

# ■ REVIEW QUESTIONS

Answer questions 1–4 using the following options.
- I.  Adjustable-rate mortgage (ARM)
- II.  Hard-money mortgage
- III.  Package mortgage
- IV.  Graduated-payment mortgage (GPM)

1. Which type of loan includes both personal property and real property?

    a.  I

    b.  II

    c.  III

    d.  IV

2. Under which type of loan is the seller cashed out?

    a.  I

    b.  II

    c.  III

    d.  IV

3. Under which type of loan are there lower payments in the early years of the loan with periodic payment increases?

    a.  I

    b.  II

    c.  III

    d.  IV

4. Under which type of loan does the lender adjust the interest rate according to a prearranged index?

    a.  I

    b.  II

    c.  III

    d.  IV

Answer questions 5–8 using the following options.

    I.      Lease option

    II.     Open-end mortgage

    III.    Bridge loan

    IV.    Reverse annuity mortgage

5. Which type of loan is known as a mortgage for future advances?

    a. I                 c. III

    b. II                d. IV

6. Under which type of loan are all payments received by the borrower?

    a. I                 c. III

    b. II                d. IV

7. Under which arrangement does a buyer lock in a seller with none, some, or all of the payments applying to the purchase price?

    a. I                 c. III

    b. II                d. IV

8. Which type of loan is short term, interest only, and is in a junior position?

    a. I                 c. III

    b. II                d. IV

9. A leasehold mortgage based essentially upon a tenant's financial strength is called a

    a. junior loan.          c. credit loan.

    b. purchase-money loan.     d. term loan.

10. With an underlying existing mortgage balance of $15,000 at 7 percent interest, the interest override earned on a $25,000 wraparound at 10 percent interest is

   a.   $1,050.                    c.   $3,000.

   b.   $1,145.                    d.   $1,450.

## ■ EXERCISES

1. Call a local mortgage banker and find out what interest rate and caps, both annual and life-of-loan, are in effect today on an ARM.

2. What yield would an investor earn on the equity in a $100,000 loan at 10 percent wrapped around an existing loan with a balance of $50,000 payable at 12 percent interest-only?

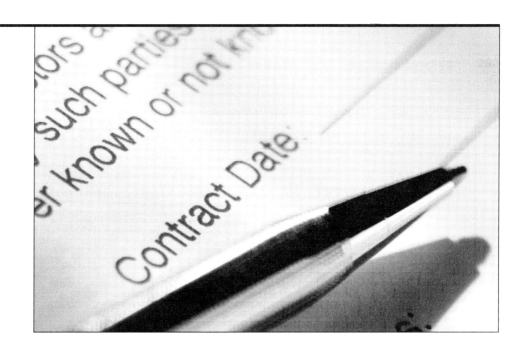

## CHAPTER NINE

# INSTRUMENTS OF REAL ESTATE FINANCE

## ■ KEY TERMS

acceleration clause
assumed
beneficiaries
blended rate
coinsured
contract for deed
cosigners
covenants that run
  with the land
deed of trust
defeasance clause
due-on-sale clause
encumbrance
equitable redemption
  rights
equitable rights
exculpatory clause
fictitious deeds of trust

judicial foreclosure
land contract
legal description
lien: voluntary, invol-
  untary, general, spe-
  cific
master trusts
mortgage
mortgagee
mortgagor
naked title
nonjudicial foreclosure
nonrecourse clause
note
novation
power-of-sale clause
prepayment penalty
  clause

real property sales
  contract
reconveys
release clause
second mortgage
security
specific performance
statutory redemption
  period
"subject to"
subordinate
title theory
trustees
trustors
vendee
vendor

An **encumbrance** is defined as a right or interest in a property held by one who is not the legal owner of the property. Encumbrances that affect the physical condition of a property may be imposed upon a parcel of land without destroying the owner's estate. These physical encumbrances do not prevent the owner from using the property or transferring it. Encumbrances of this nature include *easements*, *public and private restrictions*, and *encroachments*.

Almost every parcel of real property has some form of physical encumbrance imposed upon it. The most common physical encumbrance is the utility easement that provides the accessibility, both under and over the land, for the installation of water, gas, electric, telephone, and sewer services. These easements are recorded agreements between the property owner, usually the original subdivider, and the appropriate agency responsible for the services indicated. These recorded physical encumbrances become **covenants that run with the land** and are attached permanently to the land, following the title through to its various owners.

A property's title may also be affected by a financial encumbrance, called a **lien.** A lien is defined as a charge against a specific property wherein the property is made the security for the performance of a certain act, usually the repayment of a debt. Thus, mortgages, deeds of trusts, and contracts for deed are all forms of liens.

Liens can be either **voluntary liens**, such as financing instruments, or **involuntary liens** imposed by law, such as liens for delinquent taxes or assessments and mechanic's and judgment liens. **General liens** apply to all nonexempt property owned by a person, while **specific liens** apply only to a single property of the debtor. A mortgage loan secured by a parcel of real estate becomes a specific voluntary lien against the subject property at the time it is recorded at the courthouse of the county wherein the property is located. The recording process gives actual and constructive notice that the lender has lien rights in the property described in the loan instrument.

Lenders' rights are invariably superior to the rights of other subsequent recorded lienholders, with certain special exceptions. These exceptions include the general liens imposed by local, state, and federal governments for nonpayment of property or income taxes. Otherwise, based upon the legal recording doctrine of "first in time, first in right," lenders establish a priority lien position on the date their loan document is recorded. In the event of a foreclosure and sale of the collateral, the proceeds of the sale are distributed per the priority of the liens existing against the subject property. Lenders whose loans have the earliest recording dates are said to be in senior lien positions, and their rights take priority over those of all subsequent lienors.

Although real estate finance is in constant change, the basic instruments for executing a real estate loan have remained essentially the same over time. In this chapter, we will examine the contents of the three basic instruments used to finance real estate in California: the note and deed of trust, the note and mortgage, and the real property sales contract.

## ■ INTERESTS SECURED BY A REAL ESTATE LOAN

Any interest in real property can be security for a real estate loan. Most common to real estate finance is the pledge of a fee simple ownership as collateral to back up a promise to repay a money debt. Real property can also be pledged as collateral to secure financial lines of credit or insure the specific performance of a contract. Fee simple ownership can be enjoyed by individuals, corporations, and various forms of partnerships. Individuals, their assigns, and heirs can pledge their titles and interests in real estate in exchange for loans. Corporations, as legally created entities, may own real property and can pledge it as collateral for financing purposes. Likewise, various combinations of individuals and corporations that have joined into partnerships to own real properties can pledge their interests in these properties in order to borrow money.

Less-than-freehold interests, such as rental income from property or the leasehold rights of a tenant, can also be used as collateral for a loan. The parties to a life estate can pledge their interests for loans, even though these interests are not fully vested when the loan is secured. Most lenders are aware of the risks involved with such loans.

Other interests in real property can be owned independently from the land itself. Rights to the use of the air space over a parcel of property fall into this latter category, as do the rights to the use of water and the extraction of oil and minerals from the earth. These rights can be pledged as collateral for a loan, either singly, collectively, or jointly with other properties.

In some instances, not only is real property pledged as collateral for a loan, but personal property is also required as additional security. Thus, loans for homes might include the furnishings therein as collateral, in addition to the real estate. Commercial property loans might include trade fixtures as mortgage loan collateral.

## Title and Lien Theories

Originally, most real estate loans were designed to allow the lender to take actual physical possession of the land until the principal sum of the loan and any agreed-upon interest was derived from the proceeds of the land's production. For all intents and purposes, the lender was the owner of the land until the debt was satisfied, at which time ownership and possession were returned to the borrower. Simply put, the lender held title to the collateral.

As the system evolved, the procedure was changed to allow borrowers to remain in possession of the land as long as they kept the terms of the loan agreement. However, the borrower was still required to transfer legal ownership to the lender by snapping the symbolic twig, literally putting the title to the property in the lender's name. Thus, the lender secured legal title and the borrower retained **equitable rights** in the property.

These medieval efforts to specify which party held title to a collateral property stemmed from the demands of the lender to be put into as safe a position as possible to ensure the return of either the funds loaned or, at least, a property with value adequate to substitute for funds lost. Here we have a clear manifestation of the rights of a lender being absolutely superior to the rights of a borrower. The lender could dispossess the borrower *without notice* at the first default of the loan agreement. No compensation was made for any monies already paid to the lender. This concept has evolved into the **title theory** of real estate finance, which has been adopted in some states.

As time progressed and abuses of these lenders' powers became more prevalent, the laws were changed by the royal court to reflect a borrower's legal right to *redeem* property within some reasonable time *after* default. This right, called the **equitable redemption right**, gave defaulting borrowers time to protect their interests, but it ceased when the property was sold at a foreclosure sale.

To complement the equitable redemption right, which has come down from feudal times, more than half the states have adopted periods for redemption *after* the foreclosure sale. In California, the **statutory redemption period** ends *three months* after the auction sale, ordered by judicial foreclosure, if the proceeds have been sufficient to satisfy all creditors and the costs of the sale. If the proceeds are insufficient, the redemption period is extended to *one year*. For foreclosures other than judiciary foreclosures and/or in the event that lenders waive their rights or are prohibited from obtaining a deficiency judgment, there is no statutory redemption period. Defaults and foreclosures will be examined in Chapter 13.

Through the years, the competition between lenders' and borrowers' rights has shifted dramatically to the latter group. Most states have adopted the *lien theory*, which recognizes the rights of lenders in collateral property as being *equitable* rights, while borrowers retain their *legal* rights in their property. Thus, a borrower maintains legal interest in property while pledging it as collateral to a lender who acquires a *lien*, or an equitable interest, in the collateral property in return for the funds lent. In effect, the lien theory allows a defaulted borrower to retain possession, title, and all legal rights in the property until the lien against the collateral property is perfected by the lender according to legal foreclosure procedures, recognizing the borrower's redemption rights.

However, just as excessive power gave rise to abuse by lenders prior to the development of the concept of equity of redemption, so also does the lien theory. When coupled with the concept of statutory redemption, it provides the opportunity for *borrowers* to become abusive. Whereas previously lenders were able to dispossess their borrowers arbitrarily, now defaulted borrowers are often able to remain in possession of their properties for long periods of time without making loan payments. Long statutory redemption periods have resulted in endless problems for lenders trying to recover their collateral and minimize their losses within a reasonable time.

Therefore, California has taken a modified position between the title and lien theories. This *intermediate* position allows a lender to take possession of collateral property in the event of a loan default, often without having to wait until foreclosure proceedings have resulted in a possessory judgment. But the lender does not receive title until after any statutory redemption periods prescribed by law have expired.

## General Requirements for a Finance Instrument

Regardless of the theory practiced, all borrowers and lenders must observe the same general requirements in order to protect their rights when making a loan transaction. Real estate loans are contractual agreements that must contain certain basic elements in order to be valid. All terms of the loan transaction must be *formalized in writing* and include accurate descriptions of the interest and property being pledged as collateral as well as a complete statement detailing the loan repayment. The parties to the agreement must be legally competent, their consent must be evidenced by their signatures properly attested and affixed to the loan agreement, and a sufficient consideration must be paid.

The three basic instruments used to finance real estate—the deed of trust, note and mortgage, and real property sales contract—share the requirements listed above, but each has its own unique form and content.

## ■ NOTE AND DEED OF TRUST (TRUST DEED)

Although the mortgage was the original form for real estate finance in California, the **deed of trust** was introduced in the early 1900s and evolved to become the dominant security instrument for financiers of California real estate. The deed of trust includes a trustor/borrower, a trustee/holder of title, and a beneficiary/lender.

The advantage of a trust deed over a mortgage is a shorter foreclosure period. With the **judicial foreclosure** proceedings required under a mortgage, it may take as long as a year to acquire clear title to a defaulted property. This is due to filing and court delays and redemption periods.

Under the **nonjudicial foreclosure** trust deed's **power-of-sale clause**, this effort is reduced to as few as 120 days.

While a grant deed transfers absolute legal title (**naked title**) from the grantors to the grantees, the deed of trust is an instrument of finance. Its purpose is to encumber the collateral pledged in a loan arrangement by transferring a "quality" of title to the lender. Although the borrowers (**trustors**) still own their property, they have agreed to pass a claim against this ownership over to the lenders or their nominees (**trustees**) to hold during the term of the loan. The trustee is often a title company, attorney, or an independent corporation that is set up to act as a trustee. When the loan is fully repaid, this trust ownership is reconveyed (released) to the borrowers, clearing the records of this encumbrance. If there is a default, this trust ownership will be perfected by the trustees through the foreclosure process into full ownership or naked title.

Thus, under a deed of trust, the borrowers retain an equitable title to the collateral while the lenders secure a form of legal title. Although only the borrowers sign the note, both the borrowers and the trustees sign the deed of trust. Original notes and trust deeds are held by the trustees for the benefit of the lenders, known as **beneficiaries.**

**Note Secured by Deed of Trust**

A **note** is a promise to pay. Its terms specify the amount of money borrowed and conditions under which it will be repaid. After being signed by a borrower, without any additional signatures or acknowledgments, it becomes a legally enforceable and fully negotiable instrument of debt when in the possession of its bearer. If the terms of a note are met, the debt is discharged. If the terms of a note are broken, then a lender may choose either to sue upon the note or foreclose upon the note's collateral.

A note does not need to be tied to a deed of trust. When a note is used as a debt instrument without any related collateral, it is described as an *unsecured note*. Unsecured notes are often used by banks and other lenders to extend short-term personal loans. However, a real estate loan, described as a *secured loan*, always includes a deed of trust with a note. In fact, the note with its deed of trust is often called a **security.**

Figure 9.1 shows a typical note secured by a deed of trust on real property. Usually, this basic format is expanded to include additional provisions. However, even in its simplest form, *a note is the fundamental document upon which a deed of trust depends*. It generally incorporates the following elements.

**Date Signed.** The date of a note's origination is clearly delineated on the form. Accurate dates are vital to every legally enforceable contract because time is always of the essence to identify the chronological order of priority rights.

**FIGURE 9.1**
**Note Secured by Deed of Trust**

DO NOT DESTROY THIS NOTE: When paid, this note, with the Deed of Trust securing same, must be surrendered to Trustee for cancellation before reconveyance will be made.

**NOTE SECURED BY DEED OF TRUST**
**INSTALLMENT NOTE, INTEREST INCLUDED**

$_____, California, _____, 20 _____

In installments as herein stated, for value received, undersigned promise ____ to pay to _____

_____, or to order at

_____ the sum of

_____ Dollars

with interest from _____ on

unpaid principal at the rate of _____ percent per annum; principal and

interest in installments of _____

_____ Dollars

or more on the _____ day of each _____ month, beginning

on the _____ day of _____, 20 ____

_____

_____

_____

and continuing until said principal and interest have been paid. Each payment shall be credited first on interest then due; and the remainder on principal; and interest shall thereupon cease upon the principal so credited. Should default be made in payment of any installment, the whole sum of principal and interest shall become immediately due at the option of the holder hereof. Principal and interest payable is lawful money of the United States. If action be instituted on this note I promise to pay such sum as the Court may fix as attorney's fees. The note is secured by a DEED OF TRUST.

_____          _____

_____          _____

T-248

**Participants' Identities.**   The participants engaged in a loan contract are identified immediately at the top of the note form, and their relationship as borrower and lender is established. Some preprinted note forms identify the borrower as the undersigned and the lender's name is printed on the form.

**Promise to Pay.**   The words "promise to pay" establish the precise legal obligation of the borrower. These simple words are the heart of the entire loan arrangement. The fulfillment of the promise is the satisfaction of the obligation; a broken promise entitles the lender to seek legal remedies to recover any damages that might occur.

**Payment Due Dates.**   The specific schedule of payments must be incorporated into the note. A systematic repayment program of principal and interest over the life of the loan is described as *amortization*. A plan can be designed for a number of time intervals, such as for monthly, quarterly, semiannual, or annual payments. Semi-amortized notes call for periodic payments of principal and interest with a large principal payment, called a *balloon payment*, due at the end of the loan term. Notes can also be designed to be paid at a monthly or annual rate of interest only, with a single lump sum principal payment due at some future time. This form of finance is described as a *term loan*. In all cases, a note will specify when the payments will start, on what dates they will be due, and when they will stop.

**Amount and Terms.**   The amount of the payments is specifically a function of the terms of a loan. If a term loan for $1,000 for one year at 12 percent interest per annum is designated, then the note will stipulate a payment of $1,120, including principal and interest, to be due in full one year from the date of its inception.

The payments due on an amortized note will be based upon the length of time involved and the agreed upon interest rate.

■ **EXAMPLE**  A $200,000 note payable in monthly installments over a 30-year time span at a 5 percent annual interest rate would require a $1,073.66 regular monthly payment to satisfy the obligation. This sum represents only the monthly principal and interest amounts due to the lender. If hazard insurance premiums and property taxes are to be included in the monthly payment, these additional requirements must be described on the deed of trust form. Only the scheduled amount of principal and interest owed to the lender is specified in the note. The mathematics of amortization can be found in Chapter 15.

The terms and conditions for the repayment of a loan can be as flexible and varied as a particular situation demands. Several possibilities were examined in Chapter 8. However, the note is always held as the determining instrument in interpreting the intentions of the parties to a loan.

**Reference to Security.**  After the terms of a loan are specified, a referral is made in the note that it is secured by a deed of trust upon real property. This reference to a *security* is formalized when a copy of the note is attached to its deed of trust, thereby firmly and legally establishing the security.

The deed of trust is the liening document, the life of which depends upon the note, while the note is a freestanding contract *personally* obligating the borrower for the debt. A lender may sue for damages upon the note in the event of a borrower's default. The deed of trust is the lender's final protection and may be foreclosed if a borrower cannot fulfill the obligation under the note. Thus, the note is the power instrument in this realty lending design.

**Signatures and Endorsements.**  Although several copies of the note will be prepared and distributed to the parties in the loan transaction, only one copy will be signed. This signed copy will be delivered to the lender to be held until the debt is satisfied. This is important to a borrower because each signed note is a negotiable instrument in itself. Thus, *only one note* should be signed in any loan transaction. A note requires only the borrower's signature. The delivery of the signed note to the lender is adequate evidence of its ownership. A lender can assign it to another person by simply endorsing it on its back, much like a check. If a deed of trust is involved, the process is more complicated, but the note itself is a viable, negotiable instrument. A transfer does not affect the terms and conditions of the original agreement, except that the place to which the borrower sends payments may be changed. When the loan is repaid, the lender will mark "paid in full" across the face of the original note, sign under this comment, and return the original to the borrower.

**Cosigners.**  The lender who once made the statement that "there can never be too many signatures on a note" was referring to the fact that all signers on a note are individually and collectively responsible for its repayment. If a married couple is securing a loan, a lender will require both husband and wife to sign the note. Sometimes a lender may require the signatures of persons other than the borrower to provide additional guarantees of the repayment of the obligation. These additional signatures are usually the borrower's family or friends whose credit has been considered in qualifying the borrower for a loan. These **cosigners** share personal liability with the original maker of the note in the event of a default.

The number of signatures on a note does not have to conform with the number of persons who sign the accompanying deed of trust. Because the property in question is being pledged as collateral to back up a specific note, only the property owners will sign the deed of trust. Thus, a note may have more or fewer signatures than its deed of trust. In fact, the signatures on both instruments may be different, although this would be a rare occurrence.

**Deed of Trust**

A trust is described as a right in property, real or personal, being held by one party for the benefit of another. The parties to a trust include a trustor who grants rights to a trustee who holds the property in trust for a beneficiary. In all cases involving the establishment of a real estate trust, an instrument called a *deed of trust* is executed by the trustor to transfer a form of legal fee ownership to the trustee to be held for the beneficiary, while the trustors maintain their equitable ownership.

When a deed of trust is used for financing real estate, usually the lender-beneficiary selects a trustee. The trustee then secures title to the collateral from the trustor-borrower and the power to foreclose if necessary. However, this financing deed of trust grants ownership to the trustee only subject to the conditions agreed upon in the deed of trust note. In fact, the terms of the note are usually incorporated into the body of the deed of trust itself so that no misinterpretation will arise as to the intentions for its use.

A deed of trust has the borrower (trustor) conveying property as collateral to a trustee who holds title on behalf of the legal holder of the note (the beneficiary) until the terms of the loan are satisfied. When the loan is paid in full, the beneficiary asks the trustee to prepare and sign a deed of reconveyance, which **reconveys** the property to the trustor. If the loan goes into default, the trustee forecloses on the collateral to secure full legal title and sells the property to recover the balance of monies due to the bearer of the note.

Unlike other states, in California the trustee and the beneficiary may be one and the same. In other words, lenders may act as trustees for their own loans and not be in jeopardy of conflict of interest. The California Attorney General's office interprets each role separately; each function has its responsibilities clearly specified.

**California Deed of Trust.**   An illustration of a California Deed of Trust appears in Figure 9.2.

The first page of the instrument, entitled *Deed of Trust and Assignment of Rents*, identifies the parties to the agreement, conveys "title" to the trustee, describes the property being pledged as collateral, repeats the terms and conditions of the note, and refers to so-called fictitious deeds of trust that were recorded previously.

**Fictitious deeds of trust,** also known as **master trusts,** are comprehensive documents recorded by lenders stipulating specific details of the borrower and lender relationships under a deed of trust. The length and complexity of these master deeds are too cumbersome to reproduce for every transaction, so reference to the fictitious deeds of trust that are already of record are incorporated into each new loan agreement.

At the bottom of the page, provision is made for the signatures of the trustor(s) and proper notarization.

**FIGURE 9.2**

**Deed of Trust and Assignment of Rents**

RECORDING REQUESTED BY

AND WHEN RECORDED MAIL TO

NAME

ADDRESS

CITY
STATE & ZIP

Title Order No._____ Escrow No._____

INDEX AS ASSIGNMENT OF DEED OF TRUST AND AS REQUEST FOR SPECIAL NOTICE

SPACE ABOVE THIS LINE FOR RECORDER'S USE ——

T-504

## DEED OF TRUST AND ASSIGNMENT OF RENTS

This Deed of Trust, Made this _____ day of _____ . 20 ____ . between

_____ . herein called TRUSTOR,

whose address is _____

(Number and Street)     (City)     (State)     (Zip Code)

_____ . a California corporation, herein called TRUSTEE, and

_____ . herein called BENEFICIARY,

WITNESSETH: That Trustor irrevocably grants, transfers and assigns to trustee in trust, with power of sale, that property in _____ County, California, described as:

TOGETHER with the rents, issues and profits thereof. SUBJECT, HOWEVER, to the right, power, and authority hereinafter given to and conferred upon Beneficiary to collect and apply such rents, issues and profits.

FOR THE PURPOSE OF SECURING: 1. Performance of each agreement of Trustor herein contained; 2. payment of the indebtedness evidenced by one promissory note of even date herewith in the principal sum of $_____ executed by Trustor in favor of Beneficiary or order; 3. payment of any money that may be advanced by the Beneficiary to Trustor, or his successors with interest thereon.

TO PROTECT THE SECURITY OF THIS DEED OF TRUST, TRUSTOR AGREES: By the execution and delivery of this Deed of Trust and the note secured hereby, that provisions (1) to (13) inclusive, of the fictitious deeds of trust recorded April 10, 1969, in Book T6168 Page 257, of Official Records in the office of the Recorder of Los Angeles County, California and recorded November 20, 1968 in Book 8793 Page 602, of Official Records in the office of the Recorder of Orange County, California and recorded on February 15, 1977 in Book 1977 Page 24850 of Official Records in the office of the Recorder of Riverside County, California and recorded February 15, 1977 in Book 9115 Page 1084 of Official Records in the office of the Recorder of San Bernardino County, California and recorded February 15, 1977 as Document Number 77-057045 in the office of the Recorder of San Diego County, California and recorded on February 15, 1977 as Document Number 77-7016 in the office of the Recorder of Santa Barbara County, California and recorded February 15, 1977 in Book 4771 Page 423 in the office of the Recorder of Ventura County, California (which provisions are printed on the reverse hereof) hereby are adopted and incorporated herein and made a part hereof as fully as though set forth herein at length; that he will observe and perform said provisions; and that the references to property, obligations and parties in said provisions shall be construed to refer to the property, obligations, and parties set forth in this Deed of Trust.

The undersigned Trustor requests that a copy of any Notice of Default and of any Notice of Sale hereunder be mailed to him at his address hereinbefore set forth. For any statement regarding the obligations secured hereby, Beneficiary may charge the maximum amount permitted by law at the time of the request therefor.

STATE OF _____ } SS.

COUNTY OF _____

On this _____ day of _____ in the year _____, before me, the undersigned, a Notary Public in and for said State, personally appeared _____

☐ personally known to me
☐ proved to me on the basis of satisfactory evidence
to be the person whose name is subscribed to this instrument, and acknowledged to me that he (she or they) executed it.

Signature _____

NOTARY PUBLIC IN AND FOR SAID STATE

THIS AREA FOR OFFICIAL SEAL

**FIGURE 9.2** (CONTINUED)
**Deed of Trust and Assignment of Rents**

**DO NOT RECORD**

**To Protect the security of this Deed of Trust, Trustor agrees:**

(1) To keep said property in good condition and repair, not to remove or demolish any building thereon, to complete or restore promptly and in good and workmanlike manner any building which may be constructed, damaged or destroyed thereon and to pay when due all claims for labor performed and materials furnished therefor, to comply with all laws affecting said property or requiring any alterations or improvements to be made thereon, not to commit or permit waste thereof, not to commit, suffer or permit any act upon said property in violation of the law, to cultivate, irrigate, fertilize, fumigate, prune and do all other acts which from the character or use of said property may be reasonably necessary, the specific enumerations herein not excluding the general.

(2) To provide, maintain and deliver to Beneficiary fire insurance satisfactory to and with loss payable to Beneficiary. The amount collected under any fire or other insurance policy may be applied by Beneficiary upon any indebtedness secured hereby and in such order as Beneficiary may determine, or at option of Beneficiary the entire amount so collected or any part thereof may be released to Trustor. Such application or release shall not cure or waive any default or notice of default hereunder or invalidate any act done pursuant to such notice.

(3) To appear in and defend any action or proceeding purporting to affect the security hereof or the rights or powers of Beneficiary or Trustee, and to pay all costs and expenses, including cost of evidence of title and attorney's fees in a reasonable sum, in any such action or proceeding in which Beneficiary or Trustee may appear, and in any suit brought by Beneficiary to foreclose this Deed.

(4) To pay: at least ten days before delinquency all taxes and assessments affecting said property, including assessments on appurtenant water stock; when due, all incumbrances, charges and liens, with interest, on said property or any part thereof, which appear to be prior to superior hereto; all costs, fees and expenses of this Trust.

Should Trustor fail to make any payment or to do any act as herein provided, then Beneficiary or Trustee, but without obligation so to do and without notice to or demand upon Trustor and without releasing Trustor from any obligation hereof, may: make or do the same in such manner and to such extent as either may deem necessary to protect the security hereof, Beneficiary or Trustee being authorized to enter upon said property for such purposes; appear in and defend any action or proceeding purporting to affect the security hereof or the rights or powers of Beneficiary or Trustee; pay, purchase, contest or compromise any incumbrance, charge or lien which in the judgment of either appears to be prior or superior hereto; and, in exercising any such powers, pay necessary expenses, employ counsel and pay his reasonable fees.

(5) To pay immediately and without demand all sums so expended by Beneficiary or Trustee, with interest from date of expenditure at the amount allowed by law in effect at the date thereof, and to pay for any statement provided for by law in effect at the date hereof, regarding the obligation secured hereby, any amount demanded by the Beneficiary, not to exceed the maximum allowed by law at the time when said statement is demanded.

(6) That any award of damages in connection with any condemnation for public use of or injury to said property or any part thereof is hereby assigned and shall be paid to Beneficiary who may apply or release such moneys received by him in the same manner and with the same effect as above provided for disposition of proceeds of fire or other insurance.

(7) That by accepting payment of any sum secured hereby after its due date, Beneficiary does not waive his right either to require prompt payment when due of all other sums so secured or to declare default for failure so to pay.

(8) That, at any time or from time to time, without liability therefor and without notice, upon written request of Beneficiary and presentation of this deed of trust and the note or notes secured thereby for endorsement, and without affecting the personal liability of any person for payment of the indebtedness secured hereby, Trustee may: reconvey any part of said property; consent to the making of any map or plat thereof; join in granting any easement thereon; or join in any extension agreement or any agreement subordinating the lien or charge hereof. Trustee, and upon payment of its fees, Trustee shall reconvey, without covenant or warranty, the property then held hereunder. The recitals in any such reconveyance of any matters or facts shall be conclusive proof of the truthfulness thereof. The grantee in any such reconveyance may be described as "the person or persons legally entitled thereto." Five (5) years after issuance of a full reconveyance, Trustee may destroy said note and this deed of trust, unless directed in such request to retain them.

(9) That upon endorsement of this deed of trust and the note or notes secured thereby denoting any extension agreement or any agreement subordinating the lien or charge of said deed of trust, or any agreement modifying the note or notes secured by said deed of trust, or the deeding of any easement on said property, or the making of any map or plat of said property, the consent and joinder of the Trustee in such subordination agreement, deed or map shall not be required.

(10) That as additional security, Trustor hereby gives to and confers upon Beneficiary the right, power and authority, during the continuance of these trusts, to collect the rents, issues and profits of said property, reserving unto Trustor the right, prior to any default by Trustor in payment of any indebtedness secured hereby or in performance of any agreement hereunder, to collect and retain such rents, issues and profits as they become due and payable. Upon any such default, Beneficiary may at any time without notice, either in person, by agent, or by a receiver to be appointed by a court, and without regard to the adequacy of any security for the indebtedness hereby secured, enter upon and take possession of said property or any part thereof, in his own name sue for or otherwise collect such rents, issues and profits, including those past due and unpaid, and apply the same, less costs and expenses of operation and collection, including reasonable attorney's fees, upon any indebtedness secured hereby, and in such order as Beneficiary may determine. The entering upon and taking possession of said property, the collection of such rents, issues and profits and the application thereof as aforesaid, shall not cure or waive any default or notice of default hereunder or invalidate any act done pursuant to such notice.

(11) That upon default by Trustor in payment of any indebtedness secured hereby or in performance of any agreement hereunder, Beneficiary may declare all sums secured hereby immediately due and payable by delivery to Trustee of written declaration of default and demand for sale and of written notice of default and of election to cause to be sold said property, which notice Trustee shall cause to be filed for record. Beneficiary also shall deposit with Trustee this Deed, said note and all documents evidencing expenditures secured hereby.

After the lapse of such time as may then be required by law following the recordation of said notice of default, and notice of sale having been given as then required by law, Trustee, without demand on Trustor, shall sell said property at the time and place fixed by it in said notice of sale, either as a whole or in separate parcels, and in such order as it may determine, at public auction to the highest bidder for cash in lawful money of the United States, payable at time of sale. Trustee may postpone sale of all or any portion of said property by public announcement at such time and place of sale and from time to time thereafter may postpone such sale by public announcement at the time fixed by the preceding postponement. Trustee shall deliver to such purchaser its deed conveying the property so sold, but without any covenant or warranty, express or implied. The recitals in such deed of any matters or facts shall be conclusive proof of the truthfulness thereof. Any person, including Trustor, Trustee, or Beneficiary as hereinafter defined, may purchase at such sale.

After deducting all costs, fees and expenses of Trustee and of this Trust, including cost of evidence of title in connection with sale, Trustee shall apply the proceeds of sale to payment of: all sums expended under the terms hereof, not then repaid, with accrued interest at seven per cent per annum; all other sums then secured hereby, and the remainder, if any, to the person or persons legally entitled thereto.

(12) That this Deed applies to, inures to the benefit of, and binds all parties hereto, their heirs, legatees, devisees, administrators, executors, successors and assigns. The term Beneficiary shall mean the owner and holder, including pledgees, of the note secured hereby, whether or not named as Beneficiary herein. In this Deed, whenever the context so requires, the masculine gender includes the feminine and or neuter, and the singular number includes the plural.

(13) That Trustee accepts this Trust when this Deed, duly executed and acknowledged, is made a public record as provided by law. Trustee is not obligated to notify any party hereto of pending sale under any other Deed of Trust or of any action or proceeding in which Trustor, Beneficiary or Trustee shall be a party unless brought by Trustee.

The undersigned Trustor requests that a copy of any Notice of Default and any Notice of Sale hereunder be mailed to him at his address hereinbefore set forth.

---

# REQUEST FOR FULL RECONVEYANCE
*To be used only when note has been paid.*

Dated_____

The undersigned is the legal owner and holder of all indebtedness secured by the within Deed of Trust. All sums secured by said Deed of Trust have been fully paid and satisfied; and you are hereby requested and directed, on payment to you of any sums owing to you under the terms of said Deed of Trust, to cancel all evidences of indebtedness, secured by said Deed of Trust, delivered to you herewith together with the said Deed of Trust, and to reconvey without warranty, to the parties designated by the terms of said Deed of Trust, the estate now held by you under the same.

```
MAIL RECONVEYANCE TO:
```

*Do not lose or destroy this Deed of Trust OR THE NOTE which it secures.*
*Both must be delivered to the Trustee for cancellation before reconveyance will be made.*

**Covenants.** The various covenants pertaining to the relationship between borrowers and lenders are itemized as follows:

1. *Preservation and Maintenance.* The borrower must keep the property in good repair and not allow any waste to accumulate, nor permit deterioration to the lender's detriment.

2. *Fire Insurance.* The borrower will provide a fire insurance policy in an amount sufficient to protect the lender's interest and will name the lender as a party to the policy's proceeds in the event of a loss.

3. *Legal Action.* The borrower will defend against any action or claim on the property and agrees to pay all costs and expenses in a foreclosure against the property.

4. *Taxes and Assessments.* The borrower will pay all taxes, assessments, encumbrances, charges, and liens against the property in a timely manner, as well as all costs, fees, and expenses of the trust.

5. *Beneficiary and Trustee Expenditures.* The borrower will reimburse to the beneficiary or trustee any sums expended on behalf of the borrower.

6. *Condemnation.* All sums secured as a result of condemnation of all or part of the property will be paid to the beneficiary to reduce the loan balance.

7. *Late Payments.* Acceptance by the trustee or the beneficiary of any delinquent payments does not relieve the borrower of making subsequent payments in a timely manner.

8. *Reconveyance.* The trustee is required to reconvey the property to the trustor upon repayment of the loan amount, but must maintain records of the transaction for at least five years.

9. *Extensions, Subordination, and Modifications.* Any changes of the agreement shall occur between the trustor and beneficiary and the consent and joinder of the trustee shall not be required.

10. *Assignment of Rents.* As additional security and in the event of a default, all rents, issues, and profits that may be derived from the property shall be assigned to the beneficiary.

11. *Acceleration.* If the borrower breaches any of the covenants of this contract, the beneficiary may declare all monies owed to be due in full and the trustee may sell the property after required notices have been made.

12. *Successors and Assigns.* All successors and assigns of parties to this contract shall be bound by its terms and conditions.

13. *Trustee Acceptance.* The trustee will accept this trust when the deed, properly signed and acknowledged, is recorded.

Finally, at the bottom of the page, there is a form for full reconveyance, which will be completed when the indebtedness has been paid in full.

# ■ NOTE AND MORTGAGE

Although the deed of trust is the predominant security instrument used in California, the *Note and Mortgage* is an alternate form for financing real property.

As with the deed of trust, the note is a promise to pay a debt. However, unlike the deed of trust, the **mortgage** is a lien on the collateral property, with the legal title remaining in the name of the borrower. While a note by itself is a fully enforceable promise to pay a debt, a mortgage always needs a note to be legally valid.

## Note Secured by a Mortgage

A note secured by a mortgage is essentially the same as a note secured by a deed of trust. The terms and conditions of the loan are specified in the note form. Provisions for future advances and acceleration upon default are delineated also. Only one copy of the note will be signed by the borrower, with the original form delivered to the lender. A copy of the note will be attached to its accompanying mortgage.

## Mortgage

**Recording Information.** A mortgage is a lien upon a specific property or properties to secure the fulfillment of a promise—usually a promise to repay a debt. The only way a lender has to notify the world that there is a lien on a specific property is to record the mortgage at the office of the recorder in the county wherein the property is located.

Without a recording of the mortgage lien, only the borrower and the lender would know of the transaction. Other parties having an interest in the property would not receive notice of the lien. Thus, for its protection, a lender will absolutely insist upon recording the mortgage. Invariably, this recording will take place *before* the proceeds of a loan are distributed. By holding back the disbursement of a loan until after recording, a lender or the escrow agent has a last-minute opportunity to recheck the public records as to the condition of the collateral property's title.

Most standard mortgage forms have a space at the top of the first page devoted to specific county recording information. Others leave a blank space elsewhere on the form to be filled in at the recorder's office. In any case, the appropriate information will be included in the space provided, and the lien will be posted against the property described. This lien will vest at the date and time impressed upon the mortgage document by the recorder's clock-stamp. A copy of the original document will be made, and the original will be returned to whomever is so designated.

**Participants.** The participants to a mortgage include a borrower-mortgagor and a lender-mortgagee. In exchange for a certain consideration, usually a sum of money, a **mortgagor** will pledge property as collateral to back up the promise to repay a mortgage. The proper names of both mortgagor and **mortgagee** must appear on the mortgage form.

**Pledge.** Any rights owned by a mortgagor in real estate may be pledged as collateral for a loan. Most mortgages include the pledge of a property's fee simple ownership, although leasehold, mineral, water, and other rights less than a freehold interest can be pledged.

The words "mortgage, bargain, sell, and convey" grant quasi-legal, or equitable, form of ownership to the mortgagee, creating a lien that the mortgagee will either release when the loan is satisfied or perfect into a full legal fee if there is a default.

The equitable property interest that a mortgagee secures under the mortgage form becomes an asset that, according to the wording in the contract, inures to the benefit of the mortgagee and its "successors, heirs and assigns" forever.

**Property Description.**   All property pledged as collateral in a mortgage must be described accurately and without ambiguity to prevent any future controversies. Securing the proper *legal description* is the responsibility of the person composing the loan documents. A description used in prior transactions is usually an adequate reference and it can be copied onto the new forms. However, whenever a new subdivision is involved in a loan or some complication arises concerning a property description, a surveyor is usually engaged to provide a precise legal description.

In addition to the real property described, most mortgage forms include the pledge of all buildings and improvements now or hereafter placed thereon; all rents, issues, and profits thereof; all classes of property now, or at any time hereafter, attached to or used in any way in connection with the use, operation, or occupation of the above-described property; all property rights and privileges now or hereafter owned by a mortgagor. "All of the foregoing shall be deemed to be, remain, and form part of the realty and be subject to the lien of this mortgage."

Thus, the real property, anything that is permanently attached to it, and all of the mortgagor's rights in it are pledged as collateral for the loan.

**Covenant of Seisin.**   *The covenant of seisin* is the clause that states that the mortgagors have title to the property described and that they have the authority to pledge the property as collateral. This covenant goes one step further by specifying that the mortgagors will warrant this title and guarantee that it is being pledged free and clear of any encumbrance not described in the mortgage document.

**Note Attachment.**   It is not necessary to describe all of the terms and conditions of a note in the body of a mortgage. In fact, the parties to a loan often prefer not to reveal this information and merely indicate a reference to the note, using the phrase, "this mortgage is given to secure the payment of a certain indebtedness evidenced by a note payable to the order of the mortgagee," or words to that effect. However, some forms provide a space for the attachment of a true copy of the note. Whatever the case, the borrower agrees in the mortgage to pay the full sum due according to the terms of the note.

**Mello-Roos Disclosure.**   This nondeductible tax levy is imposed as a continuing lien upon some real property. Its purpose is to generate funds for certain public improvements and is assessed against the land rather than against property value. The sellers or their representative brokers are required to disclose to buyers when a property is subject to this tax. Additionally, The Improvement Bond Act of 1915 is a required disclosure if a property is subject to this assessment.

**Property Taxes.**   In addition to being obligated to repay a mortgagee the "just and full sum due" according to the terms and conditions of the promissory note, a mortgagor must pay all property taxes, assessments, adverse claims, charges, and liens that may jeopardize the priority position of the mortgagee. Any negligence on the part of a mortgagor to pay these claims technically puts a mortgage into default.

Depending upon specific circumstances, mortgagees may protect their interests by including, as a condition of the loan contract, that the mortgagor pay a proportionate share of the annual taxes with each monthly payment of principal and interest. These tax payments would then be held in a special impound account to accumulate over the year and be paid to the tax collector, usually the county treasurer, when they are due. This procedure has eliminated many of the problems connected with mortgagors who simply were not conditioned to put aside the funds necessary for annual property taxes. In most commercial loans and some residential loans, however, the mortgagors still retain control over these tax payments, and they are not impounded by a mortgagee.

A mortgagee will closely supervise the prompt payment of all current property taxes because a tax lien takes a priority position over any other liens, recorded or not.

**Insurance.**   Just as mortgagees must protect themselves by supervising the prompt payment of property taxes, so also must they specify in their mortgage contracts that hazard insurance is to be provided and paid for by the mortgagor in an amount and under terms adequate to protect the mortgagee's interest in the property. The insurance agency chosen by the mortgagor is subject to approval by the mortgagee.

Not only must adequate coverage be provided, but the mortgagee must also be named as a **coinsured.** The original policy must be deposited with the mortgagee, and proportionate shares of the insurance premiums must be included together with the monthly payment of principal, interest, and taxes. These hazard insurance payments are deposited in the impound account with the property taxes collected, and the funds accumulated are utilized to pay the insurance premiums as they become due. In this manner, a mortgagee can supervise the current status of the insurance coverage of the collateral.

If a loss occurs, a check for the insurance proceeds is issued either to the mortgagor and the mortgagee jointly, with the mortgagee having an opportunity to inspect the repairs prior to endorsing the check, or to the mortgagee only. In the latter case, the mortgagee usually retains the right to apply the proceeds to the indebtedness or to make the necessary repairs. Thus, a mortgagee can protect the value of the collateral during the entire life of the loan.

**Defeasance Clause and Acceleration.** A mortgage will usually include a **defeasance clause** stating that the mortgagor will regain full free and clear title upon the repayment of the debt. It has also become standard procedure to include an **acceleration clause**, which permits the lender to call the loan for four main reasons:

1. default in payment,

2. use of property for an illegal purpose,

3. nonpayment of property taxes, or

4. not maintaining adequate insurance on the property.

This acceleration clause is the heart of a mortgage in relation to a mortgagee's protection. Any of the neglects mentioned can result in a default of the contract's provisions and allows a mortgagee to accelerate the mortgage, granting the right to take the appropriate legal steps to recover the investment.

**Maintenance of the Collateral.**  As a further protection of the mortgagee's interests, a mortgagor is required by terms of a mortgage to reasonably maintain the physical condition of the premises to preserve its value. A mortgagor is charged "not to permit or commit waste on said premises and to preserve and repair said property."

**Signatures and Acknowledgment.**  Like the note, a mortgage must be signed by the mortgagors accepting the conditions of the contract. These signatures must also be dated and *acknowledged* by a notary public, attesting to their authenticity, because unacknowledged instruments are not accepted by a county recorder.

**Release of Mortgage.**  When a mortgage loan is paid in full, it is removed from the records by recording a Satisfaction of Mortgage Form. It is executed by the lender, indicating that the loan terms have been met.

## ■ REAL PROPERTY SALES CONTRACT (LAND CONTRACT)

A **real property sales contract**, also known as a **land contract**, does not have an accompanying note; it is a single, complete financing and sales agreement executed between a buyer and a seller. A land contract should not be considered a mortgage or trust deed, even though all the basic conditions included in the note and mortgage and the deed of trust are incorporated into its form. These conditions include the pledge of specific property as collateral for the loan, the terms and conditions for the loan's repayment, the enumeration of the borrower's responsibilities, and a statement of the consequences of a default. (See Figure 9.3)

A real property sales contract is an agreement drawn between two parties, the buyer-borrower **(vendee)** and the seller-lender **(vendor)**. Under this agreement, the *lender* retains the legal fee of the property, while the buyer secures an equitable interest in the property, which is one major distinction between this form of financing instrument and the mortgage and deed of trust. Although the buyer agrees to pay the seller a specific price under certain terms and conditions, thereby gaining possession of the property,

**FIGURE 9.3**
**Real Property Sales Contract**

<u>**AFTER RECORDING MAIL TO:**</u>
Name

Address

City/State

*(this space for title company use only)*

ANY OPTIONAL PROVISION NOT INITIALED BY ALL PERSONS SIGNING THIS CONTRACT -- WHETHER INDIVIDUALLY OR AS AN OFFICER OR AGENT -- IS NOT A PART OF THIS CONTRACT.

## REAL ESTATE CONTRACT
### (Residential Short Form)

1. PARTIES AND DATE. This Contract is entered into on      between      as "Seller" and      as "Buyer."

2. SALE AND LEGAL DESCRIPTION. Seller agrees to sell to Buyer and Buyer agrees to purchase from Seller the following described real estate in      County,

Assessor's Property Tax Parcel/Account Number(s):

3. PERSONAL PROPERTY. Personal property, if any, included in the sale is as follows:

No part of the purchase price is attributed to personal property.

4.      (a)      PRICE. Buyer agrees to pay:           $           Total Price
                              Less:                                 Down Payment
                              Less:                                 Assumed Obligation(s)
                              Results in                            Amount Financed by
                              Seller.

       (b)      ASSUMED OBLIGATIONS. Buyer agrees to pay the above assumed Obligation (s) assuming and agreeing to pay that certain      dated      recorded as

                Seller warrants the unpaid balance of said obligation is      which is payable      on or before the      of      [*including/plus*] interest at the rate of      % per annum on the declining balance thereof; and a like amount on or before the      day of each and every

**FIGURE 9.3   (CONTINUED)**
**Real Property Sales Contract**

*[month/year]*   thereafter until paid in full.

NOTE:  Fill in the date in the following two lines only if there is an early cash out date.

NOTWITHSTANDING THE ABOVE, THE ENTIRE BALANCE OF PRINCIPAL AND INTEREST IS DUE IN FULL NOT LATER THAN

**ANY ADDITIONAL ASSUMED OBLIGATIONS ARE INCLUDED IN ADDENDUM**

(c)      PAYMENT OF AMOUNT FINANCED BY SELLER.  Buyer agrees to pay the sum of      as follows:

or more at buyer's option on or before the             *[including/plus]*    interest from      at the rate of      % per annum on the declining balance thereof, and a like amount or more on or before the      day of each and every *[month/year]* thereafter until paid in full.

NOTE:  Fill in the date in the following two lines only if there is an early cash out date.

NOTWITHSTANDING THE ABOVE, THE ENTIRE BALANCE OF PRINCIPAL AND INTEREST IS DUE IN FULL NOT LATER THAN

Payments are applied first to interest and then to principal.  Payments shall be made at      or such other place as the Seller may hereafter indicate in writing.

5.      FAILURE TO MAKE PAYMENTS ON ASSUMED OBLIGATIONS.  If Buyer fails to make any payments on assumed obligation(s), Seller may give written notice to Buyer that unless Buyer makes the delinquent payment(s) within fifteen (15) days, Seller will make the payment(s), together with any late charge, additional interest, penalties, and costs assessed by the Holder of the assumed obligation(s).  The 15-day period may be shortened to avoid the exercise of any remedy by the Holder of the assumed obligation(s).  Buyer shall immediately after such payment by Seller reimburse Seller for the amount of such payment plus a late charge equal to five percent (5%) of the amount so paid plus all costs and attorneys' fees incurred by Seller in connection with making such payment.

6.      (a)      OBLIGATIONS TO BE PAID BY SELLER.  The Seller agrees to continue to pay from payments received hereunder the following obligation, which obligation must be paid in full when Buyer pays the purchase price in full:  That certain      dated      recorded as AF#

ANY ADDITIONAL OBLIGATIONS TO BE PAID BY SELLER ARE INCLUDED IN ADDENDUM.

(b)      EQUITY OF SELLER PAID IN FULL.  If the balance owed the Seller on the purchase price herein becomes equal to the balance owed on prior encumbrances being paid by Seller, Buyer will be deemed to have assumed said encumbrances as of that date.  Buyer shall thereafter make payments direct to the holders of said encumbrances and make no further payments to Seller.  Seller shall at that time deliver to Buyer a fulfillment deed in accordance with the provisions of Paragraph 8.

(c)      FAILURE OF SELLER TO MAKE PAYMENTS ON PRIOR ENCUMBRANCES.  If Seller fails to make any payments on any prior encumbrance, Buyer may give written notice to Seller that unless Seller makes the delinquent payments within 15 days, Buyer will make the payments together with any late charge, additional interest, penalties, and costs assessed by the holder of the prior encumbrance.  The 15-day period may be shortened to avoid the exercise of any remedy by the holder of the prior encumbrance.  Buyer may deduct the amounts so paid plus a late charge of 5% of the amount so paid and any attorneys' fees and costs incurred by Buyer in connection with the delinquency from payments next becoming due Seller on the

**FIGURE 9.3 (CONTINUED)**
**Real Property Sales**
**Contract**

purchase price. In the event Buyer makes such delinquent payments on three occasions, Buyer shall have the right to make all payments due thereafter directly to the holder of such prior encumbrance and deduct the then balance owing on such prior encumbrance from the then balance owing on the purchase price and reduce periodic payments on the balance due Seller by the payments called for in such prior encumbrance as such payments become due.

7. OTHER ENCUMBRANCES AGAINST THE PROPERTY. The property is subject to encumbrances including the following listed tenancies, easements, restrictions, and reservations in addition to the obligations assumed by Buyer and the obligations being paid by Seller:

ANY ADDITIONAL NON-MONETARY ENCUMBRANCES ARE INCLUDED IN ADDENDUM.

8. FULFILLMENT DEED. Upon payment of all amounts due Seller, Seller agrees to deliver to Buyer a Statutory Warranty Deed in fulfillment of this Contract. The covenants of warranty in said deed shall not apply to any encumbrances assumed by Buyer or to defects in title arising subsequent to the date of this Contract by, through, or under persons other than the Seller herein. Any personal property included in the sale shall be included in the fulfillment deed.

9. If any payment on the purchase price is not made within ten (10) days after the date it is due, Buyer agrees to pay a late charge equal to five percent (5%) of the amount of such payment. Such late payment charge shall be in addition to all other remedies available to Seller and the first amounts received from Buyer after such late charges are due shall be applied to the late charges.

10. NO ADVERSE EFFECT ON PRIOR ENCUMBRANCES. Seller warrants that entry into this Contract will not cause in any prior encumbrance (a) a breach, (b) accelerated payments, or (c) an increased interest rate; unless (a), (b), or (c) has been consented to by Buyer in writing.

11. POSSESSION. Buyer is entitled to possession of the property from and after the date of this Contract or whichever is later, subject to any tenancies described in paragraph 7.

12. TAXES, ASSESSMENTS, AND UTILITY LIENS. Buyer agrees to pay by the date due all taxes and assessments becoming a lien against the property after the date of this Contract. Buyer may in good faith contest any such taxes or assessments so long as no forfeiture or sale of the property is threatened as the result of such contest. Buyer agrees to pay when due any utility charges which may become liens superior to Seller's interest under this Contract. If real estate taxes and penalties are assessed against the property subsequent to date of this Contract because of a change in use prior to the date of this Contract for Open Space, Farm, Agricultural, or Timber classifications approved by the County or because of a Senior Citizen's Declaration to Defer Property Taxes filed prior to the date of this Contract, Buyer may demand in writing payment of such taxes and penalties within 30 days. If payment is not made, Buyer may pay and deduct the amount thereof plus 5% penalty from the payments next becoming due Seller under the Contract.

13. INSURANCE. Buyer agrees to keep all buildings now or hereafter erected on the property described herein continuously insured under fire and extended coverage policies in an amount not less than the balances owed on obligations assumed by Buyer plus the balance due Seller, or full insurable value, whichever is lower. All policies shall be held by the Seller and be in such companies as the Seller may approve and have loss payable first to any holders of underlying encumbrances, then to Seller as their interests may appear and then to Buyer. Buyer may within 30 days after loss negotiate a contract to substantially restore the premises to their condition before the loss. If the insurance proceeds are sufficient to pay the contract price for restoration or if the Buyer deposits in escrow any deficiency with instructions to apply the funds on the restoration contract, the property shall be restored unless the underlying encumbrances provide otherwise. Otherwise the amount collected under any insurance policy shall be applied upon any amounts due hereunder in such order as the Seller shall determine. In the event

**FIGURE 9.3** (CONTINUED)
**Real Property Sales Contract**

of forfeiture, all rights of Buyer in insurance policies then in force shall pass to Seller.

14.    NONPAYMENT OF TAXES, INSURANCE, AND UTILITIES CONSTITUTING LIENS. If Buyer fails to pay taxes or assessments, insurance premiums, or utility charges constituting liens prior to Seller's interest under this Contract,  Seller may pay such items and Buyer shall forthwith pay Seller the amount thereof plus a late charge of 5% of the amount thereof plus any costs and attorney's fees incurred in connection with making such payment.

15.    CONDITION OF PROPERTY.  Buyer accepts the property in its present condition and acknowledges that Seller, his agents, and subagents have made no representation or warranty concerning the physical condition of the property or the uses to which it may be put other than as set forth herein. Buyer agrees to maintain the property in such condition as complies with all applicable laws.

16.    RISK OF LOSS.  Buyer shall bear the risk of loss for destruction or condemnation of the property.  Any such loss shall not relieve Buyer from any of Buyer's obligations pursuant to this Contract.

17.    WASTE.  Buyer shall keep the property in good repair and shall not commit or suffer waste or willful damage to or destruction of the property.  Buyer shall not remove commercial timber without the written consent of Seller.

18.    AGRICULTURAL USE.  If this property is to be used principally for agricultural purposes, Buyer agrees to conduct farm and livestock operations in accordance with good husbandry practices.  In the event a forfeiture action is instituted, Buyer consents to Seller's entry on the premises to take any reasonable action to conserve soil, crops, trees, and livestock.

19.    CONDEMNATION.  Seller and Buyer may each appear as owners of an interest in the property in any action concerning condemnation of any part of the property. Buyer may within 30 days after condemnation and removal of improvements, negotiate a contract to substantially restore the premises to their condition before the removal. If the condemnation proceeds are sufficient to pay the contract price for restoration or if the Buyer deposits in escrow any deficiency with instructions to apply the funds on the restoration contract, the property shall be restored unless underlying encumbrances provide otherwise. Otherwise, proceeds of the award shall be applied in payment of the balance due on the purchase price, as Seller may direct.

20.    DEFAULT.  If the Buyer fails to observe or perform any term, covenant, or condition of this Contract, Seller may:

        (a)    Suit for Installments. Sue for any delinquent periodic payment; or

        (b)    Specific Performance.  Sue for specific performance of any of Buyer's obligations pursuant to this Contract; or

        (c)    Forfeit Buyer's Interest.  Forfeit this Contract · X X X X X X X X X X X X as it is presently enacted and may hereafter be amended. The effect of such forfeiture includes: (i) all right, title, and interest in the property of the Buyer and all persons claiming through the Buyer shall be terminated; (ii) the Buyer's rights under the Contract shall be cancelled; (iii) all sums previously paid under the Contract shall belong to and be retained by the Seller or other person to whom paid and entitled thereto; (iv) all improvements made to and unharvested crops on the property shall belong to the Seller; and (v) Buyer shall be required to surrender possession of the property, improvements, and unharvested crops to the Seller 10 days after the forfeiture.

        (d)    Acceleration of Balance Due.  Give Buyer written notice demanding payment of said delinquencies and payment of a late charge of 5% of the amount of such delinquent payments and payment of Seller's reasonable attorney's fees and costs incurred for services in preparing and sending such Notice and stating that if payment pursuant to said Notice is not

**FIGURE 9.3** (**CONTINUED**)
**Real Property Sales Contract**

received within thirty (30) days after the date said Notice is either deposited in the mail addressed to the Buyer or personally delivered to the Buyer, the entire balance owing, including interest, will become immediately due and payable. Seller may thereupon institute suit for payment of such balance, interest, late charge, and reasonable attorneys' fees and costs.

(e)     Judicial Foreclosure. Sue to foreclose this contract as a mortgage, in which event Buyer may be liable for a deficiency.

21.     RECEIVER. If Seller has instituted any proceedings specified in Paragraph 20 and Buyer is receiving rental or other income from the property, Buyer agrees that the appointment of a receiver for the property is necessary to protect Seller's interest.

22.     BUYER'S REMEDY FOR SELLER'S DEFAULT. If Seller fails to observe or perform any term, covenant, or condition of this Contract, Buyer may, after 30 days' written notice to Seller, institute suit for damages or specific performance unless the breaches designated in said notice are cured.

23.     NON-WAIVER. Failure of either party to insist upon strict performance of the other party's obligations hereunder shall not be construed as a waiver of strict performance thereafter of all of the other party's obligations hereunder and shall not prejudice any remedies as provided herein.

24.     ATTORNEYS' FEES AND COSTS. In the event of any breach of this Contract, the party responsible for the breach agrees to pay reasonable attorney's fees and costs, including costs of service of notices and title searches, incurred by the other party. The prevailing party in any suit instituted arising out of this Contract and in any forfeiture proceedings arising out of this Contract shall be entitled to receive reasonable attorney's fees and costs incurred in such suit or proceedings.

25.     NOTICES. Notices shall be either personally served or shall be sent certified mail, return receipt requested, and by regular first class mail to:

Buyer at:

and to:

Seller at:

or such other addresses as either party may specify in writing to the other party. Notices shall be deemed given when served or mailed. Notice to Seller shall also be sent to any institution receiving payments on the Contract.

26.     TIME FOR PERFORMANCE. Time is of the essence in performance of any obligations pursuant to this Contract.

27.     SUCCESSORS AND ASSIGNS. Subject to any restrictions against assignment, the provisions of this Contract shall be binding on the heirs, successors, and assigns of the Seller and the Buyer.

28.     OPTIONAL PROVISION — SUBSTITUTION AND SECURITY ON PERSONAL PROPERTY. Buyer may substitute for any personal property specified in Paragraph 3 herein other personal property of like nature which Buyer owns free and clear of any encumbrances. Buyer hereby grants Seller a security interest in all personal property specified in Paragraph 3 and future substitutions for such property and agrees to execute a financing statement under the Uniform Commercial Code reflecting such security interest.

| SELLER | INITIALS: | BUYER |
|---|---|---|
|  |  |  |
|  |  |  |

**FIGURE 9.3**  (CONTINUED)

**Real Property Sales Contract**

29.    OPTIONAL PROVISION -- ALTERATIONS. Buyer shall not make any substantial alteration to the improvements on the property without the prior written consent of Seller, which consent will not be unreasonably withheld.

| SELLER | INITIALS: | BUYER |
|--------|-----------|-------|
|        |           |       |

30.    OPTIONAL PROVISION -- DUE ON SALE. If Buyer, without written consent of Seller, (a) conveys, (b) sells, (c) leases, (d) assigns, (e) contracts to convey, sell, lease or assign, (f) grants an option to buy the property, (g) permits a forfeiture or foreclosure or trustee or sheriff's sale of any of the Buyer's interest in the property or this Contract, Seller may at any time thereafter either raise the interest rate on the balance of the purchase price or declare the entire balance of the purchase price due and payable. If one or more of the entities comprising the Buyer is a corporation, any transfer or successive transfers in the nature of items (a) through (g) above of 49% or more of the outstanding capital stock shall enable Seller to take the above action. A lease of less than 3 years (including options for renewals), a transfer to a spouse or child of Buyer, a transfer incident to a marriage dissolution or condemnation, and a transfer by inheritance will not enable Seller to take any action pursuant to this Paragraph; provided the transferee other than a condemnor agrees in writing that the provisions of this paragraph apply to any subsequent transaction involving the property entered into by the transferee.

| SELLER | INITIALS: | BUYER |
|--------|-----------|-------|
|        |           |       |

31.    OPTIONAL PROVISION -- PRE-PAYMENT PENALTIES ON PRIOR ENCUMBRANCES. If Buyer elects to make payments in excess of the minimum required payments on the purchase price herein, and Seller, because of such prepayments, incurs prepayment penalties on prior encumbrances, Buyer agrees to forthwith pay Seller the amount of such penalties in addition to payments on the purchase price.

| SELLER | INITIALS: | BUYER |
|--------|-----------|-------|
|        |           |       |

32.    OPTIONAL PROVISION -- PERIODIC PAYMENTS ON TAXES AND INSURANCE. In addition to the periodic payments on the purchase price, Buyer agrees to pay Seller such portion of the real estate taxes and assessments and fire insurance premium as will approximately total the amount due during the current year based on Seller's reasonable estimate.

The payments during the current year shall be      per      Such "reserve" payments from Buyer shall not accrue interest. Seller shall pay when due all real estate taxes and insurance premiums, if any, and debit the amounts so paid to the reserve account. Buyer and Seller shall adjust the reserve account in April of each year to reflect excess or deficit balances and changed costs. Buyer agrees to bring the reserve account balance to a minimum of $10 at the time of adjustment.

| SELLER | INITIALS: | BUYER |
|--------|-----------|-------|
|        |           |       |

**FIGURE 9.3** (CONTINUED)
**Real Property Sales
Contract**

33.    ADDENDA.  Any addenda attached hereto are a part of this Contract.

34.    ENTIRE AGREEMENT.  This Contract constitutes the entire agreement of the parties and supersedes all prior agreements and understandings, written or oral.  This Contract may be amended only in writing executed by Seller and Buyer.

IN WITNESS WHEREOF the parties have signed and sealed this Contract the day and year first above written.

SELLER                                          BUYER

*(Individual)*

                                      }
                                      }    SS.
County of                             }

I certify that I know or have satisfactory evidence that      is/are the person(s) who appeared before me, and said person(s) acknowledged that he/she/they signed this instrument and acknowledged it to be his/her/their free and voluntary act for the uses and purposes mentioned in this instrument.

DATED:

Name (typed or printed):
NOTARY PUBLIC in and for the State of
Residing at
My appointment expires:

*(Corporate)*

                                      }
                                      }    SS.
County of                             }

I certify that I know or have satisfactory evidence that      is/are the person(s) who appeared before me, and said person(s) acknowledged that he/she/they signed this instrument, on oath stated that he is/she is /they are authorized to execute the instrument and acknowledged it as the      of    to be the free and voluntary act of such party for the uses and purposes mentioned in this instrument.

DATED:

Name (typed or printed):
NOTARY PUBLIC in and for the State of
Residing at
My appointment expires:

the *buyer does not receive full legal title* until the terms of the contract are met. This procedure provides the seller, who is financing the sale of the property, with added protection in case of the buyer's default.

Because a land contract does not have a note accompanying it, all conditions of the sale are described in the contract form, including the purchase price and the terms of the loan. The contract specifies the buyer's responsibilities to pay the payments when due, taxes, and any special assessments or hazard insurance premiums. The contract also describes the deed that the seller will deliver to the buyer upon fulfillment of the contract or deposit with an escrow, if an escrow is used, to be held until the terms of the agreement have been met. The delivery and subsequent recording of this deed serve as proof of the satisfaction of the contract debt.

The contract directs the buyer to take possession of the subject property and maintain such possession as long as the agreed-upon terms of the contract are met. In the event of a breach of contract, all payments made by the buyer are forfeited. The seller may then elect to bring an action against the buyer for **specific performance** of the agreement or may choose to use any other legal remedies granted in the contract for recovery of the property and any losses incurred.

A real property sales contract is both a sale and financing agreement in one instrument: both the buyer and seller will sign the document and have their signatures notarized in anticipation of recording.

Under the contract, the vendees are very much the owners of the property, even though they will not receive full legal title until the terms of the contract are fulfilled. As owners, the vendees may occupy the property or rent it to others. They may change the physical characteristics of the property, but not in any way that would diminish its value or to the detriment of the vendors. The vendees may also sell the property, subject to the terms of the contract. A transfer of ownership is accomplished with a Vendee's Deed and Assignment form.

Property encumbered with a recorded real property sales contract may be sold many times, always subject to the terms of the original contract. When these terms are satisfied, the recording of the deed from the original vendor will complete the chain of title, bringing down a full legal ownership to the last vendee.

Under a real property sales contract, the vendors have really sold their property, even though they have not transferred the deed. As sellers, they must be content with receiving their payments and cannot interfere with the vendees' peaceful possession of the property. The vendors do have the right to insist on proper maintenance to preserve the value of the collateral. Vendors may sell their contracts and transfer ownership with a Vendor's Deed and Assignment form.

Most frequently, the contract for deed form is used between individuals in the purchase and sale of real property when other means of financing are not readily available. These contracts are usually junior financing instruments, established between a buyer and seller to close a particular sale when the buyer does not have sufficient cash or credit to secure a new senior mortgage or trust deed loan.

In the past, land contracts could be foreclosed in as few as 30 days under a strict forfeiture provision. This power of foreclosure was weakened considerably by *Barkis v. Scott* (34 Cal. 2d 116; 208 P. 2d 367), which held that California Civil Code Section 327.5 is a legal barrier to harsh and unreasonable foreclosure proceedings. As a result, foreclosures under a land contract must follow the rules under a mortgage—namely judicial foreclosure.

## ■ SPECIAL PROVISIONS IN REAL ESTATE FINANCE INSTRUMENTS

All three instruments for real estate financing may be enhanced and expanded by a multitude of provisions designed to serve the specific requirements of individual loans. Some of the provisions to be reviewed in this chapter have already become standard practice and are regularly incorporated into loan instruments—for example, prepayment privileges and/or penalties and due-on-sale clauses. Some special provisions are used only rarely and under unique circumstances, such as lock-in clauses, subordination, or release clauses.

**Late Payment Penalty**   Many real estate loans include a clause that imposes a penalty (called a *late charge*) on the borrower for any tardy payments. Although most lenders accept payments up to 10 or 15 days after they are due without penalty, later payments incur a penalty charge—usually a percentage of the total payment or a flat fee of a previously specified amount.

**Prepayment Privilege**   In the absence of any prepayment clause, a borrower may repay the balance of a loan at any time without any restriction or penalty. Some loans include a provision permitting certain portions of the balance to be paid in specific years. For instance, a note may include a prepayment privilege of not more than 20 percent of the original principal amount to be paid in any one year. Other loans might stipulate a fixed sum of money that can be paid in addition to the regular payments in a single year.

**Prepayment Penalties**   A lender will normally not want a borrower to repay a high-yield loan prematurely. If a borrower with a high-interest-rate loan seeks to refinance the property, the existing loan mortgage will be repaid in full, and the lender of the satisfied loan will lose the opportunity for high earnings. As a result, controls are established on prepayments when the interest rates and the resultant lenders' earnings are high.

One form of control is the inclusion of a **prepayment penalty clause** in the loan contract. This penalty usually constitutes a certain percentage of the original face amount of the loan or a percentage of the outstanding balance of the loan. If a contract includes a prepayment penalty, a borrower can be charged up to six months' interest on the loan balance if it is paid in full before it is due.

A lender will usually enforce the prepayment penalty when an existing loan is replaced by a new loan at lower interest or by a loan secured from another lender. However, the penalty is often waived when the lender of record refinances the property with a new loan at a higher interest rate. FHA, DVA, Fannie Mae, and Freddie Mac do not impose prepayment penalties.

In California, a special rule, Article 7, 10242.6 Real Estate Law, for single-family, owner-occupied dwellings, allows a prepayment penalty of up to six months' interest on any amount of principal paid in excess of 20 percent of the loan amount in any one year, but only up to seven years from the loan's inception. After seven years, no penalty may be imposed for prepayment of the loan and, under no circumstances, will there be a prepayment penalty if the dwelling securing the lien has been damaged by a natural disaster.

## Lock-In Clause

The most drastic form of prepayment control is *a lock-in clause* whereby a borrower is actually forbidden to pay a mortgage loan in full before a specific date, sometimes for as long as ten years after its inception. It seems obvious that this lock-in clause would be imposed primarily on very high-yield mortgage loans in order to preserve a lender's earning position for a prescribed time period.

Often, combinations of the prepayment privilege, prepayment penalty, and lock-in clause are melded in a single loan. For example, no prepayment would be allowed at all for a specified period of time from the date of the loan's inception, proportionate amounts of the loan would then become payable in advance according to an agreed-upon schedule, with some penalty imposed if the loan were repaid after three years but before its regularly scheduled time.

## Due-On-Sale Clause

Many financing arrangements include a **due-on-sale clause**, also known as a *call clause, right-to-sell clause, acceleration clause,* or an *alienation clause.* This condition stipulates that a borrower "shall not sell, transfer, encumber, assign, convey, or in any other manner dispose of the collateral property or any part thereof, or turn over the management or operation of any business on the collateral property to any other person, firm, or corporation without the express prior written consent of the lender."

The due-on sale clause further stipulates that if any of the foregoing events should occur *without* the lender's consent, the loan balance will become immediately due in full, with the threat of foreclosure if it is not paid.

On June 28, 1982, in the California case of *Fidelity Federal Savings and Loan Association v. de la Cuesta*, the United States Supreme Court ruled in favor of the ability of federally chartered banks and savings institutions to enforce their due-on-sale provisions.

**Assumption Versus Subject To**

In the absence of a due-on-sale clause, deeds of trust, mortgages, or real property, sales contracts are immediately assumable by buyers of the collateral property. Thus, a buyer may arrange with a seller to purchase a property, assume an existing encumbrance, and make any arrangements for financing the difference between the balance of the existing loan and the purchase price. This difference can be paid either in cash or by some form of junior financing, or both.

There are two ways for a buyer to arrange responsibility for an existing loan. The loan can be **assumed** or the property purchased **"subject to"** any existing encumbrances. If a loan is assumed, the buyer, along with the original borrower and any intervening buyers who have also assumed the loan, becomes personally liable to the lender for its full repayment. In the event of a default, the lender will foreclose, sell the collateral, and sue the original maker of the note and mortgage, as well as all subsequent persons who assumed it, for any deficiencies incurred.

On the other hand, a buyer may purchase a property with an existing encumbrance but stipulate that the purchase is *subject to* the lien of the debt. This approach eliminates the buyer's contingent personal liability in the event of a deficiency judgment. Only the original borrower and any subsequent assumers are liable. Under the subject to format, a buyer may simply walk away from the property, forfeit any equity that has accumulated, and avoid any future responsibilities in the transactions.

Knowledge of the difference between the two approaches can be extremely useful under certain circumstances. For instance, a seller in a low down payment transaction would insist that the buyer assume the underlying mortgage to bind more tightly the responsibility for the mortgage payments. Conversely, a buyer making a substantial down payment could insist upon the "subject to" approach to eliminate any contingent liability. Often, when an existing loan is assumed, the lender seeks to adjust the interest rate to more readily reflect the market. This adjustment is usually a compromise between the market rate and the loan rate and is called a **blended rate.**

No matter whether the buyer assumes the loan or buys "subject to" the lien, the original maker of the note and mortgage remains primarily responsible to the lender until the loan is paid in full or a buyer goes through a process of full substitution.

Full substitution has the seller of a property end personal legal liability as the originator of a real estate loan other than by paying it in full. This is called **novation**, in which the original borrower, as the seller, submits a request to the lender to be replaced with the new buyer as maker on the loan instrument. After the new buyer completes the qualifying process, including a credit analysis, and is accepted by the lender, the old borrower is completely released from liability. The transfer of obligation is completed by executing an amendment to the original loan contract. The new agreement is recorded to maintain the appropriate continuity of the property's title.

## Subordination Clause

To **subordinate** means to place in a lower order, class, or rank. In real estate finance, it involves placing an existing encumbrance or right in a lower priority position to a new loan secured by the same collateral property.

Any real estate finance instrument can be designed to provide for its subordination to the rights of some future lien. For example, a loan created to finance the sale of vacant land to a developer would probably include a subordination clause granting the developer an opportunity to secure new financing to construct houses on a portion of the already encumbered land. The construction lender for the houses would insist on being in *first lien* position. The existing loan given to buy the land would have to be subordinated on those specific portions to be financed with construction mortgages.

The wording used to establish this type of subordination could be: "The mortgagee shall, upon written request from the mortgagor, subordinate the lien of this mortgage on the lot or lots specified in order of release to the lien of a new construction loan or loans from a recognized lending institution."

Subordination is also employed with land leases where the interests of a landlord are subordinated to a new mortgage secured by a tenant in order to develop a parcel of land.

**Release Clause**

When two or more properties are pledged as collateral for a loan, some provision for releasing a portion of the collateral as certain amounts of the loan are repaid is usually incorporated into the financing instrument.

**Exculpatory Clause**

When securing a new real estate loan, some borrowers require that their assets, other than the property being financed, be protected from attachment in the event of a future foreclosure. This limited personal liability can be established by the inclusion of an **exculpatory clause** in the loan contract. This clause stipulates that the borrower's liability under the loan is limited to the property designated in the legal description. In the event of a default, the lender is limited to the recovery of the collateral property only and cannot pursue any deficiency judgments against the borrower's remaining assets.

**Nonrecourse Clause**

Real estate loans are often sold in the financial market (see Chapter 4). When a **nonrecourse clause** is included in the sale's agreement, the seller of the security is not liable if the borrower defaults. The buyer of the security must take action to recover the unpaid balance of the loan from the borrower or foreclose on the collateral. However, if a real estate loan is sold *with recourse*, the seller of the security is obligated to reimburse the buyer if the borrower defaults.

**Extensions and Modifications**

Some loan instruments include provisions for extensions or modifications under special circumstances. Sometimes a lender will allow an extension of time for a financially troubled borrower to continue payments beyond a specific due date. Other lenders may make adjustments and modifications in loan contracts in order to meet particular problems arising after a loan has been in effect for some time. These modifications could include adjustment in payments, interest rates, due dates, or, in extreme cases, payment moratoriums.

Two major problems may arise from an extension or modification of a real estate loan instrument. The first concerns the rights of an intervening lienor, who may move into a priority position when an existing loan is recast. Lenders usually require a complete title examination prior to modifying their loans in order to meet such contingencies. The second problem is the possibility of negating the insurance or guarantee that a mortgage may have under its original form. In the event of any modifications of an insured loan, the guarantee may be lost.

Although there are frequent occasions when a borrower experiences difficulty in meeting payments, lenders are disinclined to make any permanent alteration in the terms of a loan because of the problems mentioned above. Lenders prefer to waive temporarily either full or partial payments, as the situation dictates. After the borrower has overcome temporary difficulties, these payments can be made up over the remaining term of the loan. Under some circumstances, such as a delinquent construction loan, the lender usually continues to carry the loan until the builder can sell the property to a qualified buyer. The delinquency is preferred to a modification and recasting of the loan, which might jeopardize lien priorities.

# ■ SUMMARY

Based upon the concept of hypothecation, a person can borrow funds by pledging interests in real estate as collateral to guarantee the promise to pay. Usually, a borrower's fee simple ownership interest in property is hypothecated to a lender for this purpose. However, other property interests can also be pledged as collateral for a loan—interests such as leaseholds, life estates and mineral, air, and water rights.

The most common California financing instrument is the note and deed of trust. The participants in a deed of trust are the trustor/borrower, the trustee/holder of the deed, and the beneficiary/lender. The note is the promise to pay while the deed of trust is the security for this promise. A deed of trust is drawn in favor of a third-party trustee, signed, acknowledged, recorded, and held in trust until the terms of the loan are satisfied. When this occurs, the trust note is returned to its maker and the trustee reconveys the property to the borrower.

If a default occurs, the trustee is instructed to perfect legal fee by selling the property to recover any losses. Unlike a mortgage, in which the collateral may take up to one year to recover, a trustee may be able to perfect title and effect a sale of the collateral in approximately three months. Often lenders act in a dual capacity as lender-beneficiary *and* trustee, shortening the property recovery period even further.

In a note and mortgage arrangement, the note is a promise to pay, while the mortgage is the pledge of a specific parcel of real property as collateral to secure this promise. A note signed by a mortgagor is a negotiable instrument that specifies the terms and conditions for the repayment of a debt. A mortgage signed by both mortgagor and mortgagee establishes a lien on the collateral property as of the date it is recorded and exists because of its accompanying note. The terms of a mortgage further outline the rights and duties of the participants. When a mortgage debt is satisfied, the lender marks the note "paid in full," signs it, and returns it to its maker, along with a satisfaction of mortgage form. A recorded satisfaction piece will clear the record of the mortgage lien.

A real property sales contract is, at the same time, a sales agreement and a financing instrument between the buyer-borrower-vendee and the seller-lender-vendor. The full terms of the sale, as well as the manner in which the loan will be repaid, are elaborated in this contract financing form. The buyer is granted possession and control of the property during the terms of the payments under the conditions specified in the contract. These conditions are essentially the same as those found in the mortgage and trust deed instruments. When the terms of the contract are satisfied, the seller delivers a deed to the buyer, which transfers full legal title.

The land contract form of real estate financing is utilized primarily when other financing means are not available and is most often a junior lien, second in priority to an existing first mortgage or first deed of trust. The land contract, as a financing form, is used predominantly to facilitate sales between individuals where the buyer is short of cash or cannot obtain a new first mortgage or deed of trust loan.

All three financing instruments may be expanded by a variety of provisions designed to serve the needs of individual borrowers and lenders. Many loans include special provisions allowing for the prepayment of certain portions of the principal from time to time. Other loans assess prepayment penalties if the loan is paid prior to its regularly scheduled completion date. These penalties are usually imposed as a percentage of the principal amount due or three to six months' interest. A more severe prepayment inhibitor is a lock-in clause that prohibits any prepayment for certain specified time periods. Any penalties imposed to inhibit prepayments are designed to preserve a lender's earnings position, and these penalties are usually included in high-interest loans.

Although federally insured (FHA) or guaranteed mortgages (DVA) are generally assumable without the consent of their lenders, most conventional loans include a due-on-sale clause that stipulates a borrower cannot sell the collateral property or transfer it in any manner whatsoever without the prior written consent of the lender.

In the absence of a due-on-sale clause, property may be sold with an existing loan remaining intact. The buyer has two ways in which to arrange responsibility for an existing loan. It can be assumed, in which case the buyer, along with the original borrower, becomes personally liable for the loan or the buyer can make the purchase "subject to" this encumbrance. The latter technique eliminates the buyer's personal liability on the loan, although the seller, as originator of the loan, remains personally liable until the loan is paid in full. Infrequently, a seller will require a buyer to pursue a process of novation, which, upon its successful completion, will substitute the buyer for the seller on an existing loan contract.

Financing instruments can be subordinated to change the priority of their lien positions in relation to subsequent loan instruments. This happens when lenders on land are asked to cooperate in project development by subordinating their lien to a new loan needed to finance the construction of buildings on the subdivided property.

Lending instruments may also be extended or modified to solve unforeseen financial problems of borrowers. With the written agreement of all parties to a loan contract, a payment can be altered, waived for a certain time period, or extended or shortened as the individual case requires. However, lenders are very reluctant to make any permanent modifications to an existing loan contract because, in many instances, the loan's priority lien position and insurance or guarantee may be jeopardized by a recasting of the contract.

# ■ REVIEW QUESTIONS

1. The rights of a borrower to redeem property *after* a judicial foreclosure sale are described as

   a. foreclosure rights.

   b. equitable rights of redemption.

   c. statutory rights of redemption.

   d. statute of frauds.

2. A note has all of the following attributes *EXCEPT* it

   a. is an IOU.

   b. is a promise to pay.

   c. requires a mortgage for validity.

   d. is a negotiable instrument.

3. A covenant of seisin states that the borrower

   a. has possession of the collateral.

   b. has equitable title in the collateral.

   c. owns the collateral free and clear.

   d. warrants title, as represented, to the lender.

4. A deed of trust requires a borrower to pay all of the following *EXCEPT*

   a. property taxes.

   b. life insurance premiums.

   c. hazard insurance premiums.

   d. principal and interest payments.

5. In a deed of trust, which of the following relationships is *NOT* always correct?

   a. Borrower/trustor

   b. Lender/beneficiary

   c. Titleholder/trustee

   d. Trustee/beneficiary

6. In a real property sales contract, which of the following does *NOT* correctly define one of the parties?

   a. Buyer-vendor

   b. Seller-lender

   c. Buyer-borrower

   d. Borrower-vendee

7. A provision in a real estate loan preventing any prepayment for a specified time is called a

   a. prepayment privilege.

   b. prepayment penalty.

   c. lock-in clause.

   d. due-on-sale clause.

8. In an assumption, a due-on-sale clause in a mortgage contract allows the lender to do all of the following *EXCEPT*

   a. review the credit of the original borrower.

   b. review the credit of the buyer.

   c. call in the balance of the loan if not notified.

   d. prohibit the assumption of the mortgage.

9. To assume a loan is to do all of the following *EXCEPT*

   a. agree to make its payments.

   b. become legally liable for its provisions.

   c. relieve the liability of the original mortgagor.

   d. be responsible for maintaining the property.

10. To purchase a property "subject to" an existing mortgage is to do all of the following *EXCEPT*

    a. agree to make the mortgage payments.

    b. become legally liable for the mortgage provisions.

    c. be responsible for maintaining the property.

    d. become the property's fee simple owner.

# ■ EXERCISES

1. Interview a local lender to discover how the assumption of an existing conventional loan on real property is handled. Be specific. Is the new borrower's credit examined, property reappraised, loan terms changed, and so on?

2. Inquire of a local real estate broker about the popularity of the real property sales contract. When is it used and by whom?

# 10

# REAL ESTATE LOAN UNDERWRITING

## ■ KEY TERMS

| | | |
|---|---|---|
| appraisal | drive-by appraisal | market value |
| assets | Fair Isaac Corporation | net worth |
| cloud on the title | (FICO) | underwriting |
| cost approach | financial statements | value in exchange |
| credit report | gross rent multiplier | value in use |
| credit scoring | (GRM) | weighted average |
| depreciation | income approach | technique |
| direct sales compari- | income ratios | |
| son approach | liabilities | |

**Underwriting** a loan for real estate finance includes at least two basic evaluations: estimating the value of the property being pledged as collateral to guarantee repayment and determining the ability of a borrower to repay the loan.

These evaluations establish whether a particular borrower and the subject property will meet the minimum requirements desired by the lender, the investor, or the secondary market into which the loan will probably be sold. The loan approval process is illustrated in Figure 10.1.

# ■ QUALIFYING THE COLLATERAL

Despite the trend toward emphasizing a borrower's financial ability as the basic loan-granting criterion, real estate lenders and guarantors are practical and fully understand that life is filled with unpredictable, uncontrollable events. Death is an ever-present specter that can abruptly eliminate a family's breadwinner. Negative economic activities in a particular geographical area can exert devastating financial impacts. Applicants can be left unemployed as a result of local plant shutdowns; mistakes in personal decisions can result in bankruptcies and divorces, often damaging or destroying credit in the process. To hedge these risks and others, real estate lenders look to the value of the collateral as the final assurance for recovery of their investments in a default situation. Therefore, an accu-

**FIGURE 10.1**
**The Loan Approval Process**

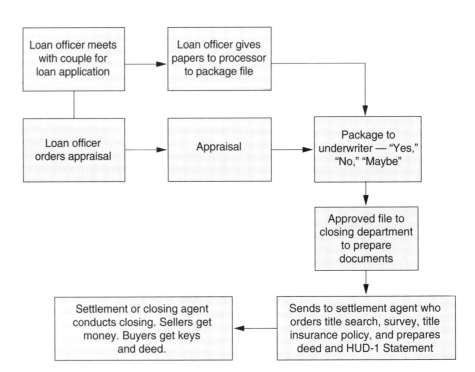

rate estimate of the value of this collateral becomes a pivotal point in the process.

**Definition of Value**

*Value* is defined as the ability of an object to satisfy, directly or indirectly, the needs or desires of human beings. As such, it is called by economists **value in use.** When the value of an object is measured in terms of its power to purchase other objects, it is called **value in exchange.**

From these definitions, it is apparent that value is a function of use and demand. As such, value is *subjective* by its very nature. A seller may have an entirely different idea of the value of a property than a potential buyer. A condemning agency's opinion of a property's value would probably be different from that of the owner. Tax assessors and property owners disagree about a particular property's value, as do many other persons under varying circumstances. However, an appraiser must make an objective estimate of value based on supply and demand in the marketplace.

■ **EXAMPLE**   Jim and Mary Smith recently made an offer on a Craftsman style house near Jim's office. Their offer of $250,000 was accepted with a $25,000 down payment and a 90 percent LTV mortgage loan of $225,000. Never having purchased a home before, Jim and Mary thought that was all they needed to start packing for the move to their new home. Over the past few weeks they have learned a lot about the pitfalls that can happen between the time of a contract acceptance and a successful closing!

First, in qualifying for their loan, they were surprised to learn that they have accumulated too much credit card debt. The lender is requiring that they pay off the outstanding balances and close out three of their credit cards.

They never realized that the property itself had to "qualify." When the appraisal came in at $240,000, the lender was no longer willing to give them a mortgage loan of $225,000! As Jim and Mary do not have the extra cash to make up the difference, they were greatly relieved when the seller eventually agreed to reduce the sales price to $240,000, leaving the down payment at $25,000 with a $215,000 loan.

With settlement only four days away, the Smiths thought they were all set when an unexpected call came from their agent telling them that the title search had come up with a **cloud on the title**. It seems that there is an outstanding mechanic's lien for $3,500 still recorded on the property! Fortunately, the sellers have canceled checks showing that the contractor who replaced their roof three years ago was in fact paid in full, although there had been lengthy arguments about the quality of the work, which had delayed payment.

Finally, 30 days from acceptance of their offer, Jim and Mary are scheduled for settlement tomorrow morning at 10:00 AM with borrowers, collateral, and title all satisfactorily qualified!

There can be only one **market value** for a specific real property at any given point in time. Market value is defined as the price a property would most likely bring if it were exposed for sale in the open market for a reasonable period of time. Implicit in this definition is that both buyer and seller are well informed and under no undue pressure to influence the decision of either party.

In terms of market value, it is important to note the fine distinctions that exist among cost, price, and value. *Cost,* a measure of past expenses, may not reflect current market value, especially if a building is fairly old. *Price,* on the other hand, is a present measure but one that may be affected by some unusual circumstances of a specific transaction. Unique financing terms or a temporarily active local housing market in which potential buyers briefly exceed available properties may cause prices to rise. Therefore, each parcel of property pledged for collateral must be inspected and appraised carefully to estimate its fair market value because this amount will be employed as the basis for determining the mortgage loan amount. Depending on the type of loan to be issued and its concurrent LTV ratio, either the amount of the formal appraisal made as part of the loan process or the purchase price, *whichever is less,* will determine the amount of the loan.

**Staff or Fee Appraisers**

Financial lenders actively engaged in making real estate loans maintain a staff of experienced appraisers whose duties include estimating and verifying property values. Lenders who are less active in the real estate market as well as the FHA and the DVA often hire professional fee appraisers. Sometimes, when very large loans are made, more than one opinion is sought and both staff and fee appraisers participate in an appraisal project.

An **appraisal** is the estimate of a property's value at a specific point in time. It must be reported in writing, in accordance with the Uniform Standards of Professional Appraisal Practice (USPAP), using the Uniform Residential Appraisal Report (see Figure 10.2), by competent individuals whose professional performance is adequately supervised.

Furthermore, to qualify, an appraiser must be state licensed and/or certified by passing an examination consistent with and equivalent to the Uniform State Certification Examination endorsed by the Appraiser Qualification Board of the Appraisal Foundation.

For loans to be issued by federally regulated banks and thrifts, appraisal documents must be provided by licensed and/or certified appraisers. Usually, standards used to certify are more stringent than those used to license. To assist in the development of these professional traits there are a number of appraisers' associations: the Appraisal Institute; the American Society of Appraisers; the National Association of Independent Fee Appraisers; and the National Association of Review Appraisers. Some of these groups maintain active education programs and award achievement designations for completing a number of formal courses and for serving a number of years as an appraiser. For example, the Appraisal Institute offers the MAI (Member, Appraisal Institute), the SRA (Senior Residential Appraiser), the SREA (Senior Real Estate Appraiser), and the SRPA (Senior Real Property Appraiser) designations.

The methods of appraisal are predominantly mathematical. Nevertheless, an appraiser relies on personal interpretive skills to a great degree. Appraising is, therefore, a science that is artfully interpreted.

**The Appraisal Process**

In most appraisals the appraiser comprehensively examines the property and provides a detailed description of its attributes and shortcomings. Based on the ability of accessing data on the Internet pertinent to appraising a specific property, sometimes an appraiser performs a drive-by appraisal of the property when more detail is not required. A **drive-by appraisal** involves the appraiser literally driving by the property for a quick inspection for an opinion of its outward appearance. If it appears to be well-kept and in good condition, it is assumed that the interior is also well maintained and the appraisal will be made on the square footage and location. If, on the other

**FIGURE 10.2**

**Uniform Residential Appraisal Report**

## Uniform Residential Appraisal Report   File #

The purpose of this summary appraisal report is to provide the lender/client with an accurate, and adequately supported, opinion of the market value of the subject property.

**SUBJECT**

| Property Address | | City | | State | Zip Code |
|---|---|---|---|---|---|
| Borrower | | Owner of Public Record | | County | |

Legal Description

| Assessor's Parcel # | | Tax Year | R.E. Taxes $ |
|---|---|---|---|
| Neighborhood Name | | Map Reference | Census Tract |

Occupant ☐ Owner ☐ Tenant ☐ Vacant   Special Assessments $   ☐ PUD   HOA $ ☐ per year ☐ per month

Property Rights Appraised ☐ Fee Simple ☐ Leasehold ☐ Other (describe)

Assignment Type ☐ Purchase Transaction ☐ Refinance Transaction ☐ Other (describe)

Lender/Client   Address

Is the subject property currently offered for sale or has it been offered for sale in the twelve months prior to the effective date of this appraisal? ☐ Yes ☐ No

Report data source(s) used, offering price(s), and date(s).

**CONTRACT**

I ☐ did ☐ did not analyze the contract for sale for the subject purchase transaction. Explain the results of the analysis of the contract for sale or why the analysis was not performed.

Contract Price $   Date of Contract   Is the property seller the owner of public record? ☐ Yes ☐ No Data Source(s)

Is there any financial assistance (loan charges, sale concessions, gift or downpayment assistance, etc.) to be paid by any party on behalf of the borrower? ☐ Yes ☐ No
If Yes, report the total dollar amount and describe the items to be paid.

**NEIGHBORHOOD**

Note: Race and the racial composition of the neighborhood are not appraisal factors.

| Neighborhood Characteristics | | | One-Unit Housing Trends | | | One-Unit Housing | | Present Land Use % | |
|---|---|---|---|---|---|---|---|---|---|
| Location ☐ Urban | ☐ Suburban | ☐ Rural | Property Values ☐ Increasing | ☐ Stable | ☐ Declining | PRICE | AGE | One-Unit | % |
| Built-Up ☐ Over 75% | ☐ 25–75% | ☐ Under 25% | Demand/Supply ☐ Shortage | ☐ In Balance | ☐ Over Supply | $ (000) | (yrs) | 2-4 Unit | % |
| Growth ☐ Rapid | ☐ Stable | ☐ Slow | Marketing Time ☐ Under 3 mths | ☐ 3–6 mths | ☐ Over 6 mths | Low | | Multi-Family | % |
| Neighborhood Boundaries | | | | | | High | | Commercial | % |
| | | | | | | Pred. | | Other | % |

Neighborhood Description

Market Conditions (including support for the above conclusions)

**SITE**

| Dimensions | Area | Shape | View |
|---|---|---|---|

Specific Zoning Classification   Zoning Description

Zoning Compliance ☐ Legal ☐ Legal Nonconforming (Grandfathered Use) ☐ No Zoning ☐ Illegal (describe)

Is the highest and best use of the subject property as improved (or as proposed per plans and specifications) the present use? ☐ Yes ☐ No If No, describe

| Utilities | Public | Other (describe) | | Public | Other (describe) | Off-site Improvements—Type | Public | Private |
|---|---|---|---|---|---|---|---|---|
| Electricity | ☐ | ☐ | Water | ☐ | ☐ | Street | ☐ | ☐ |
| Gas | ☐ | ☐ | Sanitary Sewer | ☐ | ☐ | Alley | ☐ | ☐ |

FEMA Special Flood Hazard Area ☐ Yes ☐ No FEMA Flood Zone   FEMA Map #   FEMA Map Date

Are the utilities and off-site improvements typical for the market area? ☐ Yes ☐ No If No, describe

Are there any adverse site conditions or external factors (easements, encroachments, environmental conditions, land uses, etc.)? ☐ Yes ☐ No If Yes, describe

**IMPROVEMENTS**

| General Description | | Foundation | | Exterior Description | materials/condition | Interior | materials/condition |
|---|---|---|---|---|---|---|---|
| Units ☐ One ☐ One with Accessory Unit | | ☐ Concrete Slab ☐ Crawl Space | | Foundation Walls | | Floors | |
| # of Stories | | ☐ Full Basement ☐ Partial Basement | | Exterior Walls | | Walls | |
| Type ☐ Det. ☐ Att. ☐ S-Det./End Unit | | Basement Area | sq. ft. | Roof Surface | | Trim/Finish | |
| ☐ Existing ☐ Proposed ☐ Under Const. | | Basement Finish | % | Gutters & Downspouts | | Bath Floor | |
| Design (Style) | | ☐ Outside Entry/Exit ☐ Sump Pump | | Window Type | | Bath Wainscot | |
| Year Built | | Evidence of ☐ Infestation | | Storm Sash/Insulated | | Car Storage ☐ None | |
| Effective Age (Yrs) | | ☐ Dampness ☐ Settlement | | Screens | | ☐ Driveway # of Cars | |
| Attic ☐ None | | Heating ☐ FWA ☐ HWBB ☐ Radiant | | Amenities ☐ Woodstove(s) # | | Driveway Surface | |
| ☐ Drop Stair ☐ Stairs | | ☐ Other Fuel | | ☐ Fireplace(s) # ☐ Fence | | ☐ Garage # of Cars | |
| ☐ Floor ☐ Scuttle | | Cooling ☐ Central Air Conditioning | | ☐ Patio/Deck ☐ Porch | | ☐ Carport # of Cars | |
| ☐ Finished ☐ Heated | | ☐ Individual ☐ Other | | ☐ Pool ☐ Other | | ☐ Att. ☐ Det. ☐ Built-in | |

Appliances ☐ Refrigerator ☐ Range/Oven ☐ Dishwasher ☐ Disposal ☐ Microwave ☐ Washer/Dryer ☐ Other (describe)

Finished area **above** grade contains:   Rooms   Bedrooms   Bath(s)   Square Feet of Gross Living Area Above Grade

Additional features (special energy efficient items, etc.)

Describe the condition of the property (including needed repairs, deterioration, renovations, remodeling, etc.).

Are there any physical deficiencies or adverse conditions that affect the livability, soundness, or structural integrity of the property? ☐ Yes ☐ No If Yes, describe

Does the property generally conform to the neighborhood (functional utility, style, condition, use, construction, etc.)? ☐ Yes ☐ No If No, describe

Freddie Mac Form 70  March 2005   Page 1 of 6   Fannie Mae Form 1004  March 2005

**FIGURE 10.2   (CONTINUED)**
**Uniform Residential Appraisal Report**

## Uniform Residential Appraisal Report

File #

There are _____ comparable properties currently offered for sale in the subject neighborhood ranging in price from $ _____ to $ _____

There are _____ comparable sales in the subject neighborhood within the past twelve months ranging in sale price from $ _____ to $ _____

| FEATURE | SUBJECT | COMPARABLE SALE # 1 | | COMPARABLE SALE # 2 | | COMPARABLE SALE # 3 | |
|---|---|---|---|---|---|---|---|
| Address | | | | | | | |
| Proximity to Subject | | | | | | | |
| Sale Price | $ | | $ | | $ | | $ |
| Sale Price/Gross Liv. Area | $           sq. ft. | $           sq. ft. | | $           sq. ft. | | $           sq. ft. | |
| Data Source(s) | | | | | | | |
| Verification Source(s) | | | | | | | |
| VALUE ADJUSTMENTS | DESCRIPTION | DESCRIPTION | +(-) $ Adjustment | DESCRIPTION | +(-) $ Adjustment | DESCRIPTION | +(-) $ Adjustment |
| Sale or Financing Concessions | | | | | | | |
| Date of Sale/Time | | | | | | | |
| Location | | | | | | | |
| Leasehold/Fee Simple | | | | | | | |
| Site | | | | | | | |
| View | | | | | | | |
| Design (Style) | | | | | | | |
| Quality of Construction | | | | | | | |
| Actual Age | | | | | | | |
| Condition | | | | | | | |
| Above Grade | Total  Bdrms.  Baths | Total  Bdrms.  Baths | | Total  Bdrms.  Baths | | Total  Bdrms.  Baths | |
| Room Count | | | | | | | |
| Gross Living Area | sq. ft. | sq. ft. | | sq. ft. | | sq. ft. | |
| Basement & Finished Rooms Below Grade | | | | | | | |
| Functional Utility | | | | | | | |
| Heating/Cooling | | | | | | | |
| Energy Efficient Items | | | | | | | |
| Garage/Carport | | | | | | | |
| Porch/Patio/Deck | | | | | | | |
| | | | | | | | |
| Net Adjustment (Total) | | ☐ +  ☐ - | $ | ☐ +  ☐ - | $ | ☐ +  ☐ - | $ |
| Adjusted Sale Price of Comparables | | Net Adj.        % Gross Adj.      % | $ | Net Adj.        % Gross Adj.      % | $ | Net Adj.        % Gross Adj.      % | $ |

I ☐ did ☐ did not research the sale or transfer history of the subject property and comparable sales. If not, explain

My research ☐ did ☐ did not reveal any prior sales or transfers of the subject property for the three years prior to the effective date of this appraisal.

Data source(s)

My research ☐ did ☐ did not reveal any prior sales or transfers of the comparable sales for the year prior to the date of sale of the comparable sale.

Data source(s)

Report the results of the research and analysis of the prior sale or transfer history of the subject property and comparable sales (report additional prior sales on page 3).

| ITEM | SUBJECT | COMPARABLE SALE # 1 | COMPARABLE SALE # 2 | COMPARABLE SALE # 3 |
|---|---|---|---|---|
| Date of Prior Sale/Transfer | | | | |
| Price of Prior Sale/Transfer | | | | |
| Data Source(s) | | | | |
| Effective Date of Data Source(s) | | | | |

Analysis of prior sale or transfer history of the subject property and comparable sales

Summary of Sales Comparison Approach

Indicated Value by Sales Comparison Approach  $

**Indicated Value by:  Sales Comparison Approach  $**          Cost Approach (if developed) $          Income Approach (if developed) $

This appraisal is made ☐ "as is", ☐ subject to completion per plans and specifications on the basis of a hypothetical condition that the improvements have been completed, ☐ subject to the following repairs or alterations on the basis of a hypothetical condition that the repairs or alterations have been completed, or ☐ subject to the following required inspection based on the extraordinary assumption that the condition or deficiency does not require alteration or repair:

**Based on a complete visual inspection of the interior and exterior areas of the subject property, defined scope of work, statement of assumptions and limiting conditions, and appraiser's certification, my (our) opinion of the market value, as defined, of the real property that is the subject of this report is**
**$                    , as of                    , which is the date of inspection and the effective date of this appraisal.**

Freddie Mac Form 70   March 2005                    Page 2 of 6                    Fannie Mae Form 1004   March 2005

**FIGURE 10.2   (CONTINUED)**
**Uniform Residential Appraisal Report**

# Uniform Residential Appraisal Report

File #

**ADDITIONAL COMMENTS**

### COST APPROACH TO VALUE (not required by Fannie Mae)

Provide adequate information for the lender/client to replicate the below cost figures and calculations.

Support for the opinion of site value (summary of comparable land sales or other methods for estimating site value)

| | | |
|---|---|---|
| ESTIMATED ☐ REPRODUCTION OR ☐ REPLACEMENT COST NEW | OPINION OF SITE VALUE ............................................. = $ | |
| Source of cost data | Dwelling      Sq. Ft. @ $ | = $ |
| Quality rating from cost service      Effective date of cost data | Sq. Ft. @ $ | = $ |
| Comments on Cost Approach (gross living area calculations, depreciation, etc.) | Garage/Carport      Sq. Ft. @ $ | = $ |
| | Total Estimate of Cost-New | = $ |
| | Less      Physical      Functional      External | |
| | Depreciation | = $(          ) |
| | Depreciated Cost of Improvements.......................................... | = $ |
| | As-Is" Value of Site Improvements.......... | = $ |
| Estimated Remaining Economic Life (HUD and VA only)      Years | Indicated Value By Cost Approach ............................ | = $ |

### INCOME APPROACH TO VALUE (not required by Fannie Mae)

Estimated Monthly Market Rent $      X Gross Rent Multiplier      = $      Indicated Value by Income Approach

Summary of Income Approach (including support for market rent and GRM)

### PROJECT INFORMATION FOR PUDs (if applicable)

Is the developer/builder in control of the Homeowners' Association (HOA)? ☐ Yes ☐ No   Unit type(s) ☐ Detached ☐ Attached

Provide the following information for PUDs ONLY if the developer/builder is in control of the HOA and the subject property is an attached dwelling unit.

Legal name of project

| Total number of phases | Total number of units | Total number of units sold |
|---|---|---|
| Total number of units rented | Total number of units for sale | Data source(s) |

Was the project created by the conversion of an existing building(s) into a PUD? ☐ Yes ☐ No   If Yes, date of conversion

Does the project contain any multi-dwelling units? ☐ Yes ☐ No   Data source(s)

Are the units, common elements, and recreation facilities complete? ☐ Yes ☐ No   If No, describe the status of completion.

Are the common elements leased to or by the Homeowners' Association? ☐ Yes ☐ No   If Yes, describe the rental terms and options.

Describe common elements and recreational facilities

**FIGURE 10.2** (CONTINUED)
**Uniform Residential
Appraisal Report**

## Uniform Residential Appraisal Report   File #

This report form is designed to report an appraisal of a one-unit property or a one-unit property with an accessory unit; including a unit in a planned unit development (PUD). This report form is not designed to report an appraisal of a manufactured home or a unit in a condominium or cooperative project.

This appraisal report is subject to the following scope of work, intended use, intended user, definition of market value, statement of assumptions and limiting conditions, and certifications. Modifications, additions, or deletions to the intended use, intended user, definition of market value, or assumptions and limiting conditions are not permitted. The appraiser may expand the scope of work to include any additional research or analysis necessary based on the complexity of this appraisal assignment. Modifications or deletions to the certifications are also not permitted. However, additional certifications that do not constitute material alterations to this appraisal report, such as those required by law or those related to the appraiser's continuing education or membership in an appraisal organization, are permitted.

**SCOPE OF WORK:** The scope of work for this appraisal is defined by the complexity of this appraisal assignment and the reporting requirements of this appraisal report form, including the following definition of market value, statement of assumptions and limiting conditions, and certifications. The appraiser must, at a minimum: (1) perform a complete visual inspection of the interior and exterior areas of the subject property, (2) inspect the neighborhood, (3) inspect each of the comparable sales from at least the street, (4) research, verify, and analyze data from reliable public and/or private sources, and (5) report his or her analysis, opinions, and conclusions in this appraisal report.

**INTENDED USE:** The intended use of this appraisal report is for the lender/client to evaluate the property that is the subject of this appraisal for a mortgage finance transaction.

**INTENDED USER:** The intended user of this appraisal report is the lender/client.

**DEFINITION OF MARKET VALUE:** The most probable price which a property should bring in a competitive and open market under all conditions requisite to a fair sale, the buyer and seller, each acting prudently, knowledgeably and assuming the price is not affected by undue stimulus. Implicit in this definition is the consummation of a sale as of a specified date and the passing of title from seller to buyer under conditions whereby: (1) buyer and seller are typically motivated; (2) both parties are well informed or well advised, and each acting in what he or she considers his or her own best interest; (3) a reasonable time is allowed for exposure in the open market; (4) payment is made in terms of cash in U. S. dollars or in terms of financial arrangements comparable thereto; and (5) the price represents the normal consideration for the property sold unaffected by special or creative financing or sales concessions* granted by anyone associated with the sale.

*Adjustments to the comparables must be made for special or creative financing or sales concessions. No adjustments are necessary for those costs which are normally paid by sellers as a result of tradition or law in a market area; these costs are readily identifiable since the seller pays these costs in virtually all sales transactions. Special or creative financing adjustments can be made to the comparable property by comparisons to financing terms offered by a third party institutional lender that is not already involved in the property or transaction. Any adjustment should not be calculated on a mechanical dollar for dollar cost of the financing or concession but the dollar amount of any adjustment should approximate the market's reaction to the financing or concessions based on the appraiser's judgment.

**STATEMENT OF ASSUMPTIONS AND LIMITING CONDITIONS:** The appraiser's certification in this report is subject to the following assumptions and limiting conditions:

1. The appraiser will not be responsible for matters of a legal nature that affect either the property being appraised or the title to it, except for information that he or she became aware of during the research involved in performing this appraisal. The appraiser assumes that the title is good and marketable and will not render any opinions about the title.

2. The appraiser has provided a sketch in this appraisal report to show the approximate dimensions of the improvements. The sketch is included only to assist the reader in visualizing the property and understanding the appraiser's determination of its size.

3. The appraiser has examined the available flood maps that are provided by the Federal Emergency Management Agency (or other data sources) and has noted in this appraisal report whether any portion of the subject site is located in an identified Special Flood Hazard Area. Because the appraiser is not a surveyor, he or she makes no guarantees, express or implied, regarding this determination.

4. The appraiser will not give testimony or appear in court because he or she made an appraisal of the property in question, unless specific arrangements to do so have been made beforehand, or as otherwise required by law.

5. The appraiser has noted in this appraisal report any adverse conditions (such as needed repairs, deterioration, the presence of hazardous wastes, toxic substances, etc.) observed during the inspection of the subject property or that he or she became aware of during the research involved in performing this appraisal. Unless otherwise stated in this appraisal report, the appraiser has no knowledge of any hidden or unapparent physical deficiencies or adverse conditions of the property (such as, but not limited to, needed repairs, deterioration, the presence of hazardous wastes, toxic substances, adverse environmental conditions, etc.) that would make the property less valuable, and has assumed that there are no such conditions and makes no guarantees or warranties, express or implied. The appraiser will not be responsible for any such conditions that do exist or for any engineering or testing that might be required to discover whether such conditions exist. Because the appraiser is not an expert in the field of environmental hazards, this appraisal report must not be considered as an environmental assessment of the property.

6. The appraiser has based his or her appraisal report and valuation conclusion for an appraisal that is subject to satisfactory completion, repairs, or alterations on the assumption that the completion, repairs, or alterations of the subject property will be performed in a professional manner.

**FIGURE 10.2** (CONTINUED)
**Uniform Residential Appraisal Report**

## Uniform Residential Appraisal Report    File #

**APPRAISER'S CERTIFICATION:** The Appraiser certifies and agrees that:

1. I have, at a minimum, developed and reported this appraisal in accordance with the scope of work requirements stated in this appraisal report.

2. I performed a complete visual inspection of the interior and exterior areas of the subject property. I reported the condition of the improvements in factual, specific terms. I identified and reported the physical deficiencies that could affect the livability, soundness, or structural integrity of the property.

3. I performed this appraisal in accordance with the requirements of the Uniform Standards of Professional Appraisal Practice that were adopted and promulgated by the Appraisal Standards Board of The Appraisal Foundation and that were in place at the time this appraisal report was prepared.

4. I developed my opinion of the market value of the real property that is the subject of this report based on the sales comparison approach to value. I have adequate comparable market data to develop a reliable sales comparison approach for this appraisal assignment. I further certify that I considered the cost and income approaches to value but did not develop them, unless otherwise indicated in this report.

5. I researched, verified, analyzed, and reported on any current agreement for sale for the subject property, any offering for sale of the subject property in the twelve months prior to the effective date of this appraisal, and the prior sales of the subject property for a minimum of three years prior to the effective date of this appraisal, unless otherwise indicated in this report.

6. I researched, verified, analyzed, and reported on the prior sales of the comparable sales for a minimum of one year prior to the date of sale of the comparable sale, unless otherwise indicated in this report.

7. I selected and used comparable sales that are locationally, physically, and functionally the most similar to the subject property.

8. I have not used comparable sales that were the result of combining a land sale with the contract purchase price of a home that has been built or will be built on the land.

9. I have reported adjustments to the comparable sales that reflect the market's reaction to the differences between the subject property and the comparable sales.

10. I verified, from a disinterested source, all information in this report that was provided by parties who have a financial interest in the sale or financing of the subject property.

11. I have knowledge and experience in appraising this type of property in this market area.

12. I am aware of, and have access to, the necessary and appropriate public and private data sources, such as multiple listing services, tax assessment records, public land records and other such data sources for the area in which the property is located.

13. I obtained the information, estimates, and opinions furnished by other parties and expressed in this appraisal report from reliable sources that I believe to be true and correct.

14. I have taken into consideration the factors that have an impact on value with respect to the subject neighborhood, subject property, and the proximity of the subject property to adverse influences in the development of my opinion of market value. I have noted in this appraisal report any adverse conditions (such as, but not limited to, needed repairs, deterioration, the presence of hazardous wastes, toxic substances, adverse environmental conditions, etc.) observed during the inspection of the subject property or that I became aware of during the research involved in performing this appraisal. I have considered these adverse conditions in my analysis of the property value, and have reported on the effect of the conditions on the value and marketability of the subject property.

15. I have not knowingly withheld any significant information from this appraisal report and, to the best of my knowledge, all statements and information in this appraisal report are true and correct.

16. I stated in this appraisal report my own personal, unbiased, and professional analysis, opinions, and conclusions, which are subject only to the assumptions and limiting conditions in this appraisal report.

17. I have no present or prospective interest in the property that is the subject of this report, and I have no present or prospective personal interest or bias with respect to the participants in the transaction. I did not base, either partially or completely, my analysis and/or opinion of market value in this appraisal report on the race, color, religion, sex, age, marital status, handicap, familial status, or national origin of either the prospective owners or occupants of the subject property or of the present owners or occupants of the properties in the vicinity of the subject property or on any other basis prohibited by law.

18. My employment and/or compensation for performing this appraisal or any future or anticipated appraisals was not conditioned on any agreement or understanding, written or otherwise, that I would report (or present analysis supporting) a predetermined specific value, a predetermined minimum value, a range or direction in value, a value that favors the cause of any party, or the attainment of a specific result or occurrence of a specific subsequent event (such as approval of a pending mortgage loan application).

19. I personally prepared all conclusions and opinions about the real estate that were set forth in this appraisal report. If I relied on significant real property appraisal assistance from any individual or individuals in the performance of this appraisal or the preparation of this appraisal report, I have named such individual(s) and disclosed the specific tasks performed in this appraisal report. I certify that any individual so named is qualified to perform the tasks. I have not authorized anyone to make a change to any item in this appraisal report; therefore, any change made to this appraisal is unauthorized and I will take no responsibility for it.

20. I identified the lender/client in this appraisal report who is the individual, organization, or agent for the organization that ordered and will receive this appraisal report.

Freddie Mac Form 70  March 2005                     Page 5 of 6                     Fannie Mae Form 1004  March 2005

**FIGURE 10.2** (CONTINUED)
**Uniform Residential
Appraisal Report**

## Uniform Residential Appraisal Report   File #

21. The lender/client may disclose or distribute this appraisal report to: the borrower; another lender at the request of the borrower; the mortgagee or its successors and assigns; mortgage insurers; government sponsored enterprises; other secondary market participants; data collection or reporting services; professional appraisal organizations; any department, agency, or instrumentality of the United States; and any state, the District of Columbia, or other jurisdictions; without having to obtain the appraiser's or supervisory appraiser's (if applicable) consent. Such consent must be obtained before this appraisal report may be disclosed or distributed to any other party (including, but not limited to, the public through advertising, public relations, news, sales, or other media).

22. I am aware that any disclosure or distribution of this appraisal report by me or the lender/client may be subject to certain laws and regulations. Further, I am also subject to the provisions of the Uniform Standards of Professional Appraisal Practice that pertain to disclosure or distribution by me.

23. The borrower, another lender at the request of the borrower, the mortgagee or its successors and assigns, mortgage insurers, government sponsored enterprises, and other secondary market participants may rely on this appraisal report as part of any mortgage finance transaction that involves any one or more of these parties.

24. If this appraisal report was transmitted as an "electronic record" containing my "electronic signature," as those terms are defined in applicable federal and/or state laws (excluding audio and video recordings), or a facsimile transmission of this appraisal report containing a copy or representation of my signature, the appraisal report shall be as effective, enforceable and valid as if a paper version of this appraisal report were delivered containing my original hand written signature.

25. Any intentional or negligent misrepresentation(s) contained in this appraisal report may result in civil liability and/or criminal penalties including, but not limited to, fine or imprisonment or both under the provisions of Title 18, United States Code, Section 1001, et seq., or similar state laws.

**SUPERVISORY APPRAISER'S CERTIFICATION:** The Supervisory Appraiser certifies and agrees that:

1. I directly supervised the appraiser for this appraisal assignment, have read the appraisal report, and agree with the appraiser's analysis, opinions, statements, conclusions, and the appraiser's certification.

2. I accept full responsibility for the contents of this appraisal report including, but not limited to, the appraiser's analysis, opinions, statements, conclusions, and the appraiser's certification.

3. The appraiser identified in this appraisal report is either a sub-contractor or an employee of the supervisory appraiser (or the appraisal firm), is qualified to perform this appraisal, and is acceptable to perform this appraisal under the applicable state law.

4. This appraisal report complies with the Uniform Standards of Professional Appraisal Practice that were adopted and promulgated by the Appraisal Standards Board of The Appraisal Foundation and that were in place at the time this appraisal report was prepared.

5. If this appraisal report was transmitted as an "electronic record" containing my "electronic signature," as those terms are defined in applicable federal and/or state laws (excluding audio and video recordings), or a facsimile transmission of this appraisal report containing a copy or representation of my signature, the appraisal report shall be as effective, enforceable and valid as if a paper version of this appraisal report were delivered containing my original hand written signature.

**APPRAISER**

Signature_____
Name _____
Company Name _____
Company Address_____
_____
Telephone Number _____
Email Address_____
Date of Signature and Report_____
Effective Date of Appraisal _____
State Certification #_____
or State License # _____
or Other (describe) _____ State # _____
State _____
Expiration Date of Certification or License _____

ADDRESS OF PROPERTY APPRAISED

_____
_____

APPRAISED VALUE OF SUBJECT PROPERTY $ _____
LENDER/CLIENT
Name _____
Company Name _____
Company Address_____
_____
Email Address_____

**SUPERVISORY APPRAISER (ONLY IF REQUIRED)**

Signature_____
Name _____
Company Name _____
Company Address_____
_____
Telephone Number _____
Email Address_____
Date of Signature _____
State Certification # _____
or State License # _____
State _____
Expiration Date of Certification or License _____

SUBJECT PROPERTY

☐ Did not inspect subject property
☐ Did inspect exterior of subject property from street
   Date of Inspection _____
☐ Did inspect interior and exterior of subject property
   Date of Inspection _____

COMPARABLE SALES

☐ Did not inspect exterior of comparable sales from street
☐ Did inspect exterior of comparable sales from street
   Date of Inspection _____

Freddie Mac Form 70   March 2005                    Page 6 of 6                    Fannie Mae Form 1004   March 2005

hand, the property looks worn and not well-kept, the drive-by appraiser's report would reveal this information and include a recommendation for a more comprehensive examination or even a denial of the loan.

The appraisal process generally includes defining the appraisal problem, determining the purpose for the appraisal, examining the neighborhood and property being appraised, collecting the pertinent data, applying the appropriate approaches to estimate value, reconciling these value estimates, and preparing the appraisal report.

The single most important skill in appraising is the collection of data pertinent to the problem. The appraiser estimates value primarily by carefully examining the subject property and comparing it with properties with like features (comparables, or comps). The appraiser must not only seek to find properties similar to the subject property in age, size, physical condition, location, and zoning, but must gather recent relevant data about these comparable properties to help estimate the value. The estimate of value will be based on the appraiser's opinion of the subject property's probable worth as a result of skillfully interpreting the data acquired from the most appropriate appraisal approach.

Three basic approaches are used to arrive at an estimate of a property's value. These three techniques—the direct sales comparison approach, the cost approach, and the income approach—will be described in general terms here. Any student seeking a more in-depth analysis of these approaches should consult *Fundamentals of Real Estate Appraisal.**

**Direct Sales Comparison Approach**

The **direct sales comparison approach** is based on a comparison of the subject property with similar properties in the same locale that have sold recently. An appraiser searches the records of the county recorder's office and the various multiple-listing services and maintains a comprehensive and current filing system. Thus, the appraiser is usually able to discover the sales prices and terms involved in recent transfers of properties *similar* to the property being appraised. In addition to these sources of information,

---

* William L Ventolo, Jr. and Martha R. Williams, 10th ed. Chicago: Dearborn Real Estate Education, 2008.

an appraiser can usually review the lender's files and find many comparables to use in estimating the subject property's value.

The proficiency of an appraiser is never more clearly tested than in the direct sales comparison approach. Training and experience must be employed artfully to interpret, evaluate, and reconcile the data collected from comparable sales into a dollar amount that represents the subject property's value. No two properties are exactly alike; the appraiser must make many subjective adjustments to the sales prices of the comparable properties (comps) to reflect more clearly the subject property's worth. The reasons for the various differences in the sales prices of comps must be determined and their prices adjusted to reflect what they would have sold for had they more exactly matched the subject property.

For instance, the appraiser must be able to estimate what the sales price of a comp would be if it were the same age, condition, style, floor plan, size, location, and material as the subject property and also what price it would bring on the day of the appraisal, rather than at the time of its actual sale, six months or a year ago. The appraiser must make these adjustments, all of which involve judgments based on experience, in order to estimate the subject property's value more accurately. An appraiser's efforts depend on the magnitude of the loan and the degree of risk involved. These efforts can expand from a mere impression of value, as discerned by a drive-by examination of the subject property and a recollection of other similar properties recently sold, to a massive report based on 10, 15, or more comparables. Each comparable is adjusted for significant variables to reflect the subject's value. These comprehensive appraisals are made easier by the increasing use of computer technology.

■ **EXAMPLE**   The subject house is brick, ten years old, in good condition, has three bedrooms and 1½ baths, has 1,800 square feet, and is located in a medium-quality neighborhood. Comparable "A" sold for $140,000 last week, is made of brick, 8 years old, in good condition, has three bedrooms and 1½ baths, has 1,500 square feet, and is in a good neighborhood. Comparable "B" sold for $160,000 two weeks ago, is a frame house, 10 years old, in good condition, has four bedrooms and only one bath, has 2,000 square feet, and is located in a good neighborhood.

|  | Subject House | Comp A | Comp B |
|---|---|---|---|
| Price |  | $140,000 | $160,000 |
| Material | Brick | 0 | +18,000 |
| Age | 10 years | -5,600 |  |
| Condition | Good | 0 | 0 |
| Bedrooms | 3 | 0 | -25,000 |
| Baths | 1½ | 0 | +10,000 |
| Square Feet | 1,800 | +22,500 | -15,000 |
| Adjusted Price |  | $156,900 | $138,000 |

Estimate of subject property's market value is $150,000.

A combination of the drive-by appraisal and detailed computer research is accepted by Fannie Mae and Freddie Mac lenders.

## Cost Approach

The cost approach method of estimating a property's value is based on the current value of its physical parts. In the **cost approach**, an appraiser examines and evaluates the subject property, its improvements, amenities, and land value. This technique includes an estimation of the current cost to reproduce the improvements, an estimate of the improvements' depreciation, and an estimate of the land value as derived by using the direct sales comparison approach.

An appraiser accumulates data about the current cost of building the subject property. If the property is actually newly constructed, its plans and specifications are reviewed and analyzed to estimate its value. An older property requires an examination of its design and composition to estimate its current reproduction cost. Obviously, the cost approach works best with recently built properties or unique one-of-a-kind properties.

When used properties are appraised, a depreciation allowance must be applied to the costs of reproduction. This depreciation adjustment is based on the *rule of substitution* that states that no rational, economical person would pay the same price for a used property as for the same property when new.

**Depreciation** is defined as a lessening in value from physical deterioration, functional obsolescence, or economic obsolescence. An example of physical deterioration is the six-year-old roof that may need patching or replacement. Functional obsolescence describes a situation in which access to one bedroom is available only through an adjoining bedroom. An example of economic obsolescence is a location downwind from a sewage treatment plant. The appraiser must include in the adjustments a consideration of the present physical condition of the improvements, their functional utility, and the effects of forces outside the property on its value.

After the reproduction cost is calculated and adjusted to allow for depreciation of the improvements, the value of the land, as determined by the direct sales comparison approach, is added to the depreciated figure to arrive at an estimate of the total property value. The cost approach in formula form is as follows:

$$\frac{\text{Current Replacement Cost of Improvements}}{- \text{Depreciation}}$$
$$\frac{\text{Estimate of Current value of improvements}}{+ \text{Amenities and Land Value}}$$
$$\text{Estimate of Current value of Property}$$

■ **EXAMPLE**   If a 10-year-old house with an estimated 50-year life consists of 1,800 square feet, with a current reproduction cost factor of $100 per square foot, and the lot is worth $50,000, the estimate of property value using the cost approach is $194,000.

|  |  |
|---|---|
| 1,800 | Square Feet |
| × $100 | Reproduction Cost 180,000 Value of Improvements |
| × 0.80 | Straight Line Depreciation Rate Reciprocal |
| 144,000 | Depreciated Value of Improvements |
| + 50,000 | Lot Value |
| 194,000 | Total Value of Property |

## Income Capitalization Approach

The **income approach** measures the value of a property on the basis of its ability to generate income by capitalizing the net annual income using a current market *capitalization rate*. In other words, the income approach actually measures the present worth of a property's income stream based on an investor's required rate of return.

This method is best suited to estimating the value of apartments, stores, shopping centers, and office buildings. The first factor an appraiser determines is the property's annual *gross market income*. Although a subject property may have an established rental income, an appraiser must verify whether this income is based on market rents or rents that are higher or lower than the market rate. Thus, the direct sales comparison approach is first employed to locate similar properties and analyze their rental schedules.

After the gross annual rental income has been determined, an appropriate amount must be deducted for operating expenses such as property taxes, insurance, maintenance, vacancy allowances, management, utilities, pest control, snow removal, accounting services, and advertising. Although depreciation is not considered an operating expense per se, most appraisers will include an item called *reserves for replacements* or *reserves for major repairs*. An income property should be able to support itself in every way to substantiate its value.

A *net annual market rental income* is derived when the operating expenses are deducted from the gross annual market rent. This net rental income is the amount that is capitalized into an estimate of the property's value using the formula:

$$\text{Value} = \frac{\text{Net income}}{\text{Capitalization rate}}$$

■ **EXAMPLE**  Consider an apartment house generating $250,000 gross annual income. Operating expenses, including vacancies, total 45 percent of this income. In a market that supports a 10 percent capitalization rate, this property is worth $1,375,000 using the income approach.

| | |
|---|---:|
| Gross Annual Income | $250,000 |
| Operating Ratio Reciprocal | 0.55 |
| Net Operating Income 1 | 137,500 |
| Capitalization Rate | ÷ 0.10 |
| Estimate of Value | $1,375,000 |

## Gross Rent Multiplier (GRM)

When estimating the value of single-family homes, a **gross rent multiplier (GRM)**, or *gross income multiplier (GIM)*, is often used. The GRM is derived by locating comparable properties that have sold recently, then dividing their sales prices by a monthly market gross rent to derive the multiplier.

■ **EXAMPLE**  A property that sold for $200,000 and could be rented for $1,000 per month will develop a GRM of 200 ($200,000 ÷ $1,000 = 200). Likewise, when a property similar to the property being appraised is sold for $180,000 and could be rented for $700 per month, the GRM is 257.14 ($180,000 ÷ $700 = 257.14). Therefore, if the subject property could be rented for $900 per month and the market GRM is 250, its estimated value is $225,000 ($900 × 250 = $225,000).

## Reconciliation of Data and Opinion of Value

After applying the preceding approaches pertinent to the estimate of a particular property's value, an appraiser reviews the results, reconciles or correlates the different values derived, and renders a written opinion of the property's value. This opinion may place more emphasis on one approach than another. For instance, the cost approach is more reliable when appraising a newer property than an older one. The income approach is more valid with true income property rather than with houses or vacant land on which an appraiser must impute a fictitious "rent" before this approach can be applied. The direct sales comparison approach supplies the balancing aspect to an appraisal, frequently providing the middle value in a spectrum where the cost approach is invariably high and the income approach is usually low. The direct sales comparison approach is also an integral part of the other two approaches. It is used in the cost approach to determine the value of the land and in the income approach to help derive the net annual market rental income to be capitalized. One way of reconciliation is to apply the **weighted average technique**, which assigns percentages to illustrate the importance of one approach over another.

■ **EXAMPLE** If an appraiser finds that the market, cost, and income approaches indicate $200,000, $210,000, and $220,000 respectively, and the appraiser weights them 50%, 30%, and 20% respectively, the reconciliation will be $207,000.

$$
\begin{aligned}
\$200,000 \times 0.50 &= \$100,000 \\
210,000 \times 0.30 &= 63,000 \\
220,000 \times 0.20 &= \underline{44,000} \\
\text{weighted average} &\quad 207,000
\end{aligned}
$$

When an appraisal is completed, it is delivered to the loan officer to aid in the final loan decision. As noted previously, a loan amount is based on the *lesser* of either this appraised value or the sales price of the property.

## ■ QUALIFYING THE BORROWER

Prior to the advent of high loan-to-value (L/V) ratios and long-term loan amortization, little emphasis needed to be placed on a borrower's ability to repay a real estate loan. Loans were created at 50 to 60 percent of a collateral property's value and were based upon a payment of interest-only for certain short specified periods, usually one to five years, with the entire principal due in full at the stop date. If the principal could not be paid in full, partial payment could be made and the balance of the loan amount recast for an additional five years. This five-year rollover pattern could continue until the debt was paid in full. However, if a borrower did not meet the payment obligations promptly and in the amount called for in the contract, the collateral was quickly foreclosed upon and sold for an amount sufficient to recompense the lender.

This repayment pattern has not changed much despite the 30-year amortization schedules and regular monthly payments of principal *and* interest that are the framework of the current U.S. real estate financing system. The average age of a real estate loan is still only seven to eight years, very similar to the previously established system. What has changed, and quite dramatically, is the loan-to-value (L/V) ratio. Today lenders are able to make loans of up to 100 percent or more of a property's value. As a result of increasing loans close to a collateral's total value, the emphasis has shifted from the standard past procedure of a lender placing reliance on the successful sale of the collateral to protect the investment to the more current attitude of looking to the credit of the borrower as the primary protection along with mortgage insurance and guarantees.

While lenders under insured or guaranteed programs of real estate finance do not directly bear the risks of default, they still must follow the directions of their guaranteeing agencies and carefully screen loan applicants to derive some reasonable estimate of not only the *ability* of borrowers to pay, but also their attitude about meeting their contractual obligations responsibly. Thus, a great effort is made to check and evaluate thoroughly a potential borrower's past credit history and current financial status in order to predict future economic stability.

**Loan Application**

Every formal real estate loan processing operation begins with a borrower completing a standardized loan application form and submitting it to a prospective lender. All loan application forms identify the property to be pledged and the amount of money requested. Additional facts about the prospective borrower will also be included, along with information about the loan sought. Most loan applications show the borrower's employment and income record, a statement of assets and liabilities, and a list of credit references.

Figure 10.3 is an example of a typical residential loan application. This and similar forms are used by lenders to secure pertinent information from an applicant requesting a real estate loan. The bulk of the application is devoted to securing personal information from the borrower about family size and ages of dependent children, sources of income, employment history, and a comprehensive financial statement. In addition, the property is identified by its legal description. If the borrower's credit ability is approved, a complete physical appraisal of the property will be made prior to issuing the loan. In the early stages of the loan processing procedure, however, the legal description is sufficient.

**Financial Statement.**   All **financial statements** follow a standard format that lists all assets and all liabilities. This enables a lender to assess quickly and efficiently the current financial status of an applicant.

FIGURE **10.3**
**Uniform Residential Loan Application**

## Uniform Residential Loan Application

This application is designed to be completed by the applicant(s) with the Lender's assistance. Applicants should complete this form as "Borrower" or "Co-Borrower," as applicable. Co-Borrower information must also be provided (and the appropriate box checked) when ☐ the income or assets of a person other than the Borrower (including the Borrower's spouse) will be used as a basis for loan qualification or ☐ the income or assets of the Borrower's spouse or other person who has community property rights pursuant to state law will not be used as a basis for loan qualification, but his or her liabilities must be considered because the spouse or other person has community property rights pursuant to applicable law and Borrower resides in a community property state, the security property is located in a community property state, or the Borrower is relying on other property located in a community property state as a basis for repayment of the loan.

If this is an application for joint credit, Borrower and Co-Borrower each agree that we intend to apply for joint credit (sign below):

| Borrower | Co-Borrower |
|---|---|

| **I. TYPE OF MORTGAGE AND TERMS OF LOAN** | | | | |
|---|---|---|---|---|
| **Mortgage Applied for:** ☐ VA ☐ FHA | ☐ Conventional ☐ USDA/Rural Housing Service | ☐ Other (explain): | Agency Case Number | Lender Case Number |
| Amount $ | Interest Rate % | No. of Months | **Amortization Type:** | ☐ Fixed Rate ☐ GPM | ☐ Other (explain): ☐ ARM (type): |

| **II. PROPERTY INFORMATION AND PURPOSE OF LOAN** | | |
|---|---|---|
| Subject Property Address (street, city, state & ZIP) | | No. of Units |
| Legal Description of Subject Property (attach description if necessary) | | Year Built |
| Purpose of Loan ☐ Purchase ☐ Construction ☐ Other (explain): ☐ Refinance ☐ Construction-Permanent | Property will be: ☐ Primary Residence ☐ Secondary Residence | ☐ Investment |

*Complete this line if construction or construction-permanent loan.*

| Year Lot Acquired | Original Cost $ | Amount Existing Liens $ | (a) Present Value of Lot $ | (b) Cost of Improvements $ | Total (a + b) $ 0.00 |
|---|---|---|---|---|---|

*Complete this line if this is a refinance loan.*

| Year Acquired | Original Cost $ | Amount Existing Liens $ | Purpose of Refinance | Describe Improvements ☐ made ☐ to be made | |
|---|---|---|---|---|---|
| | | | | Cost: $ | |

| Title will be held in what Name(s) | Manner in which Title will be held | Estate will be held in: ☐ Fee Simple ☐ Leasehold (show expiration date) |
|---|---|---|
| Source of Down Payment, Settlement Charges, and/or Subordinate Financing (explain) | | |

| **Borrower** | **III. BORROWER INFORMATION** | **Co-Borrower** |
|---|---|---|

| Borrower's Name (include Jr. or Sr. if applicable) | Co-Borrower's Name (include Jr. or Sr. if applicable) |
|---|---|

| Social Security Number | Home Phone (incl. area code) | DOB (mm/dd/yyyy) | Yrs. School | Social Security Number | Home Phone (incl. area code) | DOB (mm/dd/yyyy) | Yrs. School |
|---|---|---|---|---|---|---|---|

| ☐ Married ☐ Unmarried (include ☐ Separated single, divorced, widowed) | Dependents (not listed by Co-Borrower) no. ages | ☐ Married ☐ Unmarried (include ☐ Separated single, divorced, widowed) | Dependents (not listed by Borrower) no. ages |
|---|---|---|---|
| Present Address (street, city, state, ZIP) ☐ Own ☐ Rent ___No. Yrs. | | Present Address (street, city, state, ZIP) ☐ Own ☐ Rent ___No. Yrs. | |
| Mailing Address, if different from Present Address | | Mailing Address, if different from Present Address | |

*If residing at present address for less than two years, complete the following:*

| Former Address (street, city, state, ZIP) ☐ Own ☐ Rent ___No. Yrs. | Former Address (street, city, state, ZIP) ☐ Own ☐ Rent ___No. Yrs. |
|---|---|

| **Borrower** | **IV. EMPLOYMENT INFORMATION** | **Co-Borrower** |
|---|---|---|

| Name & Address of Employer | ☐ Self Employed | Yrs. on this job | Name & Address of Employer | ☐ Self Employed | Yrs. on this job |
|---|---|---|---|---|---|
| | | Yrs. employed in this line of work/profession | | | Yrs. employed in this line of work/profession |
| Position/Title/Type of Business | Business Phone (incl. area code) | | Position/Title/Type of Business | Business Phone (incl. area code) | |

*If employed in current position for less than two years or if currently employed in more than one position, complete the following:*

**FIGURE 10.3   (CONTINUED)**
## Uniform Residential Loan Application

| Borrower | | IV. EMPLOYMENT INFORMATION (cont'd) | | Co-Borrower | |
|---|---|---|---|---|---|
| Name & Address of Employer | ☐ Self Employed | Dates (from – to) | Name & Address of Employer | ☐ Self Employed | Dates (from – to) |
| | | Monthly Income $ | | | Monthly Income $ |
| Position/Title/Type of Business | | Business Phone (incl. area code) | Position/Title/Type of Business | | Business Phone (incl. area code) |
| Name & Address of Employer | ☐ Self Employed | Dates (from – to) | Name & Address of Employer | ☐ Self Employed | Dates (from – to) |
| | | Monthly Income $ | | | Monthly Income $ |
| Position/Title/Type of Business | | Business Phone (incl. area code) | Position/Title/Type of Business | | Business Phone (incl. area code) |

### V. MONTHLY INCOME AND COMBINED HOUSING EXPENSE INFORMATION

| Gross Monthly Income | Borrower | Co-Borrower | Total | Combined Monthly Housing Expense | Present | Proposed |
|---|---|---|---|---|---|---|
| Base Empl. Income* | $ | $ | $ 0.00 | Rent | $ | |
| Overtime | | | 0.00 | First Mortgage (P&I) | | $ |
| Bonuses | | | 0.00 | Other Financing (P&I) | | |
| Commissions | | | 0.00 | Hazard Insurance | | |
| Dividends/Interest | | | 0.00 | Real Estate Taxes | | |
| Net Rental Income | | | 0.00 | Mortgage Insurance | | |
| Other (before completing, see the notice in "describe other income," below) | | | 0.00 | Homeowner Assn. Dues | | |
| | | | | Other: | | |
| Total | $ 0.00 | $ 0.00 | $ 0.00 | Total | $ 0.00 | $ 0.00 |

\*   Self Employed Borrower(s) may be required to provide additional documentation such as tax returns and financial statements.

**Describe Other Income**      *Notice:*   **Alimony, child support, or separate maintenance income need not be revealed if the Borrower (B) or Co-Borrower (C) does not choose to have it considered for repaying this loan.**

| B/C | | Monthly Amount |
|---|---|---|
| | | $ |
| | | |
| | | |

### VI. ASSETS AND LIABILITIES

This Statement and any applicable supporting schedules may be completed jointly by both married and unmarried Co-Borrowers if their assets and liabilities are sufficiently joined so that the Statement can be meaningfully and fairly presented on a combined basis; otherwise, separate Statements and Schedules are required. If the Co-Borrower section was completed about a non-applicant spouse or other person, this Statement and supporting schedules must be completed about that spouse or other person also.

Completed ☐ Jointly ☐ Not Jointly

| ASSETS Description | Cash or Market Value | Liabilities and Pledged Assets. List the creditor's name, address, and account number for all outstanding debts, including automobile loans, revolving charge accounts, real estate loans, alimony, child support, stock pledges, etc. Use continuation sheet, if necessary. Indicate by (*) those liabilities, which will be satisfied upon sale of real estate owned or upon refinancing of the subject property. | | |
|---|---|---|---|---|
| Cash deposit toward purchase held by: | $ | | | |
| **List checking and savings accounts below** | | LIABILITIES | Monthly Payment & Months Left to Pay | Unpaid Balance |
| Name and address of Bank, S&L, or Credit Union | | Name and address of Company | $ Payment/Months | $ |
| Acct. no. | $ | Acct. no. | | |
| Name and address of Bank, S&L, or Credit Union | | Name and address of Company | $ Payment/Months | $ |
| Acct. no. | $ | Acct. no. | | |
| Name and address of Bank, S&L, or Credit Union | | Name and address of Company | $ Payment/Months | $ |
| Acct. no. | $ | Acct. no. | | |

**Uniform Residential Loan Application**
**Freddie Mac Form 65   7/05 (rev. 6/09)**            Page 2 of 5            **Fannie Mae Form 1003   7/05 (rev.6/09)**

**FIGURE 10.3 (CONTINUED)**
## Uniform Residential Loan Application

### VI. ASSETS AND LIABILITIES (cont'd)

| Name and address of Bank, S&L, or Credit Union | | Name and address of Company | $ Payment/Months | $ |
|---|---|---|---|---|
| Acct. no. | $ | Acct. no. | | |
| Stocks & Bonds (Company name/ number & description) | $ | Name and address of Company | $ Payment/Months | $ |
| | | Acct. no. | | |
| Life insurance net cash value | $ | Name and address of Company | $ Payment/Months | $ |
| Face amount: $ | | | | |
| **Subtotal Liquid Assets** | $ 0.00 | | | |
| Real estate owned (enter market value from schedule of real estate owned) | $ | | | |
| Vested interest in retirement fund | $ | | | |
| Net worth of business(es) owned (attach financial statement) | $ | Acct. no. | | |
| Automobiles owned (make and year) | $ | Alimony/Child Support/Separate Maintenance Payments Owed to: | $ | |
| Other Assets (itemize) | $ | Job-Related Expense (child care, union dues, etc.) | $ | |
| | | **Total Monthly Payments** | $ | |
| **Total Assets a.** $ 0.00 | | Net Worth (a minus b) ▶ $ 0.00 | **Total Liabilities b.** $ 0.00 | |

**Schedule of Real Estate Owned** (If additional properties are owned, use continuation sheet.)

| Property Address (enter S if sold, PS if pending sale or R if rental being held for income) ▼ | Type of Property | Present Market Value | Amount of Mortgages & Liens | Gross Rental Income | Mortgage Payments | Insurance, Maintenance, Taxes & Misc. | Net Rental Income |
|---|---|---|---|---|---|---|---|
| | | $ | $ | $ | $ | $ | $ |
| | | | | | | | |
| | | | | | | | |
| Totals | | $ 0.00 | $ 0.00 | $ 0.00 | $ 0.00 | $ 0.00 | $ |

List any additional names under which credit has previously been received and indicate appropriate creditor name(s) and account number(s):

| Alternate Name | Creditor Name | Account Number |
|---|---|---|
| | | |

### VII. DETAILS OF TRANSACTION

| | | |
|---|---|---|
| a. | Purchase price | $ |
| b. | Alterations, improvements, repairs | |
| c. | Land (if acquired separately) | |
| d. | Refinance (incl. debts to be paid off) | |
| e. | Estimated prepaid items | |
| f. | Estimated closing costs | |
| g. | PMI, MIP, Funding Fee | |
| h. | Discount (if Borrower will pay) | |
| i. | Total costs (add items a through h) | 0.00 |

### VIII. DECLARATIONS

| If you answer "Yes" to any questions a through i, please use continuation sheet for explanation. | Borrower Yes No | Co-Borrower Yes No |
|---|---|---|
| a. Are there any outstanding judgments against you? | ☐ ☐ | ☐ ☐ |
| b. Have you been declared bankrupt within the past 7 years? | ☐ ☐ | ☐ ☐ |
| c. Have you had property foreclosed upon or given title or deed in lieu thereof in the last 7 years? | ☐ ☐ | ☐ ☐ |
| d. Are you a party to a lawsuit? | ☐ ☐ | ☐ ☐ |
| e. Have you directly or indirectly been obligated on any loan which resulted in foreclosure, transfer of title in lieu of foreclosure, or judgment? | ☐ ☐ | ☐ ☐ |
| (This would include such loans as home mortgage loans, SBA loans, home improvement loans, educational loans, manufactured (mobile) home loans, any mortgage, financial obligation, bond, or loan guarantee. If "Yes," provide details, including date, name, and address of Lender, FHA or VA case number, if any, and reasons for the action.) | | |

Uniform Residential Loan Application
Freddie Mac Form 65   7/05 (rev.6/09)

Page 3 of 5

Fannie Mae Form 1003   7/05 (rev.6/09)

**FIGURE 10.3   (CONTINUED)**
## Uniform Residential Loan Application

| VII. DETAILS OF TRANSACTION | | | VIII. DECLARATIONS | | |
|---|---|---|---|---|---|

| | | | | Borrower | | Co-Borrower | |
|---|---|---|---|---|---|---|---|
| | | | If you answer "Yes" to any question a through i, please use continuation sheet for explanation. | Yes | No | Yes | No |
| j. | Subordinate financing | | f.   Are you presently delinquent or in default on any Federal debt or any other loan, mortgage, financial obligation, bond, or loan guarantee? | ☐ | ☐ | ☐ | ☐ |
| k. | Borrower's closing costs paid by Seller | | g.   Are you obligated to pay alimony, child support, or separate maintenance? | ☐ | ☐ | ☐ | ☐ |
| l. | Other Credits (explain) | | h.   Is any part of the down payment borrowed? | ☐ | ☐ | ☐ | ☐ |
| | | | i.   Are you a co-maker or endorser on a note? | ☐ | ☐ | ☐ | ☐ |
| m. | Loan amount (exclude PMI, MIP, Funding Fee financed) | | | | | | |
| n. | PMI, MIP, Funding Fee financed | | j.   Are you a U.S. citizen? | ☐ | ☐ | ☐ | ☐ |
| | | | k.   Are you a permanent resident alien? | ☐ | ☐ | ☐ | ☐ |
| o. | Loan amount (add m & n) | 0.00 | l.   **Do you intend to occupy the property as your primary residence?**  If "Yes," complete question m below. | ☐ | ☐ | ☐ | ☐ |
| p. | Cash from/to Borrower (subtract j, k, l & o from i) | | m.  Have you had an ownership interest in a property in the last three years? | ☐ | ☐ | ☐ | ☐ |
| | | | (1) What type of property did you own—principal residence (PR), second home (SH), or investment property (IP)? | _____ | | _____ | |
| | | | (2) How did you hold title to the home— by yourself (S), jointly with your spouse (SP), or jointly with another person (O)? | _____ | | _____ | |

| IX. ACKNOWLEDGEMENT AND AGREEMENT |
|---|

Each of the undersigned specifically represents to Lender and to Lender's actual or potential agents, brokers, processors, attorneys, insurers, servicers, successors and assigns and agrees and acknowledges that: (1) the information provided in this application is true and correct as of the date set forth opposite my signature and that any intentional or negligent misrepresentation of this information contained in this application may result in civil liability, including monetary damages, to any person who may suffer any loss due to reliance upon any misrepresentation that I have made on this application, and/or in criminal penalties including, but not limited to, fine or imprisonment or both under the provisions of Title 18, United States Code, Sec. 1001, et seq.; (2) the loan requested pursuant to this application (the "Loan") will be secured by a mortgage or deed of trust on the property described in this application; (3) the property will not be used for any illegal or prohibited purpose or use; (4) all statements made in this application are made for the purpose of obtaining a residential mortgage loan; (5) the property will be occupied as indicated in this application; (6) the Lender, its servicers, successors or assigns may retain the original and/or an electronic record of this application, whether or not the Loan is approved; (7) the Lender and its agents, brokers, insurers, servicers, successors, and assigns may continuously rely on the information contained in the application, and I am obligated to amend and/or supplement the information provided in this application if any of the material facts that I have represented herein should change prior to closing of the Loan; (8) in the event that my payments on the Loan become delinquent, the Lender, its servicers, successors or assigns may, in addition to any other rights and remedies that it may have relating to such delinquency, report my name and account information to one or more consumer reporting agencies; (9) ownership of the Loan and/or administration of the Loan account may be transferred with such notice as may be required by law; (10) neither Lender nor its agents, brokers, insurers, servicers, successors or assigns has made any representation or warranty, express or implied, to me regarding the property or the condition or value of the property; and (11) my transmission of this application as an "electronic record" containing my "electronic signature," as those terms are defined in applicable federal and/or state laws (excluding audio and video recordings), or my facsimile transmission of this application containing a facsimile of my signature, shall be as effective, enforceable and valid as if a paper version of this application were delivered containing my original written signature.

Acknowledgement. Each of the undersigned hereby acknowledges that any owner of the Loan, its servicers, successors and assigns, may verify or reverify any information contained in this application or obtain any information or data relating to the Loan, for any legitimate business purpose through any source, including a source named in this application or a consumer reporting agency.

| Borrower's Signature | Date | Co-Borrower's Signature | Date |
|---|---|---|---|
| X | | X | |

| X. INFORMATION FOR GOVERNMENT MONITORING PURPOSES |
|---|

The following information is requested by the Federal Government for certain types of loans related to a dwelling in order to monitor the lender's compliance with equal credit opportunity, fair housing and home mortgage disclosure laws. You are not required to furnish this information, but are encouraged to do so. The law provides that a lender may not discriminate either on the basis of this information, or on whether you choose to furnish it. If you furnish the information, please provide both ethnicity and race. For race, you may check more than one designation. If you do not furnish ethnicity, race, or sex, under Federal regulations, this lender is required to note the information on the basis of visual observation and surname if you have made this application in person. If you do not wish to furnish the information, please check the box below. (Lender must review the above material to assure that the disclosures satisfy all requirements to which the lender is subject under applicable state law for the particular type of loan applied for.)

| **BORROWER** | ☐ I do not wish to furnish this information | | | **CO-BORROWER** | ☐ I do not wish to furnish this information | | |
|---|---|---|---|---|---|---|---|
| Ethnicity: | ☐ Hispanic or Latino | ☐ Not Hispanic or Latino | | Ethnicity: | ☐ Hispanic or Latino | ☐ Not Hispanic or Latino | |
| Race: | ☐ American Indian or Alaska Native | ☐ Asian | ☐ Black or African American | Race: | ☐ American Indian or Alaska Native | ☐ Asian | ☐ Black or African American |
| | ☐ Native Hawaiian or Other Pacific Islander | ☐ White | | | ☐ Native Hawaiian or Other Pacific Islander | ☐ White | |
| Sex: | ☐ Female | ☐ Male | | Sex: | ☐ Female | ☐ Male | |

**To be Completed by Loan Originator:**
This information was provided:
☐ In a face-to-face interview
☐ In a telephone interview
☐ By the applicant and submitted by fax or mail
☐ By the applicant and submitted via e-mail or the Internet

| Loan Originator's Signature | | |
|---|---|---|
| X | | Date |
| Loan Originator's Name (print or type) | Loan Originator Identifier | Loan Originator's Phone Number (including area code) |
| Loan Origination Company's Name | Loan Origination Company Identifier | Loan Origination Company's Address |

**Uniform Residential Loan Application**
Freddie Mac Form 65   7/05 (rev.6/09)                    Page 4 of 5                    Fannie Mae Form 1003   7/05 (rev.6/09)

**FIGURE 10.3 (CONTINUED)**
**Uniform Residential Loan Application**

| CONTINUATION SHEET/RESIDENTIAL LOAN APPLICATION | | |
|---|---|---|
| Use this continuation sheet if you need more space to complete the Residential Loan Application. Mark **B** f or Borrower or **C** for Co-Borrower. | Borrower: | Agency Case Number: |
| | Co-Borrower: | Lender Case Number: |

I/We fully understand that it is a Federal crime punishable by fine or imprisonment, or both, to knowingly make any false statements concerning any of the above facts as applicable under the provisions of Title 18, United States Code, Section 1001, et seq.

| Borrower's Signature | Date | Co-Borrower's Signature | Date |
|---|---|---|---|
| X | | X | |

**Uniform Residential Loan Application**
**Freddie Mac Form 65   7/05 (rev.6/09)**

Page 5 of 5

**Fannie Mae Form 1003   7/05 (rev.6/09)**

**Assets** consist of all things of value, encumbered or not, owned by the applicant, and cash heads the list. Cash consists of money in hand, on deposit in checking and savings accounts, and the cash given as a deposit on the property being purchased. Lenders place great weight upon a borrower's cash position as a reflection of liquidity and money management habits. A strong cash balance develops a sense of confidence in a borrower's ability to maintain payments and meet other obligations, even in the event of temporary setbacks.

Following the entry for cash are listed all monies invested in stocks and bonds, notes or accounts receivable, personal business ventures, and other real estate. The value of the applicant's automobiles, surrender value of life insurance policies, other personal property, and any other assets are enumerated. All dollar amounts assigned to these items must reflect their realistic market value, not their purchase price or some imagined value.

When more than one bond, stock, or parcel of real estate is owned, additional spaces are provided for their itemization in an appropriate schedule on the application form. Should the applicant need more space than is provided, additional pages will be affixed to this inventory to complete these important requirements.

**Liabilities** consist of all monetary obligations of the borrower-applicant. Heading the list of liabilities are any notes payable because these are considered a priority claim against cash assets. Next in order of importance are all installment accounts, such as charge accounts and automobile payments. Other accounts payable, such as medical bills or insurance premiums, follow the list of installment accounts. Remaining long-term liabilities are then enumerated: alimony and child support payments, any encumbrances on the real estate listed as assets; accrued and unpaid real estate property and/or income taxes; security obligations on personal property such as furniture; loans on the life insurance policies listed as assets; and any other debts for which the applicant is responsible.

It is hoped that the total of the assets will exceed the total of the liabilities, with the difference being an applicant's **net worth.** The amount of net worth is added to the total liabilities in order to balance both sides of the financial statement. A 2:1 current ratio indicates that the applicant has twice as many assets as liabilities and is a good credit risk. If total liabilities exceed an applicant's total assets, a loan would probably be denied at this point and the file closed. Assuming an applicant has a positive net worth, a series of related actions will begin.

**Data Verification**

The loan officer charged with the responsibility for processing the loan will proceed to verify the information included in the application by actually checking with the various references given, the banks where deposits are held, and the applicant's employer.

**Deposits.** The borrower is obliged to sign deposit verification forms that authorize the bank to reveal to the lender the current balances in the borrower's accounts. Without a verification form, such confidential information could not be obtained. A typical form for verification of deposit is reproduced in Figure 10.4.

A deposit verification permission form must be signed by the borrower for each bank account to enable the loan processor to ascertain all the current balances. The knowledge that the loan processor can verify account amounts is usually enough incentive for the borrower to be truthful in reporting financial information. When the deposit balances are verified, the appropriate entries are made in the applicant's file.

**Employment.** Likewise, an applicant is required to sign an employment verification form similar to that illustrated in Figure 10.5. It authorizes the employer to reveal confidential information concerning the applicant's job status.

Not only will an applicant's wages and length of employment be verified, but the employer will be requested to offer an opinion of the applicant's job attitude and give a prognosis for continued employment and prospects for advancement.

**Credit Report.** Simultaneous to the gathering of financial and employment information, a loan processor will send a formal request for a borrower's **credit report** to three credit reporting agencies. Within a few days if the applicant is a local resident or longer if out-of-town credit must be checked, the credit search companies will send the loan officer a

**FIGURE 10.4**
**Request for Verification of Deposit**

## FannieMae

# Request for Verification of Deposit

**Privacy Act Notice:** This information is to be used by the agency collecting it or its assignees in determining whether you qualify as a prospective mortgagor under its program. It will not be disclosed outside the agency except as required and permitted by law. You do not have to provide this information, but if you do not your application for approval as a prospective mortgagor or borrower may be delayed or rejected. The information requested in this form is authorized by Title 38, USC, Chapter 37 (If VA); by 12 USC, Section 1701 et.seq. (If HUD/FHA); by 42 USC, Section 1452b (if HUD/CPD); and Title 42 USC, 1471 et.seq. or 7 USC, 1921 et.seq. (If USDA/FmHA).

**Instructions:**  Lender — Complete Items 1 through 8. Have applicant complete Item 9. Forward directly to depository named in Item 1.
Depository — Please complete Items 10 through 18 and return DIRECTLY to lender named in Item 2.
**The form is to be transmitted directly to the lender and is not to be transmitted through the applicant or any other party.**

### Part I — Request

| 1. To (Name and address of depository) | 2. From (Name and address of lender) |
|---|---|
| | |

I certify that this verification has been sent directly to the bank or depository and has not passed through the hands of the applicant or any other party.

| 3. Signature of lender | 4. Title | 5. Date | 6. Lender's No. (Optional) |
|---|---|---|---|
| | | | |

7. Information To Be Verified

| Type of Account | Account in Name of | Account Number | Balance |
|---|---|---|---|
| | | | $ |
| | | | $ |
| | | | $ |

**To Depository:** I/We have applied for a mortgage loan and stated in my financial statement that the balance on deposit with you is as shown above. You are authorized to verify this information and to supply the lender identified above with the information requested in Items 10 through 13. Your response is solely a matter of courtesy for which no responsibility is attached to your institution or any of your officers.

| 8. Name and Address of Applicant(s) | 9. Signature of Applicant(s) |
|---|---|
| | |

**To Be Completed by Depository**
### Part II — Verification of Depository

10. Deposit Accounts of Applicant(s)

| Type of Account | Account Number | Current Balance | Average Balance For Previous Two Months | Date Opened |
|---|---|---|---|---|
| | | $ | $ | |
| | | $ | $ | |
| | | $ | $ | |

11. Loans Outstanding To Applicant(s)

| Loan Number | Date of Loan | Original Amount | Current Balance | Installments (Monthly/Quarterly) | | Secured By | Number of Late Payments |
|---|---|---|---|---|---|---|---|
| | | $ | $ | $ | per | | |
| | | $ | $ | $ | per | | |
| | | $ | $ | $ | per | | |

12. Please include any additional information which may be of assistance in determination of credit worthiness. (Please include information on loans paid-in-full in Item 11 above.)

13. If the name(s) on the account(s) differ from those listed in Item 7, please supply the name(s) on the account(s) as reflected by your records.

### Part III — Authorized Signature - Federal statutes provide severe penalties for any fraud, intentional misrepresentation, or criminal connivance or conspiracy purposed to influence the issuance of any guaranty or insurance by the VA Secretary, the U.S.D.A., FmHA/FHA Commissioner, or the HUD/CPD Assistant Secretary.

| 14. Signature of Depository Representative | 15. Title (Please print or type) | 16. Date |
|---|---|---|
| | | |
| 17. Please print or type name signed in item 14 | 18. Phone No. | |

Fannie Mae
Form 1006   July 96

**FIGURE 10.5**

**Request for Verification of Employment**

**FannieMae**

# Request for Verification of Employment

**Privacy Act Notice:** This information is to be used by the agency collecting it or its assignees in determining whether you qualify as a prospective mortgagor under its program. It will not be disclosed outside the agency except as required and permitted by law. You do not have to provide this information, but if you do not your application for approval as a prospective mortgagor or borrower may be delayed or rejected. The information requested in this form is authorized by Title 38, USC, Chapter 37 (if VA); by 12 USC, Section 1701 et. seq. (if HUD/FHA); by 42 USC, Section 1452b (if HUD/CPD); and Title 42 USC, 1471 et. seq., or 7 USC, 1921 et. seq. (if USDA/FmHA).

**Instructions:** Lender — Complete items 1 through 7. Have applicant complete item 8. Forward directly to employer named in item 1.
Employer — Please complete either Part II or Part III as applicable. Complete Part IV and return directly to lender named in item 2.
The form is to be transmitted directly to the lender and is not to be transmitted through the applicant or any other party.

**Part I — Request**

| 1. To (Name and address of employer) | 2. From (Name and address of lender) |
|---|---|

I certify that this verification has been sent directly to the employer and has not passed through the hands of the applicant or any other interested party.

| 3. Signature of Lender | 4. Title | 5. Date | 6. Lender's Number (Optional) |
|---|---|---|---|

I have applied for a mortgage loan and stated that I am now or was formerly employed by you. My signature below authorizes verification of this information.

| 7. Name and Address of Applicant (include employee or badge number) | 8. Signature of Applicant |
|---|---|

**Part II — Verification of Present Employment**

| 9. Applicant's Date of Employment | 10. Present Position | 11. Probability of Continued Employment |
|---|---|---|

12A. Current **Gross** Base Pay (Enter Amount and Check Period)

Annual   Hourly
Monthly   Other (Specify)
$ _____   Weekly

12B. **Gross** Earnings

| Type | Year To Date | Past Year | Past Year |
|---|---|---|---|
| Base Pay | Thru _____ .__ $ | $ | $ |
| Overtime | $ | $ | $ |
| Commissions | $ | $ | $ |
| Bonus | $ | $ | $ |
| Total | $ 0.00 | $ 0.00 | $ 0.00 |

| 13. For Military Personnel Only | |
|---|---|
| Pay Grade | |
| Type | Monthly Amount |
| Base Pay | $ |
| Rations | $ |
| Flight or Hazard | $ |
| Clothing | $ |
| Quarters | $ |
| Pro Pay | $ |
| Overseas or Combat | $ |
| Variable Housing Allowance | $ |

14. If Overtime or Bonus is Applicable, Is Its Continuance Likely?
Overtime [ Yes [ No
Bonus [ Yes [ No

15. If paid hourly — average hours per week

16. Date of applicant's next pay increase

17. Projected amount of next pay increase

18. Date of applicant's last pay increase

19. Amount of last pay increase

20. Remarks (If employee was off work for any length of time, please indicate time period and reason)

**Part III — Verification of Previous Employment**

| 21. Date Hired | 23. Salary/Wage at Termination Per (Year) (Month) (Week) |
|---|---|
| 22. Date Terminated | Base _____ Overtime _____ Commissions _____ Bonus _____ |
| 24. Reason for Leaving | 25. Position Held |

**Part IV — Authorized Signature** - Federal statutes provide severe penalties for any fraud, intentional misrepresentation, or criminal connivance or conspiracy purposed to influence the issuance of any guaranty or insurance by the VA Secretary, the U.S.D.A., FmHA/FHA Commissioner, or the HUD/CPD Assistant Secretary.

| 26. Signature of Employer | 27. Title (Please print or type) | 28. Date |
|---|---|---|
| 29. Print or type name signed in Item 26 | 30. Phone No. | |

Fannie Mae
Form 1005   July 96

confidential report on their findings. A sample credit report is reproduced in Figure 10.6.

This form will usually state the applicant's age, address, status as a tenant or owner, length of residency at current address, brief employment history, and credit profile, both past and present. Most of the credit data are secured from local banks, merchants, and other cooperating local credit services. A credit report is the result of the compilation of information accumulated from a thorough check of the application and a check of the public records to discover if any suits are pending against the applicant.

The credit report itself is an itemization of the status of current and past accounts. In addition, it indicates the dates of the payments made and their regularity, delinquency, or any outstanding balances. This payment history is the most important part of the entire report. Credit managers and loan officers frequently state that a person's future attitude is, in most cases, a reflection of past behavior in meeting financial obligations. Research tends to reinforce these opinions, indicating that slow and erratic payers generally retain those attitudes when securing new loans, and prompt and steady payers are also consistent in meeting their future obligations.

**Credit Evaluation**

Not only is the quantity of an applicant's income evaluated for loan qualification, its quality is evaluated as well. The lender is looking for income that is stable, regular, and recurring. Thus, income from all sources is added together to find an acceptable total on which to apply the qualifying ratios.

In a normal transaction, the wages and earnings of the coborrowers are considered. In the event a cosigner is involved, this person's income is included as well. Extra income is considered if it is received regularly and for a period of at least three years; thus, bonuses and overtime pay can be included if they fit this criterion. Pensions, interest, and dividends are treated as regular income, although it is recognized that interest and dividends do fluctuate over time and may cease if the investment is cashed out.

A second or part-time job is accepted as part of the regular monthly income if it can be shown that the job has existed for approximately two years and there is good reason to believe it will continue. Child support can also

**FIGURE 10.6**

**Credit Report Form**

## National Credit
### STANDARD FACTUAL DATA REPORT

**CREDIT PROFILE**　　　　　　　　　　　　　　　　　　　　　**CONFIDENTIAL REPORT**

Type of Report:

| | | |
|---|---|---|
| Acct. Number: | 100 | Requested by: ABC MORTGAGE CO. |
| Date of Report: | 11/16/98 | Date Ordered: 11/16/98 |
| Name (& Spouse): | CONSUMER, JOHN A. | SALLY |
| Present Address: | 123 SECOND STREET | |
| | CHICAGO IL 60649 | |
| Property Address: | 345 THIRD STREET | |
| | CHICAGO IL 60637 | |

VA ☐　FHA ☐

FNMA ☒

This Report Contains:

☒ Joint Information　☐ Individual Information

Sources: _____

**PERSONAL**

| | |
|---|---|
| 1. Length of time at address shown above: | 1. 6 YEARS　☒ Rents　☐ Buying　☐ Owns (free & Clear) |
| 2. Former address (If less than 2 years at present address): | 2. -- |
| 3. Social Security Number(s): | 3. 123-45-6789　　Spouse:　345-67-8901 |
| 4. Approximate age of subject: | 4. 37　　Spouse:　33 |
| 5. Marital status – dependents (Exclude subject & spouse): | 5. MARRIED　　Dependents:　-1- |

**EMPLOYMENT**

| | |
|---|---|
| 6. Name of employer: | 6. XYZ CORPORATON　☒ Verified　☐ Not Verified |
| 7. Position held – length of present employment: | 7. MANAGER　Since: 1988 |
| 8. Employment verified by: | 8. HUMAN RESOURCES |
| 9. Approximate income from employment: | 9. 3300/MONTH |
| 10. Former employment (If less than 2 years above): | 10. --　☐ Verified　☒ Not Verified |

**CO. APP. EMP.**

| | |
|---|---|
| 11. Name of co-applicant's employer: | 11. SELF EMPLOYED　☐ Verified　☒ Not Verified |
| 12. Position held – length of present employment: | 12. REAL ESTATE AGENT　Since: 10/88 |
| 13. Employment verified by: | 13. SEE FINANCIAL STATEMENT |
| 14. Approximate income from employment: | 14. 3500/MONTH |
| 15. Former employment (If less than 2 years above): | 15. --　☐ Verified　☒ Not Verified |

**CERTIFICATION**

1. National Credit certifies that (a) _X_ public records have been checked for judgments, garnishments, bankruptcies, chattels, liens and other legal actions involving the subject; or, (b) equivalent information has been obtained through a qualified public records reporting service.

2. National Credit certifies that the subject's credit record in the payment of bills and other obligations has been checked; (a) ___ through credit extended by the designated credit grantors under the classes and trades identified in the contract for the community in which the subject resides; or, (b) X through accumulated credit records of such credit grantors of community in which the subject resides, with the results indicated below.

This report is provided to assist in the decision to grant credit. It is based upon information from credit grantors in good faith. The accuracy of the same, however is in no way guaranteed. The information is strictly confidential. Neither National Credit nor any of its employees shall be held responsible for violation of these conditions and by your acceptance of this report you specifically agree to the same.

### CREDIT HISTORY

| Credit Grantor | Date Opened | Date Reported | High Credit | Terms | Present Status Balance Owing | Amount Past Due | Date Last Past Due | Paying Record | Footnote Number |
|---|---|---|---|---|---|---|---|---|---|
| CITIBANK | 9/87 | 11/98 | 6000. | FLEXIBLE | 4110. | -0- | --- | SATIS | - |
| B OF A M/C | 2/85 | 11/98 | 1200. | FLEXIBLE | 556. | -0- | --- | SATIS | - |
| FINANCE AMERICA | 3/84 | 11/98 | 1000. | 84X119 | 247. | -0- | --- | SATIS | - |
| 1ST CHGO. VISA | 12/82 | 11/98 | 600. | FLEXIBLE | 125. | -0- | --- | SATIS | - |
| SEARS | 9/88 | 11/98 | 1000. | FLEXIBLE | 34. | -0- | --- | SATIS | - |
| PENNEYS | 9/87 | 11/98 | 300. | FLEXIBLE | 56. | -0- | --- | SATIS | 1 |
| WARDS | 10/89 | 11/98 | 300. | FLEXIBLE | 220. | -0- | --- | SATIS | 1 |
| CARSON PIRIE SCOTT | 8/88 | 11/98 | 1000. | FLEXIBLE | 113. | -0- | 4/90 | CURRENT | - |
| MARSHALL FIELD'S | 11/88 | 11/98 | 1500. | FLEXIBLE | 4110. | -0- | --- | PDSATIS | - |
| CHEMICAL BANK | 3/90 | 11/98 | 1500. | 36MONTHS | -0- | -0- | --- | SATIS | - |
| ROBINSON'S | 6/91 | 11/98 | 500. | FLEXIBLE | -0- | -0- | --- | SATIS | - |
| NORDSTROM | 9/89 | 11/98 | 1000. | FLEXIBLE | -0- | -0- | --- | SATIS | - |
| SAKS 5TH AVE. | 4/89 | 11/98 | 400. | FLEXIBLE | -0- | -0- | --- | SATIS | - |
| INQUIRES | | | 3/5/98 | AMERICAN EXPRESS-APPLICATION FOR CREDIT CARD. | | | | | |
| | | | 2/25/98 | AMOCO APPLICATION FOR CREDIT CARD. | | | | | |

PUBLIC RECORDS: JUDGMENT FILED 2/84 IN CHICAGO MUNICIPAL COURT, CASE #123456 FOR $450., FILED BY A&B COMPANY WAS SATISFIED 1/86.

FOOTNOTES:

1. ACCOUNT HELD IN THE NAME OF SALLY CONSUMER.

ADDITIONAL INCOME: (STATED) APPLICANT CLAIMS $500./MONTH OVERTIME.

| | | | | |
|---|---|---|---|---|
| REPORT FOR: | ABC MORTGAGE COMPANY | | | |
| PREPARED BY: | NATIONAL CREDIT | P.O.BOX 678 | CHICAGO ILLINOIS | 60657 (312)555-8916 |
| | | City | State | Zip Code |

be included in the determination of monthly income, but only if it is the result of a court order or has a proven track record. Also, under the Equal Credit Opportunity Act (ECOA), government entitlement funds must be considered. Self-employed borrowers, including commissioned wage earners, need at least two years of established income to qualify for a mortgage loan.

Divorced buyers are required to submit a copy of their decree to inform lenders which party is responsible for liabilities, how the assets are divided, and whether there are support and/or alimony obligations. For alimony to be considered as income, most lenders require a one-year history of payment receipts and reasonable assurance that payments will continue for at least three years from the date of the loan application.

On the other hand, alimony or child support payments are considered a debt of the borrower responsible for these and must be included in the financial analysis.

In addition to the total quantity of income, a loan analyst pays careful attention to its quality. An applicant's employer is asked for an opinion of job stability and possible advancement. Length of time on the job no longer carries the heavy clout it once did. Applicants whose employment records show frequent shifts in job situations that result in upward mobility each time are given full consideration. Lenders will, however, be wary of an applicant who drifts from one job classification to another and cannot seem to become established in any specific type of work.

**Credit Scoring.**   Included in the borrower qualification process is **credit scoring**, an objective method of assessing credit risk based on the statistical probability of repayment of the debt. The applicant's score is based on data included in one or more of the national credit repository files.

Credit scores reflect the combination of many risk factors. In some instances, a borrower who has had a bankruptcy with an otherwise "clean" history of making payments may have a better credit score than another borrower who has not had a bankruptcy but has a long history of delinquent payments.

Credit scores are *not* based on age, race, gender, religion, national origin, marital status, current address, or receipt of public assistance. Credit scores are based on factors such as how you pay your bills, how much outstanding debt you have, what type of credit and how long you have had established credit, and how many times you have had inquiries relative to extending credit.

The FICO scores (named after the **Fair Isaac Corporation (FICO)**, the San Rafael, California-based firm that created the FICO test) assign relative risk rankings to applicants based on statistical analyses of their credit histories. The applicants who always pay their bills on time and make moderate use of their credit cards receive the highest scores, 700 to above 800. The applicants who are late in paying bills present greater risks and get lower scores from 400 to 620.

The FICO score is based on the following percentages:

- Payment history = 35 percent; late payments, bankruptcies, and other negative items hurt score, but on-time payments help score.

- Amount owed = 30 percent; amount owed on all accounts, number of accounts with balances, and how much of available credit is being used.

- Length of credit history = 15 percent; longer credit history increases score, while a shorter history is not detrimental if a good credit record is established.

- New credit = 10 percent; multiple searches for mortgage loans should be done within 30 days.

- Other factors = 10 percent; mix of credit types (credit cards, mortgage or car loan, and personal lines of credit can add to score, while "maxed out" credit cards can lower score).

FICO scores range from 300 to 850, with most people scoring in the 600s or 700s. As of September 2005, everyone has the right to one free credit report per year from each of the three major credit reporting agencies: *Equifax* 1-800-685-1111, *www.equifax.com; Experian,* 1-866-200-6020, *www.experian.com; TransUnion,* 1-800-888-4213, *www.transunion.com.*

Congress has established an outlet to make it easier for consumers to obtain credit reports and credit scores: the Annual Credit Report Request Service, P.O. Box 105281, Atlanta, GA, 30348-5281, 1-877-322-8228, *www.annualcreditreport.com*.

Through its Web site, *www.myfico.com*, FICO offers two brochures that can be downloaded at no cost: "Your Credit Score" and "Understanding Your Credit Score."

Lenders may order credit scores electronically at relatively low cost from credit repositories or bureaus. Credit scoring speeds up the loan approval process. Most lenders today order a tri-merge credit report containing information from all three of the major credit repositories. In most cases the numerical credit score will be different on all three reports due to variations in time and content from creditors. Generally, the lender will use the middle score, not an average.

Potential misuse of credit scoring has prompted the following rules on their use:

- Never automatically disqualify anybody because of a subpar credit score (credit scores may not "single out" or prohibit low-income to moderate-income borrowers from becoming homeowners).

- Be aware of potential errors in electronic credit files.

- With a subpar score, look hard at the score factor codes and work with the applicant to clear "fixable" items.

- Three new tools are available for borrowers labeled as *unscoreables*, those who have such *thin* credit files that their traditional credit scores are too low to be considered for a loan:

  — *Anthem* is a program developed by the Massachusetts's Statewide Financing Agency to begin using a nontraditional scoring system that includes previous rental, utility, insurance, and child support payments.

— Fair Isaac Corp. is marketing a nontraditional scoring service called *Expansion Score* that includes data on the borrower's performance on payday loans, rent-to-buy agreements, rental history, and other financial accounts.

— A private national credit bureau called the *Bill Payment Scorecard* specializes in collecting data and scores a borrower's record on payments of child support, student loans, utilities, phone bills, and other similar accounts.

All three methods are available to mortgage lenders to provide home loans to creditworthy applicants who score poorly because they are virtually invisible to the national credit bureaus.

**Loan Qualifying Income Ratios.** When analyzing the borrower's ability to make the required loan payments, loan underwriters currently apply the following pairs of **income ratios**:

| Loan Type | Housing Ratio | Total Debt Ratio |
|---|---|---|
| Conventional Loans | 28 percent | 36 percent |
| Conv. Affordable Loans | 33 percent | 38 percent |
| FHA Loans | 31 percent | 43 percent |
| DVA Loans | ——— | 41 percent |

The 28, 33, and 31 percent ratios refer to the total of principal, interest, taxes, insurance, and homeowners' association fees as a percentage of acceptable gross monthly income. The 36, 38, 43, and 41 percent ratios refer to the total of the mortgage payment *plus* other monthly installment obligations such as car or furniture payments, as a percentage of acceptable gross monthly income. In this latter category, some flexibility exists, such as eliminating a car payment that will end in ten months or less.

■ **EXAMPLE**   Consider a conventional loan of $250,000 at 8 percent interest for 30 years. The property taxes are $3,600 per year, and the hazard insurance premium is $480. The homeowners' association fee is $240 for the year. The borrowers have a car payment of $400 per month with two years left to pay.

**Conventional Loan**

$250,000 @ 6% for 30 years:

| | |
|---|---|
| Principal & Interest | $1,498.90 |
| Property Taxes | 300.00 |
| Hazard Insurance | 40.00 |
| HOA Fee | 20.00 |
| Monthly Payment | $1,858.90 |
| Housing Expense Ratio | 28% |
| Required Gross Monthly Income | $6,638.93 |
| Monthly Payment | $1,858.90 |
| Car Payment | 400.00 |
| Total Housing + Debt Payment | $2,258.90 |
| Total Debt Ratio | 36% |
| Required Gross Monthly Income | $6,274.72 |

■ **EXAMPLE**

**DVA Loan**

| | |
|---|---|
| Monthly Payment | $1,858.90 |
| Car Payment | 400.00 |
| Total Housing + Debt | $2,258.90 |
| DVA Housing & Debt Ratio | 41% |
| Required Monthly Income | $5,509.51 |

Because DVA loans only use one ratio of 41 percent, less income is required. Neither example takes into account mortgage insurance or the DVA funding fee.

After reviewing all the information provided in the loan application and making the appropriate ratio analyses of the income and expense data, plus the borrower's FICO score, the loan officer collects all pertinent papers and sends the package to the company underwriters for a final determination. If a special report of unusual circumstances is warranted, it is included.

# ■ SUMMARY

This chapter described the loan underwriting process. Underwriting involves a careful examination of the ability of the value of the collateral pledged to backup the borrower's promise to pay and the ability of the borrower to make the required monthly payments on the loan. Both must be acceptable to the lender before a real estate loan can be completed.

Qualifying the collateral involves an estimate of the value of a property to be pledged as collateral for a loan. An appraiser must not only be aware of past and current value indicators, but also must pay careful consideration to what the property will be worth in the future, since a real estate loan is made for 15 to 40 years. This is not an easy task as appraising includes as many subjective variables as objective values.

Objectively, an appraiser can apply the direct sales comparison, cost, and income approaches to help evaluate a property. The appraiser will examine past sales of comparable properties, current replacement costs, and specific square and cubic footage measurements. Subjectively, the appraiser must consider appreciation, depreciation, changing locational attributes, and a constantly fluctuating capitalization rate.

Qualifying a borrower's ability to make monthly payments includes an examination of past credit history as well as current assets, payment obligations, and earnings. A borrower's record of past payments establishes a pattern of responsibility. An erratic payment history probably indicates trouble ahead and a poor risk. A stable payment record is a plus for the borrower.

If a borrower's liabilities exceed assets, the risk is considered too great to issue a new loan. Thus, a careful check of the borrower's financial statement is an integral part of the underwriting process. Likewise, a borrower's earnings must be examined in the light of existing obligations as well as the new payment burden to be incurred. These earnings must be more than adequate to cover the total payments required to ensure a safe loan.

Once the borrower and property qualify, the loan process continues toward its closing.

# ■ INTERNET RESOURCES

American Land Title Association   *www.alta.org*

American Society of Appraisers   *www.appraisers.org*

Appraisal Institute   *www.appraisalinstitute.org*

National Association of Independent Fee Appraisers   *www.naifa.com*

# ■ REVIEW QUESTIONS

1. The evaluation of the risks involved when issuing a new real estate loan is known as

   a. appraising.

   c. financing.

   b. underwriting.

   d. discounting.

2. All of the following sources of funds are usually included in a borrower's income analysis *EXCEPT*

   a. spousal earnings.

   c. part-time second jobs.

   b. regular overtime.

   d. court-ordered child support.

3. A borrower with a 2:1 current asset ratio has twice as many

   a. liabilities as assets and is probably a good credit risk.

   b. assets as liabilities and is probably an average credit risk.

   c. assets as liabilities and is probably a good credit risk.

   d. liabilities as assets and is probably a poor credit risk.

4. The direct sales comparison approach to estimating a property's value is based primarily on

   a. the property's adjusted gross income.

   b. adjusting comparable properties' recent sales prices.

   c. the property's depreciated replacement cost.

   d. the seller's adjusted book basis.

5. The income approach to the estimate of a property's value is based primarily on

   a. the property's depreciated value.

   b. the property's ability to generate net income.

   c. adjusting comparable properties' recent sales prices.

   d. discounting gross annual cash flows.

6.  The value of a 50-year-old house would probably *BEST* be estimated by using the

    a.  cost approach.

    b.  income approach.

    c.  direct sales comparison approach.

    d.  property residual approach.

7.  Using a credit ratio of 25 percent, borrowers earning $850 per week could support which of the following monthly payments?

    a.  $212.50

    b.  $850.00

    c.  $1,700.00

    d.  $3,400.00

8.  Using a debt ratio of 33 percent, borrowers earning $850 per week could support which of the following monthly payments?

    a.  $569.50

    b.  $850.00

    c.  $1,122.00

    d.  $1,700.00

9.  When applying a 10 percent capitalization rate in the income approach, an apartment property generating $100,000 gross annual income with a 40 percent operating cost ratio and a $60,000 annual interest expense is worth which of the following amounts?

    a.  $0

    b.  $400,000

    c.  $600,000

    d.  $1,000,000

10.   From the following information, what is the weighted average value of the subject property?

|        |           | Weight |
|--------|-----------|--------|
| Cost   | $125,500  | 25%    |
| Income | 140,500   | 10%    |
| Market | 125,500   | 65%    |

    a.  $125,500

    b.  $127,000

    c.  $130,000

    d.  $140,500

## ■ EXERCISES

1. Requirements to qualify for residential real estate loans vary in different areas of the state. Check with a mortgage banker in your area to determine what the earnings-to-expenses ratios are to qualify for a residential loan.

2. The efforts of appraisers in real estate finance are more complicated now than ever before. Visit with a local appraisal firm to observe what techniques are being applied to meet the new standards promulgated by the federal financing regulatory agencies.

## CHAPTER ELEVEN

# PROCESSING REAL ESTATE LOANS

## ■ KEY TERMS

abstract

actual notices

ALTA policy

annual percentage rate
 (APR)

assignment

California Land Title
 Association (CLTA)

chain of title

closing statements

cloud

constructive notice

disclosures

escrow funds

good-faith estimate

hazard insurance

hazardous waste

impound funds

mortgagee's title
 insurance

origination fee

owner's title insurance

points

preliminary report

proration

suit to quiet title

survey

title insurance

# ■ QUALIFYING THE TITLE

In anticipation of issuing a loan, the loan processor will secure a title report on the collateral property. The components of a full title report are a survey, a physical inspection of the collateral, and, most important, a search of the **chain of title** to determine all the interests in a property. Normally, property interests are perfected through the appropriate filing and the recording of standard notices. A recorded deed notifies the world that a grantee has the legal fee title to the property. A recorded mechanic's lien is notice of another's interest in a property.

These forms of recording, described as **constructive notices**, express revelations of pertinent facts that are usually matters of record. It is important that the title examiners review these recorded facts in their efforts to establish good title.

Another form of notice is where information relevant to a real estate transaction is given verbally or in writing between the parties. This is called **actual notice** and includes information as to the rights of those in possession of the property as well as the facts to be revealed under the California disclosure rules, to be described later in this chapter.

There are two methods employed for obtaining assurance of good title in California—the abstract and opinion of title and title insurance. Whichever method is used, the title report on the collateral provides the loan officer and the lender's attorney with all recorded information relevant to the legal status of the subject property, as well as any interests revealed by constructive notice. This title search requirement is yet another manifestation of a lender's efforts to protect the loan investment.

**Abstract and Opinion of Title**

An **abstract** is described as a synopsis of the recorded history of a property. Abstracting is basically the process of searching the records to accumulate information that is then distilled by the abstractor. An abstract, also known as a **preliminary report**, begins with the earliest recorded instrument pertinent to a subject property; each transaction is then listed in chronological order as it was recorded to bring the abstract up to the present date.

In the past, abstracts were given by the seller of a property to the new buyer after all transactions that occurred during the seller's ownership were added. These abstracts, in addition to the deed transferring fee title, were delivered to a buyer for approval before a transaction was closed. The attorney for the buyer signified approval through either an oral report, an informal note, or a formal written title opinion, wherein the reviewing attorney accepted personal liability if anything had been overlooked that would result in a future loss to the buyer.

In current practice, an abstract is not considered an official document because it makes no pretense of disclosing any *hidden* title hazards. The abstractor is responsible only for an accurate portrayal of documents of *record* pertinent to a property's title status. If the loan officer wishes a more expert analysis of a title, a request is made for an opinion on the condition of the collateral's title from a lawyer. This opinion is based on the facts revealed in the abstract, and all defects in the title are brought to the loan officer's attention. However, if the lender requires additional protection against hidden defects or possible errors in the abstracting process, a title insurance policy must be secured because neither the abstractor who searches the title nor the lawyer who renders an opinion of the title's condition issues a guarantee or insures against defects.

**Title Insurance**

Although the abstract together with an attorney's opinion is still used in some areas of the United States, the trend toward an expanded nationwide mortgage market has brought about the rapid growth of **title insurance** companies. These title companies combine the abstracting process with a program of insurance that guarantees the validity and accuracy of the title search. A purchaser of title insurance can rely on the assets of the insurance company to back up its guarantees of a property's marketable title. This guarantee is evidenced by a policy of title insurance.

There are two types of title insurance in California, a **California Land Title Association (CLTA)** policy and an American Land Title Association (ALTA) policy. A CLTA policy covers the value of the property from sellers to buyers, while the **ALTA policy** covers the loan amount.

The standard title coverage can be expanded to include many unusual risks, such as forgeries, incompetency of parties involved in issuing documents pertaining to the transfer of ownership, legal status of parties involved in the specific loan negotiations, surveying errors, and other possible off-record defects. Some additional risks can also be covered by special endorsements to an insurance policy. These could include protection against any unrecorded easements or liens, rights of parties in possession of the subject property, mining claims, water rights, and additional negotiated special items pertinent to the property involved. This expanded ALTA policy is generally required by participants in the secondary mortgage market for the added protection it provides.

Title insurance companies are seeking to cut costs and offer faster services through new technology. Many companies are converting to automatic indexing systems that provide instant electronic transfer of information. This shortens the title search period and reduces personnel requirements. Some title companies are developing new earnings opportunities by forming real estate services subsidiaries, such as offering property appraisals, flood plain certification, and credit reporting.

**Title Faults**

Whether the abstract and opinion or the title insurance policy is used, in all cases a property's title is searched by an experienced abstractor who prepares a report of those recorded documents that clearly affect the quality of ownership. In addition, a survey is often required. If a fault is found in the title, sometimes called a **cloud**, the loan process will not continue until this cloud is cleared to the lender's satisfaction. Such a cloud could be an unsatisfied mechanic's lien, an income tax lien, a property tax lien, an encroachment, or a zoning violation. Sometimes a borrower's name is not legally correct on the deed, or the deed has a faulty acknowledgment or does not have the appropriate signatures. Because of the many complexities in a real estate transaction, there are innumerable possibilities for faults to appear in a title search and property survey. It is the abstractor's responsibility to discover and report them.

In certain instances where clouds are difficult to remove by ordinary means, they will need to be cleared by the seller of the property or by the borrowers filing a **suit to quiet title.** After appropriate evidence is submitted, a judge will remove or modify an otherwise damaging fault in a title, and the loan process can continue. The assurance of good title is as essential to a loan's completion as are the credit of the borrower and the value of the collateral.

It is important to note that the sales of foreclosed properties create complexities that require scrupulous examinations and careful documentation of the conditions of their titles.

**Surveys**

Although many loan closings include the provision for delivery of a plat to identify where the building is on the lot, some lenders may require a **survey** of the collateral property as a condition for a new loan. Although many properties are part of subdivisions that have been engineered and described by licensed and registered surveyors and engineers, some owners might have enlarged their homes or made additions to the improvements, since the original survey was undertaken. These might not meet the various setback restrictions required in the local zoning laws. Some properties might have been resubdivided, while others might now have an encroachment problem.

Surveys often reveal errors in legal descriptions or discover encroachments and easement infractions. A few interesting lawsuits have developed as a result of the wrong properties being encumbered by a new real estate loan.

**Disclosures in California Real Estate Transactions**

Based on an increasingly effective program of providing consumers with information pertinent to their real estate purchases, the State of California and its Bureau of Real Estate require numerous **disclosures** to be made in a real estate transaction.

**Real Estate Transfer Disclosures.** These disclosures cover the material facts about a particular property that could affect its value and desirability. Disclosures include, but are not limited to: mold; the age and condition of its structural components; the presence or absence of easements, driveways, or fences; descriptions of room additions or physical alterations accomplished without required building permits; potential flooding, drainage, or soil contamination conditions; zoning violations; homeowners' association obligations; deed restrictions; and citations or lawsuits against the owner or the property. Other required disclosures include: natural hazards; the Mello-Roos Tax Lien; Alquist-Prido earthquake fault; and any other area-specific items.

**Delivery of a Pest Control Inspection Report.** Although the law *does not* require that a structural pest inspection be performed before closing, most California real estate contracts include such a provision. The seller, or the seller's agent, must deliver to the buyer a pest control report and written certification, by a registered structural pest control company, attesting to the presence or absence of wood-destroying insects in the property.

**Disclosure of Geological Hazards.** The law requires disclosure of geological conditions that may affect specific properties, such as potential hazards from earthquakes, flooding, slides, erosion, and expansive soils, such as "fault creep" caused by earthquake tremors.

**Disclosure of Hazardous Waste Deposits.** The law defines hazardous wastes as those that may cause or contribute to an increase in mortality or serious illness. **Hazardous waste** property is defined as land where a significant disposal of hazardous waste has occurred on, under, or into the earth's surface. The seller of hazardous waste property, and any property within 2,000 feet of hazardous waste land (Border Zone Property), must disclose its use to potential buyers.

**Thermal Insulation Disclosure.** The law requires sellers of new homes to include in their property reports the type, thickness, and R-value of the installed insulation, if any.

**Special Flood Area Disclosure.** The seller of a property must disclose to the buyer whether the property is included in a special flood hazard area as defined by the Flood Hazard Boundary Map identifying such areas within a California community.

**Special City and County Ordinances.** Sellers must inform buyers of any special ordinances affecting the subject property relating to occupancy, zoning and use, building code compliance, fire, and health safety code regulations.

**Foreign Investment Real Estate Tax.**\*   Title 26, U.S. Codes Section 1445 of the federal law requires that the *buyer* of a property from a foreign national must withhold 10 percent of the gross purchase price to send to the Internal Revenue Service. U.S. resident aliens are exempt from this withholding requirement.

**Condominium Documents Disclosure.**   Before the transfer of title to a condominium property, the seller must provide the buyer with: a copy of the governing documents of the development; a copy of the subdivision restrictions, including any limitations on occupancy because of age; a copy of the most recent financial statement of the homeowner's association; and a written statement from the association as to the amount of unpaid assessments, if any.

**Disclosures for Real Property Loans.**   Within 72 hours of receipt of a loan application, every borrower must receive a written statement on a form approved by the Commissioner of the California Bureau of Real Estate containing the following: expected maximum costs to be paid by the borrower to secure the loan, including fees for appraisal, settlement, credit report, title insurance, and notary service; the total amount of commissions to be received by the lender for services performed, including points, origination fees, bonuses, and other charges.

## ■ CLOSING THE LOAN TRANSACTION

Once the loan process has reached the point at which a borrower's credit has been approved, the collateral's value is acceptable and the legal title to the collateral is clear, the loan underwriter approves the loan and preparations for closing begin. An approved loan commitment is communicated to all interested parties, obligating the lender to issue the loan under the

---

\*   The California State Franchise Tax Board requires buyers of California real estate to withhold 3½ percent of the purchase price in certain sales. Sales by California residents are exempt.

terms and conditions stipulated. This commitment remains in force for only a limited time, preventing any delay in the closing. In addition, the necessary legal documents for the transaction are prepared, an escrow is established if one is to be used for the closing, and the loan closing statements allocating the appropriate charges and credits are prepared. All parties concerned are notified of the date and place of the closing. After all documents have been signed, the deed has been transferred, the loan has been recorded, and the monies have been paid, the loan process is completed.

## Costs of Securing a Loan

A number of costs are associated with securing a real estate loan. Those that are described in this chapter are not all included in each loan transaction. They do represent the normal charges a borrower will encounter when securing a mortgage loan.

The Real Estate Settlement Procedures Act (RESPA) requires a loan/escrow officer to make a **good-faith estimate** of a loan's closing costs and provide this estimate to borrowers within three business days of the loan application. This information informs the borrowers of the various costs involved and prepares them to arrange for the necessary funds to close. Figure 11.1 is a copy of the HUD good-faith estimate form. The lender must also provide the borrower with a truth-in-lending statement showing the true annual rate of interest received on the loan.

**Points.**  Some real estate loans are offered for "7.75 percent interest and no points," while others are "7.5 percent interest and one point," or "7 percent interest and two points." A **point** is actually 1 percent of the loan amount, so two points on a $100,000 loan equals $2,000. Discount points represent a sum of money paid to a lender at the inception of a loan that raises the yield on the loan without raising the interest rate. The number of points charged by a lender reflect

- the risk on the loan—the higher the risk (a borrower's weak credit), the higher the points; and

- the contract interest rate as compared to the market interest rates—the lower the contract rate, the higher the points.

**FIGURE 11.1**

**Good-Faith Estimate**

OMB Approval No. 2502-0265

# Good Faith Estimate (GFE)

| Name of Originator | Borrower |
| --- | --- |
| Originator Address | |
| Originator Phone Number | Property Address |
| Originator Email | Date of GFE |

**Purpose**    This GFE gives you an estimate of your settlement charges and loan terms if you are approved for this loan. For more information, see HUD's *Special Information Booklet* on settlement charges, your *Truth-in-Lending Disclosures,* and other consumer information at www.hud.gov/respa. If you decide you would like to proceed with this loan, contact us.

**Shopping for your loan**    Only you can shop for the best loan for you. Compare this GFE with other loan offers, so you can find the best loan. Use the shopping chart on page 3 to compare all the offers you receive.

**Important dates**

1. The interest rate for this GFE is available through ⬚ . After this time, the interest rate, some of your loan Origination Charges, and the monthly payment shown below can change until you lock your interest rate.

2. This estimate for all other settlement charges is available through ⬚

3. After you lock your interest rate, you must go to settlement within ⬚ days (your rate lock period) to receive the locked interest rate.

4. You must lock the interest rate at least ⬚ days before settlement.

**Summary of your loan**

| | |
| --- | --- |
| Your initial loan amount is | $ |
| Your loan term is | years |
| Your initial interest rate is | % |
| Your initial monthly amount owed for principal, interest, and any mortgage insurance is | $ per month |
| Can your interest rate rise? | ☐ No ☐ Yes, it can rise to a maximum of %. The first change will be in |
| Even if you make payments on time, can your loan balance rise? | ☐ No ☐ Yes, it can rise to a maximum of $ |
| Even if you make payments on time, can your monthly amount owed for principal, interest, and any mortgage insurance rise? | ☐ No ☐ Yes, the first increase can be in and the monthly amount owed can rise to $ . The maximum it can ever rise to is $ . |
| Does your loan have a prepayment penalty? | ☐ No ☐ Yes, your maximum prepayment penalty is $ |
| Does your loan have a balloon payment? | ☐ No ☐ Yes, you have a balloon payment of $ due in years. |

**Escrow account information**

Some lenders require an escrow account to hold funds for paying property taxes or other property-related charges in addition to your monthly amount owed of $ ⬚ .

Do we require you to have an escrow account for your loan?

☐ No, you do not have an escrow account. You must pay these charges directly when due.

☐ Yes, you have an escrow account. It may or may not cover all of these charges. Ask us.

**Summary of your settlement charges**

| A | Your Adjusted Origination Charges (See page 2.) | |
| --- | --- | --- |
| B | Your Charges for All Other Settlement Services (See page 2.) | |
| A + B | **Total Estimated Settlement Charges** | $ |

**FIGURE 11.1 (continued)**
**Good-Faith Estimate**

Understanding
your estimated
settlement
charges

**Your Adjusted Origination Charges**

1. **Our origination charge**
   This charge is for getting this loan for you.

2. **Your credit or charge (points) for the specific interest rate chosen**
   ☐ The credit or charge for the interest rate of [＿＿＿＿] % is included in
   "Our origination charge." (See item 1 above.)
   ☐ You receive a credit of $ [＿＿＿＿] for this interest rate of [＿＿＿] %.
   This credit **reduces** your settlement charges.
   ☐ You pay a charge of $ [＿＿＿＿] for this interest rate of [＿＿＿] %.
   This charge (points) **increases** your total settlement charges.
   The tradeoff table on page 3 shows that you can change your total settlement charges by
   choosing a different interest rate for this loan.

| A | Your Adjusted Origination Charges | $ |
|---|---|---|

**Your Charges for All Other Settlement Services**

Some of these
charges
can change
at settlement.
See the top of
page 3 for more
information.

3. **Required services that we select**
   These charges are for services we require to complete your settlement. We will choose the
   providers of these services.

   | Service | Charge |
   |---|---|
   | | |
   | | |
   | | |

4. **Title services and lender's title insurance**
   This charge includes the services of a title or settlement agent, for example, and title insurance
   to protect the lender, if required.

5. **Owner's title insurance**
   You may purchase an owner's title insurance policy to protect your interest in the property.

6. **Required services that you can shop for**
   These charges are for other services that are required to complete your settlement. We can
   identify providers of these services or you can shop for them yourself. Our estimates for
   providing these services are below.

   | Service | Charge |
   |---|---|
   | | |
   | | |

7. **Government recording charges**
   These charges are for state and local fees to record your loan and title documents.

8. **Transfer taxes**
   These charges are for state and local fees on mortgages and home sales.

9. **Initial deposit for your escrow account**
   This charge is held in an escrow account to pay future recurring charges on your property and
   includes ☐ all property taxes, ☐ all insurance, and ☐ other [＿＿＿＿] .

10. **Daily interest charges**
    This charge is for the daily interest on your loan from the day of your settlement until the first day
    of the next month or the first day of your normal mortgage payment cycle.
    This amount is $ [＿＿＿＿] per day for [＿＿＿＿] days (if your settlement is [＿＿＿＿] ).

11. **Homeowner's insurance**
    This charge is for the insurance you must buy for the property to protect from a loss, such as fire.

    | Policy | Charge |
    |---|---|
    | | |
    | | |

| B | Your Charges for All Other Settlement Services | $ |
|---|---|---|

| A + B | Total Estimated Settlement Charges | $ |
|---|---|---|

 Good Faith Estimate (HUD-GFE) 2

**FIGURE 11.1 (continued)**
**Good-Faith Estimate**

# Instructions

**Understanding which charges can change at settlement**

This GFE estimates your settlement charges. At your settlement, you will receive a HUD-1, a form that lists your actual costs. Compare the charges on the HUD-1 with the charges on this GFE. Charges can change if you select your own provider and do not use the companies we identify. (See below for details.)

| These charges **cannot increase** at settlement: | The total of these charges **can increase up to 10%** at settlement: | These charges **can change** at settlement: |
|---|---|---|
| <ul><li>Our origination charge</li><li>Your credit or charge (points) for the specific interest rate chosen *(after you lock in your interest rate)*</li><li>Your adjusted origination charges *(after you lock in your interest rate)*</li><li>Transfer taxes</li></ul> | <ul><li>Required services that we select</li><li>Title services and lender's title insurance *(if we select them or you use companies we identify)*</li><li>Owner's title insurance *(if you use companies we identify)*</li><li>Required services that you can shop for *(if you use companies we identify)*</li><li>Government recording charges</li></ul> | <ul><li>Required services that you can shop for (if you do not use companies we identify)</li><li>Title services and lender's title insurance (if you do not use companies we identify)</li><li>Owner's title insurance (if you do not use companies we identify)</li><li>Initial deposit for your escrow account</li><li>Daily interest charges</li><li>Homeowner's insurance</li></ul> |

**Using the tradeoff table**

In this GFE, we offered you this loan with a particular interest rate and estimated settlement charges. However:

- If you want to choose this same loan with **lower settlement charges,** then you will have a **higher interest rate.**
- If you want to choose this same loan with a **lower interest rate,** then you will have **higher settlement charges.**

If you would like to choose an available option, you must ask us for a new GFE.

*Loan originators have the option to complete this table. Please ask for additional information if the table is not completed.*

| | The loan in this GFE | The same loan with lower settlement charges | The same loan with a lower interest rate |
|---|---|---|---|
| Your initial loan amount | $ | $ | $ |
| Your initial interest rate [1] | % | % | % |
| Your initial monthly amount owed | $ | $ | $ |
| Change in the monthly amount owed from this GFE | No change | You will pay $ **more** every month | You will pay $ **less** every month |
| Change in the amount you will pay at settlement with this interest rate | No change | Your settlement charges will be **reduced** by $ | Your settlement charges will **increase** by $ |
| How much your total estimated settlement charges will be | $ | $ | $ |

[1]*For an adjustable rate loan, the comparisons above are for the initial interest rate before adjustments are made.*

**Using the shopping chart**

Use this chart to compare GFEs from different loan originators. Fill in the information by using a different column for each GFE you receive. By comparing loan offers, you can shop for the best loan.

| | This loan | Loan 2 | Loan 3 | Loan 4 |
|---|---|---|---|---|
| Loan originator name | | | | |
| Initial loan amount | | | | |
| Loan term | | | | |
| Initial interest rate | | | | |
| Initial monthly amount owed | | | | |
| Rate lock period | | | | |
| Can interest rate rise? | | | | |
| Can loan balance rise? | | | | |
| Can monthly amount owed rise? | | | | |
| Prepayment penalty? | | | | |
| Balloon payment? | | | | |
| **Total Estimated Settlement Charges** | | | | |

**If your loan is sold in the future**

Some lenders may sell your loan after settlement. Any fees lenders receive in the future cannot change the loan you receive or the charges you paid at settlement.

 Good Faith Estimate (HUD-GFE)   3

**Placement or Origination Fee.**   Most lenders charge the borrower a placement or **origination fee** to cover the costs of establishing a new loan. This charge pays for the services of the loan officer and others, as well as for the materials used in the loan process.

**Impound Funds (Escrow Accounts).**   The great majority of real estate loans are made on single-family, owner-occupied homes and condominiums. Invariably, lenders making these loans require borrowers to include proportionate amounts of money to be impounded monthly for payment of property taxes, insurance premiums, and any required property improvement assessments. These **impound funds**, or **escrow funds**, are deposited in a special escrow account to be held until needed. Lenders normally require that two months' taxes and insurance be left on deposit in the escrow account to offset possible tax or insurance premium increases. Regardless of the payment schedule chosen, escrow funds are collected in addition to the principal and interest and result in a total monthly payment that is familiarly labeled *PITI*, that is, principal, interest, taxes, and insurance.

**Property Taxes.**   Property taxes are imposed on private property owners as a basic source of funds to pay for the various public services of state, county, city, school district, and other local governmental jurisdictions. Liens for delinquent property taxes have priority over other liens, so lenders will often require the impounding of funds to pay property taxes to protect their position. How much each property owner contributes depends on two factors—the specific monetary requirements of the governmental bodies of the jurisdiction in which the property is located and the total market valuation of all the taxable properties within that jurisdiction.

The taxing process begins by determining the funds needed to satisfy the specific budgetary requirements of each governing body within the taxing district for the following fiscal year. At the same time, every county assessor must maintain a current inventory of the fair market value of all privately owned real property within the county's boundaries. Thus, the term coined for this form of taxation is ad valorem, that is, "according to value." Some counties use this *fair market value* when calculating the total valuation of taxable properties. Most counties, however, apply an assessor's factor to the fair market value, which reduces this amount to an *assessed valuation* of all taxable property within the county. The tax rate to be applied to individual properties is derived by dividing the total budgetary requirements of the taxing district by the total value of the taxable property within the jurisdiction. The tax rate is usually expressed in terms of so many mills (thousandths of a cent) or dollars per thousand dollars of assessed value.

■ **EXAMPLE**  A taxable property having a fair market value of $200,000 in a jurisdiction that applies a 35 percent assessor's factor would have a $70,000 assessed valuation. If the tax rate on this particular property is $50 per $1,000 of assessed value, also described as a $50-mill rate, the tax to be paid for the year is $3,500. This owner would pay $291.67 monthly for the property tax impound ($3,500 ÷ 12 = $291.67).

**Hazard Insurance.**  In addition to the property tax impound, a lender usually insists that a proportionate share of the hazard insurance premium be included in the monthly payment. Hazard insurance premiums are based on risk—the higher the risk, the higher the insurance premium. If a house were of wood-frame construction and located in a relatively isolated area far from any possible fire-fighting service, the insurance rate for this home would be higher than the rate for a brick home situated two blocks from a fire station. Also, if an area is vulnerable to hurricanes, tornadoes, excessive floods, or other natural disasters, insurance rates will reflect these risks.

Whatever method is used to determine the insurance rate, one-twelfth of the annual premium will usually be included in a monthly payment. Thus, a hazard insurance policy with a $360 annual premium will require that an additional $30 per month be included in the payment.

**Title Insurance.**  Lenders require that title insurance be issued. When a new loan is concurrently part of a property sale, *two title insurance policies are required*. The first, for the full amount of the purchase price, is called an **owner's title insurance** and is issued in favor of the buyer. The seller is usually required to pay the premium on this policy.

The second title insurance policy, called **mortgagee's title insurance**, is issued in favor of the lender. The premium for this policy is usually paid by the borrower. It is issued at a reduced rate because, when a loan is being secured as part of a property's purchase, the mortgagee's policy is issued simultaneously with an owner's policy and the coverage is only for the duration and amount of the loan.

The mortgagee's title insurance is usually issued as an American Land Title Association (ALTA) policy covering the possibility of loss to the *lender*, not the property owner. If there is a claim under this insurance, the settlement is generally for the remaining balance of the loan.

All title insurance premiums are paid only once and guarantee the named beneficiaries as long as they own the property, or as long as a loan is in existence. Once a property is resold or a loan is repaid, new policies are issued to serve any new circumstances. Title insurance premiums vary from state to state because of local regulatory requirements.

**Mortgage Insurance.** When a conventional loan is insured or an FHA loan is created, there is a charge to the borrower for the insurance premium. Except for the funding fee, the DVA has no insurance premium.

**Assessment Liens.** Occasionally, a property is charged with an assessment lien for off-site improvements, such as sewer installations or street paving. Assessment charges are calculated by dividing the total costs of the improvements by some common denominator, such as total front feet or total square feet to fairly assess those properties benefitting from the improvements. This rate is applied to the individual property, and either the charges are paid in cash or the lien goes to bond. Because these improvement district bonds are priority liens, a lender will insist that a proportionate monthly amount of the required assessment payment be impounded, along with the taxes and insurance.

**Interest Adjustments.** Most lenders arrange their mortgage payments for collection on the 1st or 15th day of the month, based to some degree on a borrower's requirements. Mortgage payments are normally paid in arrears; that is, the payment on May 1 covers the principal due on that day and the interest is charged back for the month of April. Customarily these payments start a month or two after a loan's inception, depending on when during the month the loan is closed. As a result of varying closing dates and specific mortgage starting times, interest is usually adjusted from the closing date to the end of the month and is charged to the borrower to establish the appropriate payment pattern.

■ **EXAMPLE**  Consider a $200,000 loan at 6 percent interest closed on April 15. The first payment is not due until June 1. The interest adjustment to be paid in advance at the loan closing is $533.33.

| | |
|---|---|
| Principal | $200,000 |
| Interest Rate | × 0.06 |
| Annual Interest | 12,000 |
| Pro Rata Days | ÷ 360 |
| Daily Rate | 33.33 |
| Number of Days | × 16 |
| Pro Rata Interest | $533.33 |

(Note: In those escrows not charging for the day of settlement, the charge would be $499.50 for 15 days.)

Under Regulation Z of the Federal Reserve, lenders are required to quote to the borrowers the true interest charges, called the **annual percentage rate (APR)**. The APR includes the interest paid in the settlement plus service charges, points, fees, and other costs paid by the borrower.

**Prepayment Penalties.**  Whenever an existing financial encumbrance that includes a prepayment penalty is satisfied prior to its normal time, the amount of the penalty is charged to the owner of the collateral property. Thus, if an existing loan is paid off when the seller receives funds from the buyer who has a new loan, the seller is charged the penalty. Few loans today other than jumbo ARMs have prepayment penalties. Any that do must disclose this requirement in the truth-in-lending statement provided the borrower at the loan's inception.

**Additional Charges and Requirements.**  Every real estate sale and/or loan closing will incur additional charges for services rendered. The seller usually is charged for the selling brokerage commission. However, buyer's brokers are becoming popular and if a transaction is structured as such, the buyer may be charged for all or a part of the commission.

The borrower would be charged with the costs for securing a credit report, an appraisal, and, if necessary, a survey. If an attorney's opinion is required, the borrower and seller would pay their respective costs. All parties would pay their share of the escrow and recording fees. Often new houses or remodeled houses in urban renewal areas will need documents indicating that they have met the housing code and are ready for occupancy. Also, in those parts of the country exposed to possible flooding from lakes or rivers, the Army Corps of Engineers has designated certain lands as flood areas. To secure financing for houses in these flood plains borrowers must purchase flood insurance.

**Prorations.** When closing a real estate transaction, the escrow agent prorates certain items to allocate the costs and credits to the appropriate parties. Included in the items subject to **proration** are interest to date on existing loans, property taxes, hazard insurance premiums, rents, assessments, and homeowner's fees. Prorations are usually computed on a 360-day year and a 30-day month. However, FHA and DVA loans continue to have 365-day prorations. All prorations are *through* the day of closing with the seller held responsible for that day.

**Interest.** When a buyer assumes an existing loan, the interest owed to the date of settlement is charged to the seller.

■ **EXAMPLE** Consider a loan with a balance of $115,000 and an interest rate of 6 percent. Settlement is on the 21st day with the payment having been made on the first day of the settlement month.

| | | |
|---|---|---|
| Mortgage Balance | $115,000 | |
| Interest Rate | × 0.06 | |
| Year's Interest | 6,900 | |
| Pro Rata Days | ÷ 360 | |
| Daily Rate | 19.17 | |
| Number of Days | × 21 | |
| Pro Rata Amount | $402.50 | Charge seller, credit buyer |

When a new loan is created, the interest is prorated to the date of the first payment and charged to the borrower.

■ **EXAMPLE**  Consider a $100,000 DVA or FHA loan at 7½ percent interest beginning on May 15 with the first payment due on July 1.

| | |
|---|---|
| Mortgage Amount | $100,000.00 |
| Interest Rate | × 0.075 |
| Year's Interest | 7,500.00 |
| Pro Rata Days | ÷ 365 |
| Daily Rate | 20.55 |
| Number of Days | × 15 |
| Pro Rata Amount | $308.25   Charge Borrower |

**Property Taxes.**  Because property taxes are paid in arrears, when a buyer assumes an existing loan, the taxes are prorated to the settlement date, charged to the seller, and credited to the buyer.

■ **EXAMPLE**  Consider a property with a tax of $1,650 for the year. The settlement date is May 1 and the taxes have been paid to December 31 the previous year.

| | |
|---|---|
| Property Taxes | $1,650.00 |
| Pro Rata Days | ÷ 360 |
| Daily Rate | 4.58 |
| Number of Days | × 120 |
| Pro Rata Amount | $549.60   Charge seller, credit buyer |

When a new loan is created, the borrower is required to deposit two months' taxes in advance into the escrow collection account and is charged this amount in the settlement.

■ **EXAMPLE**  Consider a property with a tax of $1,650 for the year and a two-month advance charge.

| | |
|---|---|
| Property Taxes | $1,650.00 |
| Pro Rata Months | ÷ 12 |
| Monthly Rate | 137.50 |
| Number of Months | × 2 |
| Pro Rata Amount | $275.00 |

**Insurance Premiums.**  In a sale of real estate, the existing **hazard insurance** policy is usually canceled by the seller and replaced with a new policy by the buyer. Less frequently, the existing policy is assumed by the buyer. Property insurance premiums generally are paid in advance. Thus, when a policy is assumed, the seller receives a credit for the unused portion of the premium. When a new policy is required, the buyer will pay for a full year's premium in advance and an additional two months for the escrow collection account.

■ **EXAMPLE** Consider an assumption of an insurance premium of $225 for the year and a six-month proration.

| | |
|---|---|
| Insurance Premium | $225.00 |
| Pro Rata Months | ÷ 12 |
| Monthly Rate | 18.75 |
| Number of Months | × 6 |
| Credit Seller/Charge Buyer | $112.50 |

■ **EXAMPLE** Consider a new loan and a premium of $225 for insurance for the year and a two-month advance charge.

| | |
|---|---|
| Insurance Premium | $225.00 |
| Pro Rata Months | ÷ 12 |
| Monthly Rate | 18.75 |
| Number of Prepaid Months | × 2 |
| Charge Borrower for Impounds | $37.50 |

**Additional Prorations.**   When an income property is sold, additional care must be taken in the closing to allocate the proper credits and charges for rents and deposits due and collected in advance. In addition, utility charges must be accounted for or handled outside of escrow. Sometimes a property has an outstanding balance due from an improvement district assessment. This is prorated and the proper charges and credits allocated to the appropriate parties. Also, any homeowner's association or recreational association fees and dues need to be prorated and charged or credited accordingly.

## Closing Statements

The final step in the loan process is for the escrow officer to prepare the **closing statements**, using the HUD-1 Form (Figure 11.2) as required by RESPA, allocating the appropriate charges and credits.

Effective January 1, 2010, the Department of Housing and Urban Development (HUD) enacted mortgage reforms designed to help consumers to shop for the lowest cost mortgage and avoid costly and potentially harmful loan offers. To that end, changes have been made to the Settlement Statement (HUD-1) and Good Faith Estimate (GFE) forms. For more information about the changes to these forms, visit *www.hud.gov*. Once

**FIGURE 11.2**

**HUD-1 Settlement Statement**

OMB Approval No. 2502-0265

A. **Settlement Statement (HUD-1)**

| B. Type of Loan | | | | | |
|---|---|---|---|---|---|
| 1. ☐ FHA   2. ☐ RHS   3. ☐ Conv. Unins. | | 6. File Number: | 7. Loan Number: | 8. Mortgage Insurance Case Number: | |
| 4. ☐ VA   5. ☐ Conv. Ins. | | | | | |

C. **Note:**   This form is furnished to give you a statement of actual settlement costs. Amounts paid to and by the settlement agent are shown. Items marked "(p.o.c.)" were paid outside the closing; they are shown here for informational purposes and are not included in the totals.

| D. Name & Address of Borrower: | E. Name & Address of Seller: | F. Name & Address of Lender: |
|---|---|---|
| G. Property Location: | H. Settlement Agent: | I. Settlement Date: |
| | Place of Settlement: | |

| J. Summary of Borrower's Transaction | | K. Summary of Seller's Transaction | |
|---|---|---|---|
| **100. Gross Amount Due from Borrower** | | **400. Gross Amount Due to Seller** | |
| 101. Contract sales price | | 401. Contract sales price | |
| 102. Personal property | | 402. Personal property | |
| 103. Settlement charges to borrower (line 1400) | | 403. | |
| 104. | | 404. | |
| 105. | | 405. | |
| **Adjustment for items paid by seller in advance** | | **Adjustment for items paid by seller in advance** | |
| 106. City/town taxes          to | | 406. City/town taxes          to | |
| 107. County taxes          to | | 407. County taxes          to | |
| 108. Assessments          to | | 408. Assessments          to | |
| 109. | | 409. | |
| 110. | | 410. | |
| 111. | | 411. | |
| 112. | | 412. | |
| **120. Gross Amount Due from Borrower** | | **420. Gross Amount Due to Seller** | |
| **200. Amount Paid by or in Behalf of Borrower** | | **500. Reductions In Amount Due to seller** | |
| 201. Deposit or earnest money | | 501. Excess deposit (see instructions) | |
| 202. Principal amount of new loan(s) | | 502. Settlement charges to seller (line 1400) | |
| 203. Existing loan(s) taken subject to | | 503. Existing loan(s) taken subject to | |
| 204. | | 504. Payoff of first mortgage loan | |
| 205. | | 505. Payoff of second mortgage loan | |
| 206. | | 506. | |
| 207. | | 507. | |
| 208. | | 508. | |
| 209. | | 509. | |
| **Adjustments for items unpaid by seller** | | **Adjustments for items unpaid by seller** | |
| 210. City/town taxes          to | | 510. City/town taxes          to | |
| 211. County taxes          to | | 511. County taxes          to | |
| 212. Assessments          to | | 512. Assessments          to | |
| 213. | | 513. | |
| 214. | | 514. | |
| 215. | | 515. | |
| 216. | | 516. | |
| 217. | | 517. | |
| 218. | | 518. | |
| 219. | | 519. | |
| **220. Total Paid by/for Borrower** | | **520. Total Reduction Amount Due Seller** | |
| **300. Cash at Settlement from/to Borrower** | | **600. Cash at Settlement to/from Seller** | |
| 301. Gross amount due from borrower (line 120) | | 601. Gross amount due to seller (line 420) | |
| 302. Less amounts paid by/for borrower (line 220) | (          ) | 602. Less reductions in amounts due seller (line 520) | (          ) |
| **303. Cash** ☐ From ☐ To Borrower | | **603. Cash** ☐ To ☐ From Seller | |

The Public Reporting Burden for this collection of information is estimated at 35 minutes per response for collecting, reviewing, and reporting the data. This agency may not collect this information, and you are not required to complete this form, unless it displays a currently valid OMB control number. No confidentiality is assured; this disclosure is mandatory. This is designed to provide the parties to a RESPA covered transaction with information during the settlement process.

Previous edition are obsolete                    Page 1 of 3                    HUD-1

**FIGURE 11.2** (CONTINUED)

## HUD-1 Settlement Statement

### L. Settlement Charges

| 700. Total Real Estate Broker Fees | | Paid From Borrower's Funds at Settlement | Paid From Seller's Funds at Settlement |
|---|---|---|---|
| Division of commission (line 700) as follows : | | | |
| 701. $               to | | | |
| 702. $               to | | | |
| 703. Commission paid at settlement | | | |
| 704. | | | |

| 800. Items Payable in Connection with Loan | | | |
|---|---|---|---|
| 801. Our origination charge | $               (from GFE #1) | | |
| 802. Your credit or charge (points) for the specific interest rate chosen | $               (from GFE #2) | | |
| 803. Your adjusted origination charges | (from GFE #A) | | |
| 804. Appraisal fee to | (from GFE #3) | | |
| 805. Credit report to | (from GFE #3) | | |
| 806. Tax service to | (from GFE #3) | | |
| 807. Flood certification to | (from GFE #3) | | |
| 808. | | | |
| 809. | | | |
| 810. | | | |
| 811. | | | |

| 900. Items Required by Lender to be Paid in Advance | | | |
|---|---|---|---|
| 901. Daily interest charges from          to          @ $          /day | (from GFE #10) | | |
| 902. Mortgage insurance premium for          months to | (from GFE #3) | | |
| 903. Homeowner's insurance for          years to | (from GFE #11) | | |
| 904. | | | |

| 1000. Reserves Deposited with Lender | | | |
|---|---|---|---|
| 1001. Initial deposit for your escrow account | (from GFE #9) | | |
| 1002. Homeowner's insurance          months @ $          per month $ | | | |
| 1003. Mortgage insurance          months @ $          per month $ | | | |
| 1004. Property Taxes          months @ $          per month $ | | | |
| 1005.          months @ $          per month $ | | | |
| 1006.          months @ $          per month $ | | | |
| 1007. Aggregate Adjustment          -$ | | | |

| 1100. Title Charges | | | |
|---|---|---|---|
| 1101. Title services and lender's title insurance | (from GFE #4) | | |
| 1102. Settlement or closing fee | $ | | |
| 1103. Owner's title insurance | (from GFE #5) | | |
| 1104. Lender's title insurance | $ | | |
| 1105. Lender's title policy limit $ | | | |
| 1106. Owner's title policy limit $ | | | |
| 1107. Agent's portion of the total title insurance premium to | $ | | |
| 1108. Underwriter's portion of the total title insurance premium to | $ | | |
| 1109. | | | |
| 1110. | | | |
| 1111. | | | |

| 1200. Government Recording and Transfer Charges | | | |
|---|---|---|---|
| 1201. Government recording charges | (from GFE #7) | | |
| 1202. Deed $          Mortgage $          Release $ | | | |
| 1203. Transfer taxes | (from GFE #8) | | |
| 1204. City/County tax/stamps          Deed $          Mortgage $ | | | |
| 1205. State tax/stamps          Deed $          Mortgage $ | | | |
| 1206. | | | |

| 1300. Additional Settlement Charges | | | |
|---|---|---|---|
| 1301. Required services that you can shop for | (from GFE #6) | | |
| 1302. | $ | | |
| 1303. | $ | | |
| 1304. | | | |
| 1305. | | | |

| 1400. Total Settlement Charges (enter on lines 103, Section J and 502, Section K) | | | |
|---|---|---|---|

**FIGURE 11.2   (CONTINUED)**

**HUD-1 Settlement Statement**

| Comparison of Good Faith Estimate (GFE) and HUD-1 Charrges | | Good Faith Estimate | HUD-1 |
|---|---|---|---|
| **Charges That Cannot Increase** | **HUD-1 Line Number** | | |
| Our origination charge | # 801 | | |
| Your credit or charge (points) for the specific interest rate chosen | # 802 | | |
| Your adjusted origination charges | # 803 | | |
| Transfer taxes | # 1203 | | |

| Charges That In Total Cannot Increase More Than 10% | | Good Faith Estimate | HUD-1 |
|---|---|---|---|
| Government recording charges | # 1201 | | |
| | # | | |
| | # | | |
| | # | | |
| | # | | |
| | # | | |
| | # | | |
| | # | | |
| Total | | | |
| Increase between GFE and HUD-1 Charges | | $          or          % | |

| Charges That Can Change | | Good Faith Estimate | HUD-1 |
|---|---|---|---|
| Initial deposit for your escrow account | # 1001 | | |
| Daily interest charges    $         /day | # 901 | | |
| Homeowner's insurance | # 903 | | |
| | # | | |
| | # | | |
| | # | | |

**Loan Terms**

| | |
|---|---|
| Your initial loan amount is | $ |
| Your loan term is | years |
| Your initial interest rate is | % |
| Your initial monthly amount owed for principal, interest, and any mortgage insurance is | $          includes <br> ☐ Principal <br> ☐ Interest <br> ☐ Mortgage Insurance |
| Can your interest rate rise? | ☐ No   ☐ Yes, it can rise to a maximum of          %. The first change will be on          and can change again every          after          . Every change date, your interest rate can increase or decrease by          %. Over the life of the loan, your interest rate is guaranteed to never be **lower** than          % or **higher** than          %. |
| Even if you make payments on time, can your loan balance rise? | ☐ No   ☐ Yes, it can rise to a maximum of $ |
| Even if you make payments on time, can your monthly amount owed for principal, interest, and mortgage insurance rise? | ☐ No   ☐ Yes, the first increase can be on          and the monthly amount owed can rise to $          . The maximum it can ever rise to is $ |
| Does your loan have a prepayment penalty? | ☐ No   ☐ Yes, your maximum prepayment penalty is $ |
| Does your loan have a balloon payment? | ☐ No   ☐ Yes, you have a balloon payment of $          due in          years on          . |
| Total monthly amount owed including escrow account payments | ☐ You do not have a monthly escrow payment for items, such as property taxes and homeowner's insurance. You must pay these items directly yourself. <br> ☐ You have an additional monthly escrow payment of $          that results in a total initial monthly amount owed of $          . This includes principal, interest, any mortagage insurance and any items checked below: <br> ☐ Property taxes          ☐ Homeowner's insurance <br> ☐ Flood insurance          ☐ <br> ☐ |

**Note:** If you have any questions about the Settlement Charges and Loan Terms listed on this form, please contact your lender.

the closing statements are prepared, the parties are notified of the closing date. After all the proper documents have been signed and recorded, the final settlement of funds is made and all monies are paid to the appropriate parties.

**Servicing the Loan**

Once the loan has been closed, arrangements must be made to service it. Principal and interest payments need to be collected in a timely manner and accurate records must be kept. Some loan payments include amounts for property taxes and insurance. The servicing agent not only must place these funds in a proper escrow account, but also must take responsibility for their payment, promptly and in the proper amounts. These activities are repetitious and continuing, usually on a monthly basis for many years.

Servicing duties are usually accepted by most lenders as part of the loan closing. In fact, the costs of setting up these collection escrows, as well as the monies required to prime the tax and insurance accounts, are built into a loan's closing statement. A few weeks after closing, the borrowers usually receive information as to how and where to make the payments. A coupon booklet is often included in which the borrower is instructed to send the appropriate coupon for each specific month's payment along with the check. The coupon indicates two payment amounts on its face: one amount if paid by the required date, a higher amount if paid late.

**Assignment of the Loan**

For many years, the servicing of real estate loans by financial institutions was the task of the lending institutions because they maintained ownership of the securities. This relationship changed over time as the originators of the loans found it more expedient to sell these securities in the secondary market. An **assignment** is the transfer of the right, title, and interest in the property of one person, the assignor, to another, the assignee.

Most loans today are sold or *assigned* in the secondary market, but the loan originators often retain the servicing responsibility under a contract with the new owners. For their fee, ranging from 0.25 to 0.625 percent or more, the loan originators can build up a substantial loan collection business. In fact, servicing fees are an important part of mortgage bankers' profits.

These servicing companies collect the payments and keep records for borrowers and lenders. They provide a property tax service, checking the records of the county for the amounts due and paying the taxes on time. Servicing companies are also billed directly by insurance companies for premiums due on the various policies placed on the collateral properties. Probably most important, they maintain a watchful eye on the timely receipt of loan payments.

When a payment is late, the collection manager is alerted to watch for the check. If it is not forthcoming, a letter is sent to the borrowers that notifies them of the consequences of a default. If no payments are received, the manager notifies the investors and proceeds to follow their directions to foreclose on the property.

When loan collection portfolios are sold, notices must be sent to borrowers to mail payments to the new owners of the securities. Under the loan servicing transfer provisions of the Federal Housing Law,

- lenders must give 15-day advance notice, by a Loan Transfer Disclosure statement, that the loan is changing hands;

- both the old and the new lenders must give toll-free phone numbers and the name of the person empowered to handle borrower inquiries or complaints; and

- waivers of up to 60 days after the loan assignment must be given for late fees if the borrower sent a payment on time but to the wrong lender.

## ■ HOME AFFORDABLE FORECLOSURE ALTERNATIVES PROGRAM (HAFA)

Because some homeowners are either in default or entering into default on their home loans, the U.S. Treasury introduced the Home Affordable Foreclosure Alternatives Program (HAFA) in 2009, effective April 5, 2010, which offers homeowners, mortgage servicers, and investors incentives for providing a short sale or deed-in-lieu of foreclosure to qualified homeowners. For more information, visit *www.makinghomeaffordable.gov*.

## ■ SUMMARY

Processing a real estate loan involves searching the property's chain of title and preparing the closing statements.

After searching through the history of a property's title, the examiner can verify that all matters of record are as represented by the borrowers. Careful attention is paid to the documents that were recorded in the past to determine their legal validity.

For the sake of closing a particular loan, the borrowers' rights to encumber the property must be irrefutably established. In addition, those matters of record that may affect the condition of the title must be examined to see if they could adversely affect the status of the lender. Any clouds on the title must be cleared before a loan can be issued.

Once all the title information is accumulated, the examiner prepares an opinion of the condition of the title for approval by the borrowers and their attorney. The title company will then prepare an insurance policy issued to protect the lender against any unforeseen claims against the property.

In closing the loan transaction, a statement is prepared by the escrow officer allocating the various charges and credits associated with the transaction. The lender is charged for the entire loan amount while the borrowers are charged for interest to date and all costs incurred in securing the loan. These costs include points, origination fees, recording fees, collection charges, escrow fees, and the mortgagee's title insurance premium.

When all charges and credits have been approved and all loan documents signed, notarized, and recorded, the loan proceeds are distributed and the file is closed.

## ■ REVIEW QUESTIONS

1.  An example of a constructive notice is a(n)

    a.  recorded deed.

    c.  unrecorded mechanic's lien.

    b.  property tax lien.

    d.  occupant in the property.

2.  An abstract of title is a

    a.  title insurance policy.

    b.  historical review of a property's title.

    c.  transfer of ownership.

    d.  survey of the property.

3.  A standard title insurance policy insures against

    a.  unrecorded liens.

    b.  rights of parties in possession of subject property.

    c.  water rights.

    d.  errors in matters of record.

4.  A fault in a title can be corrected by a

    a.  survey.

    c.  title insurance policy.

    b.  suit to quiet title.

    d.  sale's recession.

5.  Property surveys sometimes discover problems in all of the following categories *EXCEPT*

    a.  legal descriptions.

    c.  restrictions.

    b.  easements.

    d.  encroachments.

6. In California, real estate transfer disclosures include all of the following categories *EXCEPT* disclosures for

   a. age and condition of the structure.

   b. occupants with AIDS.

   c. soil contamination.

   d. deed restrictions.

7. Disclosures of geological hazards include all of the following events *EXCEPT* for possible

   a. flooding.

   c. tornadoes.

   b. landslides.

   d. earthquakes.

8. Prior to closing a real estate loan, every borrower must receive all of the following items *EXCEPT*

   a. an estimate of costs.

   b. a title insurance policy.

   c. an estimate of the amount of the monthly installments.

   d. information relevant under Regulation Z, RESPA, and ECOA.

9. In a loan closing, the borrower is usually charged with all of the following items *EXCEPT* the

   a. loan amount.

   c. title insurance premium.

   b. prorated interest.

   d. recording fees.

10. Which of the following amounts is the interest adjustment on a new $100,000 loan at 9 percent interest, with payments to start on March 1, if the closing is on January 15?

   a. $750

   c. $1,125

   b. $1,085

   d. $1,500

# ■ EXERCISES

1. Visit a title company and observe their techniques for examining a property's title history.

2. Review the current laws on asbestos removal from old buildings in view of the extra hazards that the physical removal creates when it spews the asbestos molecules into the atmosphere. Does the law allow an owner to forgo the removal if such a circumstance would be created?

## CHAPTER TWELVE

# THE SECONDARY MORTGAGE MARKET

## ■ KEY TERMS

administered price
system

automated
underwriting system
(AUS)

Desktop Originator®

Desktop Underwriter®

Fannie Mae

Federal Home Loan
Bank (FHLB)

Federal Housing
Finance Agency
(FHFA)

FICO

Freddie Mac

Ginnie Mae

government sponsored
enterprise (GSE)

jumbo loans

Loan Prospector®

mortgage-backed
securities (MBS)

par

pass-through
certificates

premium

real estate mortgage
investment conduits
(REMICs)

The secondary mortgage market is designed to deal in real estate mortgages, buying them from loan originators and selling them to investors or pooling them to enlarge the markets for these types of securities. When mortgages are purchased from primary lenders, also known as loan originators, the money generated acts to replenish the supply necessary for continued lending activities. When mortgages are sold to investors, funds are recirculated nationally from money-rich areas to money-poor areas.

The major participants in the secondary mortgage market are Fannie Mae (formerly the Federal National Mortgage Association), Freddie Mac (formerly the Federal Home Loan Mortgage Corporation), and Ginnie Mae (formerly the Government National Mortgage Association).

The financial market for real estate loans is based on the ability of loan originators to dispose of their new loans as quickly as possible in the secondary market, as they need to replenish funds and strive to manage the interest rate risk that arises from long-term, fixed-rate mortgages. This results in loan originators having to closely follow the loan guidelines established by the secondary market investors.

The trend toward selling real estate loans has led to the development of a major new group of investors. Based on the concept of collateralization—the pooling together of homogenous types of mortgages to use as collateral for issuing marketable securities—private companies have emerged to challenge the dominant positions of Fannie Mae and Freddie Mac. Operating as **real estate mortgage investment conduits (REMICs)**, these life insurance companies, pension funds, securities dealers, and other financial institutions are creating new loans for their own portfolios, as well as buying and selling loans from other originators.

This chapter examines the participants in the secondary mortgage market and how their activities facilitate the national distribution of funds to the primary markets. See Figure 12.1 for a diagram of the process.

**FIGURE 12.1**

**The Secondary Mortgage Market**

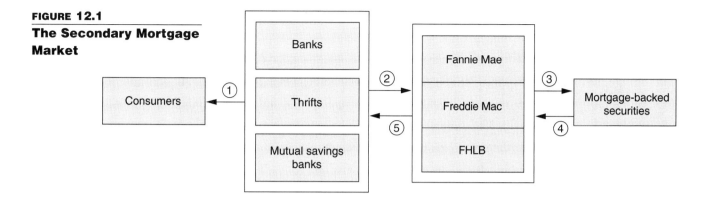

Step 1: Primary market lenders (banks, thrifts, mutual savings banks, etc.) provide mortgages to consumers.

Step 2: Primary market lenders sell loan packages to Fannie Mae, Freddie Mac, and Federal Home Loan Bank.

Step 3: Fannie Mae, Freddie Mac, and FHLB sell mortgage-backed securities on the open market.

Step 4: Monies received through the sale of mortgage-backed securities provide Fannie Mae, Freddie Mac, and FHLB with funds to purchase more loan packages from the primary lenders.

Step 5: By purchasing more loan packages, Fannie Mae, Freddie Mac, and FHLB provide the primary market lenders with additional money to fund more mortgage loans for consumers.

## ■ FEDERAL HOUSING FINANCING AGENCY

The **Federal Housing Finance Agency (FHFA)** was established under the Federal Housing Reform Act of 2007 as an independent agency to regulate the government-sponsored entities (GSE) of Fannie Mae, Freddie Mac, and the Federal Home Loan Bank (FHLB). At that point, these enterprises had $5.4 trillion of guaranteed mortgage-backed securities (MBS) and debt outstanding with an 80 percent market share of all new mortgages. Despite the best efforts of the enterprises to provide liquidity to the conforming mortgage market while raising and maintaining capital, their ability to fulfill their mission deteriorated, raising concern over both safety and soundness issues.

On September 6, 2008, Fannie Mae and Freddie Mac were placed into conservatorship. The FHFA will act as conservator until the enterprises have stabilized. In addition, the U.S. Department of the Treasury agreed to provide up to $100 billion of capital to ensure liquidity in the housing and mortgage markets. The stated goal is to restore confidence in Fannie Mae and Freddie Mac, enhance their capacity to fulfill their mission, and mitigate the systemic risk that has contributed to instability in the market. Under the conservatorship both entities will operate their business as usual but with stronger backing for the holders of MBS and other debt. The FHFA will assume the power of the board of directors and management. Common stock and preferred stock dividends will be eliminated, but all common and preferred stock will remain outstanding.

# ■ FANNIE MAE

**Fannie Mae** is a private shareholder-owned company whose stock is traded on the New York Stock Exchange and is also part of Standard and Poor's 500 Composite Stock Price Index. Fannie Mae was established by congressional charter in 1938 as the Federal National Mortgage Association (FNMA) to expand the flow of available mortgage money throughout the country by creating a secondary market for the purchase of FHA-insured mortgages. The scope of operations was broadened in 1944 to include purchasing DVA-guaranteed loans. The purchase of the FHA and DVA loans was made at **par**; that is, at full face value, making Fannie Mae a sought-after provider for the real estate mortgage market.

## Empowerment to Sell Mortgages

In 1954 Fannie Mae was rechartered as a national secondary mortgage market clearinghouse to be financed by *private capital*. Fannie Mae was empowered to *sell* its mortgages as well as purchase new FHA and DVA loans. Fannie Mae's purchases were no longer made at par but at whatever discounted price would develop a reasonable rate of return. This profit attitude was consistent with the reorganizational goal of private ownership. Fannie Mae did not have to purchase every mortgage submitted to it, only those mortgages that met its standards for marketability.

In other words, Fannie Mae imposed its own criteria for acceptance of mortgages submitted for sale, which sometimes created animosity among mortgage originators. It was argued that one federal agency should accept another's standards. Fannie Mae countered with the argument that the FHA and DVA standards for credit and appraisal were *minimum* standards and insisted that all mortgages submitted to Fannie Mae would have to meet its own standards for quality, yield, and risk. The quality and level of stability of guaranteed and insured loans were raised in order to meet these new requirements.

When Fannie Mae *purchases* mortgages, a servicing agreement is executed allowing the loan originator-seller to act as a collection agent for a specified fee. This fee, a rate of approximately one-fourth to three-eighths of 1 percent of the mortgage amount, creates a substantial source of income for the originator, depending on the size of its mortgage loan portfolio.

Loan originators derive a large portion of their mortgage investment income from origination and collection fees. In many cases, especially with the mortgage bankers who issue the bulk of FHA and DVA loans, the more loans that can be created, the higher the potential profits. Thus, the Fannie Mae secondary mortgage market allows loan originators an opportunity to "roll over" their money. By selling their mortgages, these originators can secure more funds for making additional loans, thereby collecting more origination fees.

When Fannie Mae *sells* its mortgages, it does so in open-market transactions in which the purchasers are required to pay current prices for the securities. This confirms the private ownership profit motives of this agency.

**Reorganization Under HUD**

The Housing and Urban Development Act of 1968 changed the Fannie Mae organization once again. Based on its successful operation in preceding years as a quasi-public, profitable corporation, Fannie Mae was reorganized as a fully private corporation. All Treasury-owned stock was redeemed, and a like amount of over-the-counter common stock was offered to the general public. Fannie Mae became a separate, privately owned corporation subject to federal corporate income tax and exempt from state income taxes. It retains the benefit of government "sponsorship," which includes a line of credit with the U.S. Treasury, and is referred to as a **government sponsored enterprise (GSE)**.

The 1968 reorganization was meant to enhance Fannie Mae's ability to participate in the secondary market and to encourage new money to enter the real estate mortgage market. Fannie Mae could now purchase mortgages at a **premium** (in excess of par) and was allowed to expand its own borrowing ability by floating securities backed by specific pools of mortgages in its portfolio.

The Emergency Home Finance Act of 1970 gave Fannie Mae the additional authority to purchase mortgages *other than* FHA-insured or DVA-guaranteed loans, mostly conventional loans. This further expanded Fannie Mae's impact on national real estate finance.

## Administered Price System

In the past, Fannie Mae's mortgage purchasing procedures had been handled under a free-market-system auction. Lenders offered to sell Fannie Mae their loans at acceptable discounts, with Fannie Mae buying the lowest-priced loans—those with the deepest discounts. This system has been replaced by an **administered price system** in which Fannie Mae adjusts its required yields daily in accordance with market factors and its financial needs.

Under the administered price system, lenders call a special Fannie Mae rate line to secure current yield quotes and then a separate line to place an order to sell. Lenders may order a mandatory commitment, whereby delivery of loans to Fannie Mae is *guaranteed*, or a standby commitment, in which the lender retains the *option* to deliver the loans or not, depending on the price at time of delivery.

## Fannie Mae Mortgage-Backed Securities (MBSs)

When Fannie Mae purchases mortgage loans from mortgage companies, savings institutions, credit unions, or commercial banks, they are generally packaged into **mortgage-backed securities (MBSs)** and sold in international capital markets. In June of 2005, Fannie Mae announced that first lien, fixed-rate (and some adjustable-rate) mortgages for a term of up to 40 years would be eligible for inclusion in its MBS pools. Fannie Mae also issued a variety of short- and long-term debt securities to meet investor needs. The Universal Debt Facility Offering Circular is a legal document that provides detailed information on all of Fannie Mae's funding programs. The majority of Fannie Mae's short-term funding needs are met through either Discount Notes or Benchmark Bills.

For more detailed information, see "Understanding Fannie Mae Debt" at *www.fanniemae.com.*

**Underwriting Standards**

Lenders wishing to sell their conventional loans to Fannie Mae must subscribe to their guidelines, which are revised from time to time. These include the following:

- Maximum loan amounts are set annually for single, duplex, triplex, and fourplex properties.

- Any loan with a loan-to-value (LTV) ratio of more than 80 percent must carry private mortgage insurance; cost varies according to the amount of down payment.

- A 20 percent down payment may be entirely from gift funds; gift funds are also permitted with less than 20 percent down, but some percentage may be required from borrowers' own funds, depending on the particular loan product.

- The borrowers' debt-to-income ratios must be 28 percent of their combined total gross monthly income for housing costs including principle, interest, taxes, insurance, and homeowner association fees; or 36 percent of their total monthly debt including housing costs plus other installment debt expenses. These ratios vary according to the type of loan product.

- The seller can contribute up to 3 percent of the sales price toward borrower's closing costs with a 5 percent down payment, and up to 6 percent with a 10 percent down payment.

- Fixed-rate and adjustable-rate loans are available for most loan products.

- Homebuyer education and counseling is required for first-time homebuyers obtaining a MyCommunityMortgage® or depending on non-traditional credit.

**Conforming and Nonconforming Loans.**   The terms *conforming* and *nonconforming* are used by lenders to define loans that conform to the Fannie Mae/Freddie Mac qualifying guidelines. Loans that do not meet the conforming guidelines, including maximum loan amount and down payment requirements, are called *nonconforming*.

According to the Housing and Economic Recovery Act of 2008, the national conforming loan limits are to be set annually by FHFA depending on changes in median home prices calculated by FHA over the previous year. However, they cannot decline from year to year. Two sets of limited loan amounts are provided for first mortgages: general and high-cost area.

For example, the 2009 loan limits are as follows:

|  | General | High-Cost* |
|---|---|---|
| Single unit | $417,000 | $625,500 |
| Duplex | $533,850 | $800,775 |
| Triplex | $645,300 | $967,950 |
| Fourplex | $801,950 | $1,202,925 |

*These amounts are the maximum that may apply, but they may be lower for a specific area (set at 115 percent of local median price). These limits are 50 percent higher in Alaska, Hawaii, Guam, and the U.S. Virgin Islands.

Although these are conforming conventional loan limits, buyers may pay any price for a property, making up the difference in cash. Maximum loan limits are established to set a standard for these types of loans so that they become homogeneous packages for securitization in the secondary market. Loans issued in excess of these amounts are nonconforming. They are called **jumbo loans** and are usually made by lenders for their own investment portfolios.

**Automated Underwriting System (AUS)**   Fannie Mae provides two versions of its automated underwriting system, the **Desktop Underwriter®** and the **Desktop Originator®**, for lender services and independent mortgage broker-agents respectively. Lenders access Fannie Mae's sophisticated loan analysis system through the software they offer their customers. Desktop Underwriter® is the leading automated underwriting system in the industry and is regularly updated to offer more products to more potential homebuyers.

**Fannie Mae Mortgage Loan Products**

Fannie Mae offers both fixed and adjustable-rate mortgage loans in a variety of different loan products. For the most current information on mortgage loans eligible for purchase by Fannie Mae visit *www.fanniemae.com*, or *www.efanniemae.com*. Fannie Mae also purchases home construction and renovation loans as well as reverse mortgage loans for seniors (both the FHA Home Equity Conversion Mortgage and Fannie Mae Home Keeper®).

Fannie Mae's MyCommunityMortgage® loans offer more flexibility in qualifying guidelines and credit history and have special options for teachers, police officers, firefighters, health care workers, and those with disabilities. There are also special loan products for rural housing and Native Americans.

# ■ FREDDIE MAC

The credit crunch of 1969 and 1970 gave rise to the Emergency Home Finance Act of 1970, which created, among other things, the Federal Home Loan Mortgage Corporation, now known as **Freddie Mac**. Freddie Mac was organized specifically to provide a secondary mortgage market for the U.S. savings associations and thrifts that are members of the Federal Home Loan Bank System.

**Organization**

Freddie Mac was established with an initial subscription of $100 million from the 12 Federal Home Loan district banks and placed under the direction of three members of the Federal Home Loan Bank Board. Freddie Mac was given the authority to raise additional funds by floating its own securities, which were backed by pools of its own mortgages. Since 1989, Freddie Mac has become an independent stock company and is a GSE like Fannie Mae.

As a major player in the secondary market, Freddie Mac buys mortgages that meet stated guidelines and product standards, packages the loans into MBSs, and sells the securities to investors on Wall Street.

As part of the Housing and Economic Recovery Act of 2008, Freddie Mac came under the supervision of the FHFA and in September 2008, was placed in conservatorship along with Fannie Mae.

**Underwriting Standards**   Freddie Mac generally follows the same conforming loan standards as Fannie Mae:

- Maximum loan amounts are set annually for single, duplex, triplex, and fourplex properties.

- Any loan with an LTV of more than 80 percent must carry private mortgage insurance; cost varies according to the percentage of down payment.

- A 20 percent down payment may be entirely from gift funds; gift funds are also permitted with less than 20 percent down, but some percentages may be required from the borrower's own funds, depending on the particular loan product.

- The seller can contribute up to 3 percent of the sales price toward borrower's closing costs with 5 percent down payment, and up to 6 percent with a 10 percent down payment.

One exception is that Freddie Mac only looks at total debt-to-income ratio with no set percentage for housing expense. The amount of down payment and qualifying ratios varies with different loan products.

**Electronic Underwriting System**   Freddie Mac provides its own electronic underwriting service, called **Loan Prospector®**, to participating lenders, mortgage insurers, mortgage bankers and brokers, and others in the real estate market.

The Loan Prospector® computer program evaluates a borrower's creditworthiness using statistical models and judgmental rules. The credit evaluation indicates the level of underwriting and documentation necessary to determine the investment quality of a loan. It includes the borrower's credit reputation and financial capacity as well as the estimated value of the property. The credit analysis uses information from the loan application and credit searches. The value of the property is derived from statistical models or from a traditional appraisal.

**Freddie Mac Loan Products**

Freddie Mac purchases both fixed and adjustable-rate loans for a predetermined amount of time from 15-year, 20-year, 30-year, and, in some cases, 40-year terms. Loans may be for the purchase or refinance of owner-occupied single-family dwellings, condominiums, planned unit developments (PUDs), and manufactured homes. Loans are also available for one-unit to four-unit primary residence and investment properties, and single-unit second homes. For a full description of the variety of loan products that can be purchased by Freddie Mac, see *www.freddiemac.com*.

## ■ GINNIE MAE

The Government National Mortgage Corporation was created in 1968 as a government-owned corporation under the direction of the Department of Housing and Urban Development (HUD) to provide financing for special assistance programs and operate the securities pool. Known today as **Ginnie Mae**, the stated mission is to expand affordable housing in America by linking domestic and global capital markets to the nation's housing markets.

Ginnie Mae does not buy or sell loans or issue MBSs but instead guarantees that investors will receive timely payments of principal and interest on MBSs backed by federally insured (FHA) or guaranteed (DVA) loans. Other eligible loans for Ginnie Mae MBSs include those originated by the Department of Agriculture Rural and Community Housing (RHS) and HUD's Office of Native American Programs (ONAP). Ginnie Mae MBSs are fully modified pass-through securities guaranteed by the full faith and credit of the U.S. government. Regardless of whether the mortgage payment is made, the investor receives the full principal and interest payment.

## Ginnie Mae Mortgage-Backed Securities

Mortgage-backed securities are pools of mortgages used as collateral for the issuance of securities, commonly referred to as **pass-through certificates**, as the principal and interest payments are "passed through" to the investor. The interest on the security is lower than the interest rate on the loan to cover the cost of servicing and the guaranty fee. There are two types of Ginnie Mae MBSs available. The Ginnie Mae I MBS requires that all mortgages in the pool be the same type (e.g., single-family) and that the mortgages remain insured or guaranteed by FHA, DVA, RHS, or ONAP with a minimum pool size of $1 million. Payment is made on the 15th of the month.

The Ginnie Mae II MBS provides for multiple-issue pools that allow for more geographic dispersal. Higher servicing fees are allowed, and the minimum pool size is $250,000 for multilender pools and $1 million for single-lender pools. Payment is made on the 20th of the month to allow time for payments to be consolidated by a central paying agent.

**Ginnie Mae Platinum Securities**   The Platinum Securities allow investors to combine Ginnie Mae MBS pools into a single security and receive a single payment each month rather than separate payments from individual pools. See *www.ginniemae.gov* for more information on Ginnie Mae programs.

## ■ SUMMARY

This chapter examined the roles of the various major agencies involved in the secondary mortgage market for real estate finance. These agencies are Fannie Mae, Freddie Mac, and Ginnie Mae.

Based on electronic procedures that are uniform in the evaluation of credit and collateral, a huge market for trading in securities has evolved. Local originators of loans sell them to secondary investors thereby freeing local capital for making more loans. In addition to FHA and DVA loans, the secondary mortgage market has expanded to include conventional loans on homes, condominiums, multifamily projects, and commercial developments. Operating as warehousers of money, Fannie Mae and Freddie Mac effectively redistribute funds from money-rich areas to money-poor areas.

Fannie Mae was organized in 1938 as a federal agency involved primarily in purchasing and managing FHA-insured loans. The association has evolved into a private, profit-making corporation dealing in every type of residential real estate mortgage loan.

To raise funds for the purchase of these mortgages, Fannie Mae charges fees and has the authority to borrow from the U.S. Treasury. Fannie Mae markets its own securities and is expanding its strategies to meet the pressures created by an active real estate market.

Freddie Mac was created in 1970 to provide a secondary mortgage market for the nation's savings associations. Through the years it has evolved into a private corporation, buying and selling all types of loans and adding to the effectiveness of the secondary market.

Created as a wholly owned government corporation in 1968, Ginnie Mae is under the jurisdiction of HUD. It finances special assistance programs and participates in the secondary market through its guarantee of FHA and DVA mortgage-backed securities. In addition to the three major participants in the secondary market, other public and private agencies and companies are developing under the concept of collateralization. This concept pools existing mortgages together in homogeneous packages that are then pledged as collateral to issue mortgage-backed securities (MBSs). These MBSs are, in turn, sold to investors.

## ■ INTERNET RESOURCES

Fair Isaac Co. (FICO)   *www.fico.com*

Fannie Mae   *www.fanniemae.com*

Federal Housing Finance Agency   *www.fhfa.gov*

Freddie Mac   *www.freddiemac.com*

Ginnie Mae   *www.ginniemae.gov*

# ■ REVIEW QUESTIONS

1.  Fannie Mae and Freddie Mac are able to replenish their own funds, enabling them to purchase loans from primary lenders by

    a.  borrowing from the Federal Reserve bank.

    b.  borrowing from each other.

    c.  requesting grant funds through HUD.

    d.  selling mortgage-backed securities.

2.  Lenders may order either a mandatory or standby commitment to sell loans to Fannie Mae through the

    a.  federal open market.        c.  free market auction.

    b.  stock exchange.             d.  administered price system.

3.  Which of the following statements regarding Fannie Mae guidelines is *TRUE?*

    a.  Loans with a higher than 80 percent LTV require private mortgage insurance.

    b.  Maximum loan limits are set annually by each individual lender.

    c.  The seller may contribute up to 6 percent towards borrower's closing costs.

    d.  Homebuyer education and counseling is required of all borrowers.

4.  The *BEST* description of a nonconforming loan is one that

    a.  exceeds loan limits set annually by Fannie Mae and Freddie Mac.

    b.  does not meet Fannie Mae and Freddie Mac qualifying guidelines.

    c.  is restricted to four-family units.

    d.  is limited to low-income housing.

5. Fannie Mae debt-to-income ratios requirement is

   a.  25–30.

   b.  28–36.

   c.  20–27.

   d.  30–40.

6. Freddie Mac was originally chartered to

   a.  compete with Fannie Mae.

   b.  provide a secondary market for savings associations.

   c.  purchase government loans.

   d.  provide mortgage loans for qualified applicants.

7. The agency established to ensure the financial safety and soundness of Fannie Mae and Freddie Mac is the

   a.  Federal Deposit Insurance Corporation (FDIC).

   b.  Office of Thrift Supervision (OTS).

   c.  Federal Reserve System (FED).

   d.  Federal Housing Finance Agency (FHFA).

8. The *MOST* important role played by Ginnie Mae today is

   a.  originating FHA loans.

   b.  purchasing DVA loans.

   c.  the oversight of Fannie Mae and Freddie Mac.

   d.  guaranteeing mortgage-backed securities payments.

9. Which statement regarding Ginnie Mae is *TRUE?*

   a.  Ginnie Mae purchases loans from primary market lenders.

   b.  Ginnie Mae works with both issuers and investors of mortgage-backed securities.

   c.  Ginnie Mae is an independent stockholder owner corporation.

   d.  Ginnie Mae is under the supervision of HUD.

10. Which of the following agencies is *NOT* a government-sponsored agency?

    a.  FNMA

    b.  FHMC

    c.  FHFA

    d.  GNMA

## CHAPTER THIRTEEN

# LOAN DEFAULTS AND FORECLOSURES

## ■ KEY TERMS

| | | |
|---|---|---|
| acceleration | forbearance | recast |
| auction | foreclosure | reinstate |
| crunch down | grace period | statutory redemption |
| deed in lieu of | judgment decree | period |
| foreclosure | judicial foreclosure | strict forfeiture |
| default | and sale | trustee's deed |
| deficiency judgment | late payment charge | unlawful detainer |
| delinquency | lis pendens | voluntary conveyance |
| equitable redemption | moratoriums | workouts |
| period | notice of default | |
| eviction | power-of-sale | |

The basic responsibilities of the parties to a real estate financial contract are relatively clear-cut. In exchange for money loaned, a borrower is obligated to repay the loan according to conditions stipulated in the contract and to preserve the value of the collateral and the priority lien position of the lender. In the event the borrower breaches these obligations, the lender can exercise its power of **acceleration** and insist the loan balance, accrued interest, and costs be paid immediately and in full.

In the vast majority of real estate financing arrangements, a comfortable rhythm of lending and repayment is established between the participants, with few unusual circumstances occurring to interrupt the legal relationship between these parties and to cause a breach in the loan agreement. Every lender seeks to make a "good" loan, one that will serve a borrower's financial needs, while simultaneously providing the lender with a safe and profitable yield on the investment.

Financial lenders are bound by law and company policy to display the highest ethical responsibility in granting real estate loans. The extent of their loan underwriting efforts includes an individual consideration of each applicant's ability and attitude to be qualified for a loan and the estimation of the value of the collateral to be pledged as security. A lender will establish a real estate loan on the basis of availability of funds, general economic conditions, local economic stability, and competitive lenders' actions as well as the borrower's financial position and the property's value. Thus, the terms and conditions of a particular real estate loan involve many variables that may be assessed objectively and subjectively in order to establish the payment structure and interest rate for a good loan.

Except for infrequent periods in our economic history when severe depressions or recessions created serious financial difficulties, a borrower who pledges realty as security for a loan generally enjoys the benefits of a steady inflation in the economy that usually increases the value of the property. At the same time, the balance owed on the loan is being paid down. The interaction between this growth in value and the lessening of the loan balance creates the ultimate protection for the lender against risk. The subtle, slow, and steady increase of an equity position locks the borrower into continued payments on the loan in order to protect the growing investment. Even a borrower on a 100 percent loan soon develops some measurable equity in the property and a commensurate desire to protect it. Thus, the equity position inures to the advantage of the lender by lowering the incidences of mortgage defaults. In fact, foreclosures in this country historically represent a very low percentage of the total loans.

When a real estate loan does fail, it is often the result of events that are beyond the control of the parties to the loan. As always, there are circumstances under which individuals and companies suffer personal or financial setbacks that may jeopardize their ability to maintain normal payment patterns. Some of the more readily recognized problems include loss of employment, illness, divorce, bankruptcy, loss of tenants' rent as a result of local economic setbacks (e.g., overbuilding of income properties), or ordinary mismanagement. Under such conditions, real estate loan payments usually cannot be met, and defaults and foreclosures result.

The financial crisis of 2007 and 2008 led to an alarming increase in the number of foreclosures throughout the country. The resetting of subprime loans was largely blamed for many homeowners' inability to make their mortgage payments. The Center for Responsible Lending projected that 53.6 percent of subprime loans would end in foreclosure by 2012 compared to 8.7 percent of other mortgages. Among the hardest hit states were Nevada, Florida, and California where RealtyTrak, Inc., reported that the foreclosure rate was 6.6 times the national average. Adding to the problem was the fact that tightened lending standards made it difficult for potential buyers of foreclosed properties to obtain mortgage loans.

HOPE NOW is an alliance of counselors, servicers, investors, and other market participants to maximize outreach efforts to at-risk homeowners. These homeowners are encouraged to call the HOPE Hotline at 888-995-HOPE to talk to HUD-approved credit counselors to guide them through possible options such as a loan work-out or modification.

## ■ DEFAULTS

A **default** is the breach of one or more of the conditions or terms of a loan agreement. When a default occurs, the acceleration clause contained in all loan contracts is activated, allowing the lender to declare the full amount of the debt immediately due and payable. If the borrower cannot or will not meet this requirement, the lender is empowered to foreclose against the collateral to recover any loss. Although legally any default in a loan contract enables the lender to accelerate the debt, most lenders will seek to avoid foreclosure and arrange a plan with the borrower that will protect the interests of both parties and avoid costly and time-consuming court procedures. However, in an irreconcilable situation between a defaulted borrower and the lender, acceleration and ultimate foreclosure are the lender's last resort. It is generally accepted that most lenders do not want to own the real estate that is pledged as collateral for their loans. However, defaults do occur, even though most lenders will expend every effort to qualify their borrowers in order to ensure the success of their loans.

**Delinquencies**

**Principal and Interest.**   The most common form of default **delinquency** occurs when the payment of principal and interest is not made when due.

Most loan agreements stipulate that the regular payment is due "on or before" a specified date, but lenders will allow a reasonable **grace period**, usually up to 15 days, in which to receive the regular payment. Many loan arrangements include a **late payment charge** of some specific amount that is applied if the borrower exceeds the grace period. This late payment fee is imposed to encourage promptness and to offset the extra bookkeeping costs that delinquent accounts entail. Most lenders are not disturbed by payments made within grace periods, but they will take remedial action when an account consistently incurs late charges or when a borrower exceeds a 30-day delinquency period.

**Property Taxes.**   Another frequently encountered default with real estate loans is the nonpayment or late payment of property taxes. In California, borrowers pay for a tax service that remains in effect for the life of the loan. The tax service company tracks each property and notifies the lender if the taxes are delinquent.

The nonpayment of property taxes is a technical default under a real estate loan. Property taxes represent a priority lien over most existing liens on real estate. If a tax lien is imposed, the lender's position as priority lienholder is jeopardized. If a lender is unaware of a property tax delinquency and, thus, is not protected, the collateral property may be sold for taxes, eliminating the safe lien position. As a consequence, all realty loan agreements include a clause stipulating a borrower's responsibility to pay property taxes in the amount and on the date required.

**Other Liens.** Defaults may also occur when a borrower allows other liens that have priority over the loan to vest against the collateral property. Such liens might be imposed for nonpayment of federal or state income taxes or city taxes. Under these circumstances, a lender may consider a loan in default and pursue appropriate legal remedies.

In California, mechanics' or materialmen's liens are junior in priority to existing encumbrances. However, in new construction, those liens take priority over a real estate loan that is recorded after start of construction unless the lender posts a bond with the county recorder.

**Hazard Insurance.** Another common cause of default on a real estate loan is the nonpayment of *hazard insurance* premiums required by the lender for the protection of the value of the improvements on the collateral property. The lender is named in the hazard insurance policy as an additional loss payee along with the borrower-property owner. If any losses are incurred by reason of fire, windstorm, or other insurable circumstance, the lender's collateral position is preserved. The damages are repaired to the lender's satisfaction, or the insurance proceeds are applied to reduce the balance of the loan to match the reduced value of the collateral.

**Poor Property Maintenance**

Often lenders include a provision in a formal real estate loan agreement that requires a borrower to maintain the collateral property in such a manner that its value will not diminish to the point of disturbing the lender's security position. A breach of this covenant will create a technical default of the terms of the loan. It is rather difficult to assess the amount of "waste" that would create such a defaulting situation, especially as its discovery would depend upon constant inspection by a lender, an impractical task when many loans are being serviced. Usually a lender will rely upon a borrower's pride of ownership to protect the collateral, but a serious violation can result in a loan default and acceleration of the debt.

# ■ ADJUSTMENTS

Lenders are usually reluctant to proceed with foreclosing on defaulted borrowers, and most will go to great lengths to offset their borrowers' short-term difficulties. Lenders are actually being directed by various government agencies, such as the FHA and the DVA, to extend to their delinquent borrowers every possible alternative that would prevent a foreclosure action, alternatives that are called **workouts**.

**The Soldiers and Sailors Civil Relief Act of 1940**

This act protects military personnel and their dependents from the harassment of creditors in cases where their ability to comply with financial obligations has been materially affected by military service.

The act limits the power of a creditor to sell, foreclose on, or seize the property of a member of the armed forces for nonpayment without first obtaining a court order. The courts have the right to grant relief to the borrower or make any other disposition of the case that is considered equitable.

Perhaps the most powerful provision of the act rests in giving the court the right to suspend the enforcement of any civil obligation against a service person that arose prior to entrance into the military. In all cases, however, the petitioning individual must show that the ability to meet the obligation has been materially affected by military service.

**The Housing Act of 1964**

Under the 1964 Housing Act, the FHA requires that lenders provide relief in situations in which default is beyond a borrower's control. For example, a lender might recast or extend the loan of a borrower who has defaulted because of unemployment during a serious illness. The DVA also requires leniency in the case of a borrower who is willing but unable to pay. The DVA itself may pay for such delinquencies in order to keep a loan current for a veteran, although these payments do not reduce the debtor's obligation. The DVA retains the right to collect these advances at a future date.

**Avoiding a Foreclosure**

A final foreclosure action is studiously avoided whenever possible. Before a lender decides to foreclose, full consideration will be taken of the amount of the borrower's equity in the property, the general state of the current real estate market, and the positions of any junior lienholders. The lender will also judiciously weigh the circumstances that caused the default and the attitude of the borrower concerning the repair of the breach in the contract.

The only time a foreclosure should be considered by the borrower is when the current market value of the collateral property is actually less than the balance of the indebtedness, and the borrower can no longer make the payment that has been adjusted to meet the emergency situation. Even under these extreme circumstances, a borrower should be aware that a foreclosure is not mandatory and that a **deed in lieu of foreclosure** from the borrower to the lender will end their relationship in an amicable, efficient, and legal manner.

The greatest risk to a lender making a real estate loan is that a property pledged as collateral will be abandoned by the borrower. Although this risk is considerably less when unimproved land is the collateral, any improved property left vacant becomes an immediate and irritating source of concern for a lender.

An abandoned property may well indicate the complete and total frustration that a borrower has experienced in trying to solve the problem. A borrower is logically the first person to know of the trouble and should attempt to solve the problem with the help of the lender. Failing in this attempt, the borrower should seek to sell the property at a profit. If this is not possible because of market conditions, the borrower should try to recover the equity or, at the very least, try to give the property away to someone who will assume the loan.

Only when a borrower has made every effort to give the property away and failed and when payments can no longer be made, adjusted or not, should abandonment be considered. At this point, frustration may cause a borrower to blindly seek retaliation and perhaps even physically damage the collateral. A knowledgeable lender is aware of this possibility. Even if an abandoned property is left in good condition, a vacant building is often an invitation for vandalism. In some areas, an abandoned property is considered fair game for the stripping of any valuable parts. When investigating their delinquent accounts, many lenders have discovered empty shells of buildings. The wrecking of abandoned properties is often quite vicious, the apparent motivation just plain wanton destructiveness. An abandoned property is anathema to a lender. To perfect a fee in the collateral, quick legal action must be taken to gain immediate possession of the real estate, so that it may be protected during the foreclosing procedure.

In the final analysis, most borrowers have more power than they realize and should be able to negotiate with their lenders from positions of strength rather than weakness. And increasingly, lenders *are* making every effort to cooperate and prevent a foreclosure action. These efforts include a variety of adjustments to the terms and conditions of the real estate loan contract to reflect emergency needs.

## Moratoriums and Recasting

As discussed earlier, the most common default on real estate loans is delinquent payments. These payment delinquencies can occur because of overextension of credit, loss of job, loss of earnings due to sickness or injury, personal tragedies, and other problems, such as alcoholism and drug-related problems.

When a loan becomes a problem, the person charged with the responsibility for supervising the collection of delinquent accounts will contact the borrower to discover the cause. Most lenders will attempt to cooperate with those borrowers who have legitimate excuses for failing to make payments. Sometimes a lender will waive a portion of the payment, usually the principal amount, to help a delinquent borrower regain financial balance. At other times, the interest portion of the payment is waived as well and added to the balance owed toward that time when the borrower regains financial stability. Frequently, the entire payment is waived for some reasonable length of time.

These partial or full payment waivers, described as **forbearance** or **moratoriums**, had their origins during the monetary crises of the Great Depression. A lender expects that during the moratorium period the borrower can solve the problems by securing a new job, selling the property to a buyer qualified to make the loan payments, or finding some other acceptable solution.

Granting a moratorium on payments can create peripheral problems for the borrower because these postponed amounts must eventually be paid sometime during the remaining life of the loan. Therefore, a forbearance arrangement will usually require that a borrower add extra money to the regular payments when they are reinstated. These extra monies will be applied to satisfy the bubble of principal and interest that accrued during the moratorium.

For a defaulted borrower just recovering sound economic footing, an increase in payments may present too great an additional burden. In order to offset any possible hardships that these extra payments might create, a lender may choose to extend the term of the loan by a time interval equal to the moratorium period. Then the borrower can continue to make regularly scheduled monthly payments at the same amount but for a longer period of time. Another alternative to increasing the amount of payments upon reinstatement of the loan would be for the lender to require one balloon payment for all the monies accrued during the moratorium, to be payable at the loan's scheduled expiration date.

Delinquent loans can also be **recast** to lower the payments to suit a borrower's damaged financial position. When a loan has been paid down over a period of time (e.g., five years), and a default is imminent as a result of a borrower's financial crisis, the lender may redesign the balance still owed into a new loan extending for the original time period or even longer, if feasible. This recasting would effectively reduce the payments required and relieve the pressure on the borrower.

Recasting invariably requires a new title search to discover if any intervening liens or second encumbrances have been recorded. This is especially necessary in the case of a delinquent borrower who might have sought aid from other sources. A lender may also require additional collateral and/or cosigners for the new financing agreement.

In a severely depressed market, a new form of recasting has emerged: a mortgage **crunch down**. This involves the lenders rewriting the loan at a *lower* balance to reflect its loss in value. The lender absorbs the loss, which is estimated to be less than would be incurred in a foreclosure and subsequent sale of the collateral at a substantially reduced price.

## Voluntary Conveyance of Deed

When all efforts at adjusting the terms of a loan to solve a borrower's problems have failed and the property cannot be sold to a buyer willing and able to assume the loan's balance, a lender often will seek to secure a **voluntary conveyance** from the borrower. This action prevents the costly and time-consuming process of foreclosure. By executing either a quitclaim deed or a regular deed, a borrower can eliminate the stigma of a foreclosure suit, maintain a respectable credit rating, and avoid the possibility of a deficiency judgment. On all applications for a new loan, the borrowers are asked if they ever executed a voluntary deed in lieu of foreclosure.

A deed in lieu of foreclosure is a mutual agreement under which the delinquent owners of a property deed it to the lender in return for various considerations, usually a release from liability under the terms of the loan. It can be completed quickly, without the cost of a foreclosure, and the rights of third parties having interests in the property are left undisturbed.

The efficiency of this technique for avoiding a foreclosure is sometimes offset by it being disallowed if it has been used to avoid the inclusion of the asset in a bankruptcy. It is necessary to verify that the borrower was solvent at the time of the voluntary transfer. Also, as already mentioned, the rights of third parties must be protected; hence, the borrower may still be liable for junior encumbrances not cleared prior to the transfer.

Lenders are fully aware of the difficulties with evictions as well as the costs and time involved in a full foreclosure process. Most often, a lender encourages a hopelessly defaulted borrower to transfer a deed voluntarily. Nevertheless, a lender must take care to be protected against any future claims of fraud or duress by the borrower.

## ■ FORECLOSURES

When all else has failed, a lender will pursue legal prerogatives to recover the collateral in order to sell it and recoup the investment. By definition, to foreclose means to shut out, exclude, bar, or deprive one of the right to redeem a mortgage or deed of trust. **Foreclosure**, then, is not only a process to recover a lender's collateral but also a procedure whereby a borrower's rights of redemption are eliminated and all interests in the subject property are removed.

A borrower in 14th-century England had few, if any, rights in property beyond possession. If the borrower did not pay on time and in the amount called for, any property rights were immediately forfeited and full ownership vested in the lender.

This instantaneous and often capricious deprivation of property rights aroused widespread criticism and eventually was brought before the monarch who assigned the adjudication of these grievances to a court of equity under the jurisdiction of a Lord Chancellor. Certain hardship cases were ruled upon according to their merit, rather than upon legal technicalities, and a system gradually developed wherein a distressed borrower was allowed extra time to raise the funds necessary to protect property rights. This relief was called an **equitable redemption period**, taking its name from the Lord Chancellor's court of equity. Under this ruling, a borrower could secure a certain period beyond the default time in order to redeem property. This could be accomplished either by bringing the payments current or by repaying the total amount of the principal due in addition to interest owed and any court costs incurred.

As time passed, borrowers began to abuse their equitable redemption rights. Some defaulted borrowers remained in possession of their property beyond the redemption period and otherwise created great difficulties for lenders trying to reclaim the forfeited collateral. Complaints to the court of equity resulted in the decree of foreclosure, a legal process whereby the equitable period of redemption could be terminated under appropriate conditions. This became known as strict foreclosure or **strict forfeiture**.

Present-day redemption and foreclosure processes in the United States have evolved from those medieval court decisions. However, during the 1800s, when the U.S. economy was still basically agrarian, many states expanded the strict foreclosure procedure to include additional protection for borrowers' equity interests in anticipation of better harvests in the following year. At the end of the equitable redemption period, the lender was directed to sell the property at public auction, rather than automatically take title to the collateral. It was hoped that the foreclosure sale would obtain a fair market value for the property and save part of the borrower's equity. In addition, the defaulted borrower was given another redemption period *after the sale* to recover the property before title to the collateral was transferred. This additional time period is termed the **statutory redemption period** because it came into being as a result of the enactment of state statutes. During the redemption periods, the defaulted borrower is allowed to retain possession of the property.

Lenders are concerned not only with maintaining the integrity of their collateral but also with the disposition of the income generated by the property. Therefore, in certain cases, lenders can petition the courts for the right of possession to protect the collateral. If possession is granted, and it invariably is in the case of abandoned property, the lender must maintain accurate records of the distribution of income from the property during the redemption periods. Any balance left after deductions for the required payments and property maintenance must be credited to the reduction of the debt.

The California Foreclosure Prevention Act, CFPA, enacted on June 15, 2009, may preclude a foreclosure sale for an additional 90 days beyond the current law requirements in order to allow the parties to pursue a loan modification. ABX2 7 and SBX2 7 established the California Foreclosure Prevention Act. Subchapter 14 was added to Chapter 3, Title 10 of the California Code of Regulations (CCR). These regulations clarify the application of Sections 2923.52 and 2923.53 of the Civil Code. The law and rules are available at *www.leginfo.ca.gov* or *www.oal.ca.gov*. Questions may be directed to the Mortgage Loan Activities Unit of the Bureau of Real Estate.

## Power-of-Sale Foreclosure

An alternative to the judicial foreclosure process is the **power-of-sale** method of collateral recovery. Under this form, a lender or the trustee has the right to sell the collateral property upon default without being required to spend the time and money involved in a court foreclosure suit. In fact, under this form of lender control, a borrower's redemption time frame is shortened considerably by the elimination of the statutory redemption period granted in the judicial process.

**Deeds of Trust.** The most common application of the power-of-sale foreclosure process is by exercise of the trustee's responsibility created in a deed of trust. In the event of a default, the beneficiary (lender) notifies the trustee in writing of the trustor's (borrower's) delinquency and instructs the trustee to begin the foreclosure by sale process. However, a trustee may *elect* to foreclose judicially when there may be the possibility of securing a deficiency judgment.

The beneficiary (lender) delivers the original note, trust deed, and all payment records to the trustee plus a document entitled *declaration of default*. The trustee secures a title report as to the current conditions of record and prepares a **notice of default** and *election to sell* as prescribed by statute. The notice of default is recorded in the office of the county in which the property is located at least *three months* before the notice of sale is given. Copies of the notice of default must be sent by certified or registered mail to all persons indicating an interest in the proceedings as well as to the defaulting borrower at the last known address. In addition, the notice of default must be published for three weeks in a newspaper of general circulation in the property's jurisdiction.

The deed of trust is the most common form used for real estate finance in California. The time line in the event of a default is as follows:

- beneficiary notices several months' payment delinquencies and the borrowers are unable to remedy this problem;

- beneficiary notifies trustee to foreclose;

- trustee files Notice of Default (three months prior to sale date);

- reinstatement period (up to five days before the sale);

- notice of trustee's sale and publication of date, time, and place of the sale (three weeks);

- sale is held and the highest cash bidder wins; and

- trustee's deed is given to successful bidder (sale is final, borrower has no right of redemption).

A deed of trust, unlike a mortgage, does not provide any statutory redemption period. Under a mortgage foreclosure, the borrower has prescribed time periods after the public sale to redeem the property. A deed of trust foreclosure only provides time before the public sale to **reinstate** the loan by bringing its payments current and paying any expenses incurred in the default proceedings. Deeds of trust have no rights of redemption after the trustee's sale but can be reinstated as late as five business days prior to the trustee's sale.

If the loan has not been reinstated (brought up to date) by the trustor within the three-month reinstatement period, the trustee records, mails to interested parties, and publishes a *notice of trustee's sale* with a sale date to take place not sooner than 20 days after its recording. The notice must be published at least 20 days before the sale, and notice must be posted simultaneously in a public place in the city, judicial district, or county of the sale, as well as in a conspicuous place on the subject property (e.g., if a residence, on the front door).

The sale is to be held in a public place on any business day between the hours of 9:00 AM and 5:00 PM and will be conducted as an auction. All bids must be for cash or a cash equivalent. The trustor (borrower) may redeem (pay off the entire loan balance, late charges, and trustee's fees) the property one last time before the auction.

California Civil Code 2924c, which refers to the date of recordation of the notice of default occurring on or after January 1, 1986, triggers a right to reinstate a defaulted loan secured by a deed of trust up to five business days before a trustee's sale is held. In the event of postponement of the trustee's sale, this right to reinstate is extended again up to five business days before the new trustee's sale is held.

The sale is made to the highest bidder. The successful bidder receives a **trustee's deed** to the property but without any guaranty that the title is clear. There may be some outstanding government liens still in effect. Recording the trustee's deed eliminates all junior liens, encumbrances on the property (except valid leases), and any further rights of reinstatement. The purchaser is entitled to immediate possession but may have to pursue the **eviction** of the borrower or any tenant in default by filing an **unlawful detainer** action. The proceeds from the sale are distributed in the following order:

1. To the trustee for costs and sale expenses

2. To the beneficiary for the debt

3. To junior lienholders in order of priority

4. To the borrower (if there is any surplus)

**Judicial Foreclosure and Sale**

In California, a mortgage is usually foreclosed by initiating a court action for **judicial foreclosure and sale** at public auction. Only a few mortgages include a power-of-sale clause, similar to a trust deed, which eliminates the need for a judicial action.

**Conventional Mortgages.**   Before a lender forecloses on a conventional first mortgage, the delinquent mortgagor is notified of the default and the reasons for it. An immediate solution is required, and all efforts must be expended to solve the problem as expeditiously as possible. However, if all attempts fail, a complaint is filed by the mortgagee in the county court in which the property is located and a summons is issued to the mortgagor initiating the foreclosure action.

Simultaneous with this activity, a title search is made to determine the identities of all parties having an interest in the collateral property, and a **lis pendens** is filed with the court, giving notice to the world of the pending foreclosure action. Notice is sent to all parties having an interest in the property, requesting that they appear to defend their interests or else they will be foreclosed from any future rights by judgment of the court. It is vital for the complainant-mortgagee to notify all junior lienholders of the foreclosure action lest they be enjoined from participation in the property auction and, thus, acquire the right to file suit on their own at some future time.

Depending upon the number of days required by the jurisdiction for public notice to inform any and all persons having an *unrecorded* interest in the subject property that a foreclosure suit is imminent, and depending upon the availability of a court date, the complaint is eventually aired before a presiding judge. In most instances, the defendant-mortgagor does not appear in court unless special circumstances are presented in defense of the default. Creditors who do appear to present their claims are recognized and noted, and a sale of the property at public auction by a court-appointed referee or sheriff is ordered by means of a **judgment decree**.

A public sale is necessary so the actual market value of the subject property can be established. It is unlikely the auction will generate any bids in excess of the mortgage debt balance because it is assumed that the mortgagor made every effort to recover those monies prior to the foreclosure.

Basically, a lender sues for foreclosure under the terms of the *mortgage*. If the proceeds from the auction sale are not sufficient to recover the outstanding loan balance plus costs, a mortgagee may then sue on the *note* for the deficiency. However, to establish this suit on a note, a lender *may not bid* at the auction.

If pursuing a deficiency is not anticipated, and most are not because of the apparent financial straits of the defaulted mortgagor, the mortgagee makes the opening bid at the auction. This bid is usually in an amount equal to the loan balance plus interest to date and court costs, and then the lender hopes that someone else will bid at least one dollar more to "bail the lender out." If there are any junior lienholders or other creditors who look to the property as collateral for *their* loans, they now have the opportunity to step in and bid to protect their priority positions. Their bids obligate them to repay the first mortgagee. When no junior lienholders or creditors enter a bid, the auction closes at the first mortgagee's bid price. Any interests that these creditors may have in the property are effectively eliminated. However, if any other person bids an amount above the first mortgage after the first lien is paid, the excess funds are distributed to the junior lienholders in order of their priority, with any leftover money going to the defaulted mortgagor.

**Conventional Guaranteed Mortgages.**   Under the terms of the insurance policies of most private mortgage guarantee companies, a default is interpreted to be nonpayment for four months. Within ten days of default, the mortgagee is required to notify the insurer, who will then decide whether to instruct the mortgagee to foreclose.

When a conventional guaranteed mortgage is foreclosed, the first mortgagee is the original bidder at the public auction of the collateral property. Under these circumstances, the successful bidder-mortgagee files notice with the insurance company within 60 days after the legal proceedings have transpired. If the insurance company is confident of recovering the losses by purchasing the collateral property from the mortgagee and then reselling it, it will reimburse the mortgagee for the total amount of the bid and secure title to the property. If, however, the company does not foresee any possibility for this recovery, it may elect to pay the mortgagee the agreed-upon amount of insurance, and the mortgagee retains ownership of the property. The collateral is then sold to recover any balance still unpaid.

In any and all cases of judicial foreclosure and sale, any ownership rights acquired by the successful bidder at the foreclosure auction will still be subject to the statutory redemption rights of the defaulted mortgagor. A full fee simple absolute title cannot vest in the bidder until these redemption rights have expired.

**Equitable Redemption (Reinstatement Rights).**   Under judicial foreclosure, a borrower may cure the default and reinstate the loan any time before the entry of judgment by paying the delinquencies plus costs and fees. This immediately stops the foreclosure proceedings, and the loan continues in full force and effect as though no acceleration had taken place.

**Statutory Redemption.**   After the public sale at a judicial foreclosure, the defaulted borrower may redeem the property under the following circumstances:

- Within three months if the sale proceeds satisfied the entire debt plus interest and costs of the action

- Within one year if the sale proceeds were insufficient to cover the debt plus interest and expenses

During the redemption period, the borrower may remain in possession of the property but must pay the successful bidder a reasonable rent. Sometimes a lender may take possession of the collateral under the *assignment of rents* provision in the loan contract, manage the property during the redemption period, and apply the net proceeds to the balance owed.

**FHA-Insured Loans**   Foreclosures on FHA-insured loans originate with the filing of form 2068—Notice of Default—that must be given to the local FHA administration office within 60 days of default. This notice describes the reasons for the borrower's delinquency, such as death, illness, marital difficulties, income depletion, excessive obligations, employment transfers, or military service.

In many cases involving delinquent FHA-insured loans, counselors from the local FHA offices will attempt to design an agreement between the lender and the borrower for adjustments to the loan conditions in order to prevent foreclosure. The most common technique used in circumstances when a default is beyond the borrower's control but deemed curable is forbearance of foreclosure.

If the problems causing the default are solved within a one-year period, the lender informs the local FHA office of the solution. If not, a default status report is filed and the lender must initiate foreclosure proceedings. If the bids at the auction are less than the unpaid balance, the lender is expected to bid the debt, take title, and present it to the FHA along with a claim for insurance that may be paid in cash or in government debentures. In some cases, with prior FHA approval, the lender may assign the defaulted trust deed directly to the FHA before the final foreclosure action in exchange for insurance benefits. In any case, if the property can be sold easily at a price that would repay the loan in full, the lender simply will sell the property after bidding at the auction and will not apply for FHA compensation. If the FHA ends up as the owner of the property, the collateral will be resold "as is" or repaired, refurbished, and resold at a higher price to help minimize the losses to the FHA.

**DVA-Guaranteed Loans**

Unlike the FHA-insured trust deeds, whereby a lender's entire risk is recovered from the insurance benefits, a DVA loan is similar to a privately insured loan in that a lender receives only the top portion of the outstanding loan balance. In the event of a delinquency of more than three months on a DVA loan, the lender must file proper notification with the local DVA office, which may then elect to bring the loan current if it wishes, with subrogation rights to the lender against the borrower for the amount advanced. This means that the DVA claim against the defaulted veteran takes priority over the rights of the lender to these funds.

Much like the FHA, DVA lenders are required to make every effort to offset a foreclosure through forbearance, payment adjustments, sale of the property, deed in lieu of foreclosure, or other acceptable solutions. Actual foreclosure is considered only as a last resort.

In the event of a foreclosure, the lender will usually be the original bidder at the auction and will submit a claim for losses to the local DVA office. The DVA then has the option either to pay the unpaid balance, interest, and court costs and take title to the collateral or to require that the lender retain the property and pay only the difference between the determined value of the property on the date of foreclosure and the loan balance. The latter alternative is usually chosen when the property is badly deteriorated, accenting the importance for a lender to supervise the collateral property.

**Junior Loans**

Defaults of junior loans are handled in exactly the same manner as are senior loans. Here, however, the relationship is usually between two individuals rather than between an institutional lender and individual borrower.

A junior lender will usually seek the counsel of an attorney to manage the foreclosure process. The delinquent borrower will be requested to cure the problem within a certain time period. If a cure cannot be accomplished, notice is given to all persons having an interest in the property, and the attorney then files for foreclosure.

The junior lender is generally the original bidder at the public sale and secures ownership of the collateral property subject to the lien of the existing senior loan. The junior lender can then continue to make any payments required thereon, while seeking to sell the collateral to eliminate, or at least offset, the losses.

**Tax Impacts of Foreclosure**

In a foreclosure, there may be an unexpected tax consequence for the person or entity that has borrowed the money. In the normal course of events, paying off a real estate loan has no tax consequences. When the last payment is made, all principal borrowed has been returned, plus the interest. However, in a foreclosure, the loan is retired without being paid in full.

A tax is due when the property's adjusted book value is less than the balance of the loan. As far as the IRS is concerned, a foreclosure is considered a sale; if the amount of the defaulted loan exceeds the tax basis of the property, the IRS considers that a gain.

■ **EXAMPLE** Consider the owners of an income property who have totally depreciated the improvements and who have a remaining book value on the land for $100,000. They default on a $500,000 loan and are obligated to pay income tax on the $400,000 gain. This illustration is an extreme case, but it is possible that the value of such a property could drop below the balance of the loan, and the owners would consider offering the lenders a deed in lieu of foreclosure.

■ **EXAMPLE** A more realistic example would involve a limited partnership that purchased a $1 million property with $200,000 cash and an $800,000 loan. Assuming an interest-only payment, if the loan is foreclosed at a later date, for example, when the book basis is reduced to $750,000, the individual investors would be obligated to pay income tax on the gain of $50,000.

Every borrower should try to be aware of the tax consequences in a foreclosure.

**Auctions**

Although the use of an **auction** to dispose of foreclosed properties is not a new concept, having been used extensively for years in farm and ranch finance, it is gaining new importance. Banks and savings associations are increasingly using auctions to dispose of their repossessed properties. The major reason for the interest in auctions is the pressure created by the costs for carrying defaulted properties. Auctions allow them to be sold quickly.

Carrying costs include those for mortgage insurance, maintenance, management, property taxes, and other related expenses. Usually, these costs will not be recouped in the form of a higher selling price. Add to these costs the interest rates in the current market, and you can see that holding foreclosed properties creates an enormous burden on lenders.

## ■ SUMMARY

This chapter provided an overview of the consequences of defaults in real estate finance. By far the greatest number of realty financing arrangements do not result in problems leading to foreclosure. Rising property values coupled with the systematic repayment of loans invariably create measurable equity positions for the borrower, equity "cushions" that usually inhibit the loss of property because of loan default. A troubled borrower can, in most problem situations, arrange to dispose of assets and thus maintain financial equilibrium. Occasionally, however, misfortune cannot be averted, and foreclosure develops as the sole remedy. Such a situation is most clearly recognized when property pledged as collateral is abandoned by a borrower. Here, a lender's only recourse is to immediately pursue the acquisition of the property by appropriate legal means.

Under less dramatic circumstances, a lender will usually attempt to adjust the conditions of a loan in order to help a troubled borrower over short-term difficulties. Delinquent loan payments are the most common cause for a default, although the nonpayment of property taxes or hazard insurance premiums, lack of adequate maintenance, and allowing priority liens to vest are also defaultable conditions. To offset the possibility of a foreclosure on delinquent loans, many lenders will exercise forbearance and waive the principal portion of a loan payment for a given period or even extend a moratorium on the full monthly payment. Other adjustments in the terms of a delinquent loan that might aid the defaulted borrower include an extension of time or a recasting of the loan to reflect the borrower's current ability to pay under circumstances of financial stress.

A loan will be foreclosed only if there are no alternatives. The lender notifies the defaulting borrower and arranges the advertisement necessary to inform the public that the foreclosure is in process so that all creditors having an interest may be alerted. At the foreclosure sale, the lender usually bids the outstanding balance hoping that someone will bid one dollar more and repay the loan. Invariably, however, there is no value in the defaulted property above the loan balance, and the lender becomes the property's owner. When the defaulted loan is a conventional loan, the lender assumes the risks of ownership and attempts to sell the property to minimize losses. When the defaulted loan is FHA-insured, the lender recovers any balance owed from the FHA insurance benefits. When the loan is DVA-guaranteed or privately insured, the lender will recover the top portion of the loan up to the insured amount and will sell the property to recover the balance.

The foreclosure process is designed to eliminate a borrower's rights in the collateral property. However, the laws of redemption grant the delinquent borrower certain specified times during which the property may be redeemed. Not until the redemption periods expire does the new buyer of the property receive title.

A junior lender follows essentially the same procedures in foreclosing a delinquent loan, except that the integrity of the existing senior lender's priority position must be maintained by seeing that the payments, property taxes, and insurance premiums are paid.

All deeds of trust contain a power-of-sale provision that allows a lender to pursue a somewhat faster foreclosure process than under the judicial process. Under a power-of-sale, a trustee is entitled to sell a defaulted collateral property with reduced redemption times allotted to the borrower. This is a relatively effective foreclosure tool that must follow definitive notification and advertisement procedures to be legally valid.

## ■ REVIEW QUESTIONS

1. MOST loan defaults occur when a borrower does *NOT*

   a. pay the property taxes when due.

   b. make the principal and interest payments on time.

   c. pay the hazard insurance premium when it is due.

   d. maintain the collateral.

2. A foreclosure will usually be initiated when

   a. a borrower can no longer make payments.

   b. a borrower has lost her job.

   c. the value of the collateral has dropped below the balance of the loan.

   d. a borrower can no longer make payments, even after forbearance, and the value of the collateral has dropped below the outstanding balance of the loan.

3. When all other adjustments have been made and have failed, a foreclosure procedure may still be avoided by a(n)

   a. eviction.

   b. voluntary conveyance of a deed.

   c. unlawful detainer.

   d. lis pendens.

4. After an FHA-insured loan is foreclosed, any of the following may transpire *EXCEPT*

   a. the FHA will reimburse the lender in full and in cash.

   b. the FHA will reimburse the lender in full and in debentures.

   c. the lender will secure title to the property and assign it to the FHA.

   d. the lender will secure title to the property, refurbish it, and sell it.

5. When a veteran defaults on a DVA loan and it is foreclosed, the Department of Veterans Affairs may do all of the following *EXCEPT*

   a. bring the loan current, securing subrogation rights against the borrower.

   b. pay the lender in full and in cash, allowing the lender to keep the collateral.

   c. pay the lender in full and in cash, taking title to the collateral.

   d. pay the lender the difference between the deteriorated collateral's value at the foreclosure and the balance of the loan up to the maximum limits, allowing the lender to keep the collateral.

6. The MOST common foreclosure procedure in California is the

   a. power-of-sale.

   b. strict foreclosure.

   c. judicial foreclosure and sale.

   d. voluntary conveyance of a deed.

7. Under judicial foreclosure, all of the following are true *EXCEPT* that a borrower

   a. may reinstate the loan prior to foreclosure by paying the delinquencies and costs.

   b. may redeem the property after the public sale by paying the loan in full plus costs in three months to one year, depending on circumstances.

   c. may remain in possession of the property after the public sale for a prescribed time.

   d. need not pay rent if remaining in the property after the public sale.

8.  In a foreclosure of a deed of trust, all of the following documents are utilized *EXCEPT* the

    a.  declaration of default.

    c.  notice of sale.

    b.  redemption certificate.

    d.  trustee's deed.

9.  When a deed of trust is foreclosed, the defaulting borrower has at least which of the following periods to reinstate the loan?

    a.  One month

    c.  Three months

    b.  Two months

    d.  No redemption allowed

10. When foreclosing under a deed of trust, the trustee must do all of the following *EXCEPT*

    a.  post a notice on the door of the property.

    b.  advertise in a newspaper of general circulation.

    c.  evict the errant borrower.

    d.  notify all interested parties by registered or certified mail.

## ■ EXERCISES

1.  Contact a local lender and inquire when the next public auction will be held on a foreclosed property. Attend and observe the auction.

2.  Contact the FHA and DVA offices near you to discuss what happens when a borrower defaults.

**CHAPTER FOURTEEN**

# INVESTMENT FINANCING STRATEGIES

## ■ KEY TERMS

adjusted book basis          pyramiding                    sale-leaseback-buyback
capital gains                realized capital gain         split-fee financing
estate taxes                 refinance                     tax-free gifts
joint venture                recognized capital gain
kicker                       sale-leaseback

In addition to the variations in loan payment formats already discussed, there are many special aspects of real estate that can be served through creative finance. Included in this chapter are the more esoteric arrangements that provide investment property participants with extra tax-free cash by capitalizing on equities that accumulate on properties through growth-in-value and the paydown of existing loan balances.

## ■ SALE-LEASEBACK

A creative tool of real estate finance, the **sale-leaseback**, is used for larger projects. In this situation, the owner of a property sells it to an investor and, at the same time, leases it back. This financing arrangement originated when owners of companies with considerable cash tied up in their real estate wanted to free this capital for more speculative ventures. The lease utilized for this method is usually a fully net lease that extends over a period of time long enough for the investor to recover the initial funds and to make a fair profit on the investment. However, if the lease is written for 30 years or longer, including renewal options, the IRS tends to consider this a 1031 exchange; consequently, the sellers-lessees would not get the rent deduction. In this event, the leasehold would be amortized over the term of the lease.

The sale-leaseback approach to real estate finance is applied to commercial properties because rents paid by businesses and professional persons are deductible expenses in the year in which they are incurred. Using this approach, sellers-lessees enjoy many benefits. They retain possession of the property while obtaining the full sales price and, in some cases, keep the right to repurchase the property at the end of the lease. The sellers-lessees also free capital frozen in equity, maintain an appreciable interest in realty that can be utilized by subleasing or by mortgaging the leasehold, and get a tax deduction for the full amount of the rent, which is equivalent to being able to take depreciation deductions for both the building *and* the land.

The cash secured from the sale might be utilized for plant expansion, remodeling, or investing in other opportunities. In addition, a lease appears as a contingent liability on a firm's balance sheet, whereas a mortgage or a trust deed is shown as an actual liability and adversely affects the firm's debt ratio in terms of obtaining future financing.

The advantages to the investor-landlord in this type of arrangement include a fair return *on* and *of* the investment in the form of rental income during the lease term and ownership of a depreciable asset already occupied by a "good" tenant. In other words, the investor is buying a guaranteed income stream that can be sheltered through the proper use of allowable deductions. When determining the rent to be paid on the lease, the investor can actually manage the risk by the amount of rent received. The rent for a quality tenant will be lower than the rent for a high-risk tenant.

When the lease includes an option for the tenant to repurchase the property at the end of the lease term, it is called a **sale-leaseback-buyback**. However, care must be taken to establish the buyback price for the fair market value at the time of sale. Otherwise, the arrangement is considered a long-term installment loan and any income tax benefits that might have been enjoyed during the term of the lease will be disallowed by the Internal Revenue Service.

## ■ SELLER REFINANCES PRIOR TO SALE

When a buyer cannot qualify for a new institutional first trust deed to purchase a property, the seller could refinance the property in order to secure a loan that can be assumed by the buyer. Such a situation might arise if the buyer had a prior bankruptcy or divorce, is newly employed, or is in other circumstances that limit credit ability. At the same time, the seller wishes to acquire as much cash as possible from the sale, so he secures a new loan, requires the buyer to make a cash down payment to the amount of this encumbrance, and completes the sale accordingly.

A variation of this technique, and one greatly dependent upon the sincerity and creditworthiness of the buyer, is used when a seller refinances a property and accepts a carryback wraparound contract from the buyer after receiving an acceptable down payment.

## ■ TRADING ON SELLER'S EQUITY

Reversing the previous approach in which the seller refinances prior to the sale, a buyer can secure a sizable cash amount to be paid to a seller by refinancing the subject property instead of assuming the existing loan balance. By arranging the offer accordingly, a buyer might be able to leverage and still develop cash for the seller.

■ **EXAMPLE** Assume a $200,000 property with an existing first loan balance of $125,000 and a seller who is willing to accept a second mortgage for $50,000 and a $25,000 cash down payment, if the buyer assumes the existing loan.

An enterprising buyer could offer to secure a *new* loan for $160,000, based upon the property's value of $200,000; satisfy the $125,000 existing loan; give the seller the $35,000 cash difference; and execute a $40,000 second deed of trust to the seller, as required. In effect, the seller would be securing the $35,000 cash plus the junior loan for $20,000 as agreed, but the cash down payment would be acquired by capitalizing on the seller's own equity. Under this arrangement, the seller would be relieved of any liability for the senior debt on the property, which may not have been the case had the buyer assumed the existing loan. The buyer, on the other hand, has leveraged 100 percent.

The weakness in this format, from the seller's point of view, is that the buyer has no cash invested, and the junior loan is now behind a larger senior loan, increasing the seller's risk on both counts. However, these risks can be offset with a higher interest rate on the junior loan, possibly a higher sales price, and a wrap as the junior financing alternative.

## ■ EQUITY PARTICIPATION

Lenders sometimes enlarge their earning possibilities by participating both as owners and financiers. In addition to the shared appreciation mortgage (SAM), there are several variations of this type of participation financing.

**Sale-Buyback**

Under this variation of the sale-leaseback technique, a lender, usually a life insurance company or a pension fund, agrees to purchase a completed project from the developer and then to sell it right back. The lender attains legal title to the property and profits by including a **kicker** in the payment to cover a return *of* the investment as well as regular interest *on* the investment. The developer profits through 100 percent financing and continued ownership income.

Partnership contracts are usually designed to extend 10 years longer than the financing term. The payments made during the financing period would be sufficient to repay the purchase price. The additional 10 years of payments are added compensation to the lender-participator. If a contract runs for 30 years, it might include payments for 20 years sufficient to amortize the sales price, then continue for an additional 10 years at a higher interest rate to satisfy the kicker requirements.

**Splitting Ownership**

A more common form of lender participation is **split-fee financing**. In this plan, the lender purchases the land, leases it to the developer, and then finances the improvements to be constructed.

The land lease payments are established at an agreed-upon *base rate*, plus a percentage of the tenant's rental income above a specified point. Under this arrangement, the lender-investor benefits by receiving a fixed return on the investment plus possible overages while maintaining residual property rights through ownership of the fee. The developer has the advantage of high leverage and participatory profits.

**Joint Ventures**

The most common form of equity participation is the **joint venture**, in which the lender puts 100 percent of the funds needed for a development *up front* in exchange for the expertise and time of the developer. The lender then becomes an investor in full partnership with the developer.

Some joint venture partnerships are expanded to include the landowner, the developer, the construction company, and the financier. The developer then supervises the entire project from its inception until it is completely rented, and sometimes even beyond as a permanent manager.

## ■ TAX-DEFERRED FINANCING

One of the most effective tools available to all property owners for acquiring additional funds while postponing any tax impact is to **refinance** a property that has developed an increased equity by an increase in value, and the amortization of its existing loan or both. Refinancing involves the securing of a new loan to replace an old loan. Logically, the new loan should be sufficient not only to satisfy the balance of the existing loan but also to pay all of the placement costs involved, as well as generate new cash for the borrower to use for additional investments. Any money acquired by refinancing is *not* subject to tax, even if these funds exceed the original purchase price of the specific property. This money is considered borrowed money and, as such, is not taxable.

In this regard, relevant to the discussion of income tax impacts is the distinction between two types of **capital gains** income. **Realized capital gain** is the difference between the total consideration received and the **adjusted book basis** of the property transferred. **Recognized capital gain** is that portion of the realized gain that is subject to income tax in the year received.

In the case of refinancing, any appreciation or "profit" in the property received from the proceeds of the new loan is not considered realized and is not subject to income taxes until the property is sold. Therefore, owners may periodically refinance their properties during their lifetimes, generating tax-deferred dollars for reinvestment. At the time of death, the properties would receive a step-up in basis to fair market value and could be distributed to the heirs free of potential income tax on any appreciation to time of death.

Most refinancing decisions will be governed by balancing the possible gains to be made against the known costs to be incurred. For instance, to refinance an existing 6 percent interest loan with one at 8 percent interest is not practical unless the borrower can earn more than 8 percent on a reinvestment of the new monies secured. Otherwise, the best alternative is to leave the existing financial arrangement alone. In other words, a refinancing decision should be based on the alternative investment opportunities or a measurement of opportunity costs. These measurements, like so many others in real estate finance, include subjective as well as objective inputs.

The most emotional and subjective involvement in real estate finance transpires at the home ownership level. The security of owning a home free and clear of debt is a goal that has been handed down from generation to generation and one to be sought with thrift and enterprise, even at great sacrifice. For those persons whose home will be the only substantial investment made in their lifetimes, this philosophy is comfortable and correct. However, for those persons who seek to acquire a larger real estate portfolio, free and clear ownership may not be a practical course to follow.

**Pyramiding Through Refinancing**

Real estate ownership can provide a means for accumulating great wealth. In order to establish a valuable investment portfolio, one must work hard, take carefully calculated risks, and apply appropriate leverage. One way to acquire a substantial amount of real estate is to periodically refinance those properties already owned and then use the proceeds to purchase new properties. This procedure is termed **pyramiding**.

Unlike pyramiding through *selling,* where an investor will purchase one property by conventional methods, improve it for resale at a higher price, and then purchase two properties with the gains from the sale, pyramiding through *refinancing* is based upon *retaining* all properties acquired. By not selling the properties, the investor is constantly increasing the refinancing base while capital gains taxes are postponed.

Pyramiding through refinancing begins with the purchase of a property. If more than one property can be purchased to start the plan, the refinancing base will be enhanced at the outset. The type of property to be purchased should be improved income property that has the ability to generate cash flow.

To approach pyramiding from a theoretical point of view, the investor anticipates that the original property will increase in value over time. Simultaneously, the loan payments being made will reduce the balance owed and build equity for the investor. Assuming a five-year refinancing cycle, it could be possible to secure a new loan every five years in an amount sufficient to satisfy the balance of the old loan, pay the loan acquisition costs, and return at least enough cash to make a down payment on the next purchase.

As the new loan is for a larger amount than the old one, higher payments will be required, perhaps at a higher rate of interest. The passage of five years should also provide the owner with an opportunity to raise rents commensurate with the property's increasing value and inflationary market trends in order to satisfy at least the breakeven requirements.[*]

---

[*] See David Sirota, *Essentials of Real Estate Investment, 9th Edition,* Dearborn Real Estate Education, 2010.

It is in the best interests of the pyramid investor to purchase newer properties in stable or growing areas. An older property in a declining neighborhood would make a poor investment. Rents and values of such buildings might actually fall and destroy the refinancing cycle.

After refinancing the initial property, the pyramider will then purchase an additional rental unit, either residential or commercial, with the net proceeds from the refinancing. The investor now owns two properties from the original investment. Theoretically, by continuing this sequence, the pyramider should be able to double holdings every five years. The two properties would increase to 4 at the end of 10 years, 8 in 15 years, and 16 in 20 years. Of course, there would be a substantial amount outstanding in loans against these properties, but if an estate of this size was sufficient for the investor, the rents could then be turned inward to satisfy the various balances owed and end the pyramiding process.

With the appropriate application of allowable deductions, most, if not all, of the net income earned during the years of ownership can be sheltered, as capital gains taxes are delayed through the refinancing process. The estate can then be left to the investor's heirs, without the investor ever having paid capital gains tax on any profits derived from ownership of these properties.

A deceased person's property is appraised to determine its value for estate tax purposes. The heirs take title to the property, its book value being the appraised value established as of the date of death. The old book value, which reflects the deceased owner's acquisition costs, is eliminated. If the heirs choose to sell the property at this point, the capital gains tax would be based upon any profits secured from the difference between the sale price and the *new book value*, which reflects current market value. In other words, if the heirs sell the inherited property at a price equal to its probated estate value, *no capital gains will be paid* even though the property is sold for many times more than what the deceased paid for it.

Just as important as this savings is the opportunity for the heirs to develop a larger estate. Should they decide to keep the inherited property, the heirs can refinance it, secure new tax-free cash for reinvestments, and shelter much of their earnings through allowable deductions based upon the new, and higher, book value of the inherited property.

Although the pyramiding plan is theoretical, it is completely workable if adjustments are made for those problems that will inevitably arise. For instance, depending upon money market conditions, a five-year refinancing cycle may not always be practical. A poor investment choice may be made along the acquisition route or the economy can decline to a point where there will be no increase in property value for an extended time period. These conditions, plus the risks and work involved, may exceed the rewards, but this is a decision each investor must make individually.

**Distribution to Heirs**

The ultimate capital gains tax shelter is to maintain ownership of investment property until death. At death, the property is appraised for estate tax purposes, and the deceased's heirs acquire title with the new basis of the inherited property at the fair market value established at the time of death. With the appropriate application of tax-free gift giving, taxes on the decedent's estate can be avoided.

**Federal Estate Tax.**  The 2013 exemption from federal **estate taxes** is $5 million per person. To pay estate taxes, then, a deceased's estate would have to be evaluated at more than $10 million net if owned as community property or jointly with a spouse. In other words, the gross value of the entire estate is estimated, debts against the estate, as well as all probate costs deducted, and the balance (or one-half if owned jointly or as community property) must exceed $5 million before it is subject to federal estate taxes. It is possible that Congress will adopt law changes to Federal Estate Taxes. Consult with your tax professional.

**California Inheritance Tax.**  Both the California inheritance tax law and the gift tax law were repealed as of June 8, 1982. However, upon repeal of these two tax laws, the state enacted a California estate tax that takes advantage of a provision in federal law, which allows the estate to take credit for California estate taxes paid against any federal estate taxes due. The state tax is limited to the maximum the federal government allows as a credit against any federal estate taxes due.

**Gift Tax.** With proper planning, investors may be able to distribute their entire estates by utilizing **tax-free gifts** to avoid estate taxes. The 2013 law provides gift exemptions of up to $14,000 for each donor per donee per year. Thus, a husband and wife can gift $28,000 tax free each year to each heir. Gifts in excess of the exemptions are subject to tax at the federal level and at the state level.

# ■ SUMMARY

This chapter investigates some unusual combinations and uses of traditional financing tools to meet the rapid changes in California's real estate market. Many of these financing techniques are designed to lessen the tax impact upon an investor's income.

A popular commercial property financing arrangement is the sale-leaseback technique. This plan involves a property owner selling real estate to an investor and, at the same time, leasing it back at a rent designed to develop, for the purchaser, a return *on* the investment plus a return *of* the investment. The seller-tenant benefits from the immediate cash proceeds of the sale in addition to tax deductions for the full amount of the rent and continued possession of the premises. When the sale-leaseback includes a buyback option at a fair market value upon the lease's completion, the seller-tenant can continue to control the property far into the future. This financial arrangement generates safe and profitable returns for investors; returns that can be sheltered through the application of appropriate deductions. In the absence of a buyback option, investors may also realize substantial residual benefits when the property reverts to their possession at the end of the lease.

Sellers will sometimes refinance prior to a sale in order to cash out their equity. They will obtain a new loan that can be assumed by a buyer. A variation of this approach is a buyer trading on a seller's equity and refinancing a property with all net cash proceeds from the refinancing routed to the seller as the down payment for a carryback junior loan from the seller for the difference between this new loan and the sale price. This approach gives a buyer high leverage and also offers a seller an opportunity to maximize yields with a high junior lien interest rate, an inflated sale price, and possibly a wrap arrangement to secure some override interest.

As an alternative to financing a large commercial real estate development, some financiers participate in the profits by purchasing the entire project and then reselling it to the developer on a long-term installment contract. The payments on the contract include a return *on* and *of* the investment and usually extend ten years beyond the loan amortization time period, allowing the financier-owner an opportunity to enhance the yield substantially. At the same time, the developer enjoys 100 percent leverage and participatory earnings.

A more common form of equity participation is the method of split-fee financing whereby a financier purchases the land under the project; leases it to the developer at an agreed amount of rent, sometimes including a percentage of the developer's profits; and simultaneously finances the improvements to be constructed upon the leasehold estate. This technique allows the developer to exercise high leverage and to enjoy participatory earnings. The landowner-financier earns interest and profits and anticipates a residual windfall from the ownership of the entire improved property at the end of the lease.

Probably the most complete example of equity participation is the joint venture, where a financier joins with a developer as a full partner in a commercial project. The lender will usually put up the front money needed to fund the venture; the developer contributes time and expertise.

A major source of tax-deferred dollars is available through the refinancing of the equity accumulated in real property. A property's growth in value over time and increased equity resulting from the amortization of an existing encumbrance often provides a base for securing new funds. As borrowed money, refinancing proceeds are not taxable income even when these funds exceed the original price paid for the property. However, any gains resulting from disposition of debt will be taxable when the property is sold or exchanged.

One form of investment expansion is pyramiding through refinancing. This plan begins with the purchase of a property that will grow in value and equity to a time when it will support a new and larger loan adequate to satisfy the balance of the existing encumbrance, pay all loan acquisition costs, and generate new cash flow. These cash proceeds will then be used to purchase at least one additional property, which will appreciate to the point when both properties will be refinanced to generate funds for the purchase of at least two additional properties, and so on. By periodically refinancing all properties owned and continually adding to the investment portfolio, a pyramiding investor can theoretically acquire a substantial estate. The success of this plan is based on careful investment analysis, available financing at strategic times and at reasonable costs, steady growth in value, and rentability of the property purchased.

The pyramiding through refinancing plan is also based upon maintaining ownership of the properties acquired. The strategy is to avoid the taxes that will be imposed upon the net gain when an investment property is sold. Through continued ownership, it is possible that taxes on the capital gains can be avoided throughout the lifetime of the investor. However, because laws are subject to periodic change, it is important to seek current professional advice on taxation matters before making gifts and investments in real property.

## ■ REVIEW QUESTIONS

1. Profits secured through the refinancing process are

    a. taxable at the borrower's normal rate.

    b. taxable at the borrower's capital gains rate.

    c. taxable if not reinvested in 24 months.

    d. not taxable until the property is sold.

2. When a builder, financier, and manager enter into a partnership to construct and own an office building, it is called a(n)

    a. cooperative.

    c. exchange.

    b. joint venture.

    d. land contract.

3. Realized capital gain

    a. is the portion of gain that is subject to income tax.

    b. has no effect on taxation.

    c. is the difference between the total consideration received and the adjusted book basis of the property transferred.

    d. none of the above.

4. A seller-tenant in a sale-leaseback-buyback arrangement benefits from all of the following *EXCEPT*

    a. the right to repurchase the property at the end of the lease for one dollar.

    b. immediate cash receipts.

    c. continued possession of the property.

    d. tax-deductible rent.

5. When a buyer refinances a seller's property using the proceeds from the new loan to satisfy the balance of the existing loan and to make the down payment, this buyer is

    a. splitting the ownership.

    b. creating a joint venture with the seller.

    c. practicing equity participation.

    d. trading on the seller's equity.

6. When a lender buys a project from a developer and then immediately sells it back on a contract that runs for ten years longer than the financing term, the money paid over this extra time is called the

    a. discount.              c. interest.

    b. participation fee.      d. kicker.

7. Building an estate by refinancing and purchasing additional properties is called

    a. agglomoration.         c. subordination.

    b. pyramiding.            d. impounding.

8. Equity participation includes all of the following techniques *EXCEPT*

    a. sale-buyback.          c. split-fee financing.

    b. sale-leaseback.        d. joint ventures.

9. Recognized capital gain is

    a. the portion of the realized gain that is subject to income tax in the year received.

    b. pure profit.

    c. not taxable.

    d. none of the above.

10.  When property is refinanced, any profit received from the proceeds of the new loan is

a.  taxable at the time of refinance.

b.  never taxable.

c.  not considered realized and is not subject to income taxes until the property is sold.

d.  not a way to create tax deferred dollars.

## ■ EXERCISES

1.  Using the following information, determine a 28 percent bracket taxpayer's income tax liability

(a) in the year of the sale if the property is sold for cash.

(b) in the year of the sale and subsequent years if the property is sold on an installment plan.

FACTS:   Property sells for $150,000 net. Buyer pays $20,000 cash, assumes existing loan balance of $90,000, and executes a carryback for $40,000 payable in five equal annual principal payments plus interest. The adjusted book basis is $120,000.

2.  Using the following information, determine the income tax obligations of both parties in the year of an exchange of like properties.

FACTS:   Property A price is $150,000 with a $90,000 existing loan and a $105,000 adjusted basis.
Property B price is $225,000 with a $120,000 existing loan and a $135,000 adjusted basis.

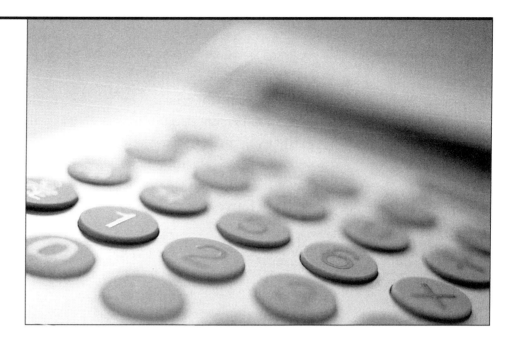

## CHAPTER FIFTEEN

# MATHEMATICS OF REAL ESTATE FINANCE

## ■ KEY TERMS

| | | |
|---|---|---|
| add-on rate | effective rate | premium |
| amortization | fixed costs | present worth |
| annuity | future worth | return on investment |
| balloon payment | interest | simple interest |
| breakeven point | interest factor (IF) | stop date |
| built-up rate | interest only | term loan |
| capitalization rate | loan constant | variable costs |
| compound interest | nominal rate | weighted rate |
| discount | opportunity cost | |
| discounted cash flow | points | |

Real estate finance, by its very nature, requires mathematical calculations. The numbers most often manipulated in this field are dollar amounts of principal, interest, payments, property taxes, income taxes, insurance premiums, assessment charges, depreciation, discounts, returns on and of investments, and other indicators of the advisability, stability, and profitability of investments.

When purchasing a home, most buyers are initially concerned with the amount of cash down payment required. Next, the buyers will look at the amount of monthly payments, including costs of utilities, as an indication of their ability to afford the property. Of course, buyers will also examine the total price, the interest on the loan, the amount of property taxes, and the insurance premiums that will have to be paid.

Commercial property purchasers have additional concerns, including cash flow and breakeven analyses used to estimate the returns on and of their investments. These purchasers must estimate the required payments to determine the feasibility of the proposed investment.

This chapter examines the methods of computing the various forms of interest, the time value of money, alternative loan repayment schedules, closing statement prorations, measurements of profitability, and discounting of mortgages and trust deeds. The rates of interest and dollar amounts used in this chapter are illustrations and may or may not reflect actual market conditions.

## ■ INTEREST

From a borrower's point of view, **interest** can be described somewhat simply as *rent paid* for the use of money. A lender views interest as money received or *earned* from a loan investment. Money is borrowed (leased) at a certain interest rate (rent) for a specified time period, during which the amount borrowed is repaid.

### Simple Interest

**Simple interest** is paid only for the amount of principal that is still owed.

The formula for computing simple interest is:

$$I = PRT$$

where:

$I$ = interest
$P$ = principal
$R$ = rate
$T$ = time

■ **EXAMPLE** Using this formula, the interest on a $1,200 loan to be repaid in one year at an 8 percent annual rate is $96.

$$I = PRT$$

$$I = \$1,200 \times 0.08 \times 1$$

$$I = \$96$$

If this $1,200 loan is to be repaid in 12 equal payments of $100, plus simple interest at the rate of 8 percent, the interest portion of the first monthly payment would be computed as follows:

$$I = PRT$$

$$I = \$1,200 \times 0.08 \times \tfrac{1}{12}$$

$$I = \$^{96}\!/_{12}$$

$$I = \$8$$

The amount of the first month's payment in this example is $108 ($1,200 ÷ 12 = $100 + $8 interest = $108). The second month's payment is $107.34 ($1,100 × 0.08 ÷ 12 = $7.34 + $100 = $107.34). The amount of the third month's payment is $106.67 ($1,000 × 0.08 ÷ 12 = $6.67 + $100 = $106.67) and so on until the loan is repaid, when the last payment of $100.67 is made ($100 × 0.08 = $0.67 + $100 = $100.67). This illustrates the fact that simple interest is charged only upon the remaining amount of principal owed and only for the time that the amount is unpaid.

**Add-on Interest**

Although the simple interest method is used for most real estate loans, some lenders occasionally employ an **add-on rate**. This technique involves the computation of interest on the total amount of the loan for the entire time period. This amount of interest is then added to the principal owed for repayment over the term of the loan before the monthly payments are calculated. This form of interest computation is used for some home improvement loans and many junior liens created by private mortgage companies. Add-on interest has the effect of almost *doubling* the simple interest rate.

■ **EXAMPLE**   Using the same figures as those in the previous example, if the add-on method of computation were employed, first the total interest on the $1,200 for the one-year period would be figured ($1,200 × 0.08 = $96). Next, this amount would be added to the total principal owed ($96 + $1,200 = $1,296). Finally, this sum would be divided by the number of required payments to derive the monthly amount due of $108 ($1,296 ÷ 12 = $108).

The borrower then pays a level $108 per month for 12 months until the loan is satisfied. A moment's reflection at this point will reveal that, although the first month's payment is a true reflection of the 8 percent per annum simple interest charge, the second and subsequent months' payments are not. The interest charged in these months did *not* stop on that portion of the principal which had been repaid. The accuracy of this observation is illustrated by examining the sixth payment of $108. The $100 principal portion of this payment repays half the total loan ($100 × 6 = $600), but the $8 interest portion still reflects the interest charge on the entire $1,200. Thus, the 8 percent add-on interest rate is, in reality, about 15 percent.

The formula for computing the add-on interest rate is:

$$AIR = \frac{2IC}{P(n+1)}$$

where:

$AIR$ = add-on interest rate
$I$ = number of installment payments per year
$C$ = total loan charge
$P$ = principal
$n$ = number of installments in the contract

Note: Wherever parentheses ( ) appears, it means multiply [e.g., 2 (50) = 100].

Substituting the figures from the previous example in this formula, the add-on interest rate would be computed as follows:

$$AIR = \frac{2IC}{P(n+1)}$$

$$AIR = \frac{2(12)(\$96)}{\$1,200\,(12+1)}$$

$$AIR = \frac{\$2,304}{\$15,600}$$

$$AIR = 0.14769 \text{ or } 14.77\% \text{ rounded}$$

The interest rate for a $3,000 home improvement loan to be repaid in monthly installments for three years at 10 percent add-on interest per year would be calculated as follows:

$$AIR = \frac{2IC}{P(n+1)}$$

$$AIR = \frac{2(12)(\$900)}{\$3,000\,(36+1)}$$

$$AIR = \frac{\$21,800}{\$111,000}$$

$$AIR = 0.19459 \text{ or } 19.46\% \text{ rounded, almost double the}$$
$$\text{10 percent rate listed on the loan agreement}$$

**Nominal and Effective Rates of Interest**

The difference between simple and add-on interest in these examples should now be quite clear. At the simple rate of 8 percent interest, the **nominal rate**, which is the rate contracted for, is the same as the **effective rate**, which is the actual rate paid by the borrower. However, the add-on rate of 8 percent interest has a nominal, or contracted, rate of 8 percent but results in an actual, or effective, rate of approximately 15 percent.

Even in simple interest rate loan agreements, the nominal rate may not always be the effective rate. For instance, when executing a new mortgage loan for $30,000, at a three-point discount fee plus other costs totaling $1,000, a borrower will only receive $29,000. However, the borrower will have to pay interest on the full $30,000 contracted for, effectively raising the interest impact.

The entire secondary mortgage market, as well as the bond and government securities markets, is based upon the concept of effective interest rates, or *yields*, as they are generally termed. When the nominal interest rate on the security instrument is *below* market interest rates, the security is usually sold at a **discount**, less than its face value, to develop the required yield. Conversely, when the nominal rate for the security is above the market rate, the security is sold for a **premium**.

## Compound Interest

**Compound interest** is generally described as interest paid on interest earned. This is demonstrated in a savings account, in which $1 deposited at the beginning of a year at 6 percent interest will have a $1.06 balance at the end of that year ($1.00 × 0.06 = $0.06 + $1.00 = $1.06). If this new $1.06 balance is allowed to remain on deposit and the interest rate continues at 6 percent, the balance in the account at the end of the second year will be $1.1236 ($1.06 × 0.06 = $0.0636 + $1.06 = $1.1236) and so on.

Compound interest may be computed by the following formula:

$$CS = BD(1 + i)^n$$

where:

$CS$ = compound sum
$BD$ = beginning deposit
$i$ = interest rate per period
$n$ = number of periods

■ **EXAMPLE** Using this formula, the compound sum of $1,000 left on deposit for ten years at 6 percent interest compounded annually would be computed as follows:

$$CS = BD(1 + i)^n$$
$$CS = \$1,000(1 + 0.06)^{10}$$
$$CS = \$1,000(1.06)^{10}$$
$$CS = \$1,000(1.79084)$$
$$CS = \$1,790.84$$

If interest is compounded more frequently, for instance, monthly or even daily as offered by many banks, then the *effective* amount of interest earnings would be slightly higher than the *nominal* rate. Thus, advertisements soliciting for insured deposits at a 6 percent annual rate indicate a 6.06 percent effective rate because of more frequent compounding periods.

The concept of compounding forms the basis for most investment decisions. Investors reason that a savings account at the current interest rate is a constant investment alternative for their money, and this interest rate constitutes a safe return. In other words, the compound interest earned on a savings account is a safe and viable investment yield against which potential earnings from other investment opportunities can be measured. Within this framework, an investor will measure the *risk* of alternative investments, assigning a required return to each alternative as a function of its specific risk. Thus, an investment in an apartment project might require at least a 10 percent return, or yield, as a function of a 6 percent *safe rate* and a 4 percent *risk rate*. This analysis is premised upon the investor's ability to reinvest profits repeatedly at the required 10 percent yield rate.

## Compound Worth of an Annuity

In addition to the effects of compound interest on a single deposit, an investor is also concerned with the compounding of a series of deposits or earnings. Any series of regular payments or receipts is termed an **annuity**.

The compound interest formula for calculating the **future worth** of a series of regular deposits, or an annuity, each made at the *beginning* of a period, is:

$$CS = RD[(1 + i)^{n-1} + (1 + i)^{n-2} + (1 + i)^{n-n} \text{ or } 1]$$

where:

$CS$ = compound sum
$RD$ = regular deposit
$i$ = interest rate per period
$n$ = number of periods

■ **EXAMPLE** A regular deposit of $1 made at the beginning of each year for three years at 6 percent compound interest will be worth $3.18 at the beginning of the third year, as shown below:

$$CS = \$1[(1 + 0.06)^{3-1} + (1 + 0.06)^{3-2} + 1]$$
$$CS = \$1[(1.06)^{2} + (1.06)^{1} + 1]$$
$$CS = \$1[(1.1236) + (1.06) + 1]$$
$$CS = \$1[3.1836]$$
$$CS = \$3.1836 \text{ or } \$3.18 \text{ rounded}$$

Using the same formula, the future worth of $1,000 deposited at the beginning of each year for ten years at 6 percent interest compounded annually is:

| | | | |
|---|---|---|---|
| $CS$ | $\$1,000[(1.06)^{9}$ | $=$ | 1.68947 |
| | $+ (1.06)^{8}$ | $=$ | 1.59384 |
| | $+ (1.06)^{7}$ | $=$ | 1.50363 |
| | $+ (1.06)^{6}$ | $=$ | 1.41851 |
| | $+ (1.06)^{5}$ | $=$ | 1.33822 |
| | $+ (1.06)^{4}$ | $=$ | 1.26247 |
| | $+ (1.06)^{3}$ | $=$ | 1.19101 |
| | $+ (1.06)^{2}$ | $=$ | 1.12360 |
| | $+ (1.06)^{1}$ | $=$ | 1.06000 |
| | $+ (1.06)^{0}$ | $=$ | 1.00000] |
| | | | 13.18079 |
| $CS$ | $\$1,000(13.18079)$ | $=$ | $13,180.79 |

These mathematical calculations of the compound future worth of a single sum of money or of an annuity involve the use of an **interest factor (IF)**. In the previous example of the compound sum of $1,000 at 6 percent for ten years, the beginning deposit was multiplied by an IF of 1.79084. Similarly, in the example of an $1,000 annuity for ten years at 6 percent, the regular deposit was multiplied by an IF of 13.18079. Thus, the $(1 + i)^{n}$ portion of these equations represents the interest factor (IF).

These interest factors are a function of interest rates and time and can be derived for any combination of these inputs. A tabular example of the future worth of $1 and the future worth of an annuity of $1, both compounded at the rate of 6 percent per year, is shown in Figure 15.2. Note the ten-year IF of 1.79084 for the future worth of $1 and the IF of 13.18079 for

**FIGURE 15.1**

**Future Worth of a Deposit of $1 Compounded at 6 Percent Interest per Period**

| Years | Growth of $1 | Growth of $1 per Period (Annuity) |
|---|---|---|
| 1 | 1.060000 | 1.000000 |
| 2 | 1.123600 | 2.060000 |
| 3 | 1.191016 | 3.183600 |
| 4 | 1.262477 | 4.374616 |
| 5 | 1.338226 | 5.637093 |
| 6 | 1.418519 | 6.975319 |
| 7 | 1.503630 | 8.393838 |
| 8 | 1.593848 | 9.897468 |
| 9 | 1.689479 | 11.491316 |
| 10 | 1.790848 | 13.180795 |
| 11 | 1.898299 | 14.971643 |
| 12 | 2.012196 | 16.869941 |
| 13 | 2.132928 | 18.882138 |
| 14 | 2.260904 | 21.015066 |
| 15 | 2.396558 | 23.275970 |
| 16 | 2.540352 | 25.672528 |
| 17 | 2.692773 | 28.212880 |
| 18 | 2.854339 | 30.905653 |
| 19 | 3.025600 | 33.759992 |
| 20 | 3.207135 | 36.785591 |
| 21 | 3.399564 | 39.992727 |
| 22 | 3.603537 | 43.392290 |
| 23 | 3.819750 | 46.995828 |
| 24 | 4.048935 | 50.815577 |
| 25 | 4.291871 | 54.864512 |

the future worth of an annuity of $1, both of which were developed in the previous examples. Tables such as those illustrated on the following pages are available for any interest rate and time combinations.

# ■ REAL ESTATE MATH FORMULAS

Real estate professionals have a number of formulas and rules to use to determine interest rates, selling prices, and costs. Following are the three-way formula concepts used in the field.

I.    Three-Way Formulas: When using this three-way formula system in solving a variety of math problems, one item is equal to the other two. Place one item in the top half of the circle, according to the formula. Place each of the other two items in adjacent quarters of the bottom half of the circle. Divide the upper half by one of the lower quarters and you will arrive at the solution for the adjacent quarter and vice versa. When multiplying a lower quarter times the adjacent quarter, you will arrive at the solution in the upper half of the circle.

A.    Interest Formula: Interest = Rate × Principal

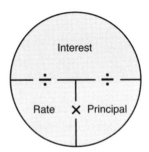

B.    Income Formula: Income = Rate × Value

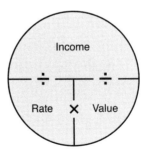

C.      Area Formula: Area = Width × Length

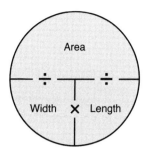

D.      Commission Formula: Commission = Rate × Sales price

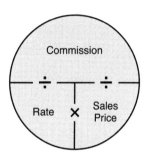

E.      Appraisal Formula:
Net operating income = Capitalization rate × Value

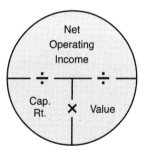

F.      Made-Percent-Paid Formula: Made = Percent × Paid

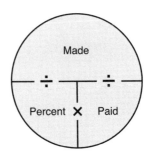

II. Selling Price Rule: To find the selling price of an item, subtract the percentage of profit desired from 100 percent and then divide the cost by the remainder. Remember that the letter *s* is in both *selling* and *subtract*. This will help you recall to subtract from 100 percent, then divide, when it is the selling price you are seeking.

A.      Selling price rule applied: Joe wishes to earn 10 percent profit over the sales price on a lot he bought for $60,000. Joe will have to pay closing costs of $460. What should he sell the lot for? 100% − 10% = 90%. Add the closing costs to the cost of $60,000 to equal $60,460. Divide $60,460 by 90 percent to arrive at the answer of $67,177.78.

B.      Selling price rule applied to discounted note problems: Norman bought a note for a 4 percent discount and paid $16,800. What is the face amount of the note? 100% − 4% = 96%. Divide the cost of the note of $16,800 by 96 percent and the answer is $17,500.

III. Cost Rule: To find the cost or net of an item, add the percentage of profit desired to 100 percent and then divide the selling price by the total percentage. Remember there are three letters in the word *net*, which is for this discussion the same as cost, and three letters in the word *add*. This will help you recall to add to 100 percent and then divide when it is the cost you are seeking.

A.      Cost rule applied: Mayme sold her property at $90,000 and made a 15 percent profit. What did the property cost?

100% + 15% = 115%. Divide $90,000 by 115 percent, and the answer is $78,260.87.

B.   Cost rule applied when closing costs are included: Mike sells his vacant lot for $45,000. He makes an 18 percent profit after paying closing costs of $350. What did the lot cost? 100% + 18% = 118%. Deduct closing costs of $350 from the selling price of $45,000 to equal $44,650. Divide $44,650 by 118 percent, and the answer is $37,838.98.

IV. Principal-Interest-Rate-Time Rule: *Principal* is the loan amount; *interest* represents the cost of borrowing money; *rate* is the cost of borrowing expressed as a percentage of the loan amount paid in interest for one year; and *time* refers to the length of the loan, usually expressed in years.

A.   Principal unknown: Principal = Interest ÷ (Rate × Time). What is the loan amount necessary to receive $1,200 interest at 12 percent if the money is loaned for three years? Solution:

$$P = \frac{\$1,200}{0.12 \times 3} \quad P = \frac{\$1,200}{0.36} \quad P = \$3,333.33$$

B.   Interest unknown: Interest = Principal × Rate × Time. Find the interest on $3,333.33 for three years at 12 percent.

$$I = \$3,333.33 \times 3 \times 0.12$$
$$I = \$1,200$$

C.   Rate unknown: Rate = Interest ÷ (Principal × Time). Find the rate on $3,333.33 that earns $1,200 interest for three years.

$$\text{Rate} = \frac{\$1,200}{\$3,333.33 \times 3} \quad \text{Rate} = 0.12 \text{ or } 12\%$$

D. Time unknown: Time = Interest ÷ (Rate × Principal). Find the time necessary to return $1,200 on a principal amount of $3,333.33 at an annual rate of 12 percent.

$$\text{Time} = \frac{\$1,200}{0.12 \times \$3,333.33} \qquad \text{Time} = 3 \text{ years}$$

# ■ TIME VALUE OF MONEY

We can observe from the previous examples of compound interest that money grows in value over time. This growth is a function of the rate of interest (yield) being earned on a deposit (investment) during the time it is invested. By the same logic, money *not* received until some time in the future must be worth *less* today. How much less is also a function of yield coupled with time.

■ **EXAMPLE** At a yield rate of 6 percent, a dollar that will not be received for one year is really worth only $0.94 today. If the dollar could be deposited today at 6 percent per annum, it would be worth $1.06 at the end of this year. By having to wait a year in order to receive the dollar, the opportunity to earn $0.06 is lost. Thus, the $0.06 can be interpreted as the **opportunity cost** or *discount rate* that diminishes the **present worth** of the subject dollar to be received at the end of the year to $0.94.

**Present Worth of a Dollar**

The present worth of a dollar is, in mathematical terms, the reciprocal of its compound worth. The formula for its derivation is then:

$$PW = A\ \frac{1}{(1+i)^n}$$

where:

$PW$ = present worth
$A$ = amount
$i$ = interest rate per period
$n$ = number of periods

■ **EXAMPLE** The present worth of $1,000 to be received ten years from today at a discount rate of 6 percent is computed as follows:

$$PW = \frac{1}{(1+i)^{10}}$$

$$PW = \$1,000 \, \frac{1}{(1+0.06)^{10}}$$

$$PW = \$1,000 \, \frac{1}{(1.790848)}$$

$$PW = \$1,000 \left[ 0.55839 \right]$$

$$PW = \$558.39, \text{or } \$558.40 \text{ rounded}$$

To verify that the $1,000 is multiplied by the reciprocal of the compound IF found in Figure 15.1: the worth of a $558.40 deposit at 6 percent interest for ten years can be calculated. If the $558.40 were deposited today into a savings account with interest at the rate of 6 percent compounded annually, this money would grow to $1,000 in ten years ($558.40 × 1.790848 = $1,000).

**Present Worth of an Annuity**

Just as the present worth of $1 is the reciprocal of its compound rate, so also is the present worth of an annuity reciprocally related to its compound formula. The present worth of an annuity is expressed as follows:

$$PWA = RA \frac{1}{(1+i)^n} + \frac{1}{(1+i)^{n-1}} \cdots + \frac{1}{(1+i)^{n-2}}$$

where:

$PWA$ = present worth of annuity
$RA$  = regular amount
$i$   = interest rate per period
$n$   = number of periods

■ **EXAMPLE** The present worth of $1 to be received at the *end* of each year for three years at 6 percent interest would be $2.67, as shown below.

$$PWA = \$1\frac{1}{(1+0.06)^3} + \frac{1}{(1+0.06)^2} + \frac{1}{(1+0.06)^1}$$

$$PWA = \$1\frac{1}{1.1910} + \frac{1}{1.1236} + \frac{1}{1.06}$$

$$PWA = \$1[0.8396 + 0.8899 + 0.9433]$$

$$PWA = \$1[2.6729]$$

$$PWA = \$2.6729 \text{ or } \$2.67 \text{ rounded}$$

Similarly, the present worth of an annuity of $1,000 to be received at the *end* of each year for ten years at 6 percent interest would be $7,360.

| $PWA$ | $\$1,000[(1.06)^{10}$ = | $1/1.790$ = | $0.558395$ |
|---|---|---|---|
| | $+ (1.06)^9$ = | $1/1.689$ = | $0.591898$ |
| | $+ (1.06)^8$ = | $1/1.593$ = | $0.627412$ |
| | $+ (1.06)^7$ = | $1/1.503$ = | $0.665057$ |
| | $+ (1.06)^6$ = | $1/1.418$ = | $0.704961$ |
| | $+ (1.06)^5$ = | $1/1.338$ = | $0.747258$ |
| | $+ (1.06)^4$ = | $1/1.262$ = | $0.792094$ |
| | $+ (1.06)^3$ = | $1/1.191$ = | $0.839619$ |
| | $+ (1.06)^2$ = | $1/1.123$ = | $0.889996$ |
| | $+ (1.06)^1$ = | $1/1.060$ = | $\underline{0.943396]}$ |
| | | | $7.360087$ |

$$PWA = \$1,000(7.360087) = \$7,360.08 \text{ or } \$7,360 \text{ rounded}$$

Thus, a contract such as a lease, or any annuity designed to develop a $1,000 net annual cash flow at a 6 percent interest over the next ten years, would be worth $7,360 today.

In order to better understand the present worth of a long-term lease agreement, it must be recognized that rent is usually paid at the *beginning* of each rental period. A ten-year lease contract established at a rate of $1,000 per year would most likely require the tenant to make a $1,000 rental payment to the landlord on the first day of the lease period. This payment would cover the rent for the first full year and would be immediately available to the landlord for reinvestment during that year. Because the other nine rental payments would not be received until stipulated future dates, the remaining $9,000 rent contracted for under the lease would not be worth as much today as it would be if the tenant paid the entire ten years' rent in advance. The landlord cannot invest this money until it is received in yearly installments from the tenant.

Thus, the present worth of a lease for ten years where the landlord would receive $1,000 at the beginning of each rental period, which would be invested at 6 percent, would be worth the full present amount of the $1,000 for the first year's payment, plus the present worth of an annuity of $1,000 at 6 percent for nine years or a total of $7,801.70, rounded [$1,000 + ($1,000 × 6.801692) = $7,801.70]. The IF of 6.801692 is derived by subtracting the last year's IF of 0.558395, found at the top of the previous example, from the total IF of 7.360087. This reduces the analysis to $1,000 cash in advance plus a nine-year, $1,000 annual annuity at 6 percent.

Paralleling the tables of interest factors for future worth, as illustrated in Figure 15.1, tables have also been developed to derive the present worth of $1 or the present worth of an annuity of $1, as shown in Figure 15.3. Note that in Figure 15.3, the IF for the present worth of $1 to be received ten years in the future is 0.558395, the same factor that was derived mathematically in the previous example. Also note that the IF of 7.360087 that appears in Figure 15.3 as the present worth of $1 to be received as an annuity for ten years is the same as the IF calculated in the preceding example, and the IF of 6.801692 is the amount derived for the ten-year lease where the rent is to be received at the beginning of each period.

With the use of tables such as those provided in this chapter, the entire process of mathematical analysis is shortened. For instance, the formulas can now be rewritten in the following abbreviated forms to reflect the availability of these tables:

1. Compound sum of $1:  $CS = BD(IF)$

2. Compound worth of annuity:  $CA = RD(IF)$

3. Present worth of $1:  $PW = A(1/IF$ from Future Worth Table) or

   $PW = A(IF$ from Present Worth Table)

4. Present worth of annuity:  $PWA = RA(1/IF$ from Future Worth Table) or

   $PWA = RA(IF$ from Present Worth Table)

# ■ PAYMENT SCHEDULES

Incorporated into the terms for borrowing money is the arrangement for its repayment. These arrangements can be varied to reflect the specific needs of the participants. Payments can be designed to be made annually, semiannually, quarterly, or monthly, and they may or may not require that the principal be paid in addition to the interest. Some schedules are level, equal payments, while others can be higher or lower at different times. Some loans are term agreements, where only the interest is paid on a regular basis and the principal amount becomes due in full in a lump sum at the end of a given period of time.

Most real estate professionals seek to prequalify their prospective buyers to discover their ability to make mortgage payments prior to submitting an offer to purchase a property.

Figure 15.2 is a prequalifying worksheet designed to aid in this effort.

**FIGURE 15.2**

**Prequalifying Worksheet for Prospective Buyers**

| | |
|---|---|
| Annual Income Divided by 12 (GMI) | $ _____ (1) |
| Gross Monthly Income × _____% (housing ratio) | $ _____ (2) |
| Gross Monthly Income × _____% (total debt ratio) | $ _____ (3) |
| Total Monthly Debt Payments | $ _____ (4) |
| Subtract Line (4) from Line (3) | $ _____ (5) |
| Enter the lesser of Line (2) or Line (5) | $ _____ (6) |

**Maximum Monthly PITI + Payment**

| | |
|---|---|
| Escrow for Taxes and Insurance (TI) | |
| Multiply Line (6) by 25% (ave.) or use actual figures if available | $ _____ (7) |
| Subtract Line (7) from Line (6) | $ _____ (8) |

**Maximum Principal and Interest Payment**

| | |
|---|---|
| Divide Line (8) by rate factor of _____ | $ _____ (9) |
| Multiply Line (9) by $1,000 | $ _____ (10) |

**Maximum Mortgage Amount ("Borrowing Power")**

| | |
|---|---|
| Cash available for Down Payment | $ _____ (11) |
| Add Line (11) to Line (10) | $ _____ (12) |

**Affordable Price Range**

## Amortization

The most common form of payment schedule for real estate loans is a system of regular level payments made over a specified time period. These payments usually include portions for both principal and interest and, when they do, the process is described as **amortization**.

**Annual Payments.** Some real estate loans are repaid in equal annual installments and are considered annuities. As such, the payments required can be derived from the use of the present worth of an annuity table (Figure 15.3). The formula for determining the present worth of an annuity can be adjusted to obtain the schedule of level payments of principal and interest necessary to repay a sum of money at a prescribed interest rate over a specified time period.

The formula for the present worth of an annuity is:

$$PWA = RA(IF)$$

where:

$$
\begin{aligned}
PWA &= \text{present worth of annuity} \\
RA &= \text{regular amount} \\
IF &= \text{interest factor}
\end{aligned}
$$

However, unlike the calculation for the present worth of an annuity, where the RA is known and the present value must be found, the determination of the *annual* payment of principal and interest needed to amortize a loan begins with the full amount of the loan being known, and the formula must be adjusted to find the RA. For instance, if a loan for $7,360 is arranged to be repaid in ten equal annual payments including 6 percent interest, the PWA of $7,360 is already known. By adjusting the formula, the unknown RA can be determined. (These numbers are the same as those found in the previous example for the present worth of an annuity.)

$$
\begin{aligned}
PWA &= RA(IF) \text{ can be written algebraically as:} \\
RA &= PWA/IF \\
IF &= \$7,360/7.3600 \ (IF = PWA \text{ of } \$1 \text{ at 6 percent} \\
& \quad \text{for ten years, Figure 15.3)} \\
RA &= \$1,000 \text{ per year level payment}
\end{aligned}
$$

Another example of this process is the determination of the level annual payment required to amortize a $20,000 loan over 25 years at 6 percent interest. The IF can be taken from the present worth of an annuity column in Figure 15.3, and the formula reads as follows:

$$
\begin{aligned}
RA &= PWA/IF \\
RA &= \$20,0000/12.7833 \ (IF = PWA \text{ of } \$1 \text{ at 6 per-} \\
& \quad \text{cent for 25 years}) \\
RA &= \$1,564.54 \text{ per year level payment}
\end{aligned}
$$

**FIGURE 15.3**

**Present Worth of a Future Amount of $1 Discounted at 6 Percent Interest per Period**

| Years | Present Worth of $1 | Present Worth of $1 per Period (Annuity) |
|---|---|---|
| 1 | 0.943396 | 0.943396 |
| 2 | 0.889996 | 1.833393 |
| 3 | 0.839619 | 2.673012 |
| 4 | 0.792094 | 3.465106 |
| 5 | 0.747258 | 4.212364 |
| 6 | 0.704961 | 4.917324 |
| 7 | 0.665057 | 5.582381 |
| 8 | 0.627412 | 6.209794 |
| 9 | 0.591898 | 6.801692 |
| 10 | 0.558395 | 7.360087 |
| 11 | 0.526788 | 7.886875 |
| 12 | 0.496969 | 8.383844 |
| 13 | 0.468839 | 8.852683 |
| 14 | 0.442301 | 9.294984 |
| 15 | 0.417265 | 9.712249 |
| 16 | 0.393646 | 10.105895 |
| 17 | 0.371364 | 10.477260 |
| 18 | 0.350344 | 10.827603 |
| 19 | 0.350513 | 11.158116 |
| 20 | 0.311805 | 11.469921 |
| 21 | 0.294155 | 11.764077 |
| 22 | 0.277505 | 12.041582 |
| 23 | 0.261797 | 12.303379 |
| 24 | 0.246979 | 12.550358 |
| 25 | 0.232999 | 12.783356 |

**Monthly Payments.**   Although some real estate loans are designed to be repaid on an annual basis, the most common amortization schedules are those paid with level *monthly* payments. The annual payments derived in the two prior examples cannot simply be divided by 12 to determine the monthly amounts, as the results of the monthly compounding process do not precisely correspond to those of annual compounding, as previously discussed. Therefore, to determine the level monthly payment more accurately, the formula must reflect the *monthly* IF, rather than the yearly factor. Figure 15.4 is a *monthly* compound interest table from which the appropriate IF can be taken.

The monthly payments for the $7,360 loan at 6 percent for ten years, which was found to require yearly payments of $1,000, will appear as follows using a monthly payment requirement:

$$RA = PWA/IF$$
$$RA = \$7,360/90.07345 \text{ (IF = PWA of \$1 at 6 percent for 120 months, Figure 15.4)}$$
$$RA = \$81.71 \text{ per month level payment}$$

If the $1,000 annual payment obtained in the previous example is divided by 12, the answer is $83.33, just a bit more than the monthly amortization amount of $81.71.

Similarly, the $20,000 loan to be repaid over 25 years at 6 percent interest, which required annual payments of $1,564.54, will have the following level monthly payment:

$$RA = PWA/IF$$
$$RA = \$20,000/155.20686 \text{ (IF = PWA of \$1 at 6 percent for 300 months)}$$
$$RA = \$128.86 \text{ per month level payment}$$

Booklets of amortization tables that have the level monthly payments are readily available.

An example of the interest rate factors available for various interest rates and times are illustrated in Figure 15.5.

**Loan Constants.**   Many real estate investors employ an annual **loan constant** as a measure of the yearly principal and interest amounts required to amortize their debt. A loan constant is an expression of the relationship between the regular level payments and the total loan amount in terms of an annual percentage rate (annual debt service loan amount = loan constant).

In the earlier example, where the $7,360, 6 percent, ten-year loan requires a $81.71 monthly principal and interest payment, the loan constant is 13.32 percent ($81.71 × 12 = $980.52 ÷ $7,360 = 0.1332). In other words, the loan is being repaid at an annual rate of 13.32 percent of the face amount, and this payment includes both principal and interest. Similarly, the annual loan constant for the $20,000, 6 percent, 25-year loan, which calls for a $128.86 monthly principal and interest payment, is 7.74% ($128.86 × 12 = $1,546.32 ÷ $20,000 = 0.0774).

**FIGURE 15.4**

**Monthly Compound Interest at 6 Percent**

| Months | Future Worth of $1 | Present Worth of $1 per Period |
|---|---|---|
| 1 | 1.005000 | 0.995025 |
| 2 | 1.010025 | 1.985099 |
| 3 | 1.015075 | 2.970248 |
| 4 | 1.020151 | 3.950496 |
| 5 | 1.025251 | 4.925866 |
| 6 | 1.030378 | 5.896384 |
| 7 | 1.035529 | 6.862074 |
| 8 | 1.040707 | 7.822959 |
| 9 | 1.045911 | 8.779064 |
| 10 | 1.051140 | 9.730412 |
| 11 | 1.056396 | 10.677027 |
| 12 | 1.061678 | 11.618932 |
| 24 | 1.127160 | 22.562866 |
| 36 | 1.196681 | 32.871016 |
| 48 | 1.270489 | 42.580318 |
| 60 | 1.348850 | 51.725561 |
| 72 | 1.432044 | 60.339514 |
| 84 | 1.520370 | 68.453042 |
| 96 | 1.614143 | 76.095218 |
| 108 | 1.713699 | 83.293424 |
| 120 | 1.819397 | **90.073453** |
| 132 | 1.931613 | 96.459599 |
| 144 | 2.050751 | 102.474743 |
| 156 | 2.177237 | 108.140440 |
| 168 | 2.311524 | 113.476990 |
| 180 | 2.454094 | 118.503514 |
| 192 | 2.605457 | 123.238025 |
| 204 | 2.766156 | 127.697486 |
| 216 | 2.936766 | 131.897876 |
| 228 | 3.117899 | 135.854246 |
| 240 | 3.310204 | 139.580771 |
| 252 | 3.514371 | 143.090806 |
| 264 | 3.731129 | 146.396926 |
| 276 | 3.961257 | 149.510979 |
| 288 | 4.205579 | 152.444121 |
| 300 | 4.464970 | **155.206864** |
| 312 | 4.740359 | 157.809106 |
| 324 | 5.032734 | 160.260171 |
| 336 | 5.343142 | 162.568843 |
| 348 | 5.672696 | 164.743393 |
| 360 | 6.022575 | 166.791614 |

**FIGURE 15.5**
**Interest Rate Factors**

| Interest Rate | 30-Year Loan | 20-Year Loan | 15-Year Loan |
|---|---|---|---|
| 4.00% | 4.77 | 6.06 | 7.40 |
| 4.50% | 5.07 | 6.33 | 7.65 |
| 5.00% | 5.37 | 6.60 | 7.91 |
| 5.50% | 5.68 | 6.88 | 8.17 |
| 6.00% | 6.00 | 7.16 | 8.44 |
| 6.50% | 6.32 | 7.46 | 8.71 |
| 7.00% | 6.65 | 7.75 | 8.99 |
| 7.50% | 6.99 | 8.06 | 9.27 |
| 8.00% | 7.34 | 8.36 | 9.56 |
| 8.50% | 7.69 | 8.68 | 9.85 |
| 9.00% | 8.05 | 9.00 | 10.14 |
| 9.50% | 8.41 | 9.32 | 10.44 |
| 10.00% | 8.78 | 9.65 | 10.75 |
| 10.50% | 9.15 | 9.98 | 11.05 |
| 11.00% | 9.52 | 10.32 | 11.37 |
| 11.50% | 9.90 | 10.66 | 11.68 |
| 12.00% | 10.29 | 11.01 | 12.00 |
| 12.50% | 10.68 | 11.37 | 12.33 |
| 13.00% | 11.07 | 11.72 | 12.66 |
| 13.50% | 11.46 | 12.08 | 12.99 |
| 14.00% | 11.85 | 12.44 | 13.32 |

Factor represents dollars paid per thousand of loan amount.

By referring to a table of mortgage constants, a borrower has the opportunity to quickly determine the amount of money that must be allocated from an investment's annual cash flow to satisfy the debt service. For instance, *any* 8¾ percent, 25-year loan will require 9.87 percent of the total loan amount as principal and interest for the year. Thus, a $100,000 loan will need $9,870.00 for its annual payment or $822.50 for its monthly payment ($100,000 × 0.0987 = $9,870 ÷ 12 = $822.50).

**Calculating Monthly Mortgage Payments.** Real estate practitioners use the worksheet in Figure 15.2 for calculating monthly mortgage payments.

The FHA recommends using the worksheet in Figure 15.2 for calculating FHA-insured monthly mortgage payments.

**Distribution of Principal and Interest.**   Intrinsic in the amortization design is the distribution of the level payments received into proportionate amounts of principal and interest. Referring once again to the $20,000, 25-year, 6 percent loan with a monthly payment of $128.86, including principal and interest, an amortization schedule can be composed to illustrate the distribution of this payment.

Normally, the first payment from the borrower is not due until one month after the loan's inception. This first payment includes a portion to cover interest during the preceding period and a portion for principal to start the repayment process. Thus, the first $128.86 payment includes $100 for interest and $28.86 for principal ($20,000 × 0.06 = $1,200 interest for one year ÷ 12 = $100 interest for one month).

Now, applying the rule of simple interest, the $28.86 is deducted from the $20,000 original loan amount, resulting in a balance of $19,971.14 for the second month. Because the amount of the amortization payment remains level at $128.86 each month, the distribution to principal and interest changes with every payment. The second $128.86 payment includes $99.85

**FIGURE 15.6**
**Loan Comparison Chart**

| | Standard Conforming | Community Homebuyer | FHA | VA |
|---|---|---|---|---|
| Maximum Loan Amount | $417,000 | $417,000 | Varies by area | $417,000 |
| Minimum Down Payment | 5% | 3% | 2.25% if more than $50,000; 1.25% if less | 0% |
| Qualifying Ratios | 28/36 | 33/38 | 31/43 | 41 |
| Mortgage Insurance | PMI (0.8 × Loan) | PMI (0.8 × Loan) | MIP (1.50 upfront + 0.5% monthly) | Funding Fee 2.15% |
| Seller Contribution | 3% with 5% down 6% with 10% DP | 3% with 5% down 6% with 10% DP | up to 6% | Unlimited |
| Reserve PITI Required | Optional | None | None | None |
| Education Requirement | None | Homebuyer class | Recommended | None |
| Assumable | Limited | Limited | With qualifying | With qualifying |

**FIGURE 15.7**
**Maximum Loan Limits**

| Fannie Mae/Freddie Mac Conforming Loan Limits | |
|---|---|
| One-family unit | $417,000 |
| Two-family unit | $533,850 |
| Three-family unit | $645,300 |
| Four-family unit | $801,950 |

Maximum loan limits are 50 percent higher in Alaska, Hawaii, and the U.S. Virgin Islands.

Second Mortgages: $208,500

| DVA entitlement—$104,250* |
|---|
| * 25% of the 2013 FHA conforming loan limit for a single family residence. |

for interest and $29.01 for principal ($19,971.14 × 0.06 = $1,198.26 ÷ 12 = $99.85 interest, and $128.86 – $99.85 = $29.01 principal).

The process of amortizing a loan is illustrated in Figure 15.8.

The schedule in Figure 15.8 can be extended for the full period of 300 months to display the total distribution of principal and interest. These schedules can be prepared on computer printouts and are often presented by lenders to individual borrowers so that they may follow the progress of their repayments.

The formula to find the principal balance of a real estate loan is:

$$B = \frac{\text{Present worth of \$1 per period of remaining term}}{\text{Present worth of \$1 for full period}} \times \frac{\text{Original}}{\text{principal}}$$

**FIGURE 15.8**
**Monthly Amortization Schedule $20,000/ 6 Percent/25 Years**

| Period | Balance | Interest | Principal |
|---|---|---|---|
| 1 | $20,000.00 | $100.00 | $28.56 |
| 2 | 19,971.14 | 99.85 | 29.01 |
| 3 | 19,942.13 | 99.71 | 29.15 |
| 4 | 19,912.98 | 99.56 | 29.30 |
| etc. to 300 | | | |

**Total Interest Costs**

To illustrate the total costs for a loan, consider a $100,000 loan at 8 percent interest for 30 years. The monthly payment required to amortize this loan is $734.17 [$100,000 × 0.0881 = $8,810 ÷ 12 = $734.17].

If the loan is paid over the prescribed time period, the total payment will equal $264,301.20, of which $164,301.20 is interest ($734.17 × 360 months = $264,301.20 – $100,000 borrowed = $164,301.20).

When faced with this apparent high cost, many people assume that by satisfying a loan as soon as possible, or better yet, by paying the total cost in cash, they can save this seemingly large amount of interest. This approach neglects to consider the opportunity cost of such a decision. If the funds are available to buy the property outright, these monies are probably deposited in a savings account earning interest—earnings that will be lost if the funds are withdrawn. Thus, at a savings interest rate of 5 percent, the withdrawal of $100,000 will result in a loss of $5,000 per year that would total $150,000 over 30 years. This sum is less than the amount of interest paid on the loan.

But this is not the complete analysis. If the $5,000 annual interest is left on deposit in the savings account together with the original $100,000 and compounded at the rate of 5 percent once a year, the $100,000 will grow to $432,194 in 30 years. This total is derived from the compound formula illustrated:

$$CS \quad = BD \times IF\ 4.32194$$
$$CS \quad = \$100,000 \times 4.32194\ (IF = \text{Future Worth of \$1}$$
$$\text{at 5.0\% compounded annually for 30 years)}$$
$$CS \quad = \$432,194$$

Thus, the opportunity cost incurred by paying cash for this property is $267,893 ($432,194 – $164,301 = $267,893). From this example, it becomes apparent that paying cash for a property may not always be to the buyer's best advantage. *Every investment*, whether it is encumbered or held free and clear, has an *opportunity cost*, which must be considered when any financial arrangements are made.

# ■ MEASURING PROFITABILITY*

The degree of underwriting effort extended by loan officers is directly related to the size of the anticipated real estate mortgage or trust deed: the larger the loan, the greater the risk and the greater the effort. Of course, every loan, despite its size, is analyzed as to the financial stability and capability of the borrower and the value of the collateral.

The problems of calculating costs for borrowers and yields for investors are closely related. Both analyses require an accurate estimate of an income stream over a specified time period and include a recognition that today's cash is worth more than tomorrow's promised money.

An analysis of a commercial loan will include a thorough examination of the borrower's financial liquidity as evidence of ability to support the payments. In addition, the profitability of the *specific project* to be financed will be reviewed as to its potential to generate the cash flow necessary for its financial success. In this endeavor, a loan analyst will be most concerned with a project's breakeven requirements as well as its potential investment returns and other variables.

**Breakeven Analysis**

The primary analysis in estimating the potential profitability of a real estate investment is to determine its **breakeven point**, that is, the point at which the gross income is equal to a total of **fixed costs** plus all **variable costs** incurred in developing that particular gross income. Only when gross income exceeds the amount required to break even will a project begin to show a profit.

Every real estate investment project has fixed costs, which continue regardless of income. Such fixed costs include property taxes, insurance premiums, loan payments, and basic property maintenance and utility charges that are incurred even in the absence of any income.

---

\* For further information, see David Sirota, *Essentials of Real Estate Investment*, 8th ed. (Chicago: Dearborn Real Estate Education, 2008).

A real estate investment project also incurs variable costs that fluctuate in proportion to the income generated. Such variable costs include managerial salaries, specialized maintenance services, bookkeeping, and advertising. Variable costs are usually expressed as a ratio of rental income, such as 20 percent for every dollar of income collected and, for ease of analysis, are applied at a set rate for any level of income.

The formula for determining a property's breakeven point can be expressed as follows:

where:

$$BE = \frac{FC}{(1-VCR)}$$

$$BE = \text{breakeven}$$
$$FC = \text{fixed costs}$$
$$VCR = \text{variable cost ratio}$$

■ **EXAMPLE**   Assuming a fixed cost requirement of $100,000 annually and a variable cost ratio of 20 percent per rental dollar, the gross income needed to break even would be calculated as follows:

$$BE = FC/(1 - VCR)$$
$$BE = \$100,000/(1 - 0.20)$$
$$BE = \$100,000/0.80$$
$$BE = \$125,000$$

If this particular project consists of 30,000 square feet of rentable space at a fair market rent of $5 per square foot per year, 83 percent of the space will have to be rented to meet the breakeven requirement ($30,000 \times \$5 = \$150,000$ and $\$125,000 \div \$150,000 = 0.8333$).

The breakeven analysis gives the loan officer and the investor a clear perspective from which to study the economic feasibility of a particular investment. If a reasonable breakeven point is determined, then the project gets the "go" signal. On the other hand, if the analysis indicates that a higher occupancy is necessary in order to break even, neither the lender nor the borrower should be interested in pursuing this venture. In such a situation, and before the project is canceled, a more intensive examination of the variables should be made to see if there is any possibility of raising the rents or lowering the payments, taxes, or other costs to achieve a more reasonable breakeven point.

## Return on Investment (ROI)

Another measurement of profitability is the ratio of pre-tax net income to money invested as a percentage **return on investment**. A deposit of $1 in a savings account at 6 percent interest will develop a $0.06 return on the $1 invested for the year. Similarly, a $0.20 return on the $1 investment would develop a 20 percent ROI.

Real estate lenders often utilize a required return on an investment as the means for estimating the value of the collateral being pledged for a loan. This required return is described as a **capitalization rate** and is usually applied on the net income before taxes.

Real estate owners also use a capitalization rate to estimate the feasibility of a specific investment. However, owners are more likely to be interested in an *after-tax* return on their actual, out-of-pocket investment. This measurement of profitability is called the *bottom-line return*.

Some lenders and owners also utilize a somewhat more sophisticated method for analyzing the profitability of a real estate investment. This approach is the net present worth method based on the concept of the present worth of an annuity.

## Lender's Profitability Calculations

The formula utilized by a lender to estimate an income property's value from its capitalization rate is:

$$V = I/R$$

where:

$V$ = value
$I$ = net annual income
$R$ = rate

■ **EXAMPLE** If a property shows a $20,000 net annual cash flow at a capitalization rate of 10 percent, its value would be calculated as follows:

$$V \ = \ I/R$$
$$V \ = \ \$20,000/0.10$$
$$V \ = \ \$200,000$$

An important factor to remember about the formula for estimating property value based on the capitalization rate is that the formula $V = I/R$ can be adjusted to find any one of its components if the other two are known. Thus, if a property is priced at $200,000 and it develops $20,000 net annual income, its rate of return is 10 percent ($R = I/V$). Similarly, a $200,000 investment at a 10 percent rate develops a $20,000 income ($I = VR$). These examples all presume that the net annual income will continue indefinitely and that the capitalization rate is an accurate reflection of the market rate of return on a total investment.

A capitalization rate can be viewed from various perspectives. From the lender's viewpoint, it can be composed of separate elements, including a safe portion, reflecting such safe investment rates as the 6 percent available on a savings account, and a risk portion, which in the 10 percent situation would be 4 percent. A capitalization rate might also include a safe portion of 6 percent, a risk portion of 2 percent, and a 2 percent portion for return of the investment.

**Investor's Profitability Calculations**

A capitalization rate may also be interpreted from an investor's point of view. This approach is called the **built-up rate**, or the **weighted rate**, and incorporates the concept of leverage. Its derivation is based upon the financing structure of a realty investment and can take the following form:

75 percent L/V senior loan requiring 9 percent interest

15 percent L/V junior loan requiring 12 percent interest

10 percent equity investment requiring 20 percent yield

Then:

$$
\begin{aligned}
0.75 \times 0.09 &= 0.0675 \\
0.15 \times 0.12 &= 0.0180 \\
0.10 \times 0.20 &= \underline{0.0200} \\
\text{Total} &\phantom{=}\ 0.1055
\end{aligned}
$$

or 10.55 percent weighted capitalization rate

This approach takes into consideration the varying yields required by each participant in a leveraged real estate investment.

**Net Present Worth (NPW) Method**

Lenders and investors recognize that a dollar received immediately is preferable to a dollar to be received at some future time. Thus, a method for determining property value and profitability has been devised that utilizes a discounted cash flow technique to analyze the present value of an investment. This technique is an application of the present worth analyses examined earlier in this chapter.

■ **EXAMPLE**   The present worth of a property that will develop a reliable net annual income of $20,000 for the next 15 years and is anticipated to have a residual value of $100,000 at the end of the 15-year period, for an investor who requires a 15 percent return on the investment, is calculated as follows:

$NPW$ = present worth of an annuity + present worth of a reversion

$NPW$ = $20,000 × 5.84737 (IF = PWA at 15% for 15 years) + $100,000 × 0.122894 (IF = PW reversion at 15% for 15 years)

$NPW$ = $116,947.40 + $12,289.40

$NPW$ = $129,236.80 or $129,000 rounded

■ **EXAMPLE** The value of this particular investment from a lender's point of view is approximately $133,000 when the simpler 15 percent capitalization rate technique is applied.

$$V \;=\; I/R$$

$$V \;=\; \$20{,}000/0.15$$

$$V \;=\; \$133{,}333 \text{ or } \$133{,}000 \text{ rounded}$$

■   **EXAMPLE**   When each year's income is discounted by the appropriate interest factor (IF), the net present worth method can also be used to estimate the value and profitability of a property generating an uneven cash flow.

## ■ DISCOUNTING TRUST DEEDS AND MORTGAGES

Buyers of real estate loans invariably pay less than the face amount of the loans. By paying less, the buyers increase their yields accordingly. Discounting involves both the imposition of points by the originator of new real estate loans as well as the analysis of how much less to pay for existing loans.

**Points**

Generally included in the costs of securing a new real estate loan are items identified as **points**. A point is 1 percent of the loan amount. Thus, a charge of two points to secure a new loan of $60,000 will generate a $1,200 cost to the borrower ($60,000 × 0.02 = $1,200).

A one-point discount is equated to raising the yield on a loan by one-eighth of one percent. Thus, a two-point imposition will raise a 10 percent loan to 10¼ percent. In effect, this is discounting before the fact, where the lender actually disburses only $58,800 while entering an account receivable in the books for the full $60,000 loan.

However, the profits generated by the imposition of points may or may not inure to the benefit of the lender. If the new loan is kept as part of the lender's investment portfolio, the increased yield is indeed the lender's profit. If the loan is to be sold in the secondary market, which is now more often the case than not, then the points charged will be the cushion that the lender needs to market the loan.

If Fannie Mae, Freddie Mac, Ginnie Mae, or any of the other participants in the secondary market will pay 98 percent for the purchase of the new $60,000 loan, the lender's profits will be limited to any origination fee charged plus collection fees to be derived from servicing the loan. The two points have been used to sell it. If the paper can be sold for more than 98 percent or the lender can charge more than two points, then the lender's profits will increase accordingly.

## Discounts

When discounting the purchase of an existing real estate loan, the buyer of the paper will be attempting to secure a return on the investment (i.e., a yield) commensurate with expectations of risk and alternative investment yield opportunities. Thus, to purchase a paper with a 10 percent nominal interest rate in the face of a 15 percent market will entail a substantial discount.

**Rule-of-Thumb Method.** A quick and often more profitable method for discounting is to take the difference of the nominal interest rate and the expected rate, multiply it by the number of years the loan has to run, and use that ratio as the discounting factor. This method is sometimes used when purchasing junior loans written for shorter time periods.

■ **EXAMPLE** Consider a new $20,000 junior loan drawn at 12 percent interest-only annually, due in full in three years. The paper buyer's required yield is 15 percent. The difference between the nominal rate of 12 percent and the required rate of 15 percent is 3 percent, and the number of years is also three, making the rule-of-thumb discount factor 9 percent (3% difference × 3 years = 9%). Applied to the $20,000 loan, the discount is $1,800 ($20,000 × 0.09 = $1,800) and the purchase price of the paper is $18,200 ($20,000 – $1,800 = $18,200).

The rule-of-thumb approach acts effectively to raise the paper buyer's yield, in this case, from 15 to 16.48 percent {[$20,000 x 0.12 = $2,400 interest only for 3 years = $7,200 + $1,800 discount when loan paid in full = $9,000 ÷ $18,200 (the invested amount) = 0.4945 ÷ 3 years = 0.1648]} annual return on investment. If the loan is paid prior to the three-year stop date, the investor's yield will increase accordingly.

**Discounted Cash Flow Method.**   A more exact approach to discounting involves the use of the present worth tables.

■ **EXAMPLE** First, discount the income stream of $2,400 interest paid annually for three years, which is $5,479.68 ($2,400 × 2.2832 *PWA IF* 15%, 3 years = $5,479.68). Then, discount the balloon payment of $20,000 to be received at the end of the third year, which is $13,150 ($20,000 × 0.6575 *PW IF* 15%, 3 years = $13,150). Finally, add these two discounted amounts to determine the purchase price of the $20,000 paper, which equals $18,629.68 ($5,479.68 + $13,150 = $18,629.68).

Notice that this amount exceeds the rule-of-thumb approach by $429.68. Thus, the **discounted cash flow** method develops exactly the 15 percent annual yield required by the buyer of the paper. Of course, if the loan is paid in full prior to the three-year stop date, the yield is increased accordingly.

## ■ SUMMARY

This chapter focused on some of the fundamental mathematical aspects of real estate finance, including interest rates, time value of money, payment schedules, profitability measurements, and discounting.

Interest charges for loans can be considered as rent for the use of money, with simple interest being the most common form of rent for real estate loans. Simple interest is charged only on the actual amount of the loan balance outstanding at each date of payment. On the other hand, add-on interest is charged on the full amount of the loan for its entire period, regardless of any periodic repayments of principal; this method almost doubles the amount of interest paid compared to simple interest. Nominal interest is the amount designated in the loan contract, while effective interest is the amount actually paid, and it is often more than the nominal rate.

Compound interest is interest paid on interest earned. A dollar deposited in a savings account at compound interest will grow in value proportionate to the interest rate and compounding period. Similarly, a series of regular deposits or an annuity will grow in value as a result of these same two factors. Conversely, a dollar to be received in the future is worth less today.

The actual amount of this difference depends on the interest rate and the length of time until the dollar is to be received. The present worth of an annuity is the total amount of the discounted annual stream of dollars for the designated term.

Amortization is the systematic repayment of a loan. A real estate loan is actually a form of annuity and can be considered a stream of income for the lender into the future in the form of payments from the borrower. As a result, loan payments can be derived by dividing the total sum of money to be amortized by an interest factor (IF) secured from the appropriate table for the present worth of an annuity.

The most widely used system of amortization is the level monthly payment schedule. Under this plan, a fixed monthly payment of principal and interest is divided into its proportionate parts, with the interest applied as "rent" on the debt balance and the principal reducing the loan balance with regularity each month. When the prescribed level payments are made over the entire loan period, the loan is said to be fully amortized.

Other arrangements can be designed to meet the varying needs of specific borrowers and lenders. Annual, semiannual, quarterly, or interest-only payments can be established to serve special circumstances. **Interest-only** payments are usually included in a **term loan**. Principal does not need to be paid until the loan's **stop date** at which time the full amount of the loan's balance is due as a **balloon payment**.

Generally, home loan payments will include not only the required principal and interest amounts, but also proportionate amounts for property taxes, hazard insurance premiums, and property improvement assessments, if applicable. These monies are identified as impound funds and are deposited into an escrow account. The lender uses these escrowed funds to pay these charges when they are due. In addition, some loans require contributions for a mortgage insurance premium.

The profitability of a commercial venture to be financed by a real estate loan can be gauged by the project's breakeven requirements and by the potential return on the investment. A breakeven analysis includes an examination of the relationship between gross income and the fixed and variable costs necessarily incurred to develop this gross income. As there is no profit until the breakeven point is passed, a careful estimate of a project's rent-up requirements to ascertain its breakeven point is imperative before a loan can be arranged. When a high rent-up ratio is needed for a project to merely break even, it is not likely to be funded.

A lender will analyze an investment property's profitability on the basis of the return required. This return depends on an amount for the return on the investment and a return of the invested principal as well. Thus, a lender can estimate the value of the collateral by dividing the project's anticipated net annual income by a capitalization rate, usually the lender's loan constant. This is an application of the formula of Value = Net income ÷ Capitalization rate. Lenders and investors can apply the present worth of money concepts to the analysis of a real estate project's potential profitability.

By measuring the present value of a project's income stream at a required return discount rate, a more realistic conclusion can be reached regarding the project's present worth.

Finally, the application of points and present worth effectively raises yields on discounting real estate loans so they may be sold in the secondary market.

# ■ REVIEW QUESTIONS

1. A homeowner secures an improvement loan for $3,600, payable over three years plus interest at 15 percent per annum. What is the amount of the third payment?

   a. $42.50

   b. $200.00

   c. $142.50

   d. $145.00

2. If the loan in Question 1 is designed to be paid monthly, interest-only, with the balance due in full at the end of three years, what is the total amount of the balloon payment?

   a. $100.00

   b. $101.25

   c. $3,600

   d. $3,645

3. If the loan in Question 1 is designed at 15 percent add-on interest, what is the amount of the third payment?

   a. $45.00

   b. $142.50

   c. $145.00

   d. $435.00

4. If the loan in Question 1 is designed at 15 percent add-on interest, what is the effective interest rate?

   a. 29.00 percent

   b. 29.19 percent

   c. 30.16 percent

   d. 31.08 percent

| | 8 Percent Annual Factors | | | |
|---|---|---|---|---|
| Years | Future Worth $1 | Future Worth Ann. $1 | Present Worth $1 | Present Worth Ann. $1 |
| 5 | 1.4693 | 5.8666 | 0.6805 | 3.9927 |
| 10 | 2.1589 | 14.4865 | 0.4631 | 6.7100 |
| 15 | 3.1721 | 27.1521 | 0.3152 | 8.5594 |
| 20 | 4.6609 | 45.7619 | 0.2145 | 9.8181 |

Answer questions 5–10 referring to the table above.

5. What is the annual payment required to amortize a $100,000 loan at 8 percent interest for 20 years?

   a. $2,145              c. $9,818

   b. $4,660              d. $10,185

6. What is the amount of a single deposit into an 8 percent interest savings account needed to accumulate $50,000 in 15 years?

   a. $1,586              c. $31,520

   b. $15,762             d. $42,797

7. What is the amount of the regular annual payments into an 8 percent interest rate savings account needed to accumulate $100,000 in 20 years?

   a. $2,185              c. $4,660

   b. $4,576              d. $9,818

8. What is the rate of the annual mortgage constant needed to amortize a $100,000 loan at 8 percent over 15 years?

   a. 8.00 percent        c. 11.68 percent

   b. 10.00 percent       d. 12.12 percent

9. At an 8 percent rate, what is the present worth of a property generating $20,000 net annual income for ten years?

   a. $43,178             c. $289,730

   b. $134,200            d. $926,400

10. At an 8 percent rate, what is the present worth of a property generating $5,000 net annual income for each of the first five years of a lease, $7,500 net for each of the next five years, and $10,000 net for each of the final five years of a 15-year lease, when the property is expected to have a residual net cash value of $100,000?

a.  $90,357.25

b.  $100,000.00

c.  $112,500.00

d.  $212,500.00

## ■ EXERCISES

1. Examine the ads in local newspapers and in other media to discover the private buyers of real estate loans. Also, accountants and attorneys may have clients who are investors. You may wish to contact them, and investors you know, to determine current yield requirements.

2. Enlist the aid of the local appraiser to provide the information you will need to analyze the breakeven point on a small apartment or commercial project.

# ANSWER KEY

**Chapter 1:**

1. b 22
2. d 22
3. d 18
4. c 11
5. c 23
6. a 18
7. a 24
8. d 25
9. a 25
10. b 27

**Chapter 2:**

1. b 36
2. d 38
3. b 37
4. d 50
5. d 50–51
6. d 40
7. d 46
8. d 45
9. a 48
10. c 51

**Chapter 3:**

1. c 66
2. b 69
3. d 61
4. a 65
5. d 67
6. b 66
7. c 71
8. d 70
9. d 71
10. b 70

**Chapter 4:**

1. b 83
2. d 83
3. a 87
4. a 84
5. b 90
6. b 92
7. c 99
8. b 94
9. d 94
10. c 97

**Chapter 5:**

1. d 114
2. d 116
3. a 116
4. a 128
5. b 140
6. d 145
7. c 131
8. c 149
9. b 146
10. a 145

**Chapter 6:**

1. c 166
2. b 167
3. b 192
4. b 185
5. d 168
6. d 175
7. c 180
8. d 172
9. c 193
10. d 182

## Chapter 7:

1. d  202
2. a  202
3. c  202
4. d  203
5. b  200
6. c  202
7. b  203
8. a  203
9. c  203
10. a  202

## Chapter 8:

1. a  229
2. b  231
3. d  213
4. a  213
5. b  221
6. d  216
7. a  236
8. c  231
9. c  229
10. d  232

## Chapter 9:

1. c  241, 249
2. c  251
3. d  262

4. b  259
5. d  256
6. a  265
7. c  276
8. a  276
9. c  277
10. b  277

## Chapter 10:

1. b  287
2. c  315
3. c  311
4. b  298
5. b  302
6. c  298
7. b  320
8. c  320
9. c  302
10. b  304

## Chapter 11:

1. a  328
2. b  328
3. d  329
4. b  330
5. c  331
6. b  331
7. c  332

8. b  333
9. b  334
10. c  340

## Chapter 12:

1. d  356
2. d  360
3. a  361
4. a  362
5. b  361
6. b  363
7. d  357
8. d  365
9. d  365
10. d  357

## Chapter 13:

1. b  376
2. d  378
3. b  379
4. d  390
5. b  391
6. a  384
7. d  387
8. d  384
9. d  386
10. c  385

## Chapter 14:

1. d  404

2. d  403

3. c  404

4. b  400, 401

5. d  401, 402

6. b  402

7. a  405

8. c  402, 403

9. b  404

10. a  404

## Chapter 15:

1. d   418
$3,600 × 0.15 = $540
$540 × 3 = $1,620 ÷ 36 = $45
$3,600 ÷ 36 = $100
$45 + $100 = $145

2. d   418
$3,600 + $45 interest = $3,645

3. c   419
$3,600 × 0.15 = $540 × 3 = $1,620;
$1,620 + $3,600 = $5,220;
$5,220 ÷ 36 = $145 equal monthly payments

4. b   419
2(12)(1620) ÷ $3,600(36 + 1) = $38,880 ÷ $133,200 = 0.29189

5. d   434
$100,000 ÷ 9.8181 = $10,185 rounded

6. b   420
$50,000 ÷ 3.1721 = $15,762 rounded

7. a   421
$100,000 ÷ 45.7619 = $2,185 rounded

8. c   437
$100,000 ÷ 8.5594 = $11,683.06;
$11,683.06 ÷ $100,000 = 0.1168 or 11.68%

9. b   445
$20,000 × 6.7100 = $134,200

10. a   445
$5,000 × 3.9927 = $19,963.50
$7,500 × 2.7173 = $20,379.75
6.7100 − 3.9927 = 2.7173
$10,000 × 1.8494 = $18,494.00(8.5594 − 6.7100 = 1.8494)
$100,000 × 0.3152 = <u>$31,520.00</u>
$90,357.25

## Exercises

8–2   8%   [$100,000 × 0.10 = $10,000 − ($50,000 × 0.12 = $6,000)$6,000 = $4,000 ÷ $50,000 = 0.08]

14–1   (a)   $8,400      [$150,000 − $120,000 = $30,000 × 0.28 = $8,400]
(b)   $2,800 in year of sale and $1,120 annually for five years.
$150,000 − $120,000 = $30,000 Gain
$150,000 − $90,000 = $60,000 Equity
$30,000 ÷ $60,000 = 0.50 Install Factor
$20,000 × 0.50 = $10,000 × 0.28 = $2,800
$8,000 × 0.50 = $4,000 × 0.28 = $1,120

14–2   (a) zero tax
(b) $75,000 taxable recognized gain

# GLOSSARY

**abstract** A condensed history of the title to a property, consisting of a summary of the original grant and all subsequent conveyances and encumbrances relating to the particular parcel of real estate.

**acceleration clause** The clause in a mortgage or trust deed that stipulates the entire debt is due immediately if the mortgagor defaults under the terms of the contract.

**acknowledgment** A notarization on a legal document attesting to the validity of the signatures affixed thereto.

**actual notice** In a real estate transaction, a presumption of knowledge (e.g., tenants in possession of house being sold).

**add-on rate** Method of computing interest whereby interest is charged on the entire principal amount for the specified term, regardless of any periodic repayments of principal that are made.

**adjustable-rate mortgage (ARM)** A variable-interest-rate loan.

**adjusted book basis** Purchase price of a property plus any capital improvements minus accrued depreciation, if any, to the date of the sale.

**administered price system** Fannie Mae securities purchasing procedure where required yields are adjusted daily to reflect financial market factors.

**allodial system** Land ownership free and clear of any rent or service due the government.

**ALTA policy** American Land Title Association title insurance policy; the most comprehensive form.

**amortization** The systematic repayment of a loan through periodic installments of principal and interest over the entire term of the loan agreement.

**annual percentage rate (APR)** The effective interest rate.

**annuity** A series of income payments or receipts over a period of years.

**appraisal** An estimate of the value of a property based upon comparison of real estate prices and the market for real estate.

**assessed value** A property's adjusted actual market value to establish property taxes.

**assets** All things of value, encumbered or not, owned by a person, corporation, or other entity.

**assignment** The transfer of an interest in a bond, mortgage, lease, or other instrument, in writing, by the assignor to the assignee.

**assumed** Buying a property and taking over or assuming the responsibility for the existing mortgage.

**automatic rate reduction** Loan interest rate reduces with clean payment record.

**auction** Selling property to the highest bidder.

**avulsion**  A sudden separation of land caused by flooding, earthquake, or other physical disruption; affects the fixity of real estate.

**baby boomer**  Name given a baby born after World War II, now a significant bubble in our population.

**balanced trust**  *See* combination trust.

**balloon payment**  The final payment of a partially amortized loan that is considerably larger than the required periodic payments.

**bankrupt**  No longer able to pay debts.

**basis points**  There are 100 basis points in one percent; thus, 50 basis points equal one-half percent.

**beneficiary**  The lender in a trust deed financing arrangement.

**bill of sale**  The document by which personal property ownership is transferred.

**biweekly loan**  A loan designed to be repaid twice monthly to match many borrowers' payroll schedules.

**blanket mortgage**  A mortgage secured by the pledging of more than one property as collateral.

**blended rate**  Adjusted rate of interest on loan assumption.

**blends**  Interest rate on refinance loans; being an average of the old rate and the new rate.

**blue-sky provision**  Requiring full disclosure of all risks in a limited partnership solicitation under the Uniform Partnership Act.

**bonds**  Securities issued to raise funds by a corporation or a governing body.

**book value**  Acquisition costs less any accrued depreciation.

**boot**  In an exchange, something of value given in addition to like-kind property, e.g., "this acre and cash to boot."

**breakeven point**  That point at which gross income equals fixed costs plus variable costs.

**bridge loan**  An equity loan made for a short time to raise money for a special purpose.

**budget loan**  Loan payments include a portion for taxes and insurance, as well as principal and interest.

**built-up rate**  *See* weighted rate.

**bullet loan**  *See* rollover loan and term loan.

**bundle of rights**  All of the ownership rights in real estate.

**buydowns**  Allows loans to be made at less-than-market interest rates by paying front-end discounts.

**California Land Title Association (CCLTA)**  Issues title insurance policies for California properties.

**Cal-Vet**  A special program for eligible California veterans to help them finance the purchase of farms and ranches within the state.

**capital gains**  Income earned from the sale of investments where the net sales price exceeds the adjusted book basis.

**capital losses**  Losses derived from the sale of investments where the net sales price is less than the adjusted book basis.

**capitalization rate**  Method of estimating a property's value by considering net annual income as a percentage of a reasonable rate of return on an investment. (Net income ÷ Capitalization rate = Property value.)

**caps** Yearly and/or life-of-loan limitations on amounts of variations allowed when adjusting interest on variable-rate loans.

**carryback** Seller agrees to finance buyer in order to complete a property sale.

**cash flow** Regular income from property rentals.

**certificate of eligibility** Entitles qualified veteran to secure DVA-guaranteed home loan.

**certificate of reasonable value (CRV)** The appraised value of a property being pledged as collateral for a DVA-guaranteed loan.

**certificate of savings** A long-term savings plan.

**chain of title** History of recordings against a specific property.

**chattel** Personal property.

**CLIC** Commercial Leasehold Insurance Corporation; owned by MGIC, it provides leasehold insurance for commercial and industrial properties, guaranteeing lease payments and leasehold improvement loans.

**closing statements** Final arrangements to transfer title of property, as well as allocate charges and credits.

**cloud on the title** An outstanding encumbrance that, if valid, would affect or impair the owner's property title.

**coinsurance** An FHA program that allows loan originators to directly underwrite housing project loans, shortening processing time considerably.

**coinsured** All parties with an interest in properties named as insureds, e.g., the owner and the lender.

**collateral** Property, real or personal, pledged as security to back up a promise.

**combination trust** A trust that participates in real estate investments as both financier and investor.

**commercial banks** Established primarily to serve the community's business needs.

**commercial leasehold insurance** *See* CLIC.

**commercial mortgage-backed securities (CMBS)** Packaged loans on commercial properties.

**commercial paper** Loans issued by banks and savings institutions for business enterprises.

**commitment** A promise by a lender to make a loan at a future date on specified terms and conditions. A promise by an investor to purchase a specified amount of mortgages from the loan originator.

**commitment fee** Charge imposed for granting an agreement either to lend or to purchase at a future date.

**common-law marriage** Recognized in California as eligible for community property.

**community property** All property acquired by either spouse during marriage and owned equally, except that received by gift, devise, or descent.

**Community Reinvestment Act (CRA)** Provides that financial institutions meet the credit needs of *all* citizens of a community.

**comp** Also known as a *comparable*; property similar to subject property used as a basis of comparison in market data appraising method.

**completion bond** A third-party guarantee that the builder will complete construction.

**compound interest** Interest paid on the original principal and also on the accrued interest.

**concurrent ownership**  Real estate ownership by more than one party, such as partnerships, tenants in common, community property, and joint tenancy.

**condemnation**  *See* eminent domain.

**condominium**  Fee simple ownership of an apartment or a unit, generally in a multiunit building, plus an undivided interest in the common elements.

**conforming loan**  Meets the maximum loan limits established by Fannie Mae.

**constant payment mortgage**  Fixed payments of principal and interest over the life of a loan.

**construction mortgage**  Open-end mortgage loan to finance construction of buildings on a property.

**construction/permanent loan**  Construction loan becomes permanent when building completed.

**constructive notice**  In a real estate transaction, matters of public record.

**Consumer Financial Protection Bureau (CFPB)**  Its mission is to make markets for consumer financial products and services (i.e., mortgages, credit cards, and other consumer financial products) work for Americans.

**contingent liability**  Responsibility that exists beyond the primary boundaries of a transaction.

**contract for deed**  *See* land contract.

**contract rate**  *See* nominal rate.

**conventional mortgage**  Mortgage loan made without any additional guarantees for repayment, such as FHA insurance, DVA guarantees, or private insurance.

**conversion**  To change from a rental format to one of individual ownership.

**convertible loan**  Borrower can change to a fixed rate any time during the life of an adjustable-rate loan.

**cooperative**  A residential multifamily building with the title in a trust or corporation that is owned and operated for the benefit of the persons living therein, each possessing a proprietary lease. All owners have joint liability for the mortgage on the property.

**corporation**  An entity created to act as an individual when engaging in business and finance but limiting the personal liability of its stockholders.

**correspondent**  A mortgage banker.

**cosigners**  Additional signers to a financial agreement adding their guarantees to that of the borrowers.

**cost approach**  Process of appraising the value of a property by adding the estimated value of the land to the appraiser's calculations of the replacement cost of the building less depreciation.

**cost recovery**  Now used to describe depreciation.

**coupon bonds**  Bonds with interest coupons attached that are removed as they become due and cashed by their bearer. Also known as bearer bonds.

**covenant of seisin**  Clause in a mortgage that warrants that the mortgagor has title to the property and the authority to pledge it as collateral.

**covenants that run with the land**  Conditions that are recorded against property that remain in effect through changes in ownership.

**credit loan**  Mortgage issued strictly upon the financial strength of a borrower without great regard for collateral.

**credit report** Document indicating credit circumstances of a borrower of a real estate loan.

**credit scoring** Used in electronic underwriting to analyze a borrower's credit.

**credit union** Organization formed by a homogeneous group for banking purposes, e.g., a government employees credit union.

**cross-defaulting clause** Usually included in a junior loan instrument; stipulates that a default in the senior encumbrance also triggers a default in the junior loan.

**crunch down** Recasting an existing loan to a lower level to avoid a foreclosure.

**customized mortgages** Individually designed loans for "desirable" borrowers.

**cycle** A period of time within which the economic ups and downs of business or real estate takes place.

**debenture** Bonds issued without any specific collateral pledge but secured by the general assets of the issuer.

**debt ratio** The relationship between a borrower's long-term debt payments and monthly income.

**deed** A document used to transfer ownership of real property.

**deed in lieu of foreclosure** Voluntarily signing over to the creditor the property pledged as collateral on a defaulted loan.

**deed of trust** A financing instrument in which the borrower/trustor conveys title of the collateral to a trustee to be held in trust for the beneficiary/lender. When the loan is repaid, title is reconveyed to the trustor. If a default occurs, the trustee exercises the power of sale on behalf of the beneficiary.

**default** Nonperformance of a duty; failure to meet an obligation when due.

**defeasance clause** Clause included in a loan instrument that provides for the cancellation of the mortgagee's interest when the debt has been paid in full.

**deficiency judgment** A personal judgment levied against the mortgagor, under the terms of the note, when a mortgage foreclosure sale does not produce sufficient funds to repay the mortgagee the outstanding loan balance, interest, and costs.

**de la Cuesta** Precedent-setting case (*Fidelity Federal Savings v. de la Cuesta*) in which the United States Supreme Court ruled on June 28, 1982, that the due-on-sale clause was legally enforceable.

**delinquency** Late payments or nonpayments of principal, interest, taxes, or insurance.

**demand deposits** Checking accounts.

**Department of Veterans Affairs (DVA)** Administers home loans for eligible veterans.

**Depository Institutions Deregulation and Monetary Control Act of 1980** Authorized deregulation of banks and savings institutions.

**depreciation** Loss of value due to all causes, but usually considered to include physical deterioration, functional obsolescence, and economic obsolescence.

**deregulation** *See* Depository Institutions Deregulation and Monetary Control Act of 1980.

**Desktop Origination®** Electronic loan processing.

**Desktop Underwriter®** Fannie Mae's electronic system for qualifying borrowers.

**direct endorsement program** An FHA special program allowing eligible lenders the right to underwrite the loans that they create.

**direct sales comparison approach** *See* market-data approach.

**disclosures**  Information pertinent to a property's value required to be imparted to buyers and borrowers in California.

**discount**  Difference between the face amount of a note or mortgage and the price at which the instrument is sold in the secondary market.

**discount rate**  The rate that the Fed charges its members for funds borrowed on collateralized loans.

**discounted cash flow**  Present value of income stream.

**discretionary income**  Earned funds left over for investment after allocations for necessities and reserves.

**disintermediation**  Rapid withdrawal of money from bank accounts.

**disposable personal income**  Total income less allocations for necessities; available for personal consumption.

**Dodd-Frank Wall Street Reform and Consumer Protection Act**  Its purpose is to promote the financial stability of the United States by improving accountability and transparency in the financial system.

**draws**  A system of payments to a contractor under a construction loan.

**drive-by appraisal**  Literally, appraising from a car window.

**due-on-sale clause**  A clause that stipulates a borrower cannot sell or transfer the property without prior written consent of the lender.

**DVA**  Department of Veterans Affairs; since 1944, the DVA has guaranteed the top portion of an eligible veteran's loan.

**easement**  Access rights over someone else's property.

**ECOA**  *See* Equal Credit Opportunity Act (ECOA).

**effective rate**  Actual interest rate paid on a loan regardless of the rate stipulated in the contract.

**electronic underwriting**  Using the Internet to analyze data to qualify a borrower's credit and the property's value.

**eminent domain**  The government's sovereign power of condemnation over private property for the benefit of the community; an example of police power.

**encroachment**  Improvements overlapping adjoining property.

**encumbrance**  Any lien against a property or any restriction in its use, such as an easement; a right or interest in a property held by one who is not the legal owner.

**endowment**  A permanent source of income.

**English Common Law**  Established allodial system of real property ownership.

**entitlement**  The amount of guarantee a veteran is eligible to secure on a DVA loan.

**Equal Credit Opportunity Act (ECOA)**  Provides for the elimination of discrimination for age, sex, and race in finance.

**equitable redemption period**  A period of time established by custom, usually six months, that allows a defaulting borrower to redeem property by bringing all payments current before foreclosure.

**equitable rights**  The rights of a less-than-fee-simple owner to occupy, lease, or sell the subject property.

**equitable title** *See* equitable rights.

**equity** The interest or value a property owner has in the property over and above any liens against it.

**equity loan** Money loaned to borrowers based on a percentage of the equity held in the collateral property.

**equity trust** An investment trust dealing in ownerships rather than in financing.

**escalator clause** Clause in a loan instrument providing for increases in payments or interest based upon predetermined schedules or upon a specific economic index, such as the consumer price index. *See* variable-rate mortgage.

**escrow** A third-party agent that receives, holds, and/or disburses certain funds or documents upon the performance of certain conditions; the closing agent in a real estate transaction.

**escrow funds** Monies collected for property taxes and insurance premiums.

**estoppel certificate** Legal form that states the unpaid balance due on the loan as of a specified date and prevents, or "stops," any purchaser of the loan from claiming that the original borrower owes more than the stated amount.

**estate tax** A tax imposed by federal and state agencies on the net value of a deceased's estate.

**eviction** Legally dispossessing occupants of real property for unlawful detainer.

**exchange** A method for postponing income taxes on capital gains by trading like-kind property. *See* Section 1031, Internal Revenue Code.

**exculpatory clause** Limits the liability of the borrower to the collateral property described in the loan agreement.

**face value** The stated amount of a security. *See* par.

**Fair Isaac Corporation (FICO)** Company which originated credit scoring.

**Fannie Mae** Formerly the Federal National Mortgage Association (FNMA); provides secondary mortgage market.

**Farm Credit System (FCS)** A complete national banking system for financing the activities of farmers and ranchers.

**Farmer Mac** The Federal Agricultural Mortgage Corporation.

**FDIC** Federal Deposit Insurance Corporation; provides insurance of $250,000 per account and supervises the operations of banks that qualify for membership in the insurance program.

**Fed** The United States Federal Reserve System.

**federal funds rate** The rate the Fed recommends that member banks charge each other.

**Federal Reserve System** The nation's economic manager, the Fed regulates its member banks.

**fee appraiser** Also known as a field appraiser. One who is not an employee of a particular lender; an independent agent.

**fee simple absolute title** The best title one can obtain.

**FHA** Federal Housing Administration; insures loans made by approved lenders to qualified borrowers in accordance with its regulations.

**FHA 203(K)** Rehabilitation mortgage insurance.

**FHLB** Federal Home Loan Bank System; serves the nation's savings associations.

**FHLMC** Federal Home Loan Mortgage Corporation; provides a secondary market for mortgages. *See* Freddie Mac.

**fictitious deeds of trust** Comprehensive master deeds of trust established by lenders to cover all areas of trust deed finance; referred to in shorter versions of trust deeds.

**fiduciary** A person in a position of trust and confidence who represents another; known as the agent.

**financial intermediary** Financial institution that accepts deposits and makes loans.

**financial service center** Provides insurance, real estate sales, real estate loans, and banking services in one location.

**financial statement** A compilation of a borrower's assets, liabilities, and earnings records.

**fine-tune** A method by which the Fed controls the nation's economy by controlling the amount of money in circulation.

**first mortgage** A loan that has priority as a lien over all other loans. *See* senior loan.

**fixed costs** Regularly impacting operating expenses such as taxes, insurance, and maintenance.

**fixed-rate loan** The interest rate remains constant over term of loan.

**fixture** Article of personal property attached permanently to a building or land so that it becomes part of the real property.

**FOMC** Federal Open Market Committee; directs and regulates the Federal Reserve System's open-market operations.

**forbearance** The postponement for a limited time of a portion or all of the payments on a loan in jeopardy of foreclosure. *See* moratorium.

**foreclosure** Court action initiated by a lender for the purpose of recovering the borrower's real estate to pay the balance owed on a defaulted loan.

**Freddie Mac** Formerly known as the Federal Home Loan Mortgage Corporation (FHLMC). Provides secondary mortgage market.

**freehold estate** *See* fee simple absolute title (fee simple).

**FSLIC** Federal Savings and Loan Insurance Corporation; provides insurance for its member savings accounts. Replaced by the FDIC.

**funding fee** A front-end charge of one percent of the loan amount paid by the borrower when securing a DVA-guaranteed loan.

**future worth** The compounding increase in the value of money over time.

**gap** A short-term, high-interest loan covering the possible gap in construction financing if rent-up requirements are not met and the long-term lender does not vest takeout mortgage in full and/or the construction mortgagee holds back a portion of the interim financing.

**Garn-St. Germain Bill** *See* Depository Institutions Deregulation and Monetary Control Act of 1980.

**general lien** A lien on all property of a debtor, both real and personal.

**general obligation bonds** Public improvement bonds to be paid from property taxes.

**general partner** In a limited partnership, the individual or company acquiring, organizing, and managing the investment.

**gift tax** A federal tax on gifts in excess of $11,000 per donee per year.

**Ginnie Mae** Government National Mortgage Association (GNMA); created in 1968 to take over special assistance and liquidation functions of Fannie Mae; participates in the secondary market through its mortgage-backed securities pools.

**good-faith estimate** An estimate of total costs for securing a real estate loan. Given to borrowers prior to closing.

**government-sponsored enterprises (GSE)** Fannie Mae and Freddie Mac.

**grace period** A time allowed, usually 15 days, for making late payments without a penalty being imposed.

**graduated payment mortgage (GPM)** Payments are adjustable.

**granting clause** Words of conveyance in a deed or mortgage.

**gross income** Total annual income before any expenses are deducted.

**gross rent multiplier (GRM)** Comparing imputed market rents to estimate the value of residential real estate by the income approach.

**ground rents** Leases given by landowners to tenants. The owner retains title, and the lessee receives the right of possession and use.

**growing equity mortgage (GEM)** A loan allowing a borrower to accelerate its satisfaction by making additional monthly principal payments.

**hard-money mortgage** Cash loan to a borrower.

**hazard insurance** Insurance covering physical damage to property.

**hazardous waste** Toxic waste materials jeopardizing the value of real estate.

**hereditaments** Things capable of being inherited.

**holdback** Funds not issued in a construction loan due to failure to lease up to required minimum.

**home equity line of credit** Pledging the equity in a home for a loan.

**Home Mortgage Disclosure Act** Lenders must report borrower's profiles to Federal Reserve.

**Housing Choice Voucher Program** Low-income borrowers receive subsidies for interest or rent if they are tenants.

**housing ratio** Costs to pay housing expenses as a percent of gross monthly income.

**HUD** Department of Housing and Urban Development; regulates FHA and GNMA.

**HUD-1 Settlement Statement** Standard settlement form.

**hybrid financing** Mixing conventional forms of finance to create a new approach; the participation loan; the convertible loan.

**hypothecation** The pledge of real estate as security without surrendering possession of the property.

**impounds** Fund set up by a lender to collect and hold monthly payments from the borrower for taxes and hazard insurance until they are due.

**income approach** Estimating the value of an income-producing property by capitalizing its net annual income.

**income ratio** The relationship between a borrower's total income and the amount needed to make one month's mortgage payment.

**index** Utilized to set interest rates.

**industrial development bond**  A bond that allows private investors to finance apartment and commercial developments by using tax-exempt, inexpensive funds. TRA '86 imposed severe restrictions on this financing technique.

**industrial revenue bonds**  Bonds issued for developing an industrial park or for constructing a building for lease to commercial tenants.

**inheritability**  The right to leave an estate to a specific designee.

**installment sale**  Paying for property over time.

**interest**  Money paid for the use of money.

**interest factor (IF)**  From a table, the numbers derived from formulas designed to indicate the present or future worth of money.

**interest only**  A term loan arrangement calling for payments of interest only, not including any amount for principal.

**intermediaries**  Financial fiduciaries including banks, savings institutions, and life insurance companies.

**Internal Revenue Code Section 1031**  Establishes tax rules for the exchange of properties.

**Interstate Land Sales Full Disclosure Act**  Establishes rules for the sale of vacant land.

**investment conduit**  *See* REIT.

**involuntary lien**  Lien imposed upon a property by law, such as a lien for delinquent taxes, a mechanic's lien, or a judgment.

**IRA**  Individual retirement account into which donors can make annual tax deferred deposits.

**joint tenancy**  Realty ownership entity with automatic survivorship.

**joint venture**  Type of equity participation in which the lender puts up the funds, the developer contributes special expertise, and the two become partners in the project.

**judgment decree**  Specifies the awards granted by the court in a civil case.

**judgment lien**  Charge upon the property of a debtor resulting from a court decree, properly entered, declaring that the owner is indebted and fixing the amount of the indebtedness.

**judicial foreclosure**  A court procedure utilized by lenders to secure clear title to a property under a defaulted real estate loan.

**jumbo loan**  A loan that exceeds the current conforming limits.

**junior loan**  A loan in subordinate position to a senior loan.

**junior mortgage**  A second mortgage; a lien subordinate to a first mortgage.

**Keogh plan**  A retirement plan for self-employed individuals who may annually deposit a percent of earned income into an approved tax deferment program.

**kicker**  A bonus paid to a lender as an enticement to make a below-market-interest rate loan.

**laissez-faire**  A free market system.

**land contract**  Real property sales contract.

**late payment charge**  Penalty imposed for late payments.

**leaseback**  *See* sale-leaseback.

**leasehold estate** An estate for a fixed length of time, established when a landlord gives up possession of real estate to a tenant; the tenant has an equitable interest in the property, defined by the terms of a lease.

**leasehold lending** Loans on leased property, with satisfaction dates usually designed to impact 10 to 20 years prior to lease expiration.

**leasehold mortgage** Mortgage loan secured by the tenant's leasehold interest in a property.

**lease option** A rental agreement including a tenant's option to purchase the property.

**legal description** Official definition of the boundaries of a parcel of real estate that is on file at the county recorder's office.

**lessee** The tenant in a leasehold estate.

**lessor** The owner or landlord in a leasehold estate.

**leverage** Using someone else's money for the purchase of property.

**liabilities** Debts incurred.

**lien** A legal claim against property as security for a debt.

**lien theory** Borrowers retain legal rights in the property pledged to the lender who has an equitable interest in the collateral.

**lien waivers** Documents signed by subcontractors and suppliers indicating they have received payments in full.

**life estate** Less than a fee simple ownership created for the life of anyone except the grantor.

**lifting clause** Clause included in a junior loan instrument that allows the underlying mortgage to be replaced or refinanced as long as the amount of the new senior mortgage does not exceed the amount of the first lien outstanding at the time the junior loan was made.

**like kind** Property in IRS Section 1031 exchange, may be any type of income-producing property.

**limited liability company (LLC)** A form of business organization with limited liability. It avoids the restrictions of limited partnerships and is taxed like a partnership.

**limited partners** In a syndicate or regular partnership, the owners other than the general partners. Liability is limited to the amount of their investment.

**line of credit** An amount stipulated by a commercial bank to an active customer on an annual basis. Must be brought to zero on an agreed upon regular date.

**liquidity** The cash position of an individual, business, or financial institution measured by cash on hand and securities that quickly convert into cash.

**lis pendens** Indicates that a lawsuit is in process.

**loan constant** *See* mortgage constant.

**Loan Prospector®** Freddie Mac's electronic underwriting source.

**loan-to-value (LTV) ratio** The relationship between the amount of a mortgage loan and the value of the collateral property; expressed as a percentage.

**lock-in clause** Clause incorporated into a loan agreement that prevents the borrower from repaying the loan prior to a specified date.

**M1, M2, M3** Measurements of the United States money supply.

**manufactured home loan** Mortgage loan on a large manufactured home considered to be real property; usually drawn for a shorter period than a conventional real estate mortgage.

**marginal index** Additional percentage added to index amount when adjusting variable rate loans.

**marginal tax** In a progressive income taxation system, such as we have in the United States, there is a point when the next dollar of income earned might be the one that places the taxpayer into a higher tax bracket. The tax that applies to the next dollar of income earned is the marginal tax.

**market value** The highest price for which a property would sell, assuming a reasonable time for the sale and a knowledgeable buyer and seller acting without duress.

**master trusts** *See* fictitious deeds of trust.

**maturity** Due date of a loan.

**mechanic's lien** Imposed against property for nonpayment of labor fees.

**MGIC** Mortgage Guaranty Insurance Corporation; provides insurance for the top 5 to 30 percent of mortgage loans made by approved lenders to qualified borrowers.

**mill** One-tenth (1/10) of a cent (0.001); used in property tax assessments.

**money** A medium of exchange; a storehouse of purchasing power; a standard of value.

**money market certificate** Special savings plan offered by thrift institutions.

**money market funds** Noninsured, nonregulated private investment pools.

**moratorium** A temporary suspension of payments due under a financing agreement in order to help a distressed borrower recover and avoid a default and foreclosure.

**mortgage** A conditional transfer or pledge of real property as security for the payment of a debt; the document used to create a mortgage lien.

**mortgage-backed securities** Mortgage pools established by Ginnie Mae that act as collateral for the sale of pass-through securities.

**mortgage banker** Financial intermediary who originates new mortgage loans, collects payments, inspects the collateral, and forecloses, if necessary.

**mortgage broker** Agent who joins borrower and lender for a real estate loan, thereby earning a placement fee.

**mortgage companies** Businesses designed to lend money on real or personal property.

**mortgage constant** Factor or multiplier used for rapid computation of the annual payment needed to amortize a loan.

**mortgage insurance premium** Payment for an FHA or private mortgage insurance policy; can be paid in cash at closing or included in monthly payments.

**mortgage participation** Condominium, cooperative, and partnership loans.

**mortgage pool** *See* mortgage-backed securities.

**mortgage release document** Filed when loan is satisfied.

**mortgage revenue bond** A type of industrial development bond that is offered by state and local governments through their housing financing agencies and is tax-exempt.

**mortgage servicing disclosure statement** Lender is required to notify borrower when their mortgage is sold.

**mortgagee**  The lender in a mortgage loan transaction.

**mortgagee's title insurance**  An insurance policy protecting the lender for the amount of the loan in the event of a future title dispute.

**mortgagor**  The borrower in a mortgage loan transaction; owner of collateral pledged as security for the mortgage.

**multiclass mortgage securities**  Short-term or long-term mortgage securities, with or without pass-through privileges.

**municipal bonds**  Bonds issued for purposes of financing public improvements, such as schools, parks, and renewal projects.

**municipal mortgage enhancement**  A Fannie Mae program in which AAA-rated mortgage-backed securities are exchanged for the underlying mortgage on a tax-exempt multifamily project, enabling the developer to secure money at the lowest rate; familiarly called a "Munie Mae."

**naked title**  Synonym for *fee simple title*.

**negative amortization**  Loan balance increases as a result of less-than-interest-only payments.

**net annual income**  Gross income less operating expenses.

**net worth**  Assets less liabilities.

**nominal rate**  The interest rate stipulated in a contract.

**nonconforming loan**  Loan exceeding limits, set by Fannie Mae or Freddie Mac.

**nonjudicial foreclosure**  *See* strict foreclosure.

**nonrecourse clause**  A lender cannot sue the borrower on a defaulted loan.

**note**  A signed instrument acknowledging a debt and promising repayment.

**notice of default**  In junior finance, where the borrower gives the senior lender permission to notify the junior lender in the event of a default.

**novation**  Full substitution of the original borrower by a new, qualified borrower; releases the original maker of the loan from all liability.

**Office of the Comptroller of the Currency (OCC)**  Federal agency that regulates national banks.

**offsite improvements**  Refers to improvements made to land outside a lot's boundaries, such as the installation of streets, sidewalks, and sewers.

**open-end mortgage**  A loan providing for future advances.

**open-market operations**  The techniques employed by the Fed in buying and selling government securities that, in turn, control the amount of money in circulation.

**opportunity cost**  Earnings available on alternative investments.

**option to buy**  *See* lease option.

**origination fee**  Fee charged by a lender or other agent for processing a loan application.

**OTS**  The Office of Thrift Supervision.

**overriding trust deed**  *See* wraparound encumbrance.

**owner's title insurance**  An insurance policy protecting the buyer for the amount of the purchase price in the event of a future title dispute.

**package mortgage**  A loan that includes certain equipment and appliances located or installed on the premises in addition to the real property itself.

**par**  The face value of a bond or security.

**partial entitlement**  Under DVA loan, the amount of guarantee still available to an eligible veteran who has used a previous entitlement.

**partial release**  Removal of a specific portion of the collateral from the lien of a mortgage.

**partially amortized**  Loan repayment schedule that provides for equal payments of principal and interest up to a certain stop date, at which time the balance of the principal is due in full. *See* balloon payment.

**participation certificate**  Shares in Ginnie Mae pools.

**participation loan**  A loan in which more than one lender or more than one borrower has an interest; a loan in which the lender receives partial ownership in the enterprise that is being financed.

**partnerships**  Two or more persons or entities joined together to own real property.

**pass-throughs**  Payments on securities sold in the secondary market that are sent directly to the investors.

**pension plans**  Public and private retirement programs wherein donations are made during the working years to develop a pool of funds to be paid to those who reach retirement age.

**personal income**  A person's gross income from all sources.

**personal property**  Movable property that does not fit the definition of realty.

**piggy-back loan**  A second mortgage created simultaneously with a first mortgage.

**placement fee**  Charge levied by a mortgage broker for joining a borrower and a lender who subsequently negotiate a loan agreement.

**points**  Amount of discount on a mortgage loan stated as a percentage; one point equals one percent of the face amount of the loan; a discount of one point raises the net yield on the loan by one-eighth of one percent.

**police power**  The government's authority to regulate the use of real estate.

**power-of-sale clause**  In a deed of trust, it authorizes a lender's attorney to confess a judgment without process to speed a foreclosure.

**predatory lending**  Loans issued at terms designed to bankrupt borrowers.

**premium**  A fee paid for an insurance policy.

**premium (in excess of par)**  A price paid for a security in excess of its face value.

**prepayment clause**  Clause that provides for a penalty to be levied against a borrower who repays a loan before the specified due date.

**present worth**  The discounted present-day value of money to be received in the future.

**primary interest rate**  *See* prime rate.

**primary lenders**  Originators of real estate loans.

**primary market**  Loan originated by local lenders to be sold to secondary market.

**prime rate**  Interest rate charged by fiduciary institutions to their AAA-rated borrowers.

**principal**  Amount of a debt; one of the parties in a financial transaction.

**priority lien position**  Established by recording loan documents—first in time, first in right.

**private mortgage insurance (PMI)**  Mortgage insurance issued by private companies.

**property**  Anything that can be controlled and owned.

**Proposition 13**  A California referendum limiting the amount of annual property tax increases.

**prorations**  At a real estate sale and/or loan closing, the allocation of charges and credits to the appropriate parties.

**purchase-money mortgage**  Loan given by a borrower to the seller as part of the purchase price of the property.

**pyramiding**  Method of acquiring additional properties through refinancing existing mortgages.

**quiet title**  A technique to clear any clouds from a property's title; a suit to quiet title.

**ranchos**  Land grants for grazing or farming issued by the King of Spain to political or military agencies in California.

**real estate**  Also termed *realty* and *real property*; a portion of the earth's surface extending downward to the center of the earth and upward into space, including all things permanently attached thereto by nature or man and all legal rights therein.

**real estate investment trust**  *See* REIT.

**real estate mortgage investment conduit (REMIC)**  Multiclass securities.

**real estate mortgage trust**  A trust dealing in financing investments rather than in owning them. *See* REMT.

**Real Estate Settlement Procedures Act (RESPA)**  An act calling for the revelation of all costs in anticipation of closing a real estate transaction.

**real property**  *See* real estate.

**real property sales contract**  Also known as a *land contract*; usually drawn between individuals. It is a contract by which the purchase price is paid in installments over a period of time during which the purchaser has possession of the property, but the seller retains title until the contract terms are completed.

**realized capital gains**  Investment profits not subject to income tax, e.g., profits from refinancing, exchanges, and installment sales.

**recast**  A redesign of an existing loan balance into a new loan for the same period or longer to reduce payments and help a distressed borrower.

**recognition clause**  Clause included in a blanket loan contract used to purchase a tract of land for subdivision and development; provides for the protection of the rights of buyers of small parcels in case of default on the part of the developer-promoter.

**recognized capital gain**  Profits from the sale of investments and subject to income tax; derived by subtracting the adjusted book basis from the net proceeds of the sale.

**reconciliation**  In appraising, estimating a single value from the different approaches. *See* weighted average technique.

**reconveys**  In satisfying a deed of trust, the trustee reconveys full title to the borrower.

**recording**  Formal filing of documents affecting a property's title.

**redemption right**  Time allotted to the borrower to redeem collateral after default by paying the debt in full, interest accrued, and all court costs.

**redlining**  The delineation by a lending institution of those areas of a community occupied by less-than-desirable borrowers; not allowed under the Community Reinvestment Act.

**refinance**  Replacing an existing mortgage; usually to gain a more favorable rate.

**registered bond**  Issued to a specific owner; it cannot be transferred without the owner's endorsement.

**rehabilitation loan**  FHA 203(k) loan to repair a collateral house.

**Regulation Z**  Truth-in-lending provision that requires lenders to reveal the actual costs of borrowing.

**reinstate**  In delinquent deeds of trust, the time prior to exercising the power of sale in which the errant borrower may bring the loan current.

**REIT**  Real estate investment trust; an unincorporated trust, set up to invest in real estate, that must have at least 100 investors; management, control, and title to the property are in the hands of trustees.

**release clause**  Provision that, upon payment of a specific sum of money, the lien on a particular parcel or portion of the collateral will be removed.

**release of liability**  Removes old borrower from further responsibility for repayment of an assumed loan.

**REMT**  Real estate mortgage trust; similar to REIT, but investment is made in mortgage securities rather than in real estate.

**renegotiable rate mortgage**  *See* rollover loan.

**rent-up**  Required pledges from lessors of commercial space before the developer will be able to obtain financing; usually represents the required rental income needed to break even.

**replacement cost**  The cost of replacing the subject property with a new property having the same amenities and utility.

**reserve requirements**  A flat percentage of deposits, required by the Federal Reserve, to be set aside by member banks as a safety measure.

**reserves**  Portion of business earnings or bank assets set aside to cover possible losses or withdrawals.

**RESPA**  *See* Real Estate Settlement Procedures Act.

**restrictions**  Rules for use of real estate in an effort to preserve value.

**return on investment**  Net annual income divided by cash investment equals a percentage return on the investment.

**revenue bonds**  Public improvement bonds to be paid from the income generated by said improvements.

**reverse annuity mortgage (RAM)**  A system developed for the elderly property owner in which regular monthly payments can be received from a lender. When the total reaches a predesignated amount, the owner then begins repaying the loan or sells the property.

**right of first refusal**  Unlike an option to buy or an option to renew a lease, which stipulates the terms in advance, this approach allows the owner to secure a market price bid that the occupant can be the first to accept or reject.

**risk-based pricing** Applying electronically-generated credit scores to estimate appropriate loan charges for degrees of risk on loans.

**ROI** Return on investment. *See* capitalization rate.

**rollover loan** A loan that includes a call date earlier than its normal amortization period; also called a renegotiable rate loan or a bullet loan.

**Roman Civil Law** Early private property ownership codes enforced on California owners by the Spanish rulers.

**sale-leaseback** Financing arrangement whereby an investor purchases real estate owned and used by a business corporation then leases the property back to the business; may include a buyback option.

**sale-leaseback-buyback** *See* sale-leaseback.

**sales contract** A financing device used mainly in low down payment transactions where the vendor retains legal title while the vendee acquires equitable ownership of the property.

**savings associations** Established primarily as savings institutions, not commercial banks. Participate heavily in residential real estate lending.

**secondary mortgage market** Source to which originators of loans may sell them, freeing funds for continued lending; aids in distributing mortgage funds on a national level from money-rich to money-poor areas.

**second mortgage** *See* junior loan.

**Section 1031, Internal Revenue Code** Permits exchanges of like kinds of property as a method to postpone paying income taxes on some capital gains.

**securitization** The pooling of real estate mortgages and trust deeds to act as collateral for the sale of securities.

**security** Something given, deposited, or pledged to make secure the fulfillment of an obligation, usually the repayment of a debt; mortgages, trust deeds, and other financing instruments backed by collateral pledges are termed securities for investment purposes.

**security agreement** Financing contract for personal property.

**senior loan** A real estate loan in first priority position.

**servicing fee** Fee charged by national lender's local representative who collects payments, disburses funds for property taxes and insurance premiums, inspects the property, and forecloses, if necessary.

**shared appreciation mortgage (SAM)** Lender participates in equity growth.

**simple interest** Interest that is charged only on the principal amount outstanding.

**sinking fund** Monies deposited in advance, in anticipation of satisfying a debt in the future.

**specific lien** Lien against a specified property of the debtor.

**specific performance** The legal obligation for the parties in a contract to fulfill their promises or be in default and subject to a lawsuit.

**split-fee financing** Type of equity participation in which the lender purchases the land, leases it to the developer, and finances the leasehold improvements in return for a basic rental plus a percentage of the profits.

**split loan** In construction financing, covers the lot and building separately.

**standby commitment** Pledge by a permanent lender to fund a long-term loan to take out the construction lender upon successful completion of the building.

**statutory redemption period** Legislated redemption period allowing borrower time to redeem defaulted property.

**stop date** Date on a term loan when the balloon payment is due.

**straight-line depreciation** TRA '86 applied to all improved investment properties put into service after January 1, 1987; 27.5 years for residential income and 31.5 years for commercial properties.

**streamline finance** FHA paper-reduction requirements.

**strict foreclosure or strict forfeiture** Under a land contract, enables a lender to foreclose in as little as 30 days when the defaulting borrower has less than 20 percent equity.

**"subject to"** The recognition by a buyer that a prior loan exists and not the legal obligation to fulfill its requirements.

**subordination** The act on the part of a lender or a landowner in the case of a leasehold mortgage, acknowledging by written recorded instrument that an existing loan or interest can be placed in an inferior position to a new loan secured by the same collateral.

**subprime loans** Borrowers have less than perfect credit, known as "B, C, or D paper."

**subrogation** In a DVA loan, the veteran preassigns all rights to the Department of Veterans Affairs at the inception of the loan, to be implemented in the event of a default.

**substitution of entitlement** Replaces one eligible veteran with another on an existing DVA loan and restores entitlement to the original veteran.

**suit to quiet title** *See* quiet title.

**survey** An engineer's description of a property's boundaries.

**sweat equity** Increase in property value due to physical efforts of owners.

**syndicate** An organization of investors who pool their capital to make a real estate investment.

**takeout** *See* takeout mortgage.

**takeout mortgage** A permanent loan, obtained by prearrangement between a builder and a financial fiduciary, to repay the interim lender at the completion of construction.

**tandem plan** Investment plan combining Fannie Mae secondary market activities with Ginnie Mae guarantees.

**tax-exempt bonds** Issued to finance public or private improvements for community benefit, interest from which may be exempt from federal, state, and local income taxes. Limited application under TRA '86.

**tax-free gifts** Gifts free from any federal gift tax imposition.

**tax-increment financing** Loans arranged by state and local industrial development boards to stimulate community growth that will, in turn, generate increased tax revenues.

**Tax Relief Act of 1987** Provides broad exeptions from capital gains taxes on the profits from the sale of personal residences.

**Tax Reform Act of 1986 (TRA '86)** Sweeping revisions of income tax laws, lowering tax rates but eliminating many tax shelters.

**tax shelter** In real estate, allowable investment losses that can be used to reduce income tax liability.

**tenants in common** Undivided ownership interests in real estate that are inheritable.

**term loan** Nonamortized loan for a specified period, at the end of which the entire principal amount is due.

**thrifts** Name for savings institutions.

**time-shares** Interval ownership of real estate, such as the right to use a resort condominium for two weeks per year.

**title insurance** Required to protect lender's position.

**title theory** Lender holds legal title to the collateral; the borrower retains equitable rights in the property.

**total obligation ratio** Total monthly payments as a percentage of gross monthly income.

**trade fixture** A commercial tenant's improvement to leased property that remains the tenant's personal property no matter how permanently it is attached.

**tranche** A portion of a multiclass security.

**transfer tax** A sales tax on real estate currently imposed at the rate of $0.55 per $500 of new money. Loans that are assumed are not taxed.

**Treasury** Nation's fiscal manager.

**Treasury bill** Issued for less than a year.

**Treasury bond** Issued for from five to ten years.

**Treasury note** Issued for from two to ten years.

**trust deed** *See* deed of trust.

**trustee** A party who administers property for the benefit of the beneficiary, such as the intermediary between a borrower and a bond owner, a bank or title company under a trust agreement, or the third-party holder of the deed under a deed of trust.

**trustee's deed** In a foreclosure, the deed given by the trustee under a deed of trust to the successful bidder at the auction.

**trustor** The grantor in a trust deed.

**truth-in-lending (TIL)** *See* Regulation Z.

**two-step mortgage** A hybrid loan between a fixed-rate and adjustable-rate loan; the lower rate remains in effect for seven years and is then automatically adjusted once for the balance of the loan period.

**underwriting** Process of evaluating borrower credit, collateral value, and risks involved in making a loan.

**unlawful detainer** Persons in default and illegally retaining possession of property.

**unrecorded contract** A written document designed to create a legal relationship between the parties but not to encumber any property. *See* recording.

**urban renewal** Programs under HUD designed to renovate substandard housing areas.

**USDA Rural Development Program** Funds housing and service projects in rural areas.

**usury** Charging more than the legal limit on interest for a loan.

**value** Present worth of future rights to income and benefits arising from ownership.

**value in exchange** Power to command other goods in exchange.

**value in use** The value of a property as it is being used for a single purpose.

**variable costs** Operating expenses that fluctuate with occupancy, such as utilities and maintenance costs.

**variable-rate mortgage (VRM)** Interest rates can be adjusted periodically, subject to certain limitations and caps.

**vendee** Purchaser-borrower under a real property sales contract.

**vendor** Seller-lender under a real property sales contract.

**voluntary conveyance** *See* deed in lieu of foreclosure.

**voluntary lien** A lien placed on a property by the owner, such as a mortgage or a deed of trust.

**warehousing** Guaranteeing for a specified time and fee, that funds will be available under certain terms and conditions; assembling into one package a number of mortgage loans, which the correspondent has originated, in anticipation of sale in the secondary market.

**weighted average technique** In appraisal, when reconciling the approaches, the application of a weight to each approach for averaging.

**weighted rate** Proportional approach to deriving overall capitalization.

**workouts** The various ways to offset a foreclosure; payment moratoriums, waivers, adjustments.

**wraparound encumbrance** Special form of junior financing instrument designed to encompass an already existing financing instrument.

**yield** Effective earnings from loans or investments.

**zero coupon bond** A single-payment bond that grows to its face value over a prescribed time period at a specified interest rate. All interim compound interest is tax-deferred until the bond is cashed.

**zoning** The right of a community, under its police power, to dictate the use of property within its boundaries.

# INDEX

# Notes

# Notes

# Notes

# Notes

# Notes

# Notes

# Notes

**Notes**

# Notes

# Notes

# Notes